PY—ARR—0043

W O R L D   B A N K

C O M P A R A T I V E   M A C R O E C O N O M I C   S T U D I E S

India

Macroeconomics

and Political Economy

1964–1991

India

Macroeconomics

and Political Economy

1964–1991

VIJAY JOSHI

I. M. D. LITTLE

THE WORLD BANK, WASHINGTON, D.C.

The World Bank Comparative Macroeconomic Studies series emerges from a research project that reviewed the macroeconomic experiences of eighteen developing countries over a period roughly from 1965 to 1990. So that the studies might be published with relatively little delay, the books have been edited outside the World Bank's Office of the Publisher by the Macroeconomic Research Department.

The complete backlist of publications from the World Bank is shown in the annual Index of Publications, which contains an alphabetical title list and indexes of subjects, authors, and countries and regions. The latest edition is available free of charge from Distribution Unit, Office of the Publisher, The World Bank, 1818 H Street, N.W., Washington, D.C. 20433, U.S.A., or from Publications, The World Bank, 66, avenue d'Iéna, 75116 Paris, France.

Cover design by Sam Ferro.

Vijay Joshi is a Fellow of Merton College, and I. M. D. Little is an Emeritus Fellow of Nuffield College, both in the University of Oxford.

Library of Congress Cataloging-in-Publication Data

Joshi, Vijay.
      India : macroeconomics and political economy, 1964–1991 / Vijay
    Joshi and I.M.D. Little.
         p.   cm. — (World Bank comparative macroeconomic studies)
    Includes bibliographical references and index.
    ISBN 0-8213-2652-X
      1. India—Economic policy—1961–1966.   2. India—Economic
    policy—1966–   3. India—Economic conditions—1947–   I. Little, Ian
    Malcolm David.   II. Title.   III. Series.
    HC435.2.J7   1994
    338.954—dc20
                                      93-33147
                                       CIP

Contents

List of Tables

List of Figures

Foreword

This volume is the product of a World Bank project on macroeconomic policy that reviewed the recent experience of eighteen countries as they attempted to maintain economic stability in the face of international price, interest rate, and demand shocks or domestic crises in the forms of investment booms and related budgetary problems. The project paid particular attention to the 1974–79 period (which included the first and second oil price shocks), the 1980–82 period of worldwide recession and external debt problems for many developing countries, and the 1983–90 period of adjustment to economic difficulties and the resumption of growth.

The objective of the project was to glean instructive lessons by analyzing the stabilization and adjustment policies pursued by these countries and assessing the outcomes. The authors of each country study were asked to deal with a common set of questions concerning the nature of the shocks or crises: their origin and degree of seriousness; the fiscal, monetary, exchange rate, and trade policies adopted in hopes of preventing permanent harm to the economy; and the results of the policies.

No single computable macroeconomic model was used in the project, but the framework of the open-economy macroeconomic model was followed to ensure consistency in generalizing about results. This intensive study of many episodes generated ideas and suggested relationships showing the cause and effect behind policies, the nature of the shocks and crises, and the governmental response to them. The overall findings of the project are presented in a synthesis volume by I. M. D. Little, Richard N. Cooper, W. Max Corden, and Sarath Rajapatirana, *Boom, Crisis, and Adjustment: The Macroeconomic Experience of Developing Countries.*

India is the largest and also one of the poorest of the eighteen countries studied. It is very dependent on fuel imports, so that the oil price rises caused serious balance of payments problems. Nevertheless India is exceptional in that external shocks are less important than the severe droughts that occur from time to time.

India's policies and experience have also been exceptional. Most countries adapted little in response to the 1973/74 oil price rise, but borrowed heavily and instigated investment booms. In contrast, India did not borrow commercially, kept inflation low, and built up reserves of food and foreign exchange. Unlike so many other countries it therefore experienced no debt crisis or recession in the early

1980s and was able to recover quickly from the external shocks of 1979/80 and from a severe drought occurring at the same time. By the later 1980s, however, India's economic conservatism had evaporated and her fiscal deficits became unsustainable. Thus, India's macroeconomic policies have been ten years out of phase with most of the eighteen countries studied. It experienced its debt crisis or associated recession in 1991.

It was once a fashionable view that India's economic policies were unsound microeconomically but sound macroeconomically, and that these aspects were linked—the forest of controls that caused resources to be used inefficiently made it easier to maintain macroeconomic balance. Contrarily, the authors of this study conclude that India's control system was not only microeconomically inefficient but that it was also macroeconomically perverse. Certainly the events of recent years have made it difficult to argue that controls ensure stability.

Publication of this study was made possible in part by a generous grant from SIDA, the Swedish International Development Authority.

Sarath Rajapatirana
Director, "Macroeconomic Policies, Crisis, and Growth
in the Long Run" Research Project
Trade and Industry Policy Adviser
Technical Department
Latin America and the Caribbean Region

Acknowledgments

This volume is a component of a research project initiated and financed by the World Bank in 1986 entitled "Macroeconomic Policies, Crisis, and Growth in the Long Run," which involved studies of the macroeconomic histories of eighteen countries. We learned much from participating in this comparative project, and from thus becoming more familiar than we otherwise would have been with the experiences of countries other than India. We remember the comments of other participants on early drafts of the book, especially those of Vittorio Corbo and Allan Meltzer. We are greatly indebted to the director of the project, Sarath Rajapatirana, and to the project coordinator, Anita Bhatia, who handled our many requests with sympathetic efficiency. We are also grateful for the assistance given by the World Bank office in New Delhi.

In the course of the research, we interviewed formally (and in some cases several times) the following persons who were involved in their official capacities in the events and policies herein described and analyzed: Shankar Acharya, Montek Singh Ahluwalia, Y. K. Alagh, S. Bhoothalingam, the late Sukhamoy Chakravarty, Raja Chelliah, Nitin Desai, P. N. Dhar, Arun Ghosh, S. Guhan, Bimal Jalan, the late L. K. Jha, V. B. Kadam, Vijay Kelkar, K. S. Krishnaswamy, P. B. Kulkarni, the late Lovraj Kumar, R. N. Malhotra, Bagicha Singh Minhas, Ajit Mozoomdar, M. Narasimham, Deepak Nayyar, I. G. Patel, C. Rangarajan, G. V. K. Rao, Arjun Sengupta, Manu Shroff, Manmohan Singh, S. S. Tarapore, A. Vaidyanathan, and S. Venkitaramanan. We are grateful to them all for giving us their time and their views so freely.

We have had useful conversations with many people, both inside and outside the Indian government. Others have helped us in other ways, such as enabling us to acquire information or documents. We would like to thank M. P. Agarwal, Isher Ahluwalia, Christopher Allsopp, Amaresh Bagchi, Pulapre Balakrishnan, Pranab Bardhan, Prahlad Basu, Jagdish Bhagwati, Surjit Bhalla, the late Krishna Bharadwaj, B. B. Bhattacharya, Pramit Chaudhuri, Vikas Chitre, S. N. Dalal, Bejoy Dasgupta, Mrinal Datta-Chaudhuri, Ravi Dayal, Ashok Desai, Meghnad Desai, Sudhir Deshpande, Jean Drèze, Hans Genberg, Ejaz Ghani, Chico Ghia, Ashok Gulati, Ravi Gulhati, Anand Gupta, Salman Haidar, Geoffrey Hawthorn, James Hanson, Prem Jha, P. C. Joshi, R. C. Joshi, S. Katyal, Deena Khatkhate, Sunil Khilnani, K. Krishamurti, Dharma Kumar, Ashok Lahiri, Deepak Lal, Michael Lipton, Srinivasa Madhur, N. A. Majumdar, Vikram Mehta, Percy Mistry, Rakesh Mohan,

Sudhir Mulji, Vineet Nayyar, V. P. Pai Panandikar, V. N. Pandit, Prabhat Patnaik, Garry Pursell, Krishna Raj, Indira Rajaraman, A. Ranganathan, D. C. Rao, J. C. Rao, M. Govinda Rao, Narahari Rao, V. J. Ravishankar, Prannoy Roy, Asha Sarabhai, Suhrid Sarabhai, Maurice Scott, Abhijit Sen, Amartya Sen, Pronab Sen, S. L. Shetty, K. Subbarow, David Taylor, Suresh Tendulkar, Gene Tidrick, John Toye, Mark Tully, T. R. Venkatachalam, Arvind Virmani, Pravin Visaria, Bevan Waide, John Williamson, and Oktay Yenal. James Manor must receive special mention for giving us illuminating advice on political economy issues. Neither the World Bank nor any of the people mentioned is responsible for the views expressed in the book.

We wish to thank Tim Jenkinson for invaluable help with the econometric appendices, M. R. Saluja for help with appendix A, and the following for providing research assistance in Oxford from time to time: Janine Aron, Sandeep Bhargava, Edmund Cannon, Sara Connolly, Bejoy Dasgupta, Ranu Dayal, and Geeta Kingdon. We are grateful for the editorial help of Connie Eysenck and the secretarial help of Elaine Herman, Judith Kirby, and the late Margaret Kitchen.

Lastly, we thank Mary Sissons Joshi and Lydia Segrave Little for their good-humored support.

Authors' Note

This book is a joint effort of both authors and they are jointly responsible for its contents. But the primary authorship was divided up as follows. Vijay Joshi drafted chapters 3, 5, 6, 7, 8, 10, and 11. I. M. D. Little drafted chapters 1, 4, 13, 14, and appendixes A and B. Chapters 2, 9, and 12 were jointly drafted.

Oxford
June 1992

Acronyms

ASI	Annual Survey of Industry
AWI	Agricultural Wages in India
BJP	Bharatiya Janata party
CAS	Credit Authorization Scheme
CFF	Compensatory Financing Facility
cif	cost, insurance, and freight
CPI	consumer price index
CRR	cash reserve ratio
DGCIS	Directorate General of Commercial Intelligence and Statistics
EFF	Extended Fund Facility
FERA	Foreign Exchange Regulation Act
GDCF	gross domestic capital formation
GDP	gross domestic product
GIC	General Insurance Corporation of India
GFCF	gross domestic fixed capital formation
GNP	gross national product
IBRD	International Bank for Reconstruction and Development
ICICI	Industrial Credit and Investment Corporation of India
ICORs	incremental capital output ratios
IDA	International Development Association
IDBI	Industrial Development Bank of India
IFCI	Industrial Finance Corporation of India
IMF	International Monetary Fund
LIC	Life Insurance Corporation of India
MRTP	Monopolies and Restrictive Trade Practices
NAS	National Accounts Statistics
NER	nominal effective exchange rate
NSS	National Sample Survey
OECD	Organization for Economic Cooperation and Development
OGL	Open General Licence
OIL	Oil India Ltd.
ONGC	Oil and Natural Gas Commission
OPEC	Organization of Petroleum Exporting Countries
PAD	Project Appraisal Division [of the Planning Commission]

PDS	public distribution system
PIB	Public Investment Board
RBI	Reserve Bank of India
RER	real effective exchange rate
RERsa	subsidy-adjusted real effective exchange rate
SDR	special drawing rights
SLR	statutory liquidity ratio
TFP	total factor productivity
TOTEFF	terms of trade effect
UTI	Unit Trust of India
UVI	unit value indices
WPI	wholesale price index

Data Notes

- *Billion* is 1,000 million throughout.
- Dates indicated with a slash (1967/68) are fiscal years.
- 100 crores = 1 billion rupees.
- *Dollars* are current U.S. dollars unless otherwise specified.
- The symbol — in tables means not available.
- n.a. means not applicable.

Introduction

This book is an analytic macroeconomic history of India from 1964 to 1991. By analytic we mean that our narrative is moulded by economic theory, which is however more pragmatic than procrustean. We pay particular attention to the policies pursued, assess their successes and failures both from the point of view of stabilization and of growth, and consider the lessons that can be drawn. We hope to be read by all those who interest themselves in macroeconomic policy, but most of all by those who may influence policy, now or in the years to come.

What is macroeconomics? It is the study of the behavior of very large economic aggregates, their relationships, and their determinants. Thus this book is about the policies that are intended to influence the values over time of gross national and domestic product, national investment and savings, imports and exports, and the balance of overseas payments.

We are concerned with both real and nominal values of these aggregates, that is with changes in price levels (inflation, or rarely, deflation). While these are the main macroeconomic magnitudes that concern us, very often their movements can be understood only when they are to some extent disaggregated or 'broken down.' One of the most important breakdowns is between the public and private sectors. Others include agriculture and industry, and some further breakdown of industry into different sectors; the subdivision of goods and services into traded and non-traded; of savings into financial and physical; and so on.

Where does disaggregation stop? That is a matter of judgment. It stops when adding to the trees obscures rather than clarifies the outline of the forest. Certainly it stops well before we reach down to the level of the individual economic decisionmaker, whether it be an individual or an institution; this is the level par excellence of microeconomics. Nevertheless, some background knowledge of the operation of markets (which consist of transactions between individual decisionmakers) may be helpful—even necessary—to an understanding of the response of the economy to changes in policy. The prime example is the extent to which a change in the monetary demand for labor will result in a change in employment or a change in wages. We have tried to give the reader an adequate account of the operation of key markets in chapter 2.

What are the instruments of macroeconomic policy that may be used to influence the main macroeconomic magnitudes? The most important instrument is the government's budget, including its collection of revenue and its expenditure (and, in a federal system, state government budgets). Within the categories of revenue and expenditure, the kinds of taxes raised and expenditures made may have significant macroeconomic implications. Even more important, the balance of revenue and expenditure is an important determinant of the overall level of demand. When, as is usual, expenditure exceeds revenue and the government must borrow, then the forms in which it borrows (by printing money, or incurring interest–bearing debt of various kinds) and from whom it borrows (foreigners, the domestic banking system, or the public) become important policy variables.

Controls over quantities and prices are the second main category of macroeconomic instruments. In many countries, controls over imports, capital movements, and exchange rates, have been the dominant control instruments, until at least very recently. In India these instruments have been used throughout the period discussed in this book. But India has many other controls, over production, investment, interest rates, credit allocation, and prices. Whatever their purpose, they have some influence on the main macroeconomic variables, and we have to take account of them.

For what purposes are the instruments of macroeconomic policy used? What, in other words, are the government's objectives? We take it that the primary short- and medium-run objective is stabilization. By stabilization, we mean both keeping inflation low (certainly less than 10 percent a year), and avoiding any depression of industrial activity that falls below some sustainable rate of long-run growth. In traditional Keynesian economics, the stabilizing role of government consists primarily of offsetting disturbances to aggregate demand that originate in the private sector. We take a broader view of stabilization as minimizing in addition the adverse consequences for output, consumption, and investment of supply-side exogenous shocks such as droughts and changes in the terms of trade. The stabilizing role of government also involves the avoidance of policy-induced shocks and this in turn requires close attention to the compatibility of policies with intertemporal constraints. Our emphasis on stabilization leads us to examine closely four macroeconomic crises that occurred during the period we analyzed. The first three crises arose from exogenous shocks associated with droughts and oil price increases. The fourth crisis (which began in 1991) did not arise from an exogenous shock but was itself the result of a failure of macroeconomic policy.

While stabilization is desirable for its own sake, we have examined the hypothesis that is is also beneficial for long-run growth and conclude that this is indeed the case. There are, of course, other ways than via the promotion of stability in which macroeconomic policy instruments may affect long-run growth, for instance their effect on savings and the efficiency of investment. We pay attention also to these effects of the government's use of the instruments of macroeconomic policy.

We have with one exception undertaken no new research into the inefficiency of the use of resources in the Indian economy, regarding this to be in the realm of microeconomics. The exception is the apparently very low yield of investment in the public sector. However, we do draw attention to the ways in which the style of macroeconomic policy, involving multiple controls, creates large price distortions that are at the heart of the problem of the inefficient use of resources. The link between macroeconomics and microeconomics is thus an important concern in this book. A fashionable view of Indian economic policy is that it was unsound microeconomically but sound macroeconomically, and further that these phenomena were positively linked—in other words, the controls that led to microeconomic inefficiency made it easier to attain macroeconomic balance. In contrast, one of our central conclusions is that India's control system was not only microeconomically inefficient but also macroeconomically perverse.

The government's objectives are not limited to the growth of the gross national product (GNP). There are other considerations that are not adequately reflected in GNP—for instance education, health, employment, and poverty alleviation. These important concerns are not our primary concern, for success or failure in these areas is largely independent of macroeconomic policy. We say "largely independent" since success in achieving stability and a high rate of growth of GNP certainly facilitates the achievement of social goals. It may also be true that some methods of achieving stability impinge more on social goals than others, and where this seems to be an important factor we take note. Finally, we are aware that the government and the ruling elite may have goals that are more self-regarding than the national welfare. In this connection, we pay attention to changes in political economy and take account of factors such as the erosion of civil service independence and the growing influence of interest groups particularly on fiscal policy. But we do not believe that understanding India's macroeconomic experience requires an outright rejection of the premise that the objectives of the government's macroeconomic policies are essentially benevolent.

Part 1 of the book is essentially introductory, and the reader who is familiar with the Indian economy may prefer to skip it. Others may find that it excites their curiosity and helps them to follow the authors' analysis of Indian macroeconomic policy that is the core of the book. Chapter 1 introduces India and gives some relevant history. Chapter 2, which describes the nature of markets and the rather dominant role of the public sector and the government, is, as already explained, pertinent to understanding the responses of the economy to the instruments of economic policy.

Part 2 is an historical account of short-run economic policy interventions and their outcomes, together with the changing political backgrounds. It starts in chapter 3 with a sketch of macroeconomic events and political economy over the entire period. The next four chapters focus in more detail on each of the four crises identified in chapter 3. Part 2 ends with an evaluation in chapter 8 of short-term economic management. The reader who is not particularly concerned with historical detail may wish to move directly from chapter 3 to chapter 8, dipping into the intervening pages selectively.

Part 3 is concerned with trends in policy and their long-run effects. The main areas of policy are treated separately—fiscal policy in chapter 9, monetary policy in chapter 10, and trade and payments policy in chapter 11. Chapters 12 and 13 are more concerned with the long run. Chapter 12 looks at the trends of savings in different sectors and at the sustainability of public sector deficits. Chapter 13 is concerned with trends in investment and with the efficiency of investment. Chapter 14 contains our concluding remarks.

Part One

History, Profile, and Institutions

Chapter One

Recent History and a Profile
of the Economy

This chapter consists of two sections. The first is a sketch of India's recent economic history before the period of our main inquiry that begins in 1964 and ends in 1991. In this we limit ourselves to certain events, a knowledge of which may help the reader to understand subsequent economic developments. The second section is a profile of the country mainly drawn for the year 1980/81, but with some reference to changes before and since. India's geography, its government, and the main features of its economic structure are described. The public sector is very important in India, and its extent is described as part of this profile. Where there have been important changes in the structure of the economy since 1965 they are noted.

In chapter 2 we describe features of capital, labor, and product markets. The pervasive influence of legislation and government controls is noted. Some knowledge of the working of the markets is of help in understanding the thrust of the government's macroeconomic policies and their effects. These two chapters are intended to give the reader who is unfamiliar with the Indian economy sufficient background to understand and appreciate our description and analysis of Indian macroeconomic policy that begins in chapter 3.

Recent History

We are not aware of any study of India with the specific focus of the influence of its history on economic institutions and economic policy formation. Rather than getting enmeshed in what could develop into an original *magnum opus*, we confine ourselves to a brief inquiry into those historical strands that might be relevant to an understanding of macroeconomic policy in our period. One feature that stands out is India's monetary and fiscal conservatism, and we pay most attention to this since it distinguishes India from most other developing countries. A second feature, which, however, it has shared with most developing countries, is the emphasis on self-reliance, that has been partly responsible for India's failure to make efficient use of foreign trade and foreign technology to help solve its problems. A third feature, also shared by many developing countries, is distrust of the price mechanism and a preference for administrative solutions to economic problems.

India inherited much from the British Raj. Before independence in August 1947, British India (that is, India and Pakistan, apart from the princely states) was a unitary state, although various measures of devolution pointed the way to the federal solution enshrined in the Constitution of 1950. Most of the panoply of central government and financial institutions that can be still observed today—the ministries, the Inland Revenue, Customs and Excise, and various other economic services—were in place. Their organization and functioning style seem very familiar to the British visitor. India also opted for cabinet rather than presidential government. Finally, the financial system evolved along British lines. The Reserve Bank had been created in 1935 and was nationalized in 1950. Its relationship to government and the Finance Ministry is much as in the United Kingdom. The banking system had also developed along British rather than German or American lines, with branch-banking and little direct involvement in industrial promotion. Only the Planning Commission, established in 1950, was a novelty, though the idea of planning was much canvassed in the 1930s and 1940s and was supported even by the British.[1] As or more important than these institutions are the higher-level bureaucrats who make them work. The British created in the Indian Civil Service a small, high-minded, highly elitist bureaucracy with a Gladstonian fiscal outlook; its successor, the Indian Administrative Service, preserved—at least initially—the same traditions.

India also inherited much from its long struggle against the British. Limited success in this struggle gave India a much longer experience of administration and government than was the case in any other British colony. The Congress party, which dominated government at least up to the beginning of our period, was founded as a nationalist movement in 1885. India therefore inherited a strong, well-established party as well as a number of highly-esteemed and experienced politicians, who were themselves imbued with Gandhian austerity and devotion to the cause of a united and prosperous India.[2]

Nehru dominated the Indian political and economic scene from 1950 until his death in 1964. His economic views were highly heterodox by British standards, but not in the fiscal sphere. Nehru was a Kashmiri Brahmin and was also a Fabian socialist with Marxist sympathies who had suffered an upper-class English education. All of these go with a distrust of business, and some of them at least with ignorance of the allocational role of the price mechanism, admiration for Russian planning, and genuine concern for the poor. Permitting inflation would harm the poor, and could be seen as a loss of control and an abrogation of the proper role of the state. He succeeded in shifting the center of gravity of the party toward a modern secular socialism and away from the Conservative, Gandhian, and Hindu-fundamentalist elements which it also embraced.

Nehru's belief in material planning, and its associated controls, did not conflict with the ethos of the Indian bureaucracy. Before independence the civil service administered law and order, with little need to understand economics or business. Faced, after independence, with the extraordinary new demands of development, it naturally thought in terms of administering it, in conformity not only with Nehru's philosophy but probably with the views of almost all members of the Congress party.[3]

India had never been a united country; even under the British, direct rule embraced only about 60 percent of the population. The partition of India that accompanied independence brought with it horror on a large scale. There were between 10 million and 15 million refugees, and murders were numbered in the hundreds of thousands. Even after this surgery, India remained divided by language, religion, and caste. However, despite this heterogeneity there were strong elements of cultural unity. Nevertheless, for about a decade after independence the most important item on the political agenda was the formation and preservation of a united nation.

The integration of the princely states was accomplished in a manner that, although rough in some cases, left no major scars except in the case of Kashmir, which was the cause of war with Pakistan at the time and again in 1965. The need both to allow for the ethnic and linguistic heterogeneity of the subcontinent and to contain the consequential separatist tendencies dominated constitution-making from 1947–50 and made the federal solution almost inevitable. The main features of the constitution that command our attention are (a) the very strong powers of the center to impose its own rule on a state; (b) the list of state subjects; and (c) the division of revenues, and other financial arrangements, as between the center and the states.

To elaborate on these features, first, the president of the republic may declare (subject to eventual parliamentary approval) an emergency on grounds of external security, or on grounds of internal instability in a state (so-called constitutional emergency), or for financial emergency. Constitutional emergency has been declared several times in our period, with the replacement of state ministerial rule by that of the president or his representative, the governor of the state. These strong, and in the event much used, powers were clearly incorporated in the constitution to ensure the ultimate power of the central government.

Second, among the state subjects is agriculture. This does not exclude important central initiatives and control, such as central finance for irrigation, subsidies, and price control, but it does preclude any central taxation of land or agricultural income. This has reduced the flexibility of central budgeting and has resulted in the continuous decline of agricultural taxation to the point of irrelevance. Furthermore, the center can promote but not implement schemes of land reform. Another important state subject is power. The inefficiency of the state enterprises is notorious, and power shortages have frequently held back production.

Third, the division of tax revenues under different heads (for example, sales, excise, and income taxes) both for collection and apportionment between center and states is decided periodically (normally quinquennially) by the independent Finance Commission appointed by the president. This, however, does not greatly reduce the fiscal power of the center over the states, since the latter still rely on the center for grants in aid and for the location of central investment projects. It must also be noted that state governments can borrow only with central permission.[4] Apart from the new constitution, the other important political events in the first decade after independence, which also responded to India's heterogeneity, were the reorganization of states on linguistic lines.[5] After Potti Sriramulu fasted to death in 1953, Andhra was created. At the time of the States Reorganization Act of 1956, there were 14 states. In 1960 Bombay State was split into Gujarat and Maharashtra, and Nagaland was created in 1963, so that there were 16 states at the beginning of our period.[6]

Prior to our period, events in the economic sphere of major importance were the creation of the Planning Commission in 1950, the Industrial Policy Resolutions of 1948 and 1956, and the second Five-Year Plan and its subsequent breakdown in 1956/57.

The Planning Commission was created to guide the economy in accordance with the socialist pattern of society to which the Congress party under Nehru's influence had come to subscribe. The same is true of the industrial policy resolutions. These divided industry into three groups. The first consisted of "commanding height" industries—those related to defense, heavy industry, most mining, aircraft, air and rail transport, communications, and power. There was no mandatory nationalization, but all future projects were to be in the public sector. The second or in-between category would be open to both public and private initiative. The third category included most consumer good industries, which were to be left to private enterprise. All might be subject to control under the Industries (Development and Regulation) Act of 1951. Although exceptions were made, these policy resolutions largely governed the public-private industrial split and the ever-increasing share of the public sector.[7]

The first Five-Year Plan (1951/52 to 1955/56) was little more than a projection of public expenditure, including investment projects that were already on the shelf or under construction. The period it covered was one of considerable liberalization of the economic controls that had been initiated during World War II (1939–45). The government did not try to stimulate demand, and prices tended to fall. The idea of an integrated model for the entire economy, the future development of which would be guided by central planning, first found expression in the second Five-Year Plan (1956/57 to 1960/61). The intellectual basis for the plan was the famous Mahalanobis model, which featured the promotion of capital-intensive industry in the public sector—especially steel, other metals, and heavy machinery. Development would require rapid rises in such modern inputs, and exports could not be expanded fast enough to buy them abroad. This would in any case make the economy too dependent on Western capitalism. A large rise in the ratio of investment to GNP was envisaged, and the need to mobilize resources (that is, to create or borrow the savings needed) was emphasized. Foreign aid was essential for some time, but in the name of self-reliance it would need to be replaced as rapidly as possible by domestic savings as the indigenous output of capital goods increased. What of consumer goods? These were supposed to emerge from traditional labor-intensive industries, including agriculture, with little investment.

The second Five-Year Plan broke down almost before it started, with the emergence of growing fiscal and balance of payment deficits. Part of the crisis reaction was the imposition of stringent import and foreign exchange controls and price controls. These controls outlasted the crisis and became a dominant feature of macroeconomic policy for the entire period of our study. The Third Five-Year Plan essentially continued the investment patterns of the second plan, together with its implicit neglect of agriculture and export opportunities. Thereafter, and during our period, plans continued to be produced, but they ceased to be of any decisive macroeconomic importance.

We discern in the first twenty years of independence a contrast between the major disturbances and policy debates at the political and microeconomic levels and a relatively quiet acceptance of macroeconomic policy. The enormous problems involved in the creation and defense of a unified Indian nation have been touched upon. In addition there were the microeconomic and political debates over land reform, over attempts to promote a grassroots democracy (*panchayat raj*), community development, and other more or less Gandhian measures to assist rural development, such as the protection of traditional industries. Progress in these areas was often limited by the fact that Congress party support was largely dependent on the dominant rural castes and their bosses, who would lose by the measures that the central government was trying to promote.

Of course, there were some macroeconomic debates and disturbances. The size of the second and third plans was quite hotly debated, with the large planners winning. But it was common to both sides of the debate that the plans must be financed in a noninflationary manner. The voices that praised inflation (or at least argued that inflation and development were inseparable), noisy in Latin America, were not heard in India. Admittedly the planners left gaps, hoping that something would turn up, but they did not praise the gaps. We have also seen that the second plan broke down, with the twin alarm bells of inflation—which was 14 percent (as measured by the wholesale price index (WPI) in 1956/57 after two years of falling prices—and a rapid loss of reserves. But in addition to the imposition of controls, the conventional remedial measures leading to a reduction in the public deficit were quite quickly taken. These measures seem to have been generally accepted as unavoidable.

Apart from occasional bubbles, India has been a relatively low inflation country during the whole period since independence. It is often suggested that past experience of very high or hyperinflation makes governments, once the inflation has been mastered or burnt itself out, particularly wary of policies that may lead in that direction. There are certainly some examples, such as the People's Republic of

China, Germany, and Taiwan (China). India experienced a fairly severe inflation (and a major famine in Bengal) during the Second World War. The inflation was around 40 percent a year from 1940–43, not in the class of hyperinflation. However it was over 100 percent in 1943, the year of the Bengal famine, and it is possible that this contributed to a lasting anti-inflationary ethos, and shaped subsequent attitudes and policies toward food prices, food supply management, and buffer stocks.

India's relative fiscal conservatism could also be attributed to the fact that India is a democracy, inflation is unpopular, and elections have to be won. But one might also plausibly expect democracy to be inflation-prone since it gives voice to many competing groups and so tempts governments to throw money at them to keep them quiet. Thus democracy is an incomplete explanation of India's fiscal prudence and low inflation. The missing element lies, as already suggested, with the inherited character of the bureaucracy, and its traditions of guardianship, as well as with the austerity of India's first generation of politicians. The bureaucrats did not even see to it that their salaries were indexed (until the 1980s) and so they imposed on themselves an incentive to keep inflation low.[8]

Distrust of the price mechanism, especially a foreign trade pattern dictated by world prices (and hence comparative advantage), is easy to explain and is a feature of most developing countries. Free trade was thought to have been the "system" by which the colonial power exploited its colonies, and in India, *swadeshi*, in effect the boycotting and destruction of foreign goods, was for a long time part of the nationalist movement of noncooperation. In addition, as we have seen, a strong central bureaucracy entrusted with development tasks tends to think in terms of administration by control—politicians, too, in the absence of a strong ethos in favor of leaving things to the market, like the power to influence some events in a direct manner, for obvious reasons. While self-reliance, interpreted as a tendency to accept autarkic arguments in defiance of comparative advantage, was partly inherited by the Congress party from the preindependence days of nationalist fervor, the same thinking (though with different roots) is shared by Hindu-fundamentalist parties and by the Communist parties. Only the weak and now defunct Swatantra party was a strong proponent of liberal market solutions during the postindependence period.

Distrust of the price mechanism extended to those prices that are among the normal levers of macroeconomic policy—the exchange rate(s) of the rupee and interest rates. Not only have these been controlled for almost the whole of our period, but there was a deep reluctance to change them. This reluctance is an important element in the macroeconomic history of the period.

A Profile of the Indian Economy

From many points of view India is a heterogenous country. Its large space includes very variable climatic conditions, and contains many ethnic and religious groups speaking a multitude of languages. The role of government and its forms are complicated. This section is designed to help the reader understand the context of economic policies and events.[9]

Geography, Demography, Government

With a population of 702 million at the time of the 1981 population census, India is the world's second most populous country. The population density is high at 214 persons per square kilometer (1981),[10] about double that of China, but about one-third that of Bangladesh. It varies greatly, of course, from state to state. Kerala's density approaches that of Bangladesh. The country is not highly urbanized by international standards, the urban percentage being about 23 percent.

The population growth rate was estimated at 2 percent a year, with crude birth and death rates of about 33 and 13 per thousand, respectively. Half the population was under 20 years of age. The sex distribution was more unusual, with men dominating in every age group. Overall there were 7 percent more men than women. Life expectancy at birth was 52 years and infant mortality was 123 per thousand. These latter figures are typical of low-income countries. Primary school gross enrollment was 76 percent (90 percent for males and 61 percent for women): secondary school enrollment was 28 percent. These figures are again typical of low-income countries, but an enrollment of 9 percent in tertiary education was exceptionally high. However, while India's health, literacy, and educational indicators are typical of many low-income countries, they are considerably worse than some others in Asia, for example China and Sri Lanka.

India is divided into twenty-five states, varying in size from the giant Uttar Pradesh with 88 million people to the dwarf Sikkim. Twelve states have over 20 million people. The principle of division is mainly linguistic, there being fourteen major languages. The languages of the northern half of the country are fairly closely related to each other, but not to those of the south, which are Dravidian in origin. The south (Andhra, Karnataka, Kerala, and Tamil Nadu) with a population of about 165 million is deeply opposed to attempts to impose Hindi as the official language for all of India. English remains the lingua franca of central government.

Sometimes India is described as a quasi-federation, presumably because the central government has exceptional powers both to create states and to override the state governments by declaring an emergency. The relative powers of the center and states are described in the following chapters where relevant to our analysis.

India is a parliamentary democracy, in that the government may be overthrown through elections that are fairly conducted on the basis of universal adult suffrage. With two brief interludes, March 1977 to December 1979 and December 1989 to June 1991, the Congress party has been in power since independence. It has usually achieved between 40 and 50 percent of the vote, giving it a large majority in Parliament (the *Lok Sabha*). However, its grip has been weakening, and since 1991 it has formed a minority government. There are a great many parties, but most of them have only state or local support. On an all-India basis, the two Communist parties—the Communist Party of India (CPI) and the CPI (Marxist)—are the runners-up, with about 9 percent of the popular vote. But the Communists are strong only in a few states, especially Kerala and West Bengal. However, in the second half of the 1980s, the Hindu fundamentalist Bharatiya Janata Party emerged as a major force.

The central government is organized essentially on British lines—with a cabinet and party government, a legislative assembly, and a permanent civil service. The upper house *(Rajya Sabha)* and the president are chosen rather differently and have different (residual) powers from those of the House of Lords and the queen, but these differences are not important for our story. In practice, though not constitutionally, the prime minister has often been rather more than *primus inter pares*. But this presidential tendency depended on the ascendancy of the Nehru dynasty (Nehru, Indira Gandhi, and Rajiv Gandhi), which ended with the assassination of Rajiv Gandhi.

Macroeconomic Decisionmaking

Short-term management is, as everywhere, the major concern of the Finance Ministry. The finance minister may take many decisions alone, but the most serious and those with important political implications will be taken by the Cabinet. The Reserve Bank will be consulted, and expects to advise on many matters, but it has very little independent authority; even on matters where it has the power and responsibility for implementation, it can do little without the approval of the Cabinet.

The Planning Commission, which has no executive responsibility and is formally an advisory body, will also be party to important decisions. Formally, again, this cannot be otherwise since the prime minister is also chairman of the Planning Commission. Less formally, the question is the extent of the influence of the secretariat of the Planning Commission. Here it is relevant that the deputy chairman, who is effectively the head of the Planning Commission and has ministerial rank, attends cabinet meetings when economic subjects are under discussion. The Planning Commission has a brief to promote development in the longer run and will fight to protect the policies and projects enshrined in the Five-Year plans that it produces. It has more say in the pattern of expenditure cuts, when these have to be proposed, than on the total; and has little voice so far as the revenue or the exchange rate is concerned. But, as always, the influence of a particular department of the civil service depends on the experience and personality of its chief. A recent deputy chairman, Dr. Manmohan Singh, had previously been governor of the Reserve Bank and, before that, secretary of the Finance Ministry. This kind of wide experience of government is not unusual in India. Dr. Singh became finance minister in July 1991.

The relative power of these three chief actors, the Ministry of Finance, the Planning Commission, and the Reserve Bank of India (RBI) have changed over the years. Under Nehru the Planning Commission was very powerful, although it always had to treat the Finance Ministry with respect. But after Nehru's death, the Planning Commission lost power, partly because it had lost its protector against those who never believed its philosophy, but also because the fallibility of its projections had become all too obvious. The RBI has always been subordinate to the others.

Some Economic Magnitudes

GNP (at market prices) per head in 1981 was $260. This was about the average of the thirty-four low-income developing countries (those with GNP per head of $400 or less). Growth of the gross domestic product (GDP) had been about 3.6 percent a year since 1965, with population growth of about 2.3 percent a year. The sources of GDP in 1980/81 were 37 percent agriculture, 26 percent industry, and 37 percent services. Close to 70 percent of the labor force was in agriculture. These figures are, again, typical of low-income developing countries.

Agricultural output in India is still very dependent on the monsoon. In a bad year there may be a fall in output of as much as 15 percent. The monsoon is the main disturbing factor for India's economy—not the terms of trade as is the case for many developing countries. This remains true despite the spread of irrigation.

India trades little of its output. Merchandise exports in 1980/81 were 5.7 percent of GDP. The figure for exports is among the lowest in the developing world. This is a consequence of India's inward-looking policies as well as the sheer size of the country.

Two-thirds of India's exports in 1980/81 were manufactures, rising to three-quarters in 1989/90. These are high figures for a low-income country, but in absolute value (in 1980/81) manufactured exports were about half those of China, a third of those of Brazil, and a quarter of those of the Republic of Korea. Textiles and garments accounted for over 20 percent of exports. Those who think of India in terms of tea should note that this commodity accounted for only 6 percent of exports. In 1980/81 petroleum and fertilizers accounted for half of total imports (petroleum 42 percent), and capital equipment and metals for a quarter of all total imports. Foodgrain imports were negligible. This composition was, however, very different from both earlier and later years (see below).

Gross domestic investment was 22.7 percent of GDP (current market prices). This was a high level for a low-income country, though lower than China and Sri Lanka among India's neighbors. The corresponding savings were sourced as shown in table 1.1. It is important to note that households include not only households in the usual sense but also unincorporated enterprises, whether agricultural or industrial. It is also important to note that these estimates are shaky.

Changes in Structure and Growth Rates, and Recent Developments

The facts we have given were for 1980/81, three-fifths of the way through our whole period. But of course there have been some changes. The basic structure of

Table 1.1   Sources of Saving, 1980–81

Source	Percentage of GDP	Percentage of gross investment
Households	16.1	70.9
Private corporate	1.7	7.5
Public	3.4	15.0
Foreign	1.5	6.6
Total	22.7	100.0

Source: Government of India, CSO (1991), *National Accounts Statistics.*

production has changed rather slowly. In 1965 agriculture, industry, and services accounted for 44, 22, and 34 percent of output, respectively; in 1989 the proportions were 30, 29, and 41 percent. Within industry, manufacturing rose only from 16 to 18 percent of GDP. Despite (or because of) the drive for import substitution in manufactures (including the prohibition of imports of virtually all consumption goods), India's relative output of manufactures is less than that of almost all South and Central American countries, and of course is much less than that of the industrialized countries of East Asia.

There has also been an increase in the proportion of output exported, but from one very low level to another very low level. Exports of goods and nonfactor services rose from 4 percent of GDP in 1965 to 8 percent in 1989. In this respect India and Brazil often score lowest in the world. Within exports, there has been a considerable rise in the proportion of manufactures.

The structure of imports shows large changes. This is mainly for two reasons. The first is India's success, dating from the second half of our period, in growing more food grains. In the 1980s, India was self-sufficient in cereals, but in the mid-1960s she was heavily dependent on imports. Thus, in 1965 food constituted 22 percent of imports, and 8 percent in 1989. The second reason is the rise in the world price of oil. Despite some success with domestic discovery and production, imports of fuel have risen from 5 to 17 percent of total imports (having been as high as 42 percent in 1980/81).

Over the whole period (1965-89) GNP per head rose at the rate of 1.8 percent a year, less than the weighted average of developing countries and much less than in most Asian countries. Investment has risen from about 17 to 24 percent of GDP. The share of public investment in the total has risen from about 42 to 48 percent. Public sector savings rose slightly from the beginning of the period until the mid-1980s, but then fell back to less than 2 percent of GDP, so that the gap between public sector investment and saving has risen from about 4 percent of GDP to about 9 percent.

In general the 1980s were very different from the earlier part of the period. After the first oil shock in 1973, India built up reserves of food and foreign currency and greatly reduced its foreign debt as a ratio of GDP and exports (as we have seen, these ratios were low in 1980/81). Inflation was low, which was in marked contrast to inflation in many developing countries. But in the 1980s India abandoned its fiscal conservatism and ran large and increasing fiscal deficits. It began to borrow heavily, both domestically and abroad. While inflation rose to about 8 percent a year, the rate of growth of real GDP rose also to over 5 percent. This again was in contrast to many developing countries, whose growth slowed (and in some cases became negative) as they struggled under the weight of debt incurred and could no longer borrow.

There was certainly progress in the 1980s. Not only did the rate of growth of GDP rise, but there were significant gains in a number of social indicators. The expectation of life at birth has risen to 59 years, while infant mortality has fallen to 95 per thousand. The population growth rate fell, albeit only a little, to 2 percent a year or slightly less. Primary school enrollment has risen to 99 percent.

In 1980/81 the total domestic debt of central and state governments was 41 percent of GDP, and the country's total foreign debt was 136 percent of the value of exports. However, because of a high proportion of concessional loans, the total debt service of the foreign debt was less than 10 percent of the value of exports. India was creditworthy. But in 1988/89 the domestic debt had risen to 55 percent of GDP, and the foreign debt to 265 percent of exports, with a total debt service of 27 percent. Moreover, these figures were rising rapidly as the central government's borrowing requirement was over 10 percent of GDP, and the current account deficit was about 33 percent of the value of exports. A crisis was pending. How all this came about is fully examined in later chapters of this book.

Extent of the Public Sector

The public sector has grown rapidly since independence, largely by investment in heavy industry and irrigation, but also by nationalization, especially of financial institutions, beginning with the Reserve Bank of India in 1948. This of course, has been in line with the economic philosophy of a socialist pattern of society. This growth of ownership was accompanied by the institution of comprehensive controls; taken together this has resulted in a rapid increase in public administration.

We turn to a description of the extent of public sector economic activities, and more narrowly to the provision of services and their financing by the central and state governments. However, the influence of government is much wider and deeper than is implied by any description of its own economic activities. This is brought out in chapter 2 where we describe the functioning of markets and the pervasiveness of economic controls.

In describing the extent of public sector activity we shall usually mean the extent of public activities at all levels—central, state, and local governments—but these will also be distinguished. We include public enterprises that are supposed to be run on commercial lines, as well as those departmental enterprises that are not. Another distinction that needs to be borne in mind is that of the organized versus the unorganized sector. The organized sector is the public sector together with all private enterprises that employ more than ten persons (or twenty if no power is used). The unorganized sector in India is large, comprising almost the whole of agriculture, which still employs nearly 70 percent of the labor force, and a large segment of industry and services. As we shall see, the public sector dominates the organized sector but seems to be of relatively modest stature when stood up against the economy as a whole.

PUBLIC SECTOR EMPLOYMENT. In 1961 (a census year) the public sector accounted for 58 percent of the labor force in the organized sector. By the 1981 census this had risen to 68 percent. But as the organized sector accounted for only 6.4 and 10 percent of the total in these years, the public sector employed only 3.8 percent and 6.8 percent of the total labor force.[11] Table 1.2 shows the division of public and private sector organized employment for selected years.

Total organized employment has risen fastest in trade and commerce (7.0 times), public utilities (3.4 times), and services (2.8 times). The public proportion has risen markedly in all sectors where it was not already very high. Public employment has risen by 13 times in trade and commerce, 7 times in mining and quarrying, and 5 times in manufacturing. The proportions in the public sector have continued to rise throughout the period.

Most labor legislation effectively applies only to the organized sector. Trade unions also are almost wholly confined to the organized sector but do not usually reach down to the smaller private enterprises. The dominance of the public sector as employer of organized labor is especially noteworthy for these reasons. To a very large extent it is responsible for the earnings and conditions of service of this relatively privileged group of workers (see also chapter 2).

PUBLIC SECTOR VALUE ADDED. Table 1.3 shows the contribution of the public sector to GDP for thirteen sectors. Since 1960/61 public sector GDP has grown from 10 to 28 percent of the total. The rate of increase has accelerated, with a growth of over 8 percentage points in the 1980s. The largest rises have been in manufacturing, mining and quarrying, and banking and insurance. Banking and insurance owe much to nationalization, while the increase in the other two sectors is explained by the reservation of many industries for the public sector, together with oil discoveries in the second half of the 1970s. Not far behind these three sectors in explaining the growth of the public sector lie the public utilities (electricity, gas, and water) and public administration and defense.

PUBLIC SECTOR INVESTMENT AND SAVINGS. Table 1.4 shows total investment and public investment and savings, as percentages of GDP, for the usual selected years. Total investment as a percentage of GDP has risen fairly steadily over the years, and public investment has kept pace. However, it has fluctuated significantly and more so than private investment. Normally it is rather less than private investment, but has occasionally exceeded it in recent years. Public savings were growing dur-

Table 1.2 Employment in the Organized Sector
(thousands)

	1960–61		1970–71		1980–81		1988–89	
	Number	*Percent public*	*Number*	*Percent public*	*Number*	*Percent public*	*Number*	*Percent public*
Services	3,707	92	6,438	85	8,577	86	10,242	86
Manufacturing	3,389	11	4,822	16	6,047	25	6,237	30
Transport and communications	1,805	96	2,290	96	2,709	98	3,077	98
Trade and commerce	254	37	581	50	1,338	65	1,789	70
Agriculture and allied services	850	21	1,078	24	1,321	35	1,435	39
Construction	842	71	949	84	1,161	94	1,244	95
Mining and quarrying	679	19	606	29	948	86	1,054	91
Public utilities (electricity and water)	264	85	446	90	718	95	907	95
Total	12,090	58	17,070	61	22,879	68	25,985	71

Note: Private organized employment is somewhat underestimated since reporting is voluntary for enterprises in the range 10-25 workers.
Source: Government of India, Ministry of Finance (various years), *Economic Survey.*

Table 1.3   GDP from Public Sector, by Industry
(percentage of GDP at factor cost, current prices)

	1960/61	1970/71	1980/81	1988/89	1989/90
Agriculture	0.2	0.4	0.8	0.9	—
Forestry	0.3	0.3	0.4	0.3	—
Mining and quarrying	0.1	0.3	1.4	3.1	—
Manufacturing	0.4	1.4	2.3	3.5	—
Electricity, gas, and water	0.4	0.9	1.5	2.5	—
Construction	0.3	0.4	0.8	1.1	—
Trade	0.0	0.2	0.7	0.6	—
Railways	2.0	1.5	0.9	1.4	—
Other transport and storage	0.5	0.7	1.6	2.1	—
Communications	0.4	0.6	0.7	1.0	—
Banks and insurance	0.4	1.1	2.4	3.4	—
Public administration and defense	3.7	4.4	4.7	5.9	—
Other services	1.2	1.8	2.3	2.6	—
Total	10.0	13.8	19.7	27.1	28.0

Source: Government of India, CSO (1989a); Government of India, CSO (1991), *National Accounts Statistics*; Government of India, CSO (1991), *Quick Estimates of National Income 1989/90.*

ing the 1970s, though not as fast as public investment, but fell in the 1980s as current expenditure rapidly rose. As a result the gap between public savings and investment reached the very high figure of 9 percent of GDP in 1989/90. The gaps were filled mainly by borrowing from the private household sector.

Public sector savings are divided in table 1.4 into government administration and public enterprises (further detail is given in chapter 14). It is the former that has been responsible for the deterioration of the public finances. In the second half of the 1980s, current revenue did not cover current expenditure, so that government was making a large negative contribution to the financing of public investment.

The savings of public enterprises improved in the second half of our period. This, however, was not because of any general improvement in their profitability. The savings of public financial enterprises rose first because of the nationalization of the commercial banks in 1969 and insurance in 1971–72, and later because of the growth of banking and insurance. The rise in the savings of nonfinancial enterprises was almost entirely due to oil discoveries in the second half of the 1970s. Indeed in the mid-1980s nonfinancial nonoil public central enterprises made a net

Table 1.4   Public Investment and Savings

(percentage of GDP, current market prices)

	1960/61	*1970/71*	*1980/81*	*1988/89*	*1989/90*
Total investment	15.7	16.6	22.7	23.9	24.1
Public investment	7.1	6.5	8.7	9.9	10.7
Public savings	2.6	2.9	3.4	2.0	1.7
of administration	1.3	1.3	1.9	−2.1	—
of enterprises	1.3	1.6	1.5	4.1	—
Public investment less public savings	4.5	3.6	5.3	7.9	9.0

Source: Government of India, CSO (1989a); Government of India, CSO (1991), *National Accounts Statistics*; Government of India, CSO (1991), *Quick Estimates of National Income 1989/90.*

loss. The poor performance of these enterprises and also of state enterprises, especially in the power and transport sectors, has been a perennial problem and is examined further in later chapters, especially chapters 12 and 13.

THE CONTROL OF PUBLIC ENTERPRISES. The departmental enterprises such as the railways and the post office (which existed before independence) are of course under full ministerial control. But the central nondepartmental enterprises constitute the bulk of the public industrial sector. They employed 2 to 3 million workers in 1990 and included twenty of the twenty-five largest companies in India. These central enterprises are subject to at least the same controls over their investment and operations as any private enterprise. Indeed, both in principle and in practice, a public sector manager's freedom to manage is much more constricted than that of his private counterpart. Borrowing requires permission of his own responsible ministry as well as the Ministry of Finance. The prices charged require ministry agreement. There are elaborate procedures that have to be followed in making purchases. Investment, above a small discretionary limit, must receive ministry approval. The same goes for the choice of technology, and any cooperative agreement with foreign firms. Pay scales for the public sector are laid down by the government. The minister will expect to be consulted on the filling of any senior executive post. Ministers can and do dismiss managing directors for reasons that bear no relation to their efficiency but to a lack of compliance with ministerial wishes, wishes that may bear a negative relation to the efficiency of the enterprise.

Management also has to cope with surveillance from the Bureau of Public Enterprises, from government officials appointed to their boards, and from parliamentary committees, as well as parliamentary questioning. Of course, some surveillance is necessary and total autonomy would be insupportable. But no one in India who does not stand to benefit doubts that the present system contributes grievously to the universally acknowledged inefficiency of the public enterprises.

Less is known about state control over state enterprises and their financial performance. We content ourselves with a few facts and judgments drawn mainly from the Centre for Monitoring the Indian Economy (1986). State electricity boards accounted for over three-quarters of generating capacity in 1980/81. Almost all have large cumulative losses, continuing at least up to and including 1983/84. The loss in 1983/84 was Rs 300 crores. Load factors are low and transmission losses so high as to be accountable for only by theft. Irrigation is the other largest sector of state activity. To quote the seventh Five-Year Plan:

> In most of the states, gross receipts from irrigation works are at present insufficient to cover even working expenses. Current water rates in many states have not been reviewed and properly updated for the past many years. The states will have to take appropriate steps in this direction.

The loss in 1984/85 amounted to Rs 700 crores, revenue covering only 22 percent of expenditure. Road transport is another favorite area of state enterprise, the loss in 1982/83 being Rs 238 crores. Our source indicated that the state enterprises function much worse even than central enterprises. The highest posts are filled by either the political bosses or their sycophants. Losses are further magnified by the politicalization of the prices charged. The Planning Commission has for decades been lecturing state governments on their losses, with no apparent effect.

Government Revenues and Expenditures

We have considered the public sector as a whole, that is including public commercial enterprises. We now consider public finance in the narrower sense of the revenue and expenditure of government as such.

The central government collects roughly twice as much tax revenue as the states—in 1980/81, for instance, the central government's take was 10.3 percent of GDP at market prices, while that of the states was 5.4 percent. However, the states are constitutionally entitled to a part of the income tax and excise duties levied by the center, this part being determined quinquennially by an autonomous finance commission appointed by the president. In recent years the states' share has risen, and since 1977/78 the revenue retained by the states has often exceeded that of the central government. In 1980/81 the center retained 7.4 percent of GDP and the states retained 8.2 percent of GDP. In 1989/90 the corresponding figures were 7.6 and 7.5 percent.

The composition of taxes collected has not changed much in recent years and is given for 1980/81 and 1989/90 in table 1.5. The exception is that customs duties have risen very rapidly since 1983/84.

Since independence it is notable that the central government's tax collection has risen more rapidly than that of the states. This is largely because the states feel

Table 1.5   Different Tax Proportions Collected by Center and States

	Center		*States*		*Total*	
	1980/81	*1989/90*	*1980/81*	*1989/90*	*1980/81*	*1989/90*
Excise duties	49	43	12	15	37	34
Sales tax	n.a.	n.a.	58	58	19	19
Customs duties	26	35	n.a.	n.a.	17	23
Income tax	11	10	1	n.a.	8	7
Corporation tax	10	9	n.a.	n.a.	7	6
Land revenue	n.a.	n.a.	2	3	1	1
Other	4	3	27	23	11	9
Total	100	100	100	100	100	100

Source: Government of India, Ministry of Finance (various years), *Indian Economic Statistics—Public Finance;* and World Bank (various years), "India: Country Economic Memorandum."

unable or are unwilling to tax agriculture and under the constitution it is only they who can. There is thus no central tax on agricultural income, which is levied only in a few states. Previously, land tax was the mainstay of the revenue in India. It is now only 2.4 percent even of the states' taxes, and as a proportion of GDP it is negligible. Apart from this, there is little of note—the low proportion of direct taxes is a common feature of poor countries, but because India is a low-trading country, excise and sales taxes are, even after very recent increases, about 2.5 times as large as customs duties, despite the very high rates of import duty levied. Taxes accounted for 75 percent of the central revenue in 1980/81. Interest payments on loans to the states accounted for 7 percent. Most of the rest were receipts from public enterprises, with foreign grants making a small 4 percent contribution.

The total current revenue of the states, which first came to exceed that of the central government in 1979/80, was accounted for in 1980/81 as 70 percent by taxation, 19 percent by grants from the central government, and 11 percent by nontax revenues (such as irrigation charges and receipts from state enterprises). Apart from grants from the center, the states also receive loans and benefit from central government investments located in their territories so that the financial and economic influence of the central government over the states is powerful. However, this can of course be nullified by the political leverage of the states.

Turning to expenditure, it should be noted that health, education, and agriculture are state subjects and that a high proportion of current expenditure under these headings is made by the states. In contrast, defense is wholly central, and borrowing is mainly central so that a high proportion of total interest is paid by the central government (excluding that paid by the states to the center). Bearing the above in mind, in table 1.6 we present the consolidated current expenditures of central and

Table 1.6   Current Government Expenditure (CGE) of Center and States

	1980/81		1989/90	
	Percent GDP	*Percent CGE*	*Percent GDP*	*Percent CGE*
Defense	2.6	14.9	2.3	9.8
Interest	2.2	12.5	4.6	19.7
General administration	2.1	11.0	1.8	7.8
Specific subsidies[a]	1.6	8.6	2.4	10.3
Social and economic services	9.9	53.0	12.3	52.4
Total	8.6	100	23.4	100

a. Center only.
Source: Government of India, Ministry of Finance (various years), *Indian Economic Statistics— Public Finance*; and World Bank (various years), "India: Country Economic Memorandum."

state governments only under a few headings of particular interest. Changes in classification, and probable differences between the center and the states, make any comparison over time (or with other countries) of the relative amount devoted to health education and other social services, or economic services to industry and agriculture, too unreliable to include usefully.

If the figures are to be believed, the proportions spent on defense and general administration are modest and actually decline over the course of the 1980s.[12] The growth in interest payments over the 1980s is alarming and is primarily the result of a rapidly rising level of debt relative to GDP. The growth in subsidies—a high proportion of which go to food, fertilizers, and exports—is also notable. The reasons for these increases in government expenditure are examined at length in later chapters, especially in chapter 9.

Chapter Two

The Structure and Working of Markets

The manner in which an economy adjusts to changes in macroeconomic policy depends on the working of markets for the basic factors of production, labor, and capital,[1] and for the products themselves. Thus the ease with which macroeconomic policy can bring about required adjustments depends very much on price flexibility and on the speed and elasticity with which production changes in response to price changes; and this in turn depends on the flexibility of real wages and on labor mobility. Interest rates and the freedom of capital to move between different domestic sectors of economic activity are also important determinants of the reaction of the economic system to changes in macroeconomic policy. Our discussion refers mainly to the early 1980s, though some changes occurring in the second half of the 1980s are noted. Changes in 1991 and later are ignored. International capital movements are discussed in chapter 11.

Indian Labor Markets

The ability of an economy to make those adjustments to its productive structure that are necessitated by exogenous events, with minimum damage to output and to employment, depends greatly on the extent to which wages are flexible. Our discussion of Indian labor markets is guided by this consideration, and therefore does not examine the manner in which relative wages or earnings are determined, or the extent to which they may fail to reflect the scarcity of labor of different kinds and in different sectors of the economy. However, the flexibility of relative wages is important as well as the flexibility of the general level of wages. The general level is of most importance when the economy has to adjust to external events that cause a change in its terms of trade or balance of payments. But desirable adjustments of productive structure, whether for these or for other reasons, are also easier if there is some flexibility between sectors that permits and encourages the transfer of labor. It should further be noted that regulations regarding hiring and firing may also make adjustment difficult.

It is real wages that matter. They may be flexible either because money wages are flexible or because prices are flexible. In any economy that suffers from a chronic high rate of inflation, the flexibility of money wages is of little interest since price movements may rapidly cause large changes in real wages despite inflexibility of money wages. In India inflation is not chronically high, and has on occasion even become negative, so that money wages are relevant in that downward inflexibility may also entail a downward inflexibility of real wages.

A major, though not the only possible, cause of inflexibility is institutional intervention in the market, whether by labor laws and other public regulation, or by trade unions. We begin our inquiry by briefly describing the scale and nature of public regulation, which, like much else in India, is complex. Useful references include Subramanian (1977), Fallon (1986), Lucas (1986a), and Fallon and Lucas (1991).

Labor Legislation and Public Regulation

Apart from minimum wages there is very little regulation—either de jure or de facto—outside the so-called "organized" sector. It is therefore important to understand the relative size of the organized sector. Essentially, it consists of industrial establishments with over ten workers, and government services, comprising about 23 million workers in 1980–81. The working population was about 250 million. Of the 23 million, about 16 million workers were in the public sector, where wages and conditions of service are directly controlled. About 6 million were in organized manufacturing (public and private)—that is the factory sector, a factory being a manufacturing establishment with over ten workers (or over twenty if no power is used). The regulations that are to be discussed probably bear most fully on this latter sector, which also comprises the largest part of the organized sector that produces tradables. The upshot is that about 9 percent of total employment and 20 percent of manufacturing employment is "organized."[2] The main regulatory features that may inhibit wage flexibility include minimum wages, indexing, and direct determination of wages (above any statutory minimum). Our description of these features refers mainly to the early 1980s; since then there has probably been some increase in indexation and in trade union power.

We have seen that the great bulk of legislative and regulatory influences applies only to the organized sector. Minimum wages is the exception. There is no general national minimum wage, nor even a set of regional minima. Each state independently lays down minimum wages for certain industries on the advice of wage boards. Originally these were limited to a small number of non-unionized, mainly traditional trades. Now the coverage is much wider, even including agriculture in some states. But although the coverage is formally wider, enforcement is probably rare outside the organized sector. On the one hand, the many studies of rural wages never mention minimum wages when investigating reasons why rural wages appear not to be market-clearing; on the other hand, it is reported that rural inspectorates have been established in a few states.[3] In manufacturing, scanty evidence suggests that the great majority of enterprises pay more than the minimum wage; but some small factories (in the range of eleven to forty-nine workers) may in recent years have paid only the minimum wages for some categories of workers.[4] But such small factories anyway account for only 15 percent of organized manufacturing employment. In unorganized manufacturing it seems unlikely that there is any enforcement. Finally, we have no evidence concerning the impact of minimum wages in the private service sector; but probably much the same remarks apply as for manufacturing. The upshot is that it is very unlikely that minimum wage legislation has inhibited wage flexibility to any significant extent.

The machinery of government intervention has consisted mainly of wage boards, and the industrial relations machinery set up in 1947. These tripartite wage boards have been responsible for advising on minimum wages, but they may also set a recommended structure of wages. Their recommendations are not binding unless implemented by the state governments, this itself often depending on trade union agitation. At the peak, nineteen industries were covered, but it is now reported that "the Wage Board System has been virtually abandoned at the present time" (Fallon 1986). Some 45,000 disputes in 1985 were referred to the industrial relations machinery, where in most cases conciliation leads to a settlement. If not, the government may refer the matter to an arbitration tribunal (about 12,000 cases in 1985). There is some evidence that wage boards and industrial tribunals have widened (but not created) the spread of wages between large and small enterprises.[5] It is also clear that wage awards and adjudications make for inflexibility of money wages, but it is not clear that such inflexibility is significantly greater than would be the case given any degree of labor organization.

Some degree of partial indexation is incorporated in most wage settlements, in the form of the charmingly named "dearness allowance." This indexation is not statutorily regulated. There is no standardized system. Different tribunals and wage boards have devised and recommended different systems. The frequency of adjustment varies from monthly to annual. Indexation is linked to various cost of living indexes and is rarely 100 percent. Boards and tribunals have often recommended 100 percent for the lowest paid only. Indexation is probably not prevalent outside organized industry, and it is only since 1980 that the stipends of senior civil servants have been partially indexed. It seems that indexation in the organized sector has been increasing and may, over short periods, limit (but not prevent) a fall in real wages consequent on price rises.[6]

Another feature of the Indian wage scene is the system of bonus payments that applies to every establishment with over twenty workers. The bonus is a statutory payment introduced in the Payment of Bonus Act of 1965. It is not a true profit-sharing scheme, since it has statutory lower and upper limits ($8\frac{1}{3}$ and 20 percent) as a proportion of non-bonus wage payments. Only within these limits is it related to profits (less some statutorily defined deductions). A firm has to make bonus payments even if it makes a loss. There is no reason to suppose that the bonus payment system makes any difference to average wages paid, and it leads to frequent disputes and complicated accountancy. It is roundly condemned by Subramanian (1977).

There is a number of statutorily imposed nonwage costs of employment; some applying to establishments with over ten workers, and others to those with over twenty workers. These include sickness insurance, provident funds, and a fund for retirement gratuity. These payments are linked to wages and do not therefore affect flexibility. Whether or not they effectively raise the cost of employing a person need not concern us here.

More important than wage regulations are the laws concerning layoffs and closure, and conditions of employment. The original Industrial Disputes Act of 1947 applied to permanent workers in establishments with fifty workers or more, and required the payment of fifteen days compensation for each year of service. Subsequent amendments are startling. In 1976 any redundancy, or total closure, was made illegal, except with the prior permission of the appropriate government department, for establishments with 300 workers or more. In 1982 this figure was reduced to 100 workers or more. Government permission to close is normally dependent on agreement with the relevant unions (usually several), whose compliance has to be bought. The constitutionality of this legislation is being challenged; in the meantime, of course, illegal closure is becoming commonplace. A much more minor legislative intervention is the limitation on overtime work, and the requirement that overtime be paid at double standard time rates.

The serious damage that such legislation must do to industrial relations, employment, and productivity, is too obvious to need comment. It also causes distortions in the establishment and firm size structure of industry. But these matters are not our concern here. However, we *are* concerned with the increased rigidity that it imposes on the structure of Indian output, thus limiting the efficacy of macroeconomic measures whose success depends on the ease with which output can adjust to changing circumstances, especially those of the external economic environment.[7]

The upshot of the above discussion has to be that government regulation probably affects wage and earnings flexibility only to a limited extent in the relatively small organized sectors of the economy, and virtually not at all outside the organized sectors. The legislation on hiring and firing is a more serious impediment to flexibility of adjustment. Apart from government, the other potentially important actor is, of course, the trade union movement, to which we now turn.

The Trade Unions and Wage Flexibility

Trade union membership is not accurately known. Verified membership at the end of 1980 was 6 million, but true membership may approach 10 million—that is between one-fifth and one-third of all organized sector employment. Growth has been rapid, probably trebling since the beginning of our period. In organized manufacturing, unionization is 30 to 45 percent. Outside the organized sector, unionization is rare, the most notable exception being the agricultural trade unions in Kerala. The movement is quite fragmented. There are often many rival unions in an establishment, which may or may not be affiliated to one of several confederations. The latter are highly political organizations linked to political parties. The growth and existence of rival unions is believed to be a major cause of worsening industrial relations. The number of staff days lost in strikes and lockouts rose from around 6 million in the first half of the 1960s to over 40 million in the 1980s. This rise was interrupted by a sharp drop during Mrs. Gandhi's emergency from 1975–77, when the government forcefully, even brutally, confronted the unions. These signs of increasing union strength have probably carried over to increasing effectiveness in collective bargaining (although this is normally at firm or plant level without regional or national agreements), and in influencing and activating awards by wage boards and arbitration tribunals.

There has certainly been a marked upward trend in real hourly wages in organized industry, as shown by Annual Survey of Industry (ASI) statistics. From 1959–60 to 1964–65 there was no growth, but from then to 1979–80 the rate of growth was 3.6 percent a year, double the rate of growth of real income per head. Such evidence as there is shows growth of less than 1 percent a year in the real agricultural daily wage over the same period.[8] Wages also probably grew in unorganized manufacturing, but at a slower rate than in the organized sector. Thus Little, Mazumdar, and Page (1987) found evidence of widening differentials across enterprise-size classes, attributing this at least partly to institutional influences on the part of both government and unions.

The evidence is thus that the growth of union power has resulted in a higher rate of growth of real wages in organized manufacturing than elsewhere. Though not the same thing, it seems likely that the growth of union power would also result in some increased inflexibility of nominal and real wages in that sector.

The proof of the pudding is in the eating. ASI figures do not record any year in which nominal wages have failed to rise. But real wages fell in 1964–65, 1967–68, 1974–75 and 1980–81 by amounts ranging from 2 to 12 percent. The series Agricultural Wages in India (AWI) also records no year in which nominal wages fell. But real wages have often fallen, and for several consecutive years. Thus between 1964–65 and 1967–68 they fell by 9 percent, between 1971–72 and 1974–75 by 26 percent, and between 1978–79 and 1980–81 by 17 percent.[9]

Agricultural Wages

Wage formation in agriculture has been the subject of much scholarly work of both a theoretical and an empirical nature. Some clues, but no very strong evidence, as to agricultural wage flexibility may be derived from these sources.[10] It appears that the same standard daily wage often applies not only to individuals of different productivity, in both peak and slack periods, but even applies for quite prolonged periods. There is thus some downward rigidity of money wages in slack periods; and even in bad years. This seems to stem from some perceived need for solidarity on the part of casual laborers. But there are exceptions—a laborer may sometimes accept a lower wage if in dire need of employment. Furthermore, earnings may be more flexible than the standard daily wage since there may be a shift to piece rates, which are more flexible; also, some daily wages are task specific, and this can result in a change in rupee earnings in slack periods without any change in any rate. Real wages are certainly more flexible than money wages. Since a good harvest produces low prices, real wages rise. A bad harvest implies both high food prices and a reduced demand for labor—in these circumstances the money wage will not rise enough to compensate for high food prices, and the real wage falls. It is possible that this effect is sometimes exacerbated by an element of upward rigidity in money wages.

The upshot seems to be that there is plenty of real wage flexibility, but falls in real wages are associated with price rises, not falls in money wages. The latter may sometimes occur, but not to the extent that real wages are market-clearing. All observers seem to agree on this; so some involuntary unemployment exists and persists.

Implications for Macroeconomic Policy

On the one hand, at the aggregate level there seems little or no reason to suppose that inflexible real wages seriously reduce the efficacy of a devaluation designed either to make Indian products more competitive in foreign markets, or to make exporting more profitable. On the other hand, Indian labor legislation must, to some degree, reduce the incentive to invest as well as the short-run flexibility of the output mix, and hence the appropriate detailed reaction to increased incentives and opportunities to export. But product market interventions, discussed later in this chapter, are probably more seriously distorting in this respect.

Indian Internal Capital Markets

There are two major segments to the financial sector—organized and informal. About the latter, little will be said here because little is known. It consists of village and urban moneylenders and the like, whose activities are outside direct government control. There are no reliable estimates of its quantitative importance. There have, however, been studies that show a connection between the organized and the informal sectors in the sense that changes in the tightness of credit in the former produce similar changes in the latter.[11] Thus, from the macroeconomic point of view, concentrating on the organized sector may not be misleading.

The government has been strongly interventionist in capital markets. Initially, the impetus for the extension of government influence and regulation came from the desire to reduce the hold of traditional moneylenders on rural credit markets. Later, in the heyday of planning, the motivation was more generally to acquire control over the disposal of the funds flowing through financial institutions. In 1955 the Imperial Bank of India, the largest Indian commercial bank, was nationalized, renamed the State Bank of India, and charged with the task of expanding into rural areas. This was followed in 1956 by the nationalization of the life insurance business and the setting up of the Life Insurance Corporation of India. Finally, in 1969 all large Indian commercial banks were nationalized. The government also created a whole array of financial institutions to perform specialized lending functions. Their deposit and lending rates and credit allocation policies are the subject of detailed government control. These controls are described later, with particular relevance to the working of macroeconomic policy. Overall, India's organized financial structure is complex. The sketch that follows does little more than highlight the most important features, and refers mainly to 1980.[12]

Traditional Banking—British Style with a Development Component

The Reserve Bank of India stands at the apex of the financial structure and performs the traditional central banking functions, but with a development orientation. Thus, in addition to conducting monetary policy, it plays a lead role in promoting the creation and development of financial institutions. The commercial banks are overwhelmingly the most important financial intermediaries in the system and hold 40 percent of the combined assets of financial institutions. There are now 201 scheduled commercial banks of which 28 are in the public sector and hold 90 percent of commercial bank assets. There are 52 private banks (of which 18 are foreign) that account for only about 9 percent of bank assets. There are also 121 "regional rural banks" set up to provide credit to the weaker sections of the rural population. Since nationalization, the number of bank offices has increased enormously, but at the same time bank profitability has declined seriously for reasons outlined later. Some financial intermediation is also carried out by nonbanking firms such as hire purchase companies and leasing companies, which compete with banks in taking deposits and making loans, but these firms are not as yet very important. More significant is the Post Office Savings Bank, run by the Post and Telegraphs Department on behalf of the Ministry of Finance, which operates through post offices and therefore can reach all over the country. Forty percent of its deposits come from rural areas. The deposits are lent entirely to the government and have become an important source of government finance in recent years.

Longer-Term Finance

Since independence, many institutions have been established to provide medium- and long-term credit to industry. Some of these operate mainly at the national level, lending mainly to large industry; others at the state level lend mainly to small industry. Apart from internal generation of funds, these institutions rely on borrowing from the Reserve Bank or other financial institutions to raise resources.

There is almost no direct borrowing from the public, and the borrowing from other financial institutions is largely on the basis of statutory provisions requiring the latter to invest in approved securities. The main national level institutions are the Industrial Development Bank of India (IDBI), the Industrial Credit and Investment Corporation of India (ICICI), and the Industrial Finance Corporation of India (IFCI). Of these, the IDBI is the largest in terms of size of assets. A borrower can in principle apply to any of these institutions, but in practice they have become quite specialized—for example, textiles are the province of IFCI, engineering that of ICICI. There is little or no competition between these institutions. Their lending rates are fixed by the Reserve Bank and they act in concert in making loans.

In addition to the above term-lending institutions, there are other institutions that provide industrial finance, mainly in the form of investment in shares and debentures. Of these the most important ones are the Life Insurance Corporation of India (LIC), the General Insurance Corporation of India (GIC), and the Unit Trust of India (UTI). Unlike the term-lending institutions, they tap funds directly from the public.

The above institutions lend mainly to industry. For agriculture there is now an extremely complex network of institutions providing both short- and longer-term finance. A multi-agency approach has been followed under which commercial banks, regional rural banks, and other field-level institutions such as cooperative banks provide rural finance, both for agriculture and small-scale industrial and service activities.

Government securities dominate the operations of the stock market. The ownership of government securities is heavily concentrated in the hands of institutional investors. As explained below, they are statutorily required to place a substantial proportion of their funds in government securities. However, the secondary market for government securities remains narrow since the holders tend to keep them until maturity. Corporate stocks and shares do not yet constitute a major instrument to mobilize household savings. In 1982/83, only 6.3 percent of the financial savings of the household sector were mobilized by the corporate sector in this way. However, the importance of new corporate issues has increased dramatically in recent years (see below).

Regulation of the Financial System

We concentrate mainly on the regulation of commercial banks since that is of most relevance for macroeconomic policy. The instruments of regulation may be divided into (a) reserve requirements, (b) interest rate controls, and (c) controls over the allocation of credit.

RESERVE REQUIREMENTS. Reserve requirements are the most important instruments of monetary policy. They consist of two different ratios which the banks have to observe—the cash reserve ratio (CRR) and the statutory liquidity ratio (SLR). The CRR, as its name suggests, specifies the proportion of their deposit liabilities that the banks must hold in the form of cash. In the late 1960s and early 1970s it stood at levels of around 5 percent, but starting in 1973 the trend has been firmly upward. In early 1991 the CRR stood at its legal upper limit of 15 percent.[13] The CRR has been quite flexibly used to control the supply of money and the total volume of credit. The SLR stipulates the proportion of their deposit liabilities that banks must invest in government and other "approved" securities. The trend in this ratio has also been firmly upward. By law, the upper limit on the SLR is 40 percent; starting from 25 percent in 1970 it was increased in steps to its 1991 level of 38.5 percent.[14]

By law and in practice, monetary arrangements in India severely constrain the scope for a monetary policy that is independent of the government budget. The government's borrowing requirement is met in substantial measure by the banking system in general and the Reserve Bank in particular. Since the Reserve Bank cannot control government deficits and is required to lend to cover them, monetary policy is largely concerned with trying to secure compatibility between fiscal deficits and an acceptable growth of the money supply. The CRR does so in a direct way by reducing the effective cash base of the banking system. The SLR does not directly affect high-powered money but captures bank credit for government use—for any given level of expenditure it indirectly reduces the government's need to borrow from the Reserve Bank and therefore limits the increase in high-powered money. Neither of these reserve ratios is fully effective in controlling the quantity of money (see chapter 10).

Open-market operations exist, but in little more than name. The market for government securities is almost entirely a captive market. This is because the government borrows at cheap administered rates. Banks therefore hold government securities only to the extent that they are compelled to hold them by SLR requirements. This applies to many other financial institutions that also have statutory requirements regarding their holdings of government securities.

Two other instruments deserve mention in connection with the overall volume of credit—discretionary lending by the Reserve Bank and quantitative credit controls. Variations in discretionary lending by the Reserve Bank ("refinance" in Indian usage) lead directly to changes in high-powered money. This is not very important in practice. Reserve Bank refinance is primarily aimed at favored "priority" activities such as food procurement and export credit and is therefore varied only within narrow limits. As far as quantitative credit controls are concerned, there used to be a certain amount of illusion. The official line of the Reserve Bank was that it could control not just the pattern of credit but the overall volume of credit by setting credit targets for banks. However, many years of overshooting of credit targets has dispelled this illusion. The Reserve Bank no longer believes that the volume of credit can be controlled independently of what is happening to high-powered money.

CONTROL OF INTEREST RATES. Almost all interest rates in organized financial markets are administratively fixed. In some cases the precise level is fixed, in others there are ceilings or floors or both. This applies not only to the interest rates that are relevant to the government's own borrowing and lending activities, but also to commercial banks and to other financial institutions. It applies even to corporate deposits, debentures, and preference shares (though in these cases only maxima are prescribed). The only "interest rate" that is not fixed is the rate of return on ordinary shares.

The government has thus not conducted interest rate policy with the object of allocating resources efficiently. (Desirable allocation is sought through direct control of credit.) Rather, the objectives of interest rate policy have been to support the activities of particular sectors and groups through preferential lending rates, and to finance the government's large borrowing programs as cheaply as possible. This is not to say that the government has not been aware of the need to offer an acceptable return to savings but that efforts in that direction have been limited by attempts to pursue the other objectives.

The structure of interest rates is complicated and what follows is only an indication of the basic thrust of the system. We take 1982/83 figures for the purpose of description. Though nominal rates have changed (mainly increased) over the years, relativities have not changed much, so a single year is enough to bring out the main points. Deposit rates in commercial banks are in the region of 8 percent for one-year deposits, going up to 11 percent for five-year deposits. The general commercial bank short-term lending rate (applicable to the private sector generally) is around 19 percent, but there are a number of exceptions. Low rates of 4 percent are available under a scheme that directs banks to lend at least 1 percent of their loan portfolio to small businesses, small farmers, and activities in areas designated by the government of India as "backward regions." Intermediate rates of 9 to 13 percent are available for exports and food procurement. As far as term loans are concerned, the general rate is 14 percent, though there are exceptions in favor of small-scale industry and certain agricultural activities, which receive loans at around 12 percent. The government borrows cheaply. The Treasury Bill rate is 4.6 percent. Rates on government bonds are in the range of 5 to 9 percent, depending on maturity.

The rate structure is dominated by the desire of the government to borrow cheaply and to secure cheap loans for favored activities. Other things being equal, the resultant rate structure reduces bank profitability—in order to limit this reduction the banks have to keep deposit rates low and general lending rates high. General lending rate ceilings have always been positive in real terms, even in years of very high inflation, but deposit rates have fluctuated widely from negative to positive as inflation waxed and waned. The real yield on government securities was negative in most years between 1970 and 1985.

CONTROLS ON THE ALLOCATION OF CREDIT. The government intervenes extensively in the allocation of credit. The two principal routes through which it does so are first, regulations governing "priority sector" lending, and second through the Credit Authorization Scheme (CAS). After nationalization in 1969, the banks were asked to ensure that total lending to "priority" sectors should by 1979 reach a level of not less than one-third of total outstanding credit. The priority sectors are defined as agriculture, small-scale industry, industrial estates, road and water transport operators, retail trade and small businesses, professionals and self-employed persons, education, and housing of weaker sections of the population. More recently, the government set a target that 40 percent of bank credit should be channeled to these sectors by 1985. In addition to these targets various subtargets have been set, of which the two most important are first that lending to agriculture should be at least 40 percent of the advances to the priority sector by 1985, and second that the ratio of credits to deposits of rural and semi-urban branches of banks should be not less than 60 percent. The targets have been met. As a result, the pattern of bank credit has changed substantially since 1969 when lending to priority sectors was only 14 percent of total lending (and lending to agriculture was about one-third of priority sector lending). The corollary is, of course, a decline in the proportion of bank credit going to "nonpriority" sectors, notably medium- and large-scale industry and wholesale trade.

The regulations of the CAS require that large individual credits made by banks be scrutinized and approved by the Reserve Bank. The credit threshold above which Reserve Bank permission is required is currently 40 million rupees. There is also a separate threshold for term lending. The objectives of the CAS are to ensure that lending is in accordance with planning priorities, to aid overall credit control in the context of the cash credit system (that is, an overdraft system) that Indian banks operate, and to curb excessive inventory holding.

The CAS introduces delays into the process of making loans since Reserve Bank approval of an individual loan takes at least one month and sometimes up to six months. Doubts have been expressed whether this measure (which reduces the flexibility of banks' operations) is desirable, given the regulations regarding priority sector lending and the various norms that have been developed over the years about the extent to which current assets of borrowers should be financed from own resources as distinct from bank credit. The CAS may, however, have some use in controlling aggregate credit in the context of the cash credit system. Under this system borrowers are given credit limits, which they utilize at their discretion. This can dilute credit control since there is the danger that borrowers with unutilized credit limits could increase their drawings without notice. Under the CAS, the Reserve Bank can prevent overgenerous credit limits being established by banks. But this is a very blunt instrument of overall credit control and was substantially liberalized in the second half of the 1980s.

Financial Deepening and the Flow of Funds

In many developing countries the phenomenon of financial repression has been observed, meaning a low degree of financial intermediation resulting from negative rates of interest on deposits and other financial assets, together with a very large spread between borrowing and lending rates. Thus private savings may be both discouraged and inefficiently transformed into investments.

The high degree of government control over interest rates, and preemption of bank lending, that we have described, does indeed amount to some degree of financial repression. Nevertheless, there has been a rapid increase of intermediation, or "financialization" of the economy. For instance the ratio of deposits to GDP rose from 13 percent in 1969 to 38 percent in 1991; and that of the ratio of advances to GDP from 10 to 25 percent.[15] In the flow of funds the main surplus sector is the household sector, and the main deficit sectors are the government and private corporations. Household funds flow mainly into bank deposits, provident funds, and cash, in that order. Stocks and shares were of little importance for most of this period. The most important source of funds for private corporations were the commercial banks and other financial institutions. However, in the late 1980s there was a phenomenal increase in new stock market issues, reaching Rs 6,500 crores in 1989.[16] The government obtains the bulk of its funds by the forced sale of treasury bills and bonds to financial institutions, again principally the commercial banks.

The increasing degree of financial intermediation was closely associated with the very rapid spread of commercial banking throughout the country (including the rural areas) after bank nationalization in 1969, though the growth of other financial institutions has also played a part. This spread has also surely contributed to the rapid rise in household financial savings and probably also to the rise in the overall rate of saving.

While the development of India's financial system has been impressive, there have been costs as well as benefits. Most notably, the profitability of the commercial banks has been seriously eroded, almost to vanishing point. The rapid expansion of branches was costly, and the quality of loan portfolios has been badly affected by the need to meet the government's lending targets. This has been on top of the unfavorable controlled interest structure described earlier. There was some reform of the system in the second half of the 1980s, mainly relating to greater interest rate flexibility. By 1991 further reform of the system had become urgent. It is ironical that severe regulation led to undercapitalization and a generally slack prudential system.

Indian Product Markets

The smoothness of macroeconomic adjustment and the effectiveness of macroeconomic policies are critically dependent on the functioning of product markets reflected in factors such as the flexibility of the aggregate price level and of relative prices, the responsiveness of output and of foreign trade to relative price changes, and the taxability of the outputs and the incomes generated. The functioning of product markets is in turn affected by government intervention as well as other factors.

Government regulation of product markets has been extensive and complicated. The following description highlights only those aspects that have important macroeconomic implications. It is valid for the early 1980s. Some liberalization has taken place since, but it has not been far-reaching at least until 1991.

Industrial Licensing

Three sets of licensing policies that control the entry and growth of firms are particularly noteworthy—capacity licensing, monopoly control, and small-scale industry reservations. Capacity licensing was originally undertaken mainly as an instrument of planning, supposedly but wholly unrealistically to ensure that supply matched demand. Under the Industries Act of 1951, prior clearance in the form of a license is required to set up a plant, expand or relocate production, or introduce a new product, for example. Despite sporadic relaxations and ex post "regularization of installed capacity," this remains an important barrier. Only half of the applications are approved and there are substantial delays in processing these. Firms frequently put in bogus applications simply to forestall competition. No consistent economic criteria were ever employed, and the need for them was not even realized. First come first served, and lobbying by large industrial concerns were probably the most important determinants.

Monopoly control was introduced to prevent the concentration of economic power and to curb restrictive practices. Under the Monopolies and Restrictive Trade Practices Act of 1969, firms with assets above a certain threshold or with a dominant market share (MRTP firms) have to receive clearances before entering or expanding any line of production. Thresholds were fixed in nominal terms for long periods, so that the regulations became increasingly restrictive. MRTP firms are generally restricted to core industries; they can enter other industries only if they comply with extremely onerous export and/or location conditions. Evidence suggests that the rate of approvals for MRTP firms is no worse than for industrial licenses generally but the delays are much longer; many applications take around two years to process. The effect of MRTP regulations has been to limit the growth of large firms and thus to prevent economies of scale being realized, and to limit expenditure on research and development. In many cases, by limiting the exercise of countervailing power, competition has been reduced, not increased.

Concessions to small-scale industry were introduced principally to promote employment on the doubtful theory that small-scale firms are labor-intensive. Assistance is given to them in many ways, including tax and interest rate concessions and guaranteed government procurement, but the most important method is that a large number of items are reserved for the small-scale sector and cannot legally be produced by larger firms. This limits competition from and expansion of large firms. The system also limits the expansion of small firms themselves since they stand to lose their concessions as soon as they reach the threshold size. It is generally agreed that there have been serious consequences in terms of inadequate economies of scale and technological obsolescence.[17]

There are many other restrictions on the expansion of industry, for example controls on location, reservation of industries for the public sector, and controls on foreign collaboration. Direct foreign investment is strictly controlled under the Foreign Exchange Regulation Act (FERA) of 1973. Companies covered by this act face even more constraints on their expansion than MRTP companies. It should also be noted that exit is as difficult in Indian industry as entry or expansion. Both labor retrenchment and bankruptcy and liquidation procedures are extremely cumbersome and politicized, making it almost impossible to close down a business legally.

Foreign Trade Controls

Import controls were brought in during the Second World War and relaxed after independence. They were reintroduced after the foreign exchange crisis of 1957. Since then there have been periods of severe tightening (1957–62 and 1968–74) and moderate relaxation (1966–68, 1975–79, and 1982–89) depending on the state of the foreign exchange reserves.

The main instrument of import control has been the import licensing system buttressed by the "actual user" policy (which forbids imports by intermediaries) and the "canalization" of many bulk imports (that is, monopoly import by public sector agencies). Imports of finished consumer goods are banned, with the exception of a few essential items such as edible oils, kerosene, and life-saving drugs. Intermediate and capital goods are divided into categories such as "banned," "restricted," and "OGL" (Open General License). There is nothing that can be freely imported. Even goods on OGL can be imported only by an actual user, that is by a firm which uses the imported item in its own production process. The intention of this policy is to control the end-use of imports and prevent profiteering by intermediaries. For imports not on OGL, there is a discretionary case-by-case approach. The actual user has to satisfy the criteria of "essentiality" and "indigenous angle clearance," the latter certifying that the item is not available locally. The industrial licensing system also has some import control features built into it. The issue of an industrial license requires clearance by special committees if the import of capital goods or technology is involved, and such clearance may be denied if the foreign exchange outlay is considered to be too large.

While imports are generally governed by the actual user rule, many key inputs are imported in bulk for resale by sixteen public canalizing agencies. (Some exports are also channeled through these agencies.) Of these canalized items, the most important are cereals, petroleum, fertilizers, iron and steel, nonferrous metals, edible oils, rubber, newsprint, cement, and sugar. It is far from clear that canalization through public agencies achieves scale economies in purchase or adequate control over quality; the policy does, however, ensure that the import, pricing, and distribution of these products is subject to government discretion.

Since 1977 there has been some relaxation of the import control system, particularly in the direction of expanding the scope of the OGL list. There has also been somewhat greater permissiveness in the administration of import licensing. But these relaxations have principally related to "noncompetitive imports," where there is no competing domestic production.

Imports are, of course, also subject to tariffs, which in some cases are well over 100 percent. Over most of the period, internal prices have been higher than landed cost (inclusive of tariff) because of quantitative import restrictions. This tendency has been partially reversed from 1980 onward since Indian tariffs have been raised substantially (the ratio of duties collected to total imports, which was around 25 percent in the 1970s, had risen to over 40 percent by 1989/90) and there is now redundancy in some tariffs. Measured effective rates of protection in India are high, particularly in the capital-intensive sectors. For these sectors, the most recent estimate of the effective rate of protection is above 70 percent;[18] when last measured by Bhagwati and Srinivasan (1975) in 1968/69 the effective rate was around 100 percent.

The discrimination implied by the above system against exports has been partially counteracted by a haphazard system of export subsidies. The principal means of subsidization have been cash assistance through the budget, duty drawbacks, and the benefit of preferential treatment as regards imports. Favored import treatment has been given in the form of import replenishment licenses. These had larger allowable shopping lists compared to actual user licenses and, in addition, could legally be sold at a premium to other users (though with many restrictions on transferability). In times of foreign exchange shortage, this premium has been high, thus providing a significant monetary incentive to exporters. Studies of the magnitude of export incentives suggest, however, that they have been too small to offset the attractiveness of producing import substitutes or of selling in the home market. The average subsidy on exports has been in the 10 to 15 percent range in the 1970s. Only engineering goods and chemicals have received substantially higher subsidies in the 40 to 50 percent range. Measured effective rates of protection on exports are much lower than on domestic sales, and are sometimes negative.[19]

Price and Distribution Controls

In addition to industrial licensing and import controls, the government has also attempted to control the prices of a range of commodities and their distribution. Though this form of intervention has been diluted in recent years, its scope nevertheless remains extensive. To quote from a recent (1986) Finance Ministry White Paper on administered prices, "The WPI consists of a total of 360 commodities of which there are 55 major items whose prices are either fully administered, partially administered or subjected to different forms of voluntary and other mechanisms of control. The total weight of these items in the WPI is 30.85 percent." Fully administered items include petroleum products, coal, electricity, fertilizers, iron and steel products, nonferrous metals, drugs and medicines, paper, and newsprint.

Partially administered items explicitly under a dual pricing scheme in which the existence of a free market is officially and legally recognized include rice, wheat, sugar, vanaspati, and cement. The avowed objectives of administered price policy have been to provide poorer groups with certain basic necessities at low prices, to provide key inputs for the development process at low prices, to encourage the use of certain commodities such as fertilizers, and to control inflation.[20]

The methods of price and distribution control in industry have varied enormously. Producer prices are generally fixed on a cost-plus basis. The objective of providing certain goods cheaply for favored uses has implications for the profitability of producers (or for the government budget). Balancing these interests has led to complicated systems of control. Sometimes (as for a long time in the case of steel) all plants in a given industry have been given a uniform price for a given product that was then allocated to consumers at a fixed price by a canalizing agency, with certain favored users being ahead in the queue. Sometimes (as in the case of fertilizers) different "retention prices" have been fixed for different plants for the same product. This in effect allows higher product prices for inefficient plants. The combined output is then pooled along with imports and sold to consumers at a subsidized price, the subsidy being partly an explicit charge on the budget and partly a concealed charge on efficient plants. Sometimes (as in the case of cement) there are different prices for the same product from a given plant—each plant has to deliver stipulated "levy" quantities at a fixed price and the rest can be sold on the free market. The levy quantities are made available to priority users.

Price intervention in industry has tended to produce the following effects.

- As one would expect, price control has led to shortages of several commodities. This was, for example, true of cement until partial decontrol led to a rapid increase in supply.
- In some cases, for example steel, the administered prices kept retained profits of steel companies at such low levels as to prevent modernization and lower costs.
- In the case of fertilizers, the "retention price" system keeps inefficient producers going. The same applies in the case of newsprint where each newspaper is required to buy a fixed proportion of its needs from each of a number of suppliers. Imports are a residual source of supply. In both cases, there is little if any competition between producers, and no competition from imports.
- Particularly in the case of fertilizers, the object of keeping prices low has led to mounting government subsidies. The fertilizer subsidy in 1991 amounted to about 1 percent of GDP.
- Price and distribution controls have led in many years to flourishing black markets that have indirectly reduced the government's tax revenue.

The basic objective of price and distribution controls in agriculture is not to even out price fluctuations but to provide grain cheaply to low-income consumers and to provide incentives to farmers. If the government were interested solely in price stabilization it would operate wholly through the market and at market prices, building up stocks in good years and selling in bad years. It would not then be necessary to retain the present system of foodgrain pricing.

The basic structure of the present system is that on the advice of the Agricultural Prices Commission the government sets procurement prices for wheat and rice at which it stands ready to acquire grain for the public distribution system. The grain thus acquired plus imports of food (a government monopoly) form the central pool from which grain is supplied to "fair price shops" at "issue prices." The logistics of buying, selling, and storing are principally the responsibility of the Food Corporation of India (and to some extent of the state governments). Procurement in India is highly concentrated in three states, which regularly have food surpluses—Punjab, Haryana, and Uttar Pradesh. In these states the procurement price quite regularly acts as a support price. In the rest of India procurement prices are below market prices except in bumper crop years (for example, in 1975/76). Issue prices are of course never higher than market prices and in general are lower.

The setting of procurement prices is a complex and intensely political matter. On the one hand if procurement prices are too far below market prices, the government cannot procure. If procurement prices are too low and also act as support prices, the incentives for farmers to grow foodgrain are adversely affected. On the other hand, if procurement prices are too high, issue prices have to be raised, which goes against the objective of protecting the poor; if issue prices are not raised, the budgetary burden goes up. Thus, the conflicting interests of producers, consumers, food-surplus states, food-deficit states, and the central government have to be reconciled in setting food prices. The consensus view is that since the mid-1960s procurement prices have kept pace with input costs. Issue prices have been set at levels that have resulted in growing food subsidies. These have now increased from about 0.1 percent of GDP at the beginning of the 1970s to about 0.6 percent of GDP in 1989/90.

The government has from time to time used direct instruments of control to buttress the procurement price system. For example, until 1977 there were segregated food zones, though their severity waxed and waned with the tightness of the food situation. A food zone was created by cordoning an area (which generally coincided with a state though sometimes it was as small as a district) so that no grain could move across the boundary except under a government license. The object of zoning was to bottle up grain in surplus areas and drive down prices, thereby making procurement easier. Food zones were, however, abolished in 1977. In addition to food zones, there have also been other nonprice methods of procurement. The setting of maximum prices and direct levies on producers and wholesalers have been tried at various times, without much success because they could not be enforced. The only direct method of control that has worked is levies on processors, whose numbers are small enough to be monitored, such as rice mills.

Product Markets and Macroeconomic Adjustment

While interventions in product markets have, in general, mainly microeconomic objectives, this was not always the case in India. For example, import controls have quite consciously been used to manage the balance of payments. Similarly, one of the objectives of price controls has been to control the rate of inflation. How far controls have helped the attainment of macroeconomic objectives is of course another matter.

The Level of Costs and Prices

It is necessary to distinguish between the level of costs and prices in particular sectors, and their flexibility. It is the latter that is relevant for short-term macroeconomic adjustment. Nevertheless, something must be said about the former, which is important from a long-term point of view. Various examples have been given above of how industrial licensing, foreign trade controls, and price controls reduce external and internal competition in manufacturing; and hence reduce the pressure to innovate and cut costs. All these factors contribute to making Indian industry high-cost, with a high ratio of capital to output. Indirectly, this is also relevant for short-term policy insofar as adjustment is easier in a fast-growing than in a slow-growing economy.

The Flexibility of Absolute Prices

The general price level is of course flexible in an upward direction. It is, however, worth asking whether the structure of product markets tends to accelerate an on-going inflation (if money supply is accommodating). The following observations may be relevant.

- The behavior of prices, in particular the extent to which a rise may become self-perpetuating, depends on how much any such rise feeds back into higher wages. Fortunately, wage indexation is limited to the organized sector in India, and is less than 100 percent even where it operates.
- The food buffer stock operations of the government can help to moderate inflation, and surely did so after the droughts of 1979 and 1987. In this connection it is perhaps ironic that the government traditionally believes that private buffer stock operations—that is speculative hoarding and dishoarding—exert an inflationary impulse. But both activities, whether public or private, will if successful result in higher prices than otherwise when prices are relatively low, and lower prices when they are relatively high, thus reducing the amplitude of a food price bubble (though the public sector may build up its stocks from imports, which the private sector is not allowed to do). Admittedly it is possible for hoarding (public or private) to

be destabilizing. But academic studies have failed to provide any conclusive evidence of such destablization.

- The government has operated under the belief that price controls on key commodities help to moderate inflation. Evidence indicates that over a run of years administered prices have increased as fast if not faster than non-administered prices. But increases in administered prices are discontinuous and their sluggishness could in principle help in the short run to dampen cost-push forces, especially in the context of India's generally conservative monetary policy. As against this, price controls in official markets during an inflationary upsurge tend to increase the inflation of black-market prices, and also to increase budgetary subsidies and therefore high-powered money.

Downward flexibility of the price level can help in macroeconomic adjustment, for example by maintaining real demand when there is a monetary contraction. Do prices in India exhibit downward flexibility?

- In agriculture, prices fall quite regularly on a seasonal basis. They can also fall on an annual basis. For example, prices of food articles have fallen four times in the last twenty-five years (1968/69, 1975/76, 1976/77, and 1978/79). It has been asserted by some that the strength of farm lobbies has led in the 1980s to procurement prices being increased even in good years, thereby reducing the downward flexibility of food prices.
- The prices of manufactured goods also sometimes fall on a seasonal basis, but not as regularly as agricultural prices do. The seasonal price falls occur particularly in the agriculture-based, labor-intensive industries—for example in food processing. Manufactured goods prices as a whole have not fallen on an annual basis in the last twenty-five years, though almost all subsectors of manufacturing have shown a drop in at least one year; for example in food processing (1975/76, 1977/78, and 1981/82), in textiles (1975/76, 1985/86, and 1986/87), in chemicals (1970/71 and 1976/77), and in machinery (1976/77). On balance, it would appear (as might be expected) that industrial prices exhibit some downward flexibility but less so than agricultural prices do. There is also some evidence of variable markup rates in industry.[21]
- It is possible that price controls would inhibit downward flexibility. But the practical importance of this point is not significant. Controlled commodities generally are also sold in black markets where prices can come down. So even if the controlled price does not decrease, the average of the controlled and the black-market price can.

The Flexibility of Relative Prices

Price controls make relative prices less responsive to changes in demand and supply conditions. This problem is less serious in cases where there is "dual pricing"—for example in foodgrains and cement. It is more serious where there is a fully administered price buttressed by a system of administrative allocation—for example in iron and steel products. Of course, even in such cases the black-market price could rise in response to a rise in demand, but that cannot act as a powerful signal for increasing total production, given the controls (though it can act as a signal for diverting existing production to the black market).

Some key relative prices of macroeconomic relevance, such as the terms of trade between agriculture and industry and the relative price of capital and consumer goods, have shown sizable movements. However, the government has been reluctant to devalue the exchange rate actively, even though a devaluation increases the price of exportables relative to nontradables.

The Elasticity of Supply of Output and Exports and of Demand for Imports

The restrictions on entry, growth, and exit in industry; the delays resulting from the industrial and import-licensing system; and the shortages caused by price controls inhibit any quick response of output to changing conditions. In particular, the elasticity of supply of exports is reduced by the above factors. This reduces the effectiveness of devaluation in increasing exports. Similarly, the fact that the import control system eliminates all except "essential" imports implies that the elasticity of demand for imports is reduced. Import restrictions can have quick effects on the balance of payments but over time they reduce the flexibility of balance of payments adjustment.

It seems fair to conclude that output prices in India are reasonably flexible but that government intervention in product markets has sharply reduced the responsiveness of output and foreign trade to price changes.

The Effects on Tax Revenue

The operation of the control systems encourages black markets and the generation of black incomes, and therefore leads to a reduction in tax revenue. Price controls of key commodities also lead to a budgetary burden through an increase in subsidies. The food and fertilizer subsidies have shown a dangerously rising trend. The same applies to budgetary support to "sick" industries. Price controls are one reason for the small contribution made by public sector enterprises to the budget. The reluctance to devalue has resulted in export subsidies that are a significant budgetary burden.

Part Two

Macroeconomic Crisis and Adjustment

Chapter Three

A Sketch of Political and Macroeconomic Developments from 1964 to 1991

In this chapter we present a sketch of political and macroeconomic developments from 1964/65 to 1990/91. We have divided the period into four subperiods, each of which includes a severe macroeconomic crisis: 1964/65 to 1970/71; 1971/72 to 1978/79; 1979/80 to 1984/85; and 1985/86 to 1990/91. The crisis episodes will be analyzed in depth in chapters 4 to 7. In the last section of this chapter we draw attention to overall trends in political economy over the whole period.

1964/65 to 1970/71

Nehru died in May 1964. As the first prime minister of independent India, he had held office continuously from 1947. During much of his lifetime the Congress was overwhelmingly the dominant political party. But toward the end of his life its hold was weakening. India's defeat at the hands of the Chinese in 1962 had shaken national confidence. After Nehru's death, the succession was managed by a caucus of state chief ministers and party bosses. This caucus (nicknamed the Syndicate) secured the election of Lal Bahadur Shastri as prime minister.

Shastri had a rural background and was not committed to Nehru's left-wing ideology. He was therefore receptive to the opposition to old-style Indian planning, both within the country (for example, from state chief ministers) and from outside (the aid donors). It was during his regime that the food minister, C. Subramaniam, began the reorientation of India's economic policy toward transforming traditional agriculture by the injection of new technology. Shastri did not have a smooth ride. Not only was there a drought in 1965, but there was also a war with Pakistan. This was followed by a suspension of U.S. aid to both India and Pakistan.

Shastri's tenure of office was cut short by his death in January 1966. After intense political maneuvering, the Syndicate was able to secure the prime ministership for Nehru's daughter, Indira Gandhi, who, it thought, would be its puppet. Morarji Desai, the defeated contender, refused a cabinet post. In June 1966 the rupee was devalued as a result of foreign pressure, and this was followed by another severe drought. National elections were held in February 1967, and they confirmed the progressive loss of support for the Congress party. Its share of the vote was reduced from 46 percent in 1962 to 41 percent in 1969, and its majority of 115 seats in Parliament to barely 25. Mrs. Gandhi was re-elected as prime minister with Morarji Desai as deputy prime minister and finance minister. In the elections to state assemblies that followed, the Congress received another setback. Opposition parties and coalitions came to power in six major states. There was, however, no coherent pattern in the swing against Congress. Gains were made by left, right, communal, and regional parties. Many observers were pessimistic about the prospects for democracy in India.

On the economic front there was a severe macroeconomic shock triggered by the two successive monsoon failures of 1965 and 1966. These droughts were superimposed on a longer-term agricultural stagnation. Indian planning, particularly in the second Five-Year Plan (1956–61), had neglected agriculture in favor of industry, particularly heavy industry. Though there was some change in this attitude during the third Five-Year Plan (1961–66), it did not go far enough. There was misplaced optimism that agricultural output could be increased at low cost by institutional changes, such as cooperative farming, and inadequate recognition that the input base of this sector was weak and needed radical improvement. While rapid population growth was adding to the demand for food, the possibilities of increasing output by an expansion of the cultivated area were diminishing, and agriculture remained highly dependent on the weather.

Agricultural production was almost stationary between 1960/61 and 1963/64. Favorable weather conditions resulted in strong growth in 1964/65, but the monsoon failure in 1965/66 reduced agricultural production by 17 percent and foodgrain output by 20 percent. The following year saw no perceptible improvement. Foodgrain production in 1965/66 and 1966/67 fell to a level lower than that of 1960/61 and per capita production fell considerably lower. The rate of inflation (WPI) rose above the politically sensitive danger-mark of 10 percent in 1966/67 and 1967/68 and food price inflation was even higher (around 20 percent). Food imports (partly financed by U.S. aid under PL 480) were critical in augmenting supply. But the importation of food was difficult because of the refusal of the U.S. administration in 1966 to renew the PL 480 agreement on a long-term basis (see below).

While the acceleration of inflation was principally caused by agricultural supply shocks, public finance was also a contributory factor. India was involved in two wars in the first half of the 1960s, with China in 1962 and with Pakistan in 1965. Defense expenditures doubled as a proportion of GDP from 1.6 percent in 1960/61 to 3.2 percent in 1965/66. The consolidated government fiscal deficit increased from 5.6 percent of GDP in 1960/61 to 6.7 percent in 1965/66. As might be expected, the worsening of the public finance position was particularly sharp in 1965/66, the year of the Indo-Pakistan War. Although fiscal deficits rose, there was in fact a substantial revenue effort in the central government budgets of 1963 and 1965. But it was politically difficult to increase tax rates year after year.

The balance of payments position had been fragile ever since the foreign exchange crisis of 1957, but it deteriorated sharply in 1965/66 and 1966/67. Exports of traditional goods slumped, and the dollar value of total exports fell for three years in succession (notwithstanding the devaluation of 1966). The current account deficit deteriorated from 43 percent of exports of goods and services in 1964/65 to 84 percent in 1966/67. The weakness of the balance of payments and the shortage of food increased the economy's dependence on foreign aid and loans. There was a sharp increase in gross external assistance from about 2 percent of GDP in 1961/62 to 3.5 percent of GDP in 1966/67. But the aid relationship was stormy. In 1965 the United States suspended its aid in response to the Indo-Pakistan war and later refused to renew the PL 480 agreement on a long-term basis, preferring to keep India "on a short leash" (in President Johnson's words) in order to exercise leverage over its policies. There was a concerted effort by the United States, the World Bank, and the IMF to use external assistance as an instrument to induce India (a) to adopt a new agricultural strategy and (b) to liberalize its network of industrial and trade controls and to devalue the rupee. The rupee was devalued by 36.5 percent in June 1966, and tariffs and export subsidies were simultaneously rationalized, on the understanding that the inflow of aid would be substantially increased.

While the country faced a severe inflation and balance of payments crisis, the government's room for maneuver was limited. Food stocks and foreign exchange reserves were very low, food imports were needed to prevent starvation, and since import controls were already severe, they could not be tightened further without serious dislocation of industrial production. Imports were covered roughly half and half by exports and foreign aid, and the actions of the aid donors—particularly the United States—further emphasized the vulnerability of the economy. Moreover, the government was weaker than it had ever been since independence. The Congress party's majority in parliament was slender, there was considerable intra-party strife quite apart from the challenge posed by other parties, and the position of the prime minister, Indira Gandhi, was very shaky.

The government's response to the macroeconomic crisis was complex, and three strands can be distinguished. First, restrictive fiscal policies were adopted. Second, the rupee was devalued along with some import liberalization and rationalization of import duties and export subsidies. Third, a new agricultural strategy encouraged the use of fertilizers and high-yielding seeds. The second and third of these were measures of a longer-term variety that the aid donors had insisted upon. Domestically, there was support for the change in agricultural strategy but almost none for the devaluation.

The government's fiscal restriction operated principally through restraint of expenditure, particularly capital expenditure, which was politically easier to axe than current expenditure. There were some measures to increase government revenues, but it was not easy for a rather weak government to increase tax rates after the hefty increases in the early 1960s. The rate of growth of consolidated government current expenditure was lower than in the first half of the decade, but capital expenditure fell by a third in *nominal* terms from 1966/67 to 1970/71, with a real decline of about 50 percent. Real gross fixed capital formation in the public sector fell about 20 percent during 1966/67 and 1967/68 and remained roughly constant at this level over the next three years. This is in contrast to the first half of the decade when it grew by 9 percent a year. The deficits of the government and the public sector were brought down sharply both in nominal terms and as a proportion of GDP. The same applies to government borrowing from the Reserve Bank, with the exception of the year 1968/69 when there was a bumper crop and the government felt more relaxed about letting the money supply increase.

The decline in aid inflows after 1966/67 was a contributory cause of the decline in public investment. In that year, gross aid disbursements reached $1.6 billion (3.5 percent of GDP). They declined to $1.2 billion (2 percent of GDP) by 1970/71. The effect on aid net of debt service was sharper still, from 2.7 percent of GDP to 1 percent of GDP. Statistically, this accounts for the entire decline in public investment. Maintaining public investment would have required higher domestic taxation, either explicit or through higher inflation.

The restrictive fiscal policies had a procyclical effect on the industrial sector, which was already suffering from a reduction in demand from the agricultural sector and shortages of agricultural raw materials and imported inputs. Though the industrial recession was mild, the capital goods sector suffered badly. Capital goods production fell by 17 percent over the two-year period 1966/67 and 1967/68 and rose very gradually after that, not reaching the 1965/66 level until 1973/74.

The balance of payments improved after 1966/67 but largely because of the decline in imports. Food imports fell after the agricultural recovery in 1968, and capital goods imports fell with the fall in investment. Such import liberalization as there was (and it affected only noncompetitive imports) was reversed toward the end of the decade. This was because aid flows were declining and it was feared that imports would surge as the economy emerged from the recession. Exports performed indifferently despite the devaluation. Export value fell in 1966/67 and in 1967/68 because of the droughts, increased by 14 percent in 1968/69 after a good crop year, and then grew only marginally until 1970/71.

Politically, devaluation was a disaster, being attacked on all sides as a surrender to reactionary capitalist pressure from the World Bank. It was blamed for recession, inflation, and the reduction in exports, though these were mainly the result of the drought and the government's restrictive policies. The reduction in aid confirmed the belief that devaluation was a sellout. There was little appreciation of the longer-term resource allocation benefits of the devaluation-liberalization package, and by the end of the decade the liberalization was aborted. This episode and the political difficulties it generated made a deep impression on Mrs. Gandhi and delayed the adoption of liberal economic policies for many years.

Inflation ceased during calendar 1967 along with the agricultural recovery in that year. The droughts and large grain imports of the mid-1960s reinforced the shift of attention toward agriculture that had begun during Shastri's premiership. The "green revolution" received rapid official acceptance and encouragement. From 1967/68 to 1970/71 foodgrain production rose by 35 percent (the wisdom of hindsight shows, however, that there was no change in the long-run trend). GDP also staged a recovery in these years, growing at 6 percent a year, though industrial performance was sluggish.

We saw above that the fiscal response to the shocks of the mid-1960s was contractionary. One reason for this was disillusionment with foreign aid and the desire for "self-reliance." Another reason, however, was a certain disenchantment with planning, which had come to be associated with expansionist policies. Accordingly, the Planning Commission declined in importance. Droughts and devaluation in any case made nonsense of the draft fourth Five-Year Plan. A "plan holiday" was declared from 1966 to 1969. The Planning Commission lost prestige. Power passed to the Finance Ministry, which from 1967–69 was headed by Morarji Desai, a financial conservative. At the same time, the Congress party and the government were politically in a weak position. So it is not surprising that the contraction took the form of expenditure cuts rather than tax increases.

Ironically, while financially conservative and cautiously liberal policies were being followed, politics was taking a radical turn. The election of 1967 shook the credibility of the Syndicate and convinced Mrs. Gandhi that the Congress needed a new image. Moreover, she needed a new base of support in order to free herself from the Syndicate, who she suspected would oust her if she did not toe their line. She therefore turned increasingly in a populist direction. In July 1969 she relieved Desai of the finance portfolio, thereby precipitating his resignation from the cabinet. The government then announced the nationalization of domestically-owned commercial banks by presidential ordinance (soon followed by parliamentary legislation) and passed the MRTP act regulating closely the activities of business houses.

These populist measures increased the Prime Minister's support and led inexorably to a split in the Congress party in November 1969. Mrs. Gandhi's wing of the Congress Party came to be known as Congress (R) and the conservative wing as Congress (O). The government was able to retain its parliamentary majority only with the support of two Communist and two regional parties. Throughout 1970 Mrs. Gandhi continued to emphasize her commitment to radical and socialist policies such as abolishing the privy purses of princes and redistributing land and wealth. In December 1970 she dissolved parliament and called a general election to consolidate her position.

The election was held in March 1971. It was different from previous elections because it was delinked from state elections so that national issues and personalities figured prominently, and Mrs. Gandhi was able to appeal directly to the voters in a "presidential" manner above the heads of party bosses. She campaigned on the slogan of *garibi hatao* (abolish poverty). The election resulted in a landslide victory for Congress (R), which with its allies secured a clear two-thirds majority in parliament. The radical turn in economic policy from 1969 led to a proliferation of controls and dilution of fiscal caution for several years.

1971/72 to 1978/79

Hard on the heels of the election of March 1971 came a crisis in foreign relations. The intervention of the Pakistani army in East Pakistan (now Bangladesh) resulted in an immense refugee problem in West Bengal. In response to a possible war and the long-standing alliance between Pakistan and the United States, Mrs. Gandhi concluded a treaty with the Soviet Union in August 1971. The two countries promised mutual support, short of actual military involvement, in the event of either being attacked by a third. When Pakistan launched an air attack against India in early December, the Indian army counterattacked in East Pakistan and won an unconditional surrender in two weeks.

Mrs. Gandhi's standing rose enormously as a result of this successful war. A decisive victory over India's traditional enemy was something that neither Nehru nor Shastri had accomplished. Mrs. Gandhi's personal position was further strengthened by the state elections of 1972 in which Congress (R) again swept the polls. The above events strengthened the hand of the left-radicals such as P. N. Haksar, D. P. Dhar, and Mohan Kumaramangalam, who had supported the prime minister during her intraparty struggles. The populist policies initiated in 1969 and 1970 were continued. Insurance companies were nationalized in 1972, followed by the coal industry in 1973. The government took over the management of many "sick" companies including a number of textile mills. The Foreign Exchange Regulation Act was passed in 1973, controlling foreign investment in India in a comprehensive manner. An array of regulatory measures was added on to an already over-regulated economy. This "radical-populist" phase lasted until 1974.

The mood of euphoria that attended Mrs. Gandhi's election and military victories had some macroeconomic consequences. It bred a rather cavalier attitude toward government expenditure and also led to various problems in managing food supplies. The radical rhetoric emphasized self-sufficiency in food and independence from the United States in this regard. A reluctance to refute this rhetoric contributed to delays in importing food after the droughts of 1972/73. The brief but disastrous episode of nationalization of the wholesale wheat trade (see below) was also a direct outgrowth of this populist phase.

Following the excellent crops of 1970/71, agricultural and foodgrain production fell in 1971/72 but was still above trend. The harvests in 1972/73 were very bad, with an 8 percent drop in agricultural production. Though there was some recovery in the following year, foodgrain production in 1973/74 was nevertheless lower than it had been in 1970/71. In 1974/75 there was a further sizable drop in agricultural output. This shock was accompanied by a sharp increase in the pressure of domestic demand. The war increased government current expenditure not only for the usual reasons but also because it left a costly legacy of 10 million refugees. The droughts, as always, led to expenditure on drought relief. In addition, there was a marked step-up in public investment from 1971/72 to revive the pace of development after the stagnation of the late 1960s. This was understandable, indeed desirable, but it went too far. Money supply grew rapidly, fueled by rising fiscal deficits.

The warning signs of macroeconomic problems were present in 1972/73 when food prices rose by 9 percent. (Averaging over months conceals some information—food prices rose by 25 percent between July 1972 and July 1973.) The government's response appears to have been delayed, uncoordinated, and even perverse. The Food Corporation of India appears not to have informed the planners of the true position regarding food stocks. When the problem began to be understood, the government responded with a scheme to nationalize the wheat trade in the spring of 1973. Here the influence of the left-radical group surrounding Mrs. Gandhi was clearly important, particularly D. P. Dhar who was then the planning minister. The logic of this move was said to be to enable the government to capture a commanding position in the wheat trade by eliminating middlemen. The whole exercise made the situation worse, and it was abandoned after a few months. Imports of food were also mishandled. The world price of wheat (like that of many other commodities) began a sensational rise in the summer of 1972. Unfortunately, the government delayed purchases, and somehow less was bought than had been authorized, so that food availability fell more than necessary in 1973. Finally, India ended up paying very high prices on the world market. Lack of information, lack of interministerial coordination, and wishful thinking about the next monsoon and about wheat nationalization all seem to have played a part. Ironically, while India was nationalizing the grain trade, the Soviet Union was buying cheap grain from the United States. Another policy mistake was the delay in the monetary policy response to inflation. Money supply was allowed to grow very rapidly in 1973/74 while the price situation was worsening.

As a final turn of the screw, India was hit by the oil shock as oil prices rose from $2.70 per barrel in September 1973 to $11.20 per barrel in September 1974. It must be noted that in September 1973 domestic inflation (WPI) was already running at 17 percent a year. Expressed as a proportion of GDP, the deterioration in India's terms of trade was small compared to many other oil-importing developing countries. But India is a low-trading country, and the balance of payments effects were large. The current account changed from a deficit of $450 million in 1972/73 to a deficit of $950 million in 1974/75, representing only 1.1 percent of

GDP but 21 percent of the value of exports. This change could be accounted for almost entirely by the price of oil. If oil prices had risen only as much as other import prices, there would have been a negligible worsening of the current account deficit in 1974/75 since exports were growing at a reasonably satisfactory rate.

Inflation worsened in 1973/74 (the WPI rose 25 percent) and the political situation deteriorated with it. Mrs. Gandhi's populist promises had led to high expectations, which were now replaced by feelings of frustration. In some states (for example, Maharashtra, Gujarat, and Bihar) food shortages were acute, and prices of critical commodities rose much more than the wholesale price index would suggest. (To give only one example, the national average price of wheat rose by 90 percent between September 1973 and September 1974.) These cost of living increases sparked riots and encouraged political movements led by frustrated middle-class idealists. A political solution was difficult because Mrs. Gandhi had overturned the party organization and installed her own people. When things went wrong, she and her protegés became the focus of discontent, and the police force was increasingly used to restore law and order.

The years 1973 and 1974 were turbulent. There were food riots in some states and an enormous increase in student unrest and industrial strikes. A large number of organized worker groups, particularly in the public sector, struck for higher wages—these included employees of nationalized banks and insurance companies; central and state government employees; employees of steel mills and other public sector undertakings; and even airline pilots, government doctors, and engineers. Table 3.1 gives some indicators.

The turning point came in May 1974 with the threatened strike by 2 million railway employees who were demanding large improvements in wages, dearness

Table 3.1   Indicators of Unrest, 1971–78

Year	Riots (thousands)	"Student indiscipline" (reported incidents)	Workdays lost (millions)
1971	64	4,380	16.5
1972	—	6,355	20.5
1973	—	5,551	20.6
1974	81	115,440	40.3
1975	67	3,847	21.9
1976	63	1,190	12.8
1977	80	7,520	25.3
1978	—	9,174	29.7

Source: Rudolph and Rudolph (1987).

allowance, and bonuses. This was the first national political challenge by a trade union to the central government since independence, and in that sense it was unprecedented and promised to destabilize the country. The strike never took place. The government declared it illegal under Defense of India Rules and arrested 20,000 workers and trade union leaders, with some display of brutality.

The agitation against Mrs. Gandhi found a focus in the leadership of Jayaprakash Narayan, a Gandhian socialist of national stature. His message of "total revolution" struck a chord with many people who were disenchanted with the promises of Mrs. Gandhi's radical rhetoric. But the high inflation of these years certainly fueled this movement. When inflation began to decline after September 1974, the opposition to Mrs. Gandhi began to wane. In retrospect, it appears that she would have been able to reassert her authority within a democratic framework were it not for certain fortuitous events connected with her conviction for some minor election offenses.

There were some anti-inflationary measures in 1973/74 but of a rather ambiguous variety. Government expenditure was cut, but money supply accelerated and inflation speeded up. Around the time of the rail strike, Mrs. Gandhi decided that inflation had reached the limits of political tolerance and had to be dealt with. Breaking the strike was itself an anti-inflationary measure; if it had succeeded, there would have been a wage-bargaining spree in other sectors. After the strike was broken, an interministerial task force of senior bureaucrats was formed to devise an anti-inflationary policy. When it came, the crackdown was savage. There was a series of tax measures (introduced in a supplementary budget in July 1974), nontax fiscal measures (promulgated by presidential ordinance though later ratified by acts of parliament), monetary measures, and measures to increase food availability.

Following this package of policies, inflation abruptly came to a halt and prices actually started falling from September 1974 (even though harvests in 1974/75 were poor). Wholesale price inflation averaged −1 percent in 1975/76 and 2 percent in 1976/77, and food prices fell 4.5 and 7 percent respectively in those two years. The disinflationary policies were surprisingly mild in their effects on output, though they were quite brutal in design. Manufacturing GDP rose by 4.5 percent in 1973/74 and by 3 and 2 percent in the following two years, respectively. Inflation continued to be low until the beginning of 1979 in spite of rapid money supply growth from 1976/77. The fact that the weather gods were smiling during these years has something to do with this outcome. But as we shall see in chapter 5 that is by no means a complete explanation.

We now turn to the evolution of the balance of payments. In the short run the current account deficit of 1974/75 was financed by increased aid from the traditional donors and the Organization of Petroleum Exporting Countries (OPEC), and by drawings on the unconditional and low-conditionality facilities of the IMF (including the newly set up Oil Facility) so that foreign exchange reserves did not fall. But the current account soon turned round in a most remarkable manner, and by 1976/77 there was a large surplus of $1,250 million (18 percent of exports) that persisted for the next two years. The main factor underlying this dramatic change was the rapid growth in exports and remittances. The latter was an unanticipated consequence of the oil price rise, the result of the emigration of Indian workers to the Middle East in search of opportunities created by the oil boom. The former owed a great deal to exchange rate policy.

The exchange rate story is interesting. As we saw earlier, after the 1966 devaluation Mrs. Gandhi would not have permitted an *overt* devaluation. After the dollar cut loose from gold in August 1971, the rupee was briefly pegged to the dollar. But in December 1971, after the so-called Smithsonian realignment, the pound sterling was chosen as the peg and remained so until 1975. Sterling was a weak currency at that time, and the rupee depreciated with it. The nominal effective exchange rate (against a trade-weighted basket of ten currencies) depreciated by 20 percent from 1971 to 1975, but there was no explicit devaluation. As a result, the competitiveness of exports was maintained during the inflationary surge; indeed, the real effective exchange rate fell during the period. The decision to link sterling was ex post a good one; its wisdom stands out in the rather muddled policymaking in the early 1970s. No doubt the very bad relations between the United States and India in 1971 had something to do with the change from a dollar to a sterling peg, but we believe there was also some clever anticipation on the part of a few senior bureaucrats who saw the importance of devaluing the rupee by stealth. After September 1975 the peg was altered to a basket of currencies with undisclosed weights, though sterling remained the currency in which the exchange rate was officially quoted. The sensible reason given was that this would reduce undesirable variations in the nominal effective rate (though it seems likely also that a further effective devaluation, which was anticipated if sterling had remained the peg, was thought to be undesirable). By then, inflation had fallen so sharply that the real exchange rate continued to depreciate though the nominal effective rate was held steady.

The period of the turnaround in the current account overlaps with Mrs. Gandhi's national emergency (June 1975 to March 1977). The emergency was not directly caused by macroeconomic events, though inflation did contribute indirectly to starting the political ferment. We saw that in 1974 there was considerable political instability. After September 1974 prices began to fall, but the momentum of the agitation continued. As part of the political maneuvering, Mrs. Gandhi was challenged in the courts for some election offenses. The ruling went against her and, though the charges were minor, she could have been unseated. In response, claiming that democracy and national unity were threatened, she imposed an emergency on 26 June 1975 (observing, however, the legal niceties in so doing). Individual rights were suspended, and the country acquired many of the characteristics of a police state. The emergency did not have direct macroeconomic effects of any significance. (It did however encourage the "deinstitutionalization of politics." As discussed in the last section of this chapter, this was to have indirect macroeconomic effects over the longer run.) Mrs. Gandhi claimed that it brought down inflation, but in fact the fight against inflation was really won in 1974. It was also claimed that the emergency scared tax evaders and hoarders of food stocks but, though useful, this was not critical. When the balance of payments situation improved in 1975 the deflationary policies were reversed, but liberalization of trade and other controls was slow to take place. It has been suggested that the pace of liberalization would have been faster if Mrs. Gandhi had not had to rely for support on the Communists, the leaders of all other parties having been locked up.

In January 1977 Mrs. Gandhi announced an election in order to secure legitimacy. There were also several other reasons behind her decision to hold elections—a wish to promote the political advance of her son Sanjay, the need to outflank opponents such as Jagjivan Ram in her own party, and plain misinformation about her popularity. Jagjivan Ram resigned from the cabinet and formed another party, the Congress for Democracy, as soon as the election was declared. The elections were held in March and the Congress was comprehensively defeated. People rejected the assault on individual rights and the controversial population policies (including "voluntary" sterilization) that had been followed. As, if not more, important was simple arithmetic. The opposition parties succeeded in combining either formally in the Janata party or, on the basis of electoral agreements, with Jagjivan Ram's new party. The Congress vote went down to 35 percent, and the Janata party secured 43 percent; in terms of parliamentary seats the Congress lost half its strength, and the Janata party won a very large majority. The emergency was over.

The Janata government took over in March 1977 with the aged Morarji Desai as prime minister and H. M. Patel as finance minister, both financial conservatives of the old school. The government was lucky with the rains in its first two years in office, and agricultural production increased at a very satisfactory rate, which permitted a reduction of food imports and a buildup of food stocks to record levels (21 million tonnes in July 1979). Export growth continued, though at a slower rate; imports rose strongly as a result of some import liberalization, and gross aid and loans fell after 1976. But remittances remained so buoyant that foreign exchange reserves rose to more than $7 billion in 1978, providing 9 months of import cover. Inflation was moderate despite the fact that money supply grew at around 20 percent a year, fueled by the rising foreign exchange reserves. The reasons underlying this puzzling phenomenon are discussed in chapter 5.

A striking feature of economic policy during 1977/78 and 1978/79 was that India was slow to make use of the large reserves of food and foreign exchange that continued to accumulate until the second oil price shock and the disastrous harvest of 1979/80. Real gross fixed investment fell as a proportion of GDP and so did its public component. Consolidated government and public sector deficits fell as a proportion of GDP in 1977/78, though they recovered partially in 1978/79. Three reasons can be advanced for the lack of expansion. First, the government's own import control policies prevented higher imports, an example of how microeconomic policies can affect or inhibit macroeconomic flexibility. Second, policymakers ex ante took a very cautious view of the growth of remittances. (Indeed, in criticizing policymakers for not using foreign exchange reserves, one has to bear in mind that such reserves came in very handy in the aftermath of 1979.) Finally, when the Janata government came in, it spent too much time devising a new plan and thus created delays in the expansion of investment.

From the beginning the Janata government and the Janata coalition in parliament were plagued by factionalism. There were three Janata leaders of considerable stature—Morarji Desai, Charan Singh, and Jagjivan Ram—but their personal ambitions kept them at loggerheads. In June 1978 Desai dismissed Charan Singh from the cabinet. Mrs. Gandhi began a comeback and returned to parliament by winning a by-election in the southern state of Karnataka. In January 1979 Desai was forced to take Charan Singh back into the cabinet as deputy prime minister and finance minister. But at the end of 1978/79 the government looked distinctly unstable.

1979/80 to 1984/85

By July 1979 the government was virtually immobilized by quarrels within the Janata party. Parliament presented an unsavory spectacle of byzantine intrigue, defections, and counterdefections. Charan Singh finally succeeded in forcing Morarji Desai out of office in July 1979 and becoming prime minister in his place. In doing so, however, he broke the Janata party and had to rely on parliamentary support from Mrs. Gandhi and her followers. This support was withdrawn after 28 days, and in due course the president decided to dissolve parliament and call fresh elections.

The economic situation deteriorated in 1979. Inflation accelerated as a result of a severe drought, the doubling of world oil prices, and the lagged effect of the rapid monetary expansion of the preceding years. The 1979 budget showed a very large increase in the fiscal deficit and in government borrowing from the Reserve Bank and the banking system generally. (In retrospect, this budget appears as a watershed marking the change from previous fiscal conservatism.) Mrs. Gandhi fought her election campaign focusing on the deteriorating law and order situation, the steep rise in the cost of living (the price of onions was an emotional issue), and the Janata government's inability to govern. The opposition parties could not muster a united front. In the national elections held at the beginning of 1980, Mrs. Gandhi won a sweeping victory. Her party, named after her as Congress (I), secured 43 percent of the votes cast and a two-thirds majority in parliament, a dramatic reversal of the result in the March 1977 election. Mrs. Gandhi remained in office until her assassination in October 1984.

During 1979/80 and 1980/81 the economy suffered from both internal and external shocks. The drought in 1979 was the worst since independence. In that year, agricultural production fell by 15.2 percent and foodgrain production by 17.6 percent. The terms of trade deteriorated by 33 percent during 1979 and 1980 as a result of the rise in oil prices. Domestic oil supplies were further disrupted by the agitation in Assam (a state that supplied one-third of India's oil production) against the inclusion in electoral registers of migrants into the state. This agitation began in 1979 and continued into 1980. The picketing of oil pipeline headquarters, followed by strikes by oil workers, led to refineries being shut down; consequently, an acute shortage of petroleum products developed. The drought and the disruption of fuel supplies led to power shortages, which in turn led to shortages of coal and transport facilities, adding to the infrastructure bottlenecks that had built up over the years. The combined effects of the drought and the shortages of key inputs led to an industrial recession in 1979/80 and 1980/81. Inflation accelerated sharply. Wholesale prices rose by 17 and 18 percent respectively in these two years. It is worth noting, however, that food articles rose in price somewhat less rapidly (8 and 11 percent respectively in the two periods) than the general index because the government sold food stocks on a large scale. The main contribution to the price rise came from manufactured goods and fuel.

The oil price rise and the accompanying world recession led to a significant deterioration in the balance of payments. The oil import bill increased from $2 billion in 1978/79 to $6.6 billion in 1980/81, and total imports rose over the same period from $8.3 billion to $15.8 billion. The current account changed from a small deficit of $350 million in 1978/79 (0.3 percent of GDP and 4 percent of exports) to a deficit of $2.9 billion in 1980/81 (1.7 percent of GDP and 26 percent of exports). The deterioration in the current account was thus somewhat greater than after the first oil shock. (It remains true, however, that India suffered less than other oil-importing developing countries, one reason being the negligibly small commercial borrowing during the 1970s. The "interest rate shock" did not affect India at all.) The overall foreign exchange situation, however, was more comfortable than in 1973/74 because reserves had piled up during the intervening years.

In sharp contrast to what happened after the first oil shock, there was little or no current account adjustment. (In 1984/85, the current account deficit was still running at 1.8 percent of GDP and 26 percent of exports.) The government's response to the shock was quite different. There was little fiscal restriction except in 1981 and no intensification of import controls. The government's stated intention was to bring about an "expansionary adjustment" by (a) increasing investment, (b) changing the pattern of investment to increase oil production and break infrastructure constraints, and (c) taking measures to increase public savings and exports. It was for such a program that the government negotiated a massive loan from the IMF under its Extended Fund Facility (EFF).

In 1980 India drew SDR 530 million from the IMF's Trust Fund and SDR 266 million from the Compensatory Financing Facility (CFF), both low-conditionality facilities. In the autumn of 1980 negotiations were started to obtain a large extended loan. The intention was to borrow preemptively to support a program of investment, growth, and structural adjustment as part of the sixth Five-Year Plan. At the beginning, the IMF negotiators were concerned about the seriousness of domestic resource mobilization efforts, but worries on this score were removed by the tough budget of 1981, which increased indirect taxes sharply, supplemented in the middle of the year by steep increases in administered prices of domestic crude oil, kerosene, electricity, and fertilizers. As a result of these measures, the credit ceilings in the IMF program, which in any case were rather generous, appeared to be well within reach. The government thus avoided the impression of submitting to foreign pressure. There was nevertheless considerable domestic opposition to the loan, particularly but not exclusively from the left, on the grounds that it was too large, too conditional, and would hurt the poorer sections of society. The government argued in response that the loan would reduce the burden on the poor by avoiding a recession, and that its conditions were no tougher than the requirements imposed by the country's own sixth Five-Year plan. Within the IMF there was strong opposition to the loan from the United States, which argued that it was too large, not conditional enough, and not specific enough about the conditions that the government should meet to show success in structural adjustment. In the final vote in the IMF's executive board in November 1981, the United States abstained, but India got the loan of SDR 5 billion, payable in three installments. India drew the first two installments of the EFF loan on schedule. In May 1984, India terminated the program, having drawn SDR 3.9 billion out of the SDR 5 billion authorized.

Notwithstanding the EFF program, the fiscal stance of the government was considerably more relaxed than it had been in 1973/74 to 1978/79. This is true of the whole period 1979/80 to 1984/85 and also of the period 1982/83 to 1984/85 (for example, after the EFF program came into operation). The more relaxed fiscal attitude of the 1980s can partly be explained by the desire to pursue an expansionary investment path, but it is also related to the shift toward populism and the dilution of the traditional political and bureaucratic austerity. The move away from fiscal conservatism was reflected in growing government subsidies, which increased from 1.7 percent of GDP in 1973–78 to 2.5 percent in 1979–84.

It is possible to check whether the intention to increase investment in the post-second oil shock period was in fact fulfilled. Table 3.2 presents data on public and private fixed capital formation in the 1973/74 to1978/79 and 1979/80 to 1984/85 periods. It can be seen that public fixed investment did indeed grow more rapidly, but this was accompanied by a reduction in the growth of private fixed investment. This is consistent with some crowding out as a result of the growing public deficit.

We saw above that there was little adjustment of the current account. The deficit was financed by borrowing, largely from the IMF but also from commercial sources. The lack of current account adjustment cannot be attributed to imports, which fell in value, helped by import substitution in oil and falling oil prices after 1982. The main culprit was exports whose growth was sluggish in sharp contrast to the 1973–78 period. Though partly due to a slowdown of world trade, it should be noticed that exports received no boost from a depreciating real exchange rate, since on this occasion India's inflation exceeded that of its main trading partners. The real exchange rate appreciated by 14 percent between 1979 and 1981. This appreciation was slightly offset by an increase in export incentives, but the contrast with the second half of the 1970s remains. After 1981 the real exchange rate

Table 3.2   Real Fixed Investment before and after 1979/80

	1973/74 to 1978/79	1979/80 to 1984/85
Average annual growth rates		
Real GFCF	4.8	4.1
Real public GFCF	5.3	7.3
Real private GFCF	4.8	1.3
Percentage of real GDP at market prices		
Real GFCF	17.8	19.0
Real public GFCF	7.7	9.4
Real private GFCF	10.1	9.6

Source: Tables 5.16 and 6.15.

was kept roughly constant, but Indian exports continued to suffer from the competitive disadvantage created in 1979–81 when the adverse change in the terms of trade would normally have called for a further real depreciation.

There were two other notable developments in the balance of payments. First, remittances stopped growing after 1981/82. Unlike the post-first oil shock period, there was no sustained boom in the Middle East. Most countries in the region were becoming more restrictive in their immigration policies, and some of them were disrupted by the Iran-Iraq war. Second, India for the first time resorted to commercial borrowing on a significant scale, reflecting not merely the need to cover current account deficits but "the lack of rupee resources" (that is, the government's budgetary problems). The expansionary policies in the first half of the 1980s (combined with modest liberalization) did lead to faster growth. But problems were stored up for the future by the fiscal deterioration and the lack of current account adjustment.

The economic events discussed above were played out against a political backdrop of increasing tension. Mrs. Gandhi returned triumphantly in 1980, but the following years were marked by growing center-state conflicts and communal problems, particularly the separatist (and partly terrorist) movement in the Punjab. In the course of trying to stamp out this movement, Mrs. Gandhi ordered the Indian army to assault the Golden Temple in Amritsar, which had become the terrorist headquarters. In revenge, she was assassinated by one of her own bodyguards on 31 October 1984. Her son Rajiv Gandhi succeeded her as prime minister and called a national election shortly thereafter. Elections were held at the end of the year and the Congress (I), whose election prospects looked distinctly uncertain before Mrs. Gandhi's death, was returned to power on the crest of a wave of sympathy, with a massive near four-fifths majority in parliament. The new government was sworn in on 1 January 1985, with Rajiv Gandhi as prime minister and V. P. Singh as finance minister. The landslide victory of Congress (I) was followed by state elections in March 1985. Congress did not sweep the board (opposition parties won in Andhra Pradesh, Karnataka, and West Bengal), but it won handsomely enough.

1985/86 to 1990/91

Rajiv Gandhi's first year in office began in a blaze of hope and high expectations. He had a modern, managerial style and clearly wanted to shed the ideological baggage of the past. The new government moved fast in the first few months and successfully undertook a number of political and economic initiatives. There were political agreements in both Punjab and Assam. The budget of 1985 reduced rates of direct taxation and introduced a number of significant measures of liberalization of industrial and trade policy. Later in the year the government issued a White Paper entitled *Long-Term Fiscal Policy*, setting out both its tax reform proposals and its plans to curb fiscal deficits of the center.[1] Some progress was made in the following year with reform of indirect taxation, but the intention to reduce fiscal deficits was to remain spectacularly unfulfilled.

The liberalizing measures of the Gandhi government from 1985/86 to 1989/90 can be summed up as follows. Many of them were undertaken early in the life of the government; from the middle of 1986/87 resistance to the program began and its pace slowed down considerably. After that there was no reversal but only minor advances.

- *Industrial deregulation.* There was some dilution of licensing requirements as regards entry and expansion of capacity. The list of industries open to large firms was extended. The asset threshold above which firms are subject to monopoly regulation was raised.
- *Import deregulation.* Restrictions on imports of capital goods were somewhat eased to encourage technological modernization. There was some replacement of quantitative import restrictions by tariffs, primarily in cases where there was no competing domestic production.
- *Export incentives.* These were substantially increased. Cash assistance and duty drawbacks went up. There was a widening of the coverage of products available to exporters against import replenishment licenses. Very substantial income tax concessions were given to business profits attributable to exports.
- *Exchange rate policy.* From 1986 there was a policy of active exchange rate depreciation.
- *Financial liberalization.* The yield on long-term government securities was raised a little, in the direction of market rates. There were some moves to develop the money market.
- *Taxation.* Rates of direct taxation were lowered to increase incentives and reduce evasion. The excise tax structure was modified to some extent in

the direction of value added taxation in order to reduce inefficiencies resulting from the erstwhile cascading system that provided tax offsets for only a limited range of products. The import tariff structure was somewhat simplified (but the average tariff rate went up).

The above liberalization was not all that bold looked at from the vantage point of the 1990s, but it was certainly faster than the funereal pace of 1975/76 to 1984/85. While it can be criticized as being lopsided in some respects (see chapter 7), it was largely pointed in the right direction from the viewpoint of efficiency and growth. But a stabilization program was also required since the underlying macroeconomic position was unsound. Both fiscal deficits and current account deficits needed correction. In this respect the government's performance in 1985/86 and 1986/87 was extremely poor. Admittedly the government was not lucky with the rains. Foodgrain output fell by 5 percent in 1986/87. (As is frequently the case in India, estimates of food production were far off the mark. The Economic Survey for 1986/87 estimated that food production had increased by 1 percent during the year.) But GDP grew by 4 percent, thanks to rapid growth in industry and services. There was a large increase in central and consolidated government fiscal deficits as a proportion of GDP, an outcome mainly to be attributed to the growth of current expenditure driven by the familiar troika of defense, interest, and subsidies but also by higher wages following the report of the Fourth Pay Commission. The current account deficit also worsened sharply, compared to 1984/85, in spite of falling oil prices and fast export growth in 1986/87. But the reserves did not fall as the inflow of nonresident deposits continued, and there was resort to more external commercial borrowing, both long and short term.

Politically, disillusionment with Rajiv Gandhi's government had already begun to set in by 1986/87. There was mounting regional and ethnic assertiveness, especially in Punjab where the progress of 1985 was not sustained. But the real turning point for Rajiv Gandhi came in 1987/88. In that year his reputation as an honest prime minister at the head of an essentially "clean" government was brought into question by allegations of corruption relating to the purchase of field artillery from the Swedish firm, Bofors. V. P. Singh resigned over this issue in April 1987. The Punjab problem was no nearer to a solution (partly because Rajiv Gandhi himself veered away from accommodating Sikh demands) and the Indian army became embroiled in Sri Lanka. In June 1987 the government lost a crucial midterm election in Haryana. Faced with manifold political problems and challenges to his authority, Rajiv Gandhi gave up any further substantive liberalization of the economy.

On the macroeconomic front, the year was dominated by what was initially thought to be "one of the worst monsoon failures on record." In the event, it turned out not to be a serious drought; in fact, agricultural output fell less than in the previous year. Some researchers (see Bhalla 1989) have claimed that it was the *least* bad of the droughts since independence. The government's own figures in the Economic Survey of 1988/89 show a weighted rainfall index of 88.7 in 1987/88 (normal = 100) as against 85.3 in 1986/87 and 77.0 in 1979/80. Even so, the government must be given some credit for handling a second successive drought skillfully. A successful effort was made in quickly increasing the coverage of the public distribution system. Food stocks were ample (as a matter of deliberate anticipatory policy) and enabled 4 million tonnes more to be distributed in 1987 as compared to 1986. Imports of edible oils and pulses were increased. Income support was also provided by stepping up employment creation and relief works programs—an additional Rs 1,800 crores (about 0.50 percent of GDP) was spent for this purpose. Fiscal policy was slightly tightened in September 1987 by surcharges on income tax, wealth tax, and import duties. Expenditure cuts, as usual, fell more on capital than on current expenditure. As a consequence there was a small fall in the central fiscal deficit as a proportion of GDP. But it remained much too high to be sustainable in the long run. It is notable that manufacturing output continued to grow strongly in 1987/88. This is not surprising—the drought was not severe, exports were growing rapidly, the fiscal stance was expansionary, and there was industrial deregulation.

In 1988/89 and 1989/90 there was a strong agricultural recovery, helped by good weather. Exports also boomed as a result of a depreciating real exchange rate and growth in industrial countries. Expansionist policies and deregulation contributed to fast growth of manufacturing output. But all the while the underlying macroeconomic position was getting worse. Fiscal deficits and current account deficits remained high. Public debt and external debt continued along a dangerous track. Although the Economic Surveys made ritual references to these problems, there was no determined attempt to resolve them.

Politically, the government lost confidence and was unable to act decisively. In August 1988, seven opposition parties formed the National Front with V. P. Singh as convener. There was a spurt in extremist activities in the North East and in Kashmir. Punjab continued its gruesome record of violence and terrorism. Communal tensions were also high, a new twist being provided by the "temple-mosque" affair. This arose from the attempt of Hindu extremists, led by the fundamentalist Bharatiya Janata party (BJP) to demolish a sixteenth-century mosque that they alleged was built on the site of the birthplace of the god Rama. Rajiv Gandhi dissolved parliament in October and called for elections, hoping to get a new and convincing mandate. But the popularity of the government was very low. The National Front formed an electoral alliance with the BJP and the Communists, and campaigned on the issue of corruption. In the elections that followed the Congress (I) suffered a humiliating defeat. It won 192 out of 525 seats in parliament, followed by the National Front (144 seats), BJP (88 seats), and the Communists (51 seats). V. P. Singh formed a minority government on 2 December 1989 with parliamentary support from the BJP and the Communists. The deputy prime minister and minister for agriculture was Devi Lal, ex-chief minister of Haryana and a representative of middle and rich farmer interests.

V. P. Singh began with the promise of starting a new era of clean politics and providing a healing touch to solve the Punjab problem. His public statement that "the coffers of the nation are empty" also suggested awareness of the need to re-orient macroeconomic policy. In the event, no progress was made on any outstanding problems, political or economic, and after eleven months in office the government collapsed.

As seen above, the underlying macroeconomic situation was fragile when the National Front government took office, but there was as yet no overt crisis. Food prices had risen very moderately after the bumper harvest of the previous year. Foreign exchange reserves were down to $3.7 billion (about two months of imports), but nonresident deposits were still flowing in, and though external commercial borrowing was becoming more difficult and expensive, it was still possible. The central budget of 1990 was fairly tight though not nearly tight enough, given the underlying macroeconomic disequilibrium. There was some tax effort (as usual, heavily directed to customs duties, rail fares, and postal charges). Expenditure control was more than usually difficult because of a pre-election commitment to write off the debts of small farmers, and the presence of Devi Lal in a key position in the cabinet did not help with the problem of reducing fertilizer subsidies. Even so, the budget planned to bring the central fiscal deficit down by 1 percent of GDP, an intention that proved to be little more than a pious hope.

The government was lucky with the monsoon, which was satisfactory for a third successive year. But in August 1990 the Gulf crisis erupted following the Iraqi invasion of Kuwait. The price of crude oil rose from $15 per barrel in July to $35 per barrel in October. Petroleum-product prices rose even more sharply. These price rises were to last only five months, but this was not known at the time and the situation looked threatening. Iraq and Kuwait were major sources of India's oil imports and the war made it necessary to buy oil on the spot market. Exports to and remittances from the Gulf region were adversely affected. Earnings from tourism also fell. In addition, India's own oil production declined because of civil disturbances in Assam, adding to oil and petroleum-product imports.

The government responded to the oil shock in October by (a) imposing a "Gulf surcharge" of 25 percent on domestic prices of most petroleum products; (b) levying an additional surcharge of 7 percent on the corporation tax for one year (specifically earmarked for defraying the cost of evacuating Indian residents from the Gulf); (c) slowing canalized imports and delaying approvals of imports of capital goods; and (d) raising the statutory liquidity ratio of banks from 38 to 38.5 percent. These measures were perfectly sensible but clearly stop-gap in nature. Given the unsound macroeconomic position before the Gulf war, the mini oil shock led to a rapid deterioration of the capital account. Acute difficulties began to be experienced in new commercial borrowing and even in rolling over existing short-term loans and trade credit. In October the net inflow of nonresident deposits, which had provided strong support to the balance of payments in recent years, turned negative. Foreign exchange reserves fell by more than $1 billion between July and October, of which $660 million came from India's reserve tranche with the IMF. A revaluation of India's gold reserves (from the erstwhile $35 per ounce to a market valuation) did not impress anybody, and in November India's credit rating was sharply downgraded in New York by Moodys bond rating agency.

The political situation was very disturbed and occupied most of the government's energies. Regional and ethnic tensions worsened in Punjab, Assam, and Kashmir; in all these states, parliamentary government was suspended during the year and replaced by president's rule. Progress was difficult because the alliance between the National Front and the BJP was uneasy; the BJP was inclined to be more hawkish than the government. Communal and caste conflicts also grew apace. Partly out of conviction but partly also to expand his base of support, V. P. Singh announced that the government would implement the recommendations of the Mandal Commission regarding the reservation of public sector jobs. This would have implied setting aside 27 percent of government posts for "Other Backward Castes" in addition to the 22.5 percent already reserved for the "Scheduled Castes and Tribes." This announcement led to violent protests, demonstrations, even self-immolations by higher-caste Hindus in north India. In response, the BJP bid for support from all Hindus by agitating again on the temple-mosque issue. The agitation led to more violence and many deaths.

Finally, the government collapsed. The occasion was the arrest on "public order" grounds of L. K. Advani, the leader of the BJP, who had embarked on a march with thousands of followers to the temple-mosque site. Following his arrest, the BJP withdrew its parliamentary support of the government, and the government lost a vote of confidence in early November 1990. Rajiv Gandhi did not want to form a government, preferring to bide his time and win a general election in due course. Chandra Shekhar, a veteran politician, broke away from V. P. Singh's National Front and formed a minority government. But his party had only seventy members of parliament, and the government could function only with support in parliament from Rajiv Gandhi and Congress (I).

By now it was clear that India was facing a full-scale macroeconomic crisis, but it was also clear that the country had a lame-duck government. It did its best, given the constraints. There was a round of tax increases in December involving customs duties, excise duties, and a surcharge on personal income tax. Across-the-board expenditure cuts of 10 percent were announced. Of course, implementation was difficult and, unsurprisingly, the cuts fell mainly on capital expenditure. Import curbs were progressively tightened, principally by the imposition of cash-margin requirements on imports of raw materials and selective credit controls on imports of capital goods. Agreement was reached with the IMF in January 1991 on a loan of $1.8 billion, partly out of the Compensatory Financing Facility (to offset increased oil import costs) and partly as a first credit tranche standby. The latter involved assurances regarding fiscal consolidation in the forthcoming budget but the government was too weak to deliver on these promises. The budget, due at the end of February 1991, had to be postponed at the behest of Rajiv Gandhi. A vote-on-account was presented on 4 March. In it the finance minister bravely announced his plans to reduce the fiscal deficit from an anticipated 8.5 percent in 1990/91 to 6.5 percent in 1991/92, but his words had a hollow ring.

Two days after the budget, Chandra Shekhar resigned following a brouhaha caused by alleged police surveillance of Rajiv Gandhi's house. A week later the president dissolved parliament and called elections to be held from May 20 to 26. The existing government remained on a caretaker basis. The balance of payments position continued to be desperate. There was a further downgrading of India's credit rating in March. Cash margins on imports were raised to draconian levels (50 to 200 percent). The trade deficit began to fall, but the import curbs were beginning to hurt exports. The government sold 20 tonnes of gold (with a repurchase option) to the Union Bank of Switzerland, enabling it to borrow $200 million for six months. The RBI tightened monetary policy in May, imposing an incremental CRR of 10 percent on top of the 15 percent average. But international confidence was at a very low ebb. The hemorrhage of nonresident deposits continued, and foreign lending completely dried up. The country was teetering on the edge of default.

On May 21, a day after polling began, Rajiv Gandhi was assassinated by Tamil militants. The rest of the election was adjourned to June 12 to 15. In the election Congress (I) won 226 seats, 30 short of an overall majority. P. V. Narasimha Rao formed a minority government with Manmohan Singh, a distinguished economist of wide domestic and international experience, as finance minister. The government's inheritance was grim. The highlights of the situation at the beginning of July 1991 were as follows. Inflation was 13 percent a year and rising. Food prices were rising even faster in spite of three successive good harvests. The current account deficit was about $10 billion (3.5 percent of GDP, 44 percent of exports). Reserves equaled only two weeks of imports in spite of the IMF loan. The recent import curbs were hurting industrial production and exports. Industrial growth had been surprisingly rapid in 1990/91, but there were now evident signs of a recession. The central fiscal deficit was 8.4 percent of GDP, little changed from the previous year; the consolidated government deficit was around 11 percent. The country's external debt-to-export ratio was in excess of 250 percent as compared with about 150 percent in 1980/81.

The new government moved swiftly and announced a program of macroeconomic stabilization and structural adjustment.

Overall Trends in Political Economy, 1964/65 to 1990/91

Two developments of significance for macroeconomic policy took place during this period that invite a "political economy" explanation. There was an erosion of fiscal conservatism; and there was a gradual and piecemeal liberalization of controls, but without any fundamental reform of the system. We examine these trends below.

Nehru's death in 1964 symbolizes the divide between the old and the new order in Indian politics. Since then, the country has become less easily governable. Conflicts are nothing new in India's complex and heterogeneous society. But the intensity of caste, communal, ethnic, religious, and regional conflicts has sharpened. Violence and breakdowns of law and order have become more frequent. Corruption has increased and standards of integrity have declined in public life. Though India is unlikely to fall apart, its democracy is under growing strain. This is not the place for an extensive discussion of these changes. But there is clearly some commonality between the causes of the above changes and the erosion of fiscal conservatism on which we focus here.

Erosion of Fiscal Conservatism

The dilution of fiscal conservatism was clearly manifested in the upward creep in fiscal deficits after the mid-1970s. But we should note that it did not lead to more than a small increase in inflation or inflation-tolerance. (Leaving aside falling prices in the early 1950s as exceptional, the trend rates of inflation from 1956/57 to 1964/65 and 1965/66 to 1989/90 were approximately 6 and 8 percent a year, respectively. Note also that the period beginning 1965/66 contains three severe droughts and two oil shocks.) Fiscal and monetary policies continued to react vigorously to overt inflation. The reasons for the inflation-sensitivity of the authorities (see chapter 1) continued to be relevant. Governments could not afford to be complacent about inflation in a functioning democracy with periodic elections. Moreover, as compared to some inflation-prone democracies, India had, for most of our period, a dominant party at the center with comfortable parliamentary majorities, capable of weathering the short-term unpopularity of anti-inflationary policies. Compared with the early postindependence period, the "guardian" mentality of politicians and bureaucrats declined (see below) but democratic imperatives kept them committed to low inflation (see Joshi and Little 1987). The more narrowly economic question of how and why inflation was kept in reasonable check despite rapidly rising fiscal deficits is discussed extensively in later chapters.

Though the rate of inflation did not increase much, fiscal deterioration was unmistakable. The consolidated government's fiscal deficit, which was about 5 percent of GDP in the mid-1970s, rose persistently to reach about 10 percent of GDP at the end of the 1980s. At that level it clearly threatened to explode into high inflation or a balance of payments crisis. In accounting for the deterioration in the public finances, it is helpful to consider the explanations given by some political scientists of the decline in India's governability. They have summed up the changes in India's democracy as characterized by "political awakening" and "political decay."[2] The basic argument is that India has become turbulent because the self-assertion and political participation ("awakening") of hitherto silent and inactive groups have been combined with a sharp decline in the capacity of political institutions to manage these growing demands ("decay"). We examine the fiscal aspects of these changes and why these became evident particularly from the mid 1970s.

Consider·"political awakening" first. In a very real sense this was an aspect of the growing democratization of India, a working-out of the representational aspect of democracy. Various "demand groups" became stronger and more organized in promoting their own interests and came to realize that they could influence the distribution of benefits by offering or withholding their political support. Interestingly, these new groups mostly came not from the severely disadvantaged and downtrodden sections of society but from the middle ranges of the social hierarchy. At the time of independence, the dominant groups of significance were the big industrial capitalists, the rural rich, and the political and bureaucratic elites. These groups continued to be important, but over time others—numerically much larger—emerged to make claims on state resources. In particular, three may be mentioned.

- The abolition of *zamindari* in the early years after independence and the state-supported green revolution in the 1960s brought into prominence "middle peasants" and "bullock capitalists" who campaigned vigorously for output and input prices favorable to themselves. In these matters, their interests were congruent with those of the larger landlords who had managed to evade the legislation on land ceilings. A growing number of members of parliament of all parties came from these groups.[3] In 1977, when the Janata party acquired power in New Delhi, they achieved representation in the cabinet itself.
- The government began to encourage small-scale industry after independence because it was thought to make lower demands on scarce investible resources. In due course, small businessmen and traders became an important pressure group, demanding tax concessions and the reservation of products for small-enterprise production. These groups also made large strides during the Janata regime when reservations for small-scale industry were greatly expanded.
- Professionals in the public sector expanded rapidly in numbers and acquired enormous influence because they were in charge of managing the system of control. More generally, organized sector workers also became a significant "demand group." Their claims were pressed by trade unions with political party affiliations. The public sector, which had pretensions of being a model employer, was particularly affected in this respect.

While demands on state resources were thus increasing from a variety of politicized social groups, the capacity of the state to manage these demands was progressively weakened. Any democracy needs some institutions that can mediate between competing demands and other institutions that can "stand above" sectional interests. At independence, India was fortunate in having two such institutions—the Congress party and the civil service. The Congress party had deep roots in Indian society and its leaders had inherited the legitimacy of the national movement. The organization of the party was a highly complex, subtle, and resilient network of patronage and bargaining. The civil service had a tradition of neutrality and independence and was reckoned to be among the world's best. From about the mid-1960s, these great institutions began to deteriorate.

This deterioration resulted largely from the self-seeking actions of political leaders themselves. The organization of the Congress party was gravely weakened by Mrs. Gandhi who undertook a process of centralization of power after she returned as prime minister in 1971. She bypassed the democratic procedures of the party and abandoned intraparty elections. Chief ministers, cabinets of states, and local party leaders were appointed by her or her nominees. This process gathered pace during the emergency when personal loyalty to Mrs Gandhi and Sanjay Gandhi became the passport to power. It continued again right through the 1980s under Mrs. Gandhi and Rajiv Gandhi, notwithstanding the latter's announced intention to reintroduce intraparty elections. A similar story can be told with regard to the bureaucracy. Mrs Gandhi wanted a 'committed' bureaucracy, loyal to her personally, and used summary transfers and other such devices to achieve this end. This tendency began during the emergency and continued thereafter even during the Janata interregnum.

The fiscal effect of awakening and decay was that the increasingly insistent claims of various politicized groups could not be contained. The lack of party organization prevented political settlement of the various claims outside the budgetary process. Instead, they were managed by handouts, measures that increased government expenditures or reduced tax and nontax receipts. In addition, having weakened party organizations, leaders at both central and state levels had to resort to populist promises in order to win electoral support. These changes acted slowly and were sometimes interrupted by fiscal retrenchment in response to inflation (for example, in 1974 and 1981) or by the temporary ascendancy of individual fiscal conservatives (for example, Morarji Desai in 1977/78). But the general trend in the 1970s and 1980s is unmistakable.

Some of the obvious fiscal manifestations of the above pressures are listed below.

- Phenomenal growth of food and fertilizer subsidies; subsidies (explicit and hidden) on the use of water and electricity; concessional credit to farmers; failure to tax agricultural incomes or wealth (it should be noted that these benefits do not in general go to the poorest in the rural sector)
- Excise tax, sales tax, and interest rate concessions to small business and traders, and the failure to tax them adequately
- Rampant overstaffing in the public sector
- Large tax breaks for savings by middle-income groups
- Blatant populism—"loan *melas*" where loans are given without proper investigation; schemes in some states to provide free milk, or saris, for example; writeoffs of rural loans
- Trend toward higher center-state transfers
- Takeovers of "sick" firms

- Failure to wind up loss-making public sector enterprises.

At one remove, fiscal deterioration also resulted from India's pervasive controls which encouraged kickbacks and generated "black incomes" that escaped the tax net. But the persistence of the control system was in turn another manifestation of the sociopolitical pressures described above.

Liberalization of Controls

It has long been clear to thoughtful observers that India's economy has been stifled by controls. So the interesting question is not why there was some liberalization but why there was so little of it.

We saw in chapter 1 that controls in India, as in many developing countries, were the product of an interventionist ideology. Once established, they grew ever more elaborate. This was because dominant groups were able to manipulate them to their own advantage. Controls generated rents; the recipients of the rents had a vested interest in keeping the system going. The business classes in India have always had a pragmatic attitude to controls. Controls can be an irritant; but, if successfully manipulated, they can also provide large profitmaking opportunities.

In the 1970s some liberalization occurred. This was largely a "top-down" affair led by some bureaucrats who had begun to appreciate the inefficiencies of controls. One obvious example is the greater flexibility in the use of the exchange rate, which is extensively discussed in forthcoming chapters. This came in stealthily, first under the cover of a sterling peg, later under the guise of a multicurrency basket. (It should be noted that it was only in the late 1980s that a policy of active exchange rate depreciation was pursued.)

More liberalization occurred after Mrs. Gandhi returned to power in 1980. It has been alleged that her motive was to cultivate new sources of support, and the business community was one such source (Kohli 1989). This seems plausible because liberalization was of the kind that brought very little pain. It was mainly concerned with deregulation of industrial licensing and softening of the restrictions on monopolies. Both these measures had big business support because they were not accompanied by any serious trade liberalization. At the same time, Mrs. Gandhi gave several sweeteners to small-scale industry, notably with regard to expanding the scope of reservations.

The same story continues, broadly speaking, with Rajiv Gandhi. In the initial honeymoon period, the pace of industrial deregulation was much faster. But again very little was done to open up Indian industry to foreign competition. The import liberalization related mainly to inputs and components and thus increased the effective protection of final products.

In summary, liberalization in our period consisted of little more than the piecemeal deregulation of industrial licensing and the introduction of a measure of exchange rate flexibility. These changes were not trivial and did improve economic performance. But ideology and vested interests prevented any significant action in the more difficult areas such as trade liberalization, financial liberalization, and reform of the labor market and public sector enterprises.

Chapter Four

The Crisis of 1965–67: Antecedents and Consequences

The crisis was triggered by two severe droughts in succession. In 1965/66 foodgrain output fell by 20 percent, and total agricultural value added by 13.5 percent. There was a poor monsoon again in 1966/67; foodgrain production recovered by only 1.7 percent, and agricultural value added actually fell again by about 2 percent. Real GDP in 1966/67 was 3 percent lower than in 1964/65. Famine was avoided only by increased foodgrain imports, partly financed by PL 480 aid, which peaked at $565 million in 1966/67. Despite these imports, foodgrain availability per head fell about 10 percent from average levels in the first half of the 1960s. Largely as a result, wholesale prices rose more than 10 percent in 1966/67 (and foodgrain prices by 18 percent), a rate regarded at the time as dangerous and intolerable.[1] Exports also suffered from the drought, and despite the rise in total net aid to $1.3 billion in 1965/66 (about 2.4 percent of GDP), the balance of payments was under severe strain with foreign exchange reserves hovering close to their statutory minimum of Rs 200 crores, equal to about two months of imports.

Droughts and Public Deficits Superimposed on a "Quiet Crisis"

Clearly, 1965/66 and 1966/67 were years of crisis. But this crisis was superimposed upon a "quiet crisis," or a creeping paralysis that had been evident for several years.[2] The slow growth of agriculture and exports, together with the endeavor to continue with the investment programs of the Third Plan, resulted in an underlying balance of payments deficit that was contained only by import controls of such severity that production and exports were hampered. Matters were made worse by the growth of defense expenditure set off by the war with China in 1962. Public deficits and inflation were already rising before the years of drought. The following paragraph briefly fills in the above broadbrush picture.

Agricultural production was virtually flat from 1960/61 to 1963/64. The year 1964/65 was exceptionally good, but even so output was only 11 percent above the level of 1960/61, a growth rate of 2.7 percent a year. The 1960/61 level was next exceeded only in 1967/68. In these seven years the growth rate was only 1.2 percent, well below the population growth rate. From 1960/61 to 1965/66 the dollar value of exports rose at a rate of 4.2 percent. Public fixed investment under the Third Plan was slow to get under way, but then rose rapidly from 1961/62 to 1965/66, at a rate of 11.2 percent a year, to reach a peak of 9.6 percent of GDP, a record not surmounted until 1982/83. Government consumption rose from 6.7 to 8.9 percent of GDP. Defense expenditure rose from only 2 percent of GDP in 1960/61 to just over 4 percent in 1963/64, after the war with China. The consolidated government fiscal deficit rose from 5.6 percent of GDP in 1960/61 to 6.7 percent in 1965/66. Inflation of the WPI was imperceptible at the beginning of the decade, but rose to 11 percent in 1964/65; foodgrain prices actually rose by 20 percent in this year, when output jumped. It appears that there may be a lag of up to a year before changes in foodgrain production have their full effect on prices. Foodgrain-price inflation moderated to 6 percent in 1965/66 but shot up to 18 and 25 percent in the following two years.

The Donors' Concern with the Quiet Crisis: The Bell Mission

The aid consortium formed the view by 1964 that India was in an impasse, and the World Bank's Bell mission was appointed in September 1964 and reluctantly accepted by the Indian government. Mr. Bell made an interim report to the president of the World Bank in May 1965, and a final personal report in August 1965. The report was directed toward curing the "quiet crisis" we have described. It came before there was even a hint of the 1965 drought.

The diagnosis was very closely in line with the description given above of India's impasse. Stress was laid on the lack of "maintenance" imports, including fertilizers for agriculture. This lack, according to the report, was caused by growing cereal imports, which were in turn caused by the slow growth of agricultural output; by too much emphasis on capital good imports (the fault of both aid donors and the government); and finally, of course, by sluggish exports, themselves held back partly by the inadequate supply of both agricultural and imported inputs.

There was no official disagreement with this diagnosis. The Economic Survey of March 1965 stressed the very low level of the reserves; called attention to the virtual stagnation in the output of foodgrains and the disturbing rise in prices; and stated that shortages of imported materials and components had become an important brake on production.

The Bell mission's report formed the basis of the dialogue with aid donors over the succeeding nine months. One of the main macroeconomic recommendations was that there should be a major shift of inputs, investment, and the high level of attention of policymakers and bureaucrats toward agriculture. This recommendation was pushing at a door that was already ajar. The prime minister, Lal Bahadur Shastri, was not so addicted to the "heavy-industry-first" Mahalanobis model as Nehru had been, and his food minister, C. Subramaniam, had already begun, as it were, to sow the seeds of the green revolution.

The other main recommendations proved more troublesome. Among the reccomendations were that the rupee should be devalued. The devaluation would take the place of the highly selective and inefficient (so the members of the mission believed) system of export subsidies, which should be abandoned. At the same time controls over imports of most raw materials and components (but not major items of machinery and equipment, and consumption goods) should also be eliminated. The devaluation was not so much to cure the current account deficit (controls already suppressed that), but to achieve a balance at a higher level with a much more limited set of controls. At the same time the level of nonproject aid should be raised to permit a larger and freer flow of maintenance imports in the period before the reforms could be expected to secure a substantial improvement.

Most of these recommendations were adopted in June 1966 after protracted discussion and negotiation. In the meantime the first great drought had occurred, reserves were at rock bottom, inflation was accelerating, and famine was feared. The crisis was no longer quiet.

The Devaluation Negotiations and Their Effects

The devaluation of June 1966 was later widely resented and criticized as having been imposed by foreign agencies, which, moreover, reneged on their side of a bargain. These impressions had a lasting influence on the management of the economy. We first address this issue, and then return to the real crisis and the fiscal measures taken to deal with it.[3]

On the Indian side, negotiations were complicated and delayed by the domestic political situation. It is believed that Shastri felt that devaluation was acceptable if it was necessary to ensure sufficient imports of cereals; but that T. T. Krishnamachari, the finance minister in 1965, was resolutely opposed to it. Krishnamachari resigned at the end of the year and was succeeded by Sachin Chaudhuri in January 1966. But Shastri died soon after, and after a few weeks of intense political manoeuvering in congress circles, Mrs. Gandhi succeeded at the end of the month. It appears that devaluation had been agreed in principle before Mrs. Gandhi's accession, but there was no firm decision until after she visited the United States in April.

Details of the complex devaluation package, which included many other adjustments to the trade regime (see below), were worked out and agreed with the World Bank and the IMF in the course of several missions to Washington. Although the IMF favored devaluation, and agreed with the package, the World Bank, representing itself and the aid consortium, was the prime mover.[4]

The package was agreed to on the understanding that $900 million of nonproject aid would be provided, apparently for several years, from 1966/67 onward. All the four Indians we have interviewed who were closely concerned with the devaluation package believe that the donors let them down to the tune of $200 million to $300 million a year. Particular blame was attached to George Woods, president of the World Bank, but President L. B. Johnson was also blamed. This belief clearly engendered serious ill-feeling, which persisted and continued to influence Indian macroeconomic policy for some years.

Table 4.1 gives figures for aid authorizations and disbursements, and makes it clear that about $900 million of nonproject aid *was* authorized in 1966/67 but that authorizations fell away sharply after then. This agrees with the accounts given by the *Economic Survey* for 1967/68 and by Mason and Asher (1973), and J. P. Lewis (1970).[5] Disbursements of nonproject aid averaged about $550 million a year from 1966/67 and 1969/70.

There is little dispute about the figures for authorizations and disbursements. The question remains as to what exactly was "promised" and not just "understood" in the devaluation discussions.[6] For our purposes here, the truth does not matter very much. What matters is that highly responsible Indian civil servants thought that the donors shortchanged them and there can be no doubt that key politicians, including Mrs. Gandhi, thought the same. There was also a souring of the aid relationship due to the temporary stop to U.S. nonfood aid authorizations as a result of the Indo-Pakistan war in the summer of 1965. At the same time, President Johnson refused to renew food aid (PL 480) on a long-term basis. In fact, food aid was provided on a scale generous enough for India to survive the drought years without serious famine, except in Bihar, and then to begin at last to build a buffer stock. Johnson's supposed intention was to ensure that India maintained the momentum of its new policies in favor of agriculture. But the uncertainty that was created probably exacerbated the price inflation at the time and—for good or ill—strengthened India's determination to rely in the future as little as possible on aid, and even on trade.

The Crisis Itself: The Policy Response

The government's response to the crisis had several components: the devaluation-liberalization-aid package, the management of food supplies, and conventional demand management. The devaluation package had of course been negotiated before the crisis and was seen as a long-term measure. So it was a "response" only

Table 4.1 Commitments and Disbursements of Aid, 1961/62 to 1969/70

(millions of dollars)

	1961/62	1962/63	1963/64	1964/65	1965/66	1966/67	1967/68	1968/69	1969/70
New commitments of aid	874	1,387	993	1,560	1,146	2,135	1,047	926	1,080
Project aid	874[a]	1,296[a]	983[a]	1,087[a]	990[a]	723	108	164	306
Nonproject aid						888	534	595	525
PL 480 (food and nonfood)	—	91	10	473	246	524	405	167	249
Gross disbursements of aid	711	933	1,239	1,519	1,623	1,494	1,575	1,211	1,201
Project aid	262	383	548	701	684	497	380	368	307
Nonproject aid [b]	257	292	301	352	421	424	672	548	598
Food aid	144	227	300	446	476	538	447	260	227
Nonfood PL 480	48	31	90	20	42	35	76	35	69
Debt service payments[c]	191	182	209	255	315	365	444	500	550
Net transfer	520	751	1,030	1,264	1,308	1,129	1,131	711	651

a. Breakdown of project and nonproject aid is not available. Figures give total of the two.
b. Includes debt relief.
c. Excludes debt relief, which is included under nonproject aid.
Source: Government of India, Ministry of Finance (various years), *Economic Survey;* and World Bank (1971, 1974), "India: Country Economic Memorandum."

in the sense that it was introduced after the onset of the crisis, though it was no doubt hoped that it would ease the balance of payments problem. The package itself has been described above; its effects are further discussed later. Here we concentrate on the other two strands of the policy response.

The Management of Food Supplies

In the absence of a buffer stock, food prices and consumption could be cushioned from the effects of the drought by imports of food. But imports were constrained by lack of foreign exchange. Even so, they were increased by about 5 million tonnes from 1965 to 1967, financed by PL 480 and free foreign exchange (see table 4.9).

The main plank of food policy in famine-affected states such as Bihar was free-feeding programs, though public works also played a part.[7] The movement of food from surplus to deficit states through private channels was hampered by the existence of "food zones." Since public procurement in the surplus states fell sharply with the droughts, transfer of food to states like Bihar depended on the convoying of food by official agencies all the way from the United States, a process that was fraught with difficulties such as the closure of the Suez Canal, quite apart from President Johnson's "short leash" policy. The limitations on supply-management policies increased the pressure for a fiscal response to the crisis.

The Fiscal Reaction

We have seen that the *Economic Survey* for 1964/65 (March 1965) recognized that the pressure of demand was strong and that there was no scope for relief on the international front. However, there was no great alarm, since prices had not risen significantly in the previous six months. The budget was framed to result in a small surplus, but this turned out to be very optimistic. In August 1965 a supplementary central budget was introduced by Finance Minister T. T. Krishnamachari since expenditures were outrunning the estimates and prices had begun to rise more ominously. Customs and excise duties were raised to yield an estimated Rs 167 crores in a full year (0.7 percent of GDP).

Despite the August budget, 1965/66 turned out to be a year when most indicators of the public sector's demand pressure were at a peak. Real public sector investment rose by 5.2 percent, and real government consumption by 9.7 percent. This was against the background of a fall in real GDP of 3.7 percent (agricultural GDP fell by 13.5 percent, industrial GDP and services rose 3 percent each). Monetary GDP rose 4.6 percent. Total government expenditure rose by 12.9 percent, and revenue receipts by 10.8 percent. Real government consumption rose—partly as a result of the war with Pakistan—and the drought also increased expenditures on subsidies and relief schemes. There was some budgetary relief from increased PL 480 aid, but the consolidated government fiscal deficit rose to 6.7 percent of

GDP.[8] (Most of this increase was the result of larger deficits of state governments. The central government's fiscal deficit fell as a proportion of GDP and even in absolute terms.) As a proportion of GDP, public investment peaked at 8.5 percent, and the gap between public savings and investment also peaked at 5.4 percent. Net RBI credit to the government rose by 14.3 percent; as a proportion of GDP the rise was 1.2 percent.

From March 1965 to March 1966 the wholesale price index (WPI) rose 11.5 percent; but at the time of Chaudhuri's budget speech of February 1966, he could say that the January to January price rise had been only 7.6 percent. However, it should be recalled that the full extent of the drought affecting the *kharif* (summer monsoon) crop was known. The country was living hand-to-mouth for grain supplies. The budgetary situation had, as we have seen, worsened since the midcourse budget correction of August 1965. Taxes were modestly increased (by about Rs 100 crores), but a further fall in the current (revenue) surplus was expected. The finance minister said that the utmost caution in both plan and nonplan expenditure must be exercised. A quite large cut in capital expenditure (including loans) of around Rs 300 crores was budgeted, to arrive at a virtual "balance."[9] Evidently a beginning was to be made in the reduction of real government expenditure, especially central government investment, that was to be the main feature of the next few years. As we shall see, the public sector's positive influence on demand was eventually to be much reduced.

The following year, 1966/67, saw little relief for the real economy. The *kharif* harvest was again bad and agricultural GDP fell slightly, even from its nearly catastrophic level of the previous year, though cereal output rose slightly. The public expenditure cuts began to take effect. Public sector investment fell to 7.2 percent of GDP, the lowest level since 1961/62. In real terms it fell by 13 percent. But the gap between public sector savings and investment fell only slightly as a proportion of GDP. Real government consumption was stationary. Total real GDP was virtually unchanged, a small rise in industry and services canceling a small fall in agricultural GDP. Inflation continued, and monetary GDP rose 13.8 percent. The WPI and the consumer price index (CPI) rose by about 14 percent, an inflation rate regarded as unacceptable in India. The consolidated government fiscal deficit actually rose slightly as a proportion of GDP (to 7.3 percent) as the increase in revenue lagged behind expenditure. But net foreign aid receipts in rupee terms rose dramatically.[10] So RBI credit to the government rose only by 4.7 percent, the lowest figure for a long time.

A general election was held in February 1967 before the next budget. The congress lost ground and Morarji Desai became finance minister (and deputy prime minister). His main budget was delayed until May to allow the new government to take stock. Inflation was still the main concern. There was some reduction of export duties, but this was more than balanced by widespread increases in excise duties. The total increase was modest (about Rs 100 crores). But the finance minister was determined that the budget would be balanced (see endnote 9). Nonplan outlays could not be prevented from rising, although this was deplored. He admitted that balance would be achieved "primarily by keeping the plan outlays strictly in check."

By the autumn the crisis was over. There was a bumper *kharif* harvest, and prices began to fall. For the financial year 1967/68 as a whole the rise in the WPI was 11.6 percent, but from March 1967 to March 1968 it was zero. Real GDP rose 8.2 percent, and its agricultural component by 17 percent. Nominal GDP rose by 17.5 percent. But the impact of government remained very restrictive, indeed much more restrictive than in the previous year. Total nominal government expenditure rose by the remarkably low figure of only 1.2 percent, while revenue rose by 8.2 percent. Government real consumption grew only slightly, but public fixed investment fell by another 7.0 percent (after a fall of 13 percent in the previous year). In relation to nominal GDP, it was reduced to 6.7 percent. The consolidated government fiscal deficit fell from 7.3 to 5.5 percent of GDP. The Finance Ministry was certainly showing its power to implement the minister's word. More detail of the fiscal changes and their consequences are given in the next section.

It may seem rather surprising that real nonagricultural GDP rose by 3.7 percent in 1967/68 (against 2.9 percent in the previous year) in the face of the above figures. There was a small reduction in the resource gap (imports minus exports), which had been rising since 1963/64, but this represented only 0.4 percent of GDP. Private fixed investment was more important, rising by 13.7 percent, so that total gross fixed real capital formation (before an error correction) actually rose by 4 percent, or 0.7 percent of GDP. But errors were still more important. Between the two years, they added 1.8 percent to GDP. This warns us not to fine-tune our account, or our explanations.

Table 4.2 gives the figures quoted in the text, and in effect summarizes the discussion of the years 1965/66 through 1967/68 (more detail is given in tables 4.10 to 4.14). In 1966/67 it is notable that the large fall in real public investment (and the small rise in real consumption) was accompanied by a rise in the fiscal deficit. Part of the reason was that revenue was lagging behind nominal GDP despite the tax increases; here it must be noted that the rise in food prices does nothing for the revenue, while nonagricultural output was growing only sluggishly. On the expenditure side, the public wage bill is virtually indexed, while there was a large rise in subsidies (half the saving on investment was "spent" on increased subsidies), itself largely explained by the drought, and by devaluation (for the rupee price of imported grain was not increased). Thus it was not until 1967/68 that there was a pronounced fiscal impact, when the subsidies were reduced and the fiscal deficit fell sharply.

Another point to note is that there was a large change in the financing of the fiscal deficit. The jump in PL 480 in 1966/67 permitted a fall in RBI credit to the government. But this was not reflected in a similarly large fall in the growth of monetary aggregates. However, the rate of growth of M1 was falling over the period, and both M1 and M3 grew less than the growth of nominal GDP in 1966/67 and in 1967/68. To this extent the authorities were not accommodating inflation, but the monetary squeeze was not severe.

Table 4.2 Selected Macroeconomic Indicators

	1965/66	1966/67	1967/68	1968/69	1969/70	1970/71
Nominal percentage changes						
Consolidated government expenditure	12.9	13.2	1.2	2.7	6.8	14.2
Consolidated government revenue	10.8	8.9	8.2	10.3	10.7	10.0
Consolidated government fiscal deficit	17.7	22.3	-11.9	-14.9	-4.8	12.9
Net aid and foreign borrowing excluding IMF (rupees)	3.5	36.0	0.2	37.1	-8.4	—
RBI credit to government	14.4	4.1	5.4	10.7	-2.5	8.8
M1	8.2	7.3	6.5	8.4	11.4	11.8
Reserve money	7.6	7.6	6.1	8.5	10.2	10.3
M3	10.2	11.2	9.2	10.7	13.2	13.3
WPI	7.7	13.9	11.6	-1.2	3.8	5.5
Real percentage changes						
GDP at factor cost	3.7	1.0	8.1	2.6	6.5	5.0
Agricultural GDP	-13.5	-2.3	17.1	-0.4	7.3	7.4
Manufacturing GDP	0.9	0.8	0.4	5.5	10.7	2.4
Public fixed investment	5.2	-13.1	-8.0	1.2	-2.1	2.5
Government consumption	9.7	0.9	2.0	5.5	9.8	9.4
Percentage of nominal GDP at market prices						
Public investment	8.5	7.2	6.7	5.9	5.6	6.5
Government consumption	8.8	8.5	8.1	8.4	8.5	8.5
Public saving	3.1	2.3	1.9	2.3	2.6	2.9
Public deficit (gap between investment and saving)	5.4	5.0	4.8	3.6	3.0	3.6
Consolidated government fiscal deficit	6.7	7.3	5.5	4.4	3.8	4.6
Net aid and foreign borrowing	2.5	2.5	2.2	1.2	1.5	0.9

Source: Tables 4.10, 4.11, 4.12, 4.13, and 4.14.

The extent to which the fiscal-monetary squeeze helped to put an end to the price rise is an interesting question. At first glance, it looks as if it began to operate seriously just when agricultural output recovered.

The Aftermath of the Crisis: 1968–69 to 1970–71

Two medium-run effects of the crisis years and the measures taken need to be examined—those of the devaluation and those of the new fiscal stance.[11] We first deal with the devaluation and the accompanying changes in the trade regime.

The Devaluation

The exchange rate was altered from 4.76 to 7.50 rupees to the dollar on 6 June 1966, a massive nominal devaluation of 36.5 percent. (The devaluation was 36.5 percent using the definition of the exchange rate in the present study, that is dollars per rupee. The devaluation was 57.6 percent if measured using the alternative definition of the exchange rate, that is rupees per dollar.) This was accompanied by the elimination of export subsidies (mainly the import entitlement scheme, but also various tax credits), some increase in export duties, and a reduction in tariffs, which greatly reduced the effective devaluation. The net effective devaluation has been estimated by Bhagwati and Srinivasan, both overall and for various individual products or product groups.[12] For exports, they arrived at a figure of 17.8 percent for all commodities. (Their figure of 21.6 percent was based on defining the exchange rate as rupees per dollar. This equals 17.8 percent using the definition of the exchange rate in the present study, that is dollars per rupee.) But for some important nontraditional manufactures—for example, chemicals, engineering goods, books and journals, and wood manufactures—there was a substantial revaluation. It also has to be remembered that India was in the throes of a growing inflation at the time of devaluation. We have estimated the subsidy-adjusted real effective exchange rate for exports. Between the years 1965/66 and 1966/67, the estimated increase in competitiveness was only 7 percent (see table 11.3).

On the import side, the devaluation was larger and more uniform, and was estimated at 29.7 percent (defining the exchange rate as dollars per rupee). In line with the rationale of the devaluation there was some delicensing of noncompetitive imports (Indian producers could still rely on virtually complete protection from import competition).

In 1966/67 many exports were severely hampered by the drought. India was then still heavily dependent on agriculture-based exports. The volume of exports of jute and cotton manufactures, tea, oil cakes, tobacco, and pepper all declined. The index weight of these was 48.5 percent. The *Economic Survey* of March 1968 also stated that slack internal demand and idle capacity in 1966/67 did not give the expected push to export sales. Engineering and chemical exports declined by about 10 percent. We have noted that the devaluation package actually reduced export incentives for these industries, that is until export promotion was resumed, already in the summer of 1966, in the new form of selective and variable cash subsidies.[13]

In the face of the fall in exports, it was doubtless difficult to resist resuming special export incentives. The value of exports fell from $2,058 million in 1965/66 to $1,882 million in 1966/67, and to $1,851 million in 1967/68 (see table 4.15). Exports improved with the agricultural recovery in 1968/69, but the rate of growth of the dollar value from 1965/66 to 1970/71 was a mere 0.6 percent a year. This stagnation, however, was the net result of large falls in the dollar value of traditional exports of cotton and jute fabrics, and tea, and large rises in engineering goods after 1967/68 (iron and steel, and chemical exports also rose, but much less).

The balance of payments situation did improve in the period 1967/68 to 1969/70 despite considerable falls in net aid from about $1.1 billion to $650 million (see tables 4.1 and 4.15). Reserves rose by $450 million, and repayment of earlier IMF drawings began ($518 million was repaid from 1968/69 to 1970/71). This, however, was mainly due to a fall in merchandise imports, the value of which fell by $820 million from 1966/67 to 1969/70, that is by 27 percent (20 percent in volume).

The fall in imports came as a result of the agricultural recovery. Cereal imports fell from about 10 million tonnes in 1966/67 to about 3.5 million tonnes in 1970/71. Capital good imports also fell as a result of the fall in public investment, which we examine in the next section. So far as the total of maintenance imports is concerned, the 1966 liberalization had little effect because of the recession; by the time the economy recovered the liberalization had been reversed (and by 1970/71 the control system was as comprehensive as it had ever been). Within the total there was, however, a large increase in fertilizer imports (a state trading business) over the 1967/68 to1970/71 period.

With the Indian system of controls and state trading one cannot expect to be able to relate imports to the exchange rate. But given the complexity of the changes it is also extremely difficult to estimate the effect on exports. Initially there were severe supply-side problems. In addition to this, the change in incentives, both from the original devaluation package and the subsequent reintroduction of export promotion, differed markedly from industry to industry. For instance, cotton textile exports were on a declining trend throughout the 1960s and their competitiveness was not enhanced by the devaluation package and subsequent export promotion.[14]

Bhagwati and Srinivasan (1975:145) conclude from their detailed examination of this complexity that there was probably some positive effect on exports, and above all that

> Clearly, the fear that export supplies would be inelastic was vastly exaggerated. The presence of excess capacity, admittedly aided by the

jolt from the domestic recession, led to increased export sales as the relative profitability of the foreign market improved.

The Indian devaluation experience, therefore, underlines the fact that the view generally held by large developing countries that the price in-elasticity of export supply and/or demand will make devaluation a necessarily harmful policy is not empirically sustainable.

Our own concurrence with this view is based partly on common sense and the experience of other countries, but also on the econometric model of Indian exports presented in the appendix to chapter 11. This suggests that while both world de-mand and the domestic supply situation are relevant, the medium-run price elas-ticity of demand is probably about 3.

Of course, a major devaluation might be expected to have *some* effect on ev-ery macroeconomic variable. But these possible effects are mostly subject to cor-rection by other economic policies, and in the Indian case were so overlain by the droughts, and by fiscal policies that were dominated by the droughts and the infla-tion they caused, that they are untraceable, and probably very small (recall that trade is a small part of the Indian economy).

Given also that the devaluation package was untied within a very few years, and trade policies reverted to the strong control cum subsidization regime previ-ously in force, one cannot go far wrong in treating the devaluation package as a non-event in the realm of economics, certainly in the long term and even in the medium run of four to five years.

In the realm of politics it was a different matter. Devaluations are always like-ly to be unpopular, and this was even more true in the 1960s than in the 1980s when par values (where they existed) lost much of their significance and people became used in many countries to floating rates and crawling pegs. But in India there were a number of specific reasons why the devaluation of 1966 provoked the intense political opposition that it did.[15]

First, and probably most important, the devaluation was seen as having been imposed by foreigners. The government had for years been promoting propaganda to the effect that a devaluation would be unsound economics. Such propaganda found ready listeners, for distrust of the price mechanism and a belief in structural planning was widespread among Indian elites and intellectuals. The suggestion that the government had given way, against its better judgment, to foreign influ-ence that was inspired by neo-imperialist motives, was therefore difficult to re-but.[16] Even within the ruling Congress party there was little support. Only a few ministers had been consulted. Other ministers, and other prominent members of the party, were at best lukewarm in support, and at worst openly hostile. They doubtless feared that the devaluation would be a vote-loser in the forthcoming 1967 election, as indeed it probably was.

Of course, any major price change provokes opposition from those who ex-pect to lose. This should normally be offset by support from those who expect to gain. But the very complicated nature of the devaluation package made it difficult to be sure *who* would gain. Some manufacturers should have gained from import liberalization, but this was probably offset by the fear that liberalization would lead to increased competition. The devaluation taken alone made exports more profitable, but we have seen that it was accompanied by the removal of subsidies, which many exporters may have regarded as a more sure guarantee that they could sell profitably abroad. There was thus some scattered support from industrialists, but it did not amount to much.

The rationale and nature of the complex devaluation package was also misunderstood. A major objective was to achieve a more rational system of promoting exports and limiting imports. Its economic outcome should not therefore have been judged, as it often was, solely by the subsequent inflation and performance of exports, both of which were, as we have seen, very adversely affected by the droughts.[17]

To the critics, the large fall in aid in 1968/69 was further confirmation of the folly of succumbing to foreign influence. The political backlash (which occurred as a result of the 1965–66 negotiations with the World Bank and the aid consortium), the worsened aid relations described above, and the devaluation itself were all to have lasting effects. Mrs. Gandhi was doubtless surprised that devaluation could cause such a furor, and she was not to forget it. She would henceforth be opposed to any economic measures that could be presented as including devaluation, and this was to be important both in 1972 and in the early 1980s.[18] The devaluation-liberalization episode does raise the question whether India would have been better off without devaluation or with a different kind of policy package. Discussion of this question is postponed to chapter 8.

The Changed Fiscal Stance, and its Effects

In the face of the inflation caused by the severe fall in agricultural output in 1965/66 and 1966/67, the government tried hard to be deflationary. Until 1967/68 it was not overtly successful. The fiscal deficit rose in 1965/66 and 1966/67 as a proportion of GDP, though the "fiscal impulse" in these two years was mildly negative.[19] In 1966/67 there were substantial cuts in real public investment and consumption—which did not translate into a fall in the fiscal deficit because of lagging revenue (despite tax rate increases) and increasing subsidies. These falls in public investment and consumption (predominantly the former) carried through into 1967/68. It was only in this year that government policy became sharply contractionary; both the fiscal stance and the conventionally measured fiscal deficit fell substantially. (See chapter 9 for an estimate of the fiscal stance.)

Halfway through the year, in October, prices stopped rising. The WPI did not again exceed the October level until March 1970, almost two and a half years later. Foodgrain prices peaked in August, earlier than the WPI, and remained well below the levels of 1967/68 right through 1970/71. Nonfood agricultural prices (that is, prices of industrial raw materials) peaked even earlier in February. Budgetary policies, however, remained deflationary in 1968/69 and 1969/70. By the latter year the fiscal deficit had fallen to 3.8 percent of GDP (from 7.3 percent in 1966/67) and the fiscal stance to –0.2 percent of GDP from 2.5 percent in 1964/65 (see chapter 9).

It is difficult to apportion the temporary ending of inflation as between the operation of the fiscal squeeze and the recovery of agricultural output. The *kharif* harvest of 1967 was very good, but prices of foodgrains stopped rising months before the harvest could have reached the market. They stopped rising almost before it could have been known for sure that there was going to be a bumper crop; and while expectations no doubt played a part it must be remembered that private stocks were low after two successive bad harvests. A further point is that prices of industrial raw materials and manufactured goods stabilized early in calendar 1967 in spite of the fall in the output of industrial raw materials in 1966/67.[20] But the WPI also stopped rising. The evidence is thus consistent with the budgetary measures of 1965–67 having a significant impact on demand. Fiscal policy did most of the running. Monetary policy played a secondary role. In 1966/67 and 1967/68 it was nonaccommodating without being severe. Growth of monetary aggregates slowed down until 1967/68 but accelerated over the next three years to 1970/71.

The buoyancy of agricultural output was of course critical in maintaining low inflation. The great leap in output in 1967/68, which brought the level almost back to that of the pre-crisis year 1964/65, was maintained in 1968/69, and succeeded by two more good harvests in 1969/70 and 1970/71. By the latter year output was 13 percent higher than in 1964/65. During these years imports of grain under PL 480 were continued but mainly used to begin at last the long-heralded policy of building a buffer stock.

We next need to examine the particular manner in which the fiscal deficit was reduced, and relate this to the relative stagnation of industrial output and manufacturing over these years. There had been a steady rise in revenue as a proportion of GDP during the first half of the 1960s, but this trend was broken by the drought years. Every central budget in the second half of the 1960s tried to raise revenue; but as a proportion of GDP there was a fall in 1966/67 and 1967/68, followed by a recovery to about 13.1 percent in 1968/69, which was maintained in 1969/70 and 1970/71.

There was some success in cutting current expenditures in 1967/68, but thereafter they resumed their slow but almost inexorable rise. More detail is given in table 4.3. Except in 1966/67 and 1967/68 public consumption continued to rise as a proportion of GDP. Finance ministers always rued the dearness allowances, which prevented them from cutting real wages (and the number of public servants went on rising). Subsidies leapt in 1966/67 with the rise in foodgrain prices, were slowly reduced again, but not to pre-crisis levels. Interest fell slowly as public sector borrowing fell (all these as a proportion of GDP).

It is now clear that the change in fiscal stance does not show up in revenues or current expenditures. The whole change lies with public investment to which we now turn. Table 4.4 shows the course of gross fixed public investment from 1964/65 to 1970/71 at 1970/71 prices.[21] The total peaked in 1965/66, then fell by

**Table 4.3   Consolidated Government Current Expenditure,
1964/65 to 1970/71**

(percentage of GDP at market prices)

	1964/65	1965/66	1966/67	1967/68	1968/69	1969/70	1970/71
Consumption	8.10	8.78	8.46	8.05	8.32	8.46	8.81
Wage bill	4.82	5.16	5.16	5.06	5.29	5.36	5.49
Supplies	3.28	3.62	3.30	2.96	3.02	3.10	3.32
Transfers	2.03	2.44	3.27	2.82	2.58	2.64	2.68
Subsidies	0.59	0.73	1.39	1.03	0.77	0.73	0.78
Interest	0.50	0.67	0.79	0.70	0.57	0.62	0.50
Other transfers	0.94	1.04	1.09	1.09	1.24	1.29	1.40
Total	10.14	11.22	11.73	10.86	10.89	11.10	11.48

Note: This table is not entirely accurate since the expenditure figures come from the old series of national accounts. But the errors are very small.

Source: Government expenditure figures come from Government of India, CSO (various years), *National Accounts Statistics* (old series), and GDP figures from Government of India, CSO (1989a). A breakdown of government expenditures for these years is not available in the new series.

13 percent during the next four years before recovering slightly in 1970/71. The falls were sectorally very selective. The large falls were in manufacturing and the railways. Manufacturing was the only sector where the decline in public investment continued into 1970/71; by then public investment was 40 percent less than what it had been in 1965/66. Railway investment began to fall before the finance minister decreed investment cuts. It peaked in 1964/65 after a long period of rapid rises and it is evident that the railways considered that they had overinvested. In 1969/70 the level of investment was less than half that of 1964/65. There had been a cyclical bunching of railway investment that was independent of general fiscal policy.

In 1967/68, while the stance of fiscal policy was generally deflationary, some efforts were made to raise demand very selectively in favor of depressed industrial subsectors. For instance, in the *Economic Survey* of March 1968 it is stated that the railways as well as other public authorities were instructed to place firm orders with private firms for delivery in the next fiscal year (1968/69). Accordingly, the railways placed orders for 16,000 wagons against the 1968/69 rolling stock program, although a preliminary assessment of traffic suggested that only 10,000 new wagons would be required in that year.[22] Apart from manufacturing and railways, the sector electricity, gas, and water shows some fall in investment in 1966/67 and

Table 4.4 Gross Fixed Capital Formation (GFCF) in the Public Sector, by Industry, 1960/61 to 1970/71
(Rs crores in 1970/71 prices)

	1960/61	1961/62	1962/63	1963/64	1964/65	1965/66	1966/67	1967/68	1968/69	1969/70	1970/71
Primary											
Agriculture	218	208	222	240	265	289	260	270	305	307	327
Mining	32	39	57	80	87	54	95	82	67	85	76
Forestry	12	11	14	13	16	19	15	19	16	17	18
Secondary											
Manufacturing	348	258	297	339	431	554	531	427	419	364	315
Electricity, gas, and water	175	286	314	382	415	465	426	419	476	524	586
Construction	11	12	17	19	17	22	20	28	32	33	-4
Tertiary											
Railways	334	347	431	478	496	453	305	272	241	208	224
Other transport	61	86	71	78	81	93	133	108	143	129	187
Communication	28	30	39	55	64	46	68	69	68	73	55
Public administration and defense	440	425	481	520	570	565	528	523	454	472	495
Trade and hotels	2	3	5	6	8	19	16	10	19	22	28
Banking and insurance	10	6	6	4	10	13	15	11	13	10	17
Other services	19	29	30	37	34	45	56	41	72	54	67
Total	1,691	1,734	1,980	2,244	2,491	2,627	2,453	2,274	2,311	2,297	2,391

Source: Government of India, CSO (1983).

**Table 4.5   Public Gross Fixed Capital Formation (GFCF), by Level
of Authority, 1964/65 to 1970/71**

(Rs crores in 1980/81 prices)

	1964/65	1965/66	1966/67	1967/68	1968/69	1969/70	1970/71
GFCF	7,411	7,798	6,778	6,237	6,312	6,179	6,335
Center	2,398	2,165	1,759	1,462	1,390	1,275	1,268
States	2,418	2,519	2,315	2,322	2,394	2,379	2,480
Nondepartmental enterprises	2,595	3,114	2,704	2,453	2,528	2,525	2,587

Source: Figures for the total come from table 4.14. The new series of national accounts (Government of India, CSO (1989a), does not give the breakdown of public capital formation by levels of authority. We assume that the breakdown is in the same proportion as that available at 1970/71 prices. The latter is available in the National Accounts old series (Government of India, CSO 1983).

1967/68, and a recovery thereafter. Public administration and defense also show some fall until 1968/69. Other sectors just about held their own, though in a somewhat erratic manner. (The above account is further confirmed in chapter 13.) Another feature of the fall in public investment is that it was concentrated at the central government level. Table 4.5 illustrates this.

Central fixed capital formation had already begun to fall before the crisis, though this is more than accounted for by the fall in railway investment that we have already discussed. But the investment of both state and nondepartmental enterprises (which, however, are predominantly central) rose in 1965/66. From then until 1970/71, central investment fell by about 40 percent, that of the states was virtually unchanged, while that of the nondepartmental enterprises fell by 17 percent. Thus the second half of the 1960s saw a major, almost dramatic, change in both the amount, the direction, and the provenance of public investment.

Before examining the reasons for these changes, and the extent to which they can be related to the crisis of 1965/67, we need to glance at the performance of the private economy and at the industrial recession (or if not recession, stagnation) for which the fall in public investment was surely at least partly responsible. Private investment did not fall like public investment.[23] Table 4.6 illustrates, and also gives periodically corresponding growth rates for nonagricultural and manufacturing GDP.

Both nonagricultural GDP and manufacturing growth declined after 1965/66, and this is often referred to as the recession of the late 1960s. Indeed some authors have seen, in the industrial sphere, the mid-1960s as a watershed between the Nehru era of high planning and performance and a period of planning decline and low performance.

Table 4.6   Growth Rates of Gross Fixed Capital Formation and GDP, 1961/62 to 1970/71

(1980/81 prices)

Period	GFCF			GDP	
	Public	*Private*	*Total*	*Nonagricultural*	*Manufacturing*
1961/62 to 1965/66	8.8	8.5	8.6	5.3	6.6
1966/67	–13.1	3.4	–4.7	3.0	0.8
1967/68 to 1970/71	–1.6	5.6	2.5	4.3	4.8

Source: Tables 4.10 and 4.14.

We cannot here try to assess in any definitive manner the total causal or systemic connection between the reduction in public investment and the slowdown in the growth of nonagricultural GDP and manufacturing. The public sector deficit is probably more relevant than investment alone. The deficit was reduced from 5.4 percent of GDP in 1965/66 to 3 percent in 1969/70, a significant deflationary influence. But this was largely offset by a fall in the external resource deficit (by 1.5 percent of GDP from 1966/67 to 1970/71).

Value added in the manufacturing sector as a whole did not fall in any year but there was a sharp slowdown in growth for three years. Registered (that is organized) manufacturing, however, fell by 3 percent in 1967/68. The industrial slowdown hardly needs explaining. Industry was squeezed by a fall in demand (arising from the reduction in rural incomes and the fiscal contraction) and by a rise in the cost of raw materials. The immediate impact of devaluation may also have been mildly deflationary since there was a large trade deficit. There was a severe recession in the capital goods sector, which can be closely related to the fall in public investment. The index of industrial production for capital goods fell from 109 in 1965/66 to 91 in 1967/68.

Fiscal policy remained deflationary for about two and a half years after inflation had ended and agriculture had recovered. The reason for this stern behavior will be examined below. But the recovery in agriculture, together with an easy monetary policy and the return to a restrictive import policy, offset the deflationary effects. Nonagricultural GDP grew at about 4.7 percent a year from 1968/69 to 1970/71 and manufacturing at 6.7 percent, though exports were not buoyant. Production of capital goods, however, continued to stagnate. The index of industrial production for capital goods did not recover its 1965/66 level until 1973/74.[24] In explaining this, one must remember that the capital goods industry suffered from serious excess capacity even at the peak of its output. The projections of the second and third plans had resulted in capacity that would never be used.[25]

We need to take note of monetary events and policy as well as fiscal policy. We saw above that the monetary policy reaction to the crisis was nonaccommo-

Table 4.7   Summary Monetary Indicators, 1962/63 to 1970/71

	1962/63 to 1965/66	*1966/67 to 1967/68*	*1968/69 to 1970/71*
Annual percentage changes (average)			
M1	8.8	6.9	10.5
M3	9.8	10.2	12.4
Reserve money	8.0	6.9	9.7
RBI credit to government	9.6	4.8	5.7
RBI credit to commercial sector	12.7	18.7	29.5
Net foreign exchange assets of RBI	−12.4	66.4	61.5
Absolute values (average)			
Velocity of M1	6.60	7.50	7.52
Velocity of M3	4.33	4.60	4.39

Source: Table 4.11.

dating but not fierce. From 1968/69, however, money supply grew faster compared to both crisis and pre-crisis rates. This was largely because reserve money grew faster. While the squeeze on government borrowing from the Reserve Bank continued, Reserve Bank lending to the commercial sector speeded up considerably and the level of foreign exchange reserves recovered. Table 4.7 refers. Inflation remained moderate from 1968/69 to 1970/71 in spite of monetary acceleration.[26]

Finally, we would like to know the effects on personal incomes of the fall in output in 1965/66 and 1966/67 and the resultant shifts in policy. Who bore the losses? Unfortunately, little can be said with confidence. Table 4.8 shows real annual earnings per worker in the organized manufacturing sector. There is a fall of 7 percent in real earnings in 1964/65, followed by two years of constancy and then another drop of 4 percent in 1967/68.[27] Real product earnings rose continuously from 1960/61 to 1970/71 but the rate of growth fell in 1966/67 and 1967/68.[28] There is some evidence that profit margins were squeezed.[29]

In the case of agricultural earnings, it is much easier to discern a connection between output, inflation, and daily earnings.[30] Nominal earnings never show a fall, but when output fails and inflation soars they do not keep pace. Thus real earnings fell 9 percent from 1964/65 to 1966/67. But in 1968/69 the cost of living

Table 4.8   Real Wages in Agriculture and Organized Manufacturing, 1960/61 to 1970/71

(1960 prices)

Year	Agriculture	Organized manufacturing	
	Real wage[a] (rupees per day)	Real wage[b] (rupees per year)	Product wage[c] (rupees per year)
1960/61	1.43	1,197	1,197
1961/62	1.51	1,261	1,302
1962/63	1.48	1,292	1,317
1963/64	1.48	1,363	1,356
1964/65	1.37	1,263	1,394
1965/66	1.32	1,262	1,450
1966/67	1.25	1,264	1,457
1967/68	1.24	1,215	1,482
1968/69	1.47	1,230	1,557
1969/70	1.49	1,345	1,596
1970/71	1.58	1,387	1,650

a. Nominal wages in agriculture from Government of India, Ministry of Agriculture (various years), *Agricultural Wages in India*, deflated by CPI for agricultural workers.

b. See Tulpule and Datta (1988). Nominal wage in organized manufacturing deflated by CPI for industrial workers.

c. Nominal wage in organized manufacturing from Tulpule and Datta (1988), deflated by GDP deflator for manufacturing.

index for agricultural workers fell 10 percent, and real earnings rose 19 percent as nominal wages rose at their trend rate of about 6 to 7 percent.

In estimating gains and losses one must also take account of hours and days worked. It is obvious that when agricultural output falls there is less work obtainable. This reinforces the already clear evidence that agricultural laborers (and very small farmers) suffer seriously when output falls, while organized industrial workers and civil servants are more protected, against both inflation and unemployment. In the unorganized sector, there is no protection and no evidence.

We have no empirical evidence that makes it possible to estimate the distributional effects of the changes in fiscal policy. Insofar as it was successful in reducing inflation, it would have helped the rural poor. In the organized sector of industry, and in government, no one was sacked, and real wages continued to rise (in industry, anyway). We have no evidence for the unorganized sectors of the economy, but the slowdown of industrial growth may well have resulted in reduced earnings there.

The Reasons for the Changed Fiscal Stance, and the Form It Took

Let us review the features that seem to require some explanation:

- The fiscal stance was deflationary.
- The deflation took the form mainly of cuts in public investment.
- The cuts were mainly in central investment.
- Monetary policy was relatively relaxed.

We shall discuss these in turn, although the reasons tend to overlap the features requiring explanation.

That the stance was deflationary may seem hardly to require explanation. Inflation had risen above the level regarded as critical in India. Riding out the crisis was thought to be impossible because food and foreign exchange reserves were exhausted. But this is not a sufficient reason, since the deflationary stance continued for at least two years after inflation had been eliminated. We believe that the main reason for the continued fiscal caution was a change of mood engendered by the worsened aid relations, and increased distrust of foreigners engendered by the devaluation and its surrounding negotiations, as already described. One can call this an increased emphasis on self-reliance. But "self-reliance" underwent a certain shift of meaning. In the Mahalanobis-Nehru planning era, the essence of self-reliance had been seen as the creation of capital goods industries. Admittedly, the second and third Five-Year plans promised eventually an end to foreign aid—but meanwhile aid was necessary to put an end to aid. But now India had had the experience of extreme reliance on foreign aid to avert starvation, and to supply the inputs to keep industrial output from receding; and also, of course, the experience of the power of intervention in policymaking which this dependence gave to the aid agencies. To this may be added a certain disillusionment among the more conservative members of the Congress party with the Mahalanobis-Nehru philosophy, and some understanding that indiscriminate import substitution, especially in the public sector, could lead to trouble. So self-reliance came to mean retrenchment, taking no risks with the balance of payments, restoring foreign exchange reserves, and beginning to build up food reserves. A "plan holiday" was declared in 1966. The fourth plan was delayed until 1969.

The next question is why public investment took the brunt. First, of course, it is politically much easier to cut investment than anything else—taxation is unpopular and in any case rates were very high, while current expenditure consists largely of wages. The government was too weak to increase public savings in a determined manner. Public savings as a proportion of GDP fell in the second half of the 1960s. Second, project aid was falling (from \$684 million in 1965/66 to \$368 million in 1968/69). In that sense, public investment cuts constituted an adaptation to the changed availability of foreign aid that was easier than other alternatives (such as increasing public savings). Moreover, some pause in the institution of new public manufacturing projects was probably not greatly regretted in view of the shift in philosophy, and such projects were likely to be very im-port-intensive (an improvement of the balance of payments was an objective, as well as the reduction of inflation). Third, railway investment did not have to be cut by the Ministry of Finance. The railway authorities wanted less investment themselves.

The above reasons also partly answer the question why it was central invest-ment that mostly suffered. The railways are wholly a central concern, as are most of the big manufacturing investments. The main state reductions were probably in power, especially transmission including rural electrification (but we do not have details).

Some authors have suggested that a shift of power from the Planning Com-mission to the Ministry of Finance should be included as a cause of both the above features. It seems to us that this is not an independent explanation; rather the same events that resulted in the change of fiscal stance, and its concentration on a slow-ing up of central public investment, also resulted in the shift of power from the Planning Commission to the Ministry of Finance.[31] In any case, the shift of power to the Finance Ministry cannot fully explain the concentration of cuts at the central government level. After all, the capital programs of the states depend largely on loans from the center and on market borrowing permitted by the center. The center chose not to cut these sources of state finance, presumably because the erosion of Congress dominance had increased the bargaining power of both Congress and non-Congress state governments.

Lastly, we noted the relative laxity of monetary policy. We have no evidence of any conflict between the RBI and the Ministry of Finance. Monetary targeting was not in vogue in this period. Although Indian policy has always been essential-ly monetarist, it seems almost as if it were assumed that if the government did not borrow too much from the RBI, monetary policy looked after itself (for example, there was no mention of it in budget speeches). It is also possible that it was hoped that monetary relaxation would enable private investment to offset some of the public investment cuts.

Should It Have Been Different? Could It Have Been Different?

The most obvious comment is that an economy that is predictably subject to occa-sional severe falls in agricultural output should keep adequate reserves, of cereals (and possibly some other agricultural products), or foreign exchange, or both. But there was a tendency among aid donors, and the development establishment in the 1950s and beyond, to regard reserves as wasted resources. Short-term manage-ment of the economy was an almost totally neglected subject during this period. India had virtually no reserves when the droughts came.

The next question is whether deflationary action is appropriate when loss of output causes a rise in agricultural prices. Such action as the government took directly caused some loss of nonagricultural output. Could this loss, which at first view does nobody any good, not have been avoided?

It is possible to imagine an economy where the necessary relative rise in food and other agricultural prices would leave the real demand for nonagricultural output unaffected. Perfect wage and price flexibility could produce this result even given the fact that nonwage costs in some industrial sectors that use agricultural inputs must rise. When agricultural output recovered, prices would fall back to their old level.

In reality, we have seen that wages are significantly indexed, especially in government, but also in the organized industrial sectors. The inflation was obviously far from being limited to food prices, and to passing on the increased costs of agricultural inputs. From 1964/65 to 1967/68 food prices rose 49 percent, while both nonfood agricultural and manufactured product prices rose by 32 percent. In this period any explanation of the rises in manufacturing prices is complicated by the devaluation, which has some positive but quantitatively unknown effect on costs. But manufacturing earnings, at least in organized industry, kept pace with inflation (except in 1967/68).

A much more reasonable suggestion would be that if no deflationary action were taken the inflation would be stopped when agricultural output recovered, though it would not significantly reverse itself. The food price inflation would have distributional effects, with differential shifts in demand that would result in some loss of output, given limited price flexibility. However, deflationary action (especially in the form it took) would have very little effect on prices, given the low price elasticity of demand for food, but would exacerbate the loss of industrial output. Anyone holding these views has, of course, a relatively strong case against the continuation of the deflationary fiscal stance after inflation had been stopped.[32]

These arguments are very theoretical, since we cannot say how much effect the deflationary action had on prices and output respectively. But it should be pointed out that, as we have seen, the main sufferers from inflation are the poor, and that any reduction of inflation is to be commended on that account.

It must be recognized that there was a political compulsion to take action, not unconnected with the distributional effects mentioned above. The form that the deflationary action took is perhaps open to stronger criticism. Insofar as the primary objective was to limit the food price inflation (and its spread effects), the need was to reduce purchasing power. Reducing investment in railway equipment, electric power, and heavy industry, does very little to reduce incomes (especially in view of the extreme difficulty of sacking anyone in India). Much more obvious would be increases in taxation, and some direct action on incomes (for example, deferral of dearness allowance, or dividend limitation)—the kind of measure that was indeed taken in the crackdown of 1974. It is not that taxation was not increased, but nonetheless the main emphasis was, as we have seen, on reducing investment. However, there was a subsidiary aim of improving the balance of payments, and for this purpose the action taken was appropriate. The question remains of the longer run damage that the reduction of infrastructure investment may have done. This issue will be most appropriately dealt with in chapter 13, and discussion of it is therefore deferred.

Finally, we must note that the conduct of fiscal policy in the late 1960s was not completely independent of the shape of the devaluation-liberalization package. If the aid component of the package had been more generous, the government would have had an extra degree of freedom, and fiscal policy could have been less deflationary. Discussion of this counterfactual case is postponed to chapter 8.

Appendix

Appendix tables 4.9 to 4.15 follow.

Table 4.9   Foodgrain Availability, 1961–70
(millions of tonnes)

Year	Net production	Net imports	Public procurement	Public distribution	Net availability[a]
1961	72.0	3.5	0.5	4.0	75.7
1962	72.1	3.6	0.5	4.4	76.1
1963	70.3	4.5	0.8	5.2	74.9
1964	70.6	6.3	1.4	8.7	78.1
1965	78.2	7.4	4.0	10.1	84.6
1966	63.3	10.3	4.0	14.1	73.5
1967	65.0	8.7	4.5	13.2	73.9
1968	83.2	5.7	6.8	10.2	86.8
1969	82.3	3.8	6.4	9.4	85.6
1970	87.1	3.6	6.7	8.8	89.5

a. Net availability = net production + net imports – change in government stocks.

Note: Production figures relate to the agricultural year just finished. Thus 1961 figures relate to 1960/61 and so forth. Net production equals gross production minus a 12.5 percent allowance for seed requirements and waste. Figures for procurement and public distribution relate to calendar years.

Source: Government of India, Ministry of Finance (various years), *Economic Survey.*

Table 4.10 Output and Price Indicators, 1961/62 to 1970/71
(*annual percentage changes*)

	1961/62	1962/63	1963/64	1964/65	1965/66	1966/67	1967/68	1968/69	1969/70	1970/71
Real GDP[a]	3.1	2.1	5.1	7.6	-3.7	1.0	8.1	2.6	6.5	5.0
Real GDP (agriculture)[a]	-0.3	0.0	-0.3	10.3	-13.5	-2.3	17.1	-0.4	7.3	7.4
Real GDP (manufacturing)[a]	8.5	7.3	9.5	6.9	0.9	0.8	0.4	5.5	10.7	2.4
Real GDP (registered manufacturing)[a]	9.1	9.7	11.3	8.3	3.3	0.1	-3.3	6.8	17.4	2.4
Real GDP (unregistered manufacturing)[a]	7.9	4.5	7.3	5.3	-2.0	1.7	5.1	4.1	2.6	2.3
Food production	0.8	-3.5	1.8	10.6	-19.6	1.7	28.0	-1.7	7.2	8.6
Agricultural production	0.1	-1.7	2.2	11.1	-16.6	-0.1	22.6	-1.6	6.7	7.4
Foodgrain availability	—	0.5	-1.6	4.4	8.3	-13.1	0.5	17.5	-1.4	4.5
WPI (overall index)	0.2	3.8	6.3	10.8	7.7	13.9	11.6	-1.2	3.8	5.5
WPI (foodgrains)	-1.3	5.4	9.2	26.4	6.0	18.5	25.0	-12.0	3.6	-0.7

(table continues on next page)

97

Table 4.10 (continued)

	1961/62	1962/63	1963/64	1964/65	1965/66	1966/67	1967/68	1968/69	1969/70	1970/71
WPI ("food articles")	0.8	6.0	5.8	20.5	8.4	16.3	18.3	-5.4	5.4	2.6
WPI (nonfood agriculture)	-2.7	-2.8	4.2	16.1	13.6	16.9	-0.9	4.4	11.9	7.6
WPI (manufac- tured products)	1.2	4.3	5.7	5.4	6.3	12.1	11.2	0.0	0.3	7.4
CPI (industrial workers)	2.0	3.9	4.6	14.2	7.8	13.0	11.5	-0.6	1.7	5.1

a. At factor cost.
Source: GDP: Government of India, CSO (1989a). Food and agriculture: table 4.1 in this book. Wholesale prices (Base 1970/71, average of weeks), and consumer prices (Base 1960, average of months), from Government of India, Ministry of Finance (various years), *Economic Survey*; and Chandok (1978).

Table 4.11 Monetary Indicators, 1960/61 to 1970/71

	1960/61	1961/62	1962/63	1963/64	1964/65	1965/66	1966/67	1967/68	1968/69	1969/70	1970/71
Annual percentage changes											
M1[a]	n.a.	3.4	8.3	9.7	8.8	8.2	7.3	6.5	8.4	11.4	11.8
M3[a]	n.a.	1.6	9.9	8.8	10.3	10.2	11.2	9.2	10.7	13.2	13.3
Reserve money[a]	n.a.	5.1	6.9	9.3	8.3	7.6	7.6	6.1	8.5	10.2	10.3
RBI credit to government[b]	n.a.	8.4	10.1	8.6	5.2	14.4	4.1	5.4	10.7	-2.5	8.8
RBI credit to commercial sector[b]	n.a.	-2.1	16.8	10.4	40.0	-16.6	34.3	-3.1	14.5	39.0	35.1
RBI net foreign exchange assets[b]	n.a.	-35.7	-22.7	33.7	-22.0	-38.5	111.9	20.8	100.0	91.4	-6.9
Absolute values											
Velocity of M1	6.07	6.23	6.19	6.49	6.95	6.79	7.15	7.86	7.69	7.60	7.27
Velocity of M3	4.00	4.17	4.08	4.31	4.56	4.37	4.44	4.76	4.55	4.43	4.18
Money multiplier (M1)	1.26	1.23	1.25	1.25	1.26	1.27	1.26	1.27	1.27	1.28	1.30
Money multiplier (M3)	1.90	1.84	1.90	1.89	1.92	1.97	2.04	2.10	2.14	2.20	2.26

a. Average of months.
b. Last Friday of financial year.
Source: Reserve Bank of India (various years), *Report on Currency and Finance;* Table 10.1; and Singh, Shetty, and Venkatachalam (1982).

Table 4.12 Fiscal Indicators: Consolidated Government, 1960/61 to 1970/71

	1960/61	1961/62	1962/63	1063/64	1964/65	1965/66	1966/67	1967/68	1968/69	1969/70	1970/71
Annual percentage changes											
Current expenditure	—	13.3	19.9	17.5	11.2	13.5	12.8	10.5	10.6	11.9	8.5
Capital expenditure	—	-1.5	26.1	26.7	19.0	12.0	13.9	-14.1	-14.2	-7.0	33.4
Total expenditure	—	7.9	22.0	20.7	14.0	12.9	13.2	1.2	2.7	6.8	14.2
Revenue	—	12.9	22.0	21.9	12.2	10.8	8.9	8.2	10.3	10.7	10.0
Fiscal deficit	—	-2.1	21.9	17.8	18.2	17.7	22.3	-11.9	-14.9	-4.8	12.9
Percentage of GDP at market prices											
Current expenditure	10.5	11.2	12.5	12.8	12.2	13.1	13.0	12.3	12.9	13.1	13.3
Capital expenditure	6.0	5.6	6.6	7.2	7.4	7.8	7.9	5.8	4.7	3.9	4.9
Total expenditure	16.5	16.8	19.0	20.0	19.5	20.9	20.9	18.1	17.5	17.0	18.2
Revenue	10.9	11.7	13.2	14.0	13.5	14.2	13.6	12.6	13.1	13.2	13.6
Fiscal deficit	5.6	5.1	5.8	6.0	6.0	6.7	7.3	5.5	4.4	3.8	4.6
Primary fiscal deficit	5.2	4.7	5.2	5.7	5.7	6.3	6.7	5.0	4.2	3.6	4.3

Source: Government of India, Ministry of Finance (various years), *Indian Economic Statistics—Public Finance.*

Table 4.13   Investment and Saving, 1960/61 to 1970/71
(percentage of GDP at market prices)

	1960/61	1961/62	1962/63	1963/64	1964/65	1965/66	1966/67	1967/68	1968/69	1969/70	1970/71
GDCF (adjusted)	15.7	14.2	15.8	15.4	15.1	16.8	18.4	15.4	13.9	15.6	16.6
GDCF (unadjusted)	15.9	15.6	16.5	16.6	16.4	16.9	18.0	16.5	15.1	16.0	17.1
Public	7.1	6.7	7.8	7.9	7.9	8.5	7.2	6.7	5.9	5.6	6.5
Private corporate	3.3	4.3	2.9	4.1	3.6	2.7	2.1	2.3	2.1	1.6	2.4
Private household	5.6	4.6	5.8	4.6	4.9	5.8	8.7	7.4	7.1	8.8	8.2
Gross domestic savings	12.7	12.2	13.4	13.3	12.7	14.5	15.3	13.0	12.8	15.0	15.7
Public	2.6	2.9	3.1	3.3	3.3	3.1	2.3	1.9	2.3	2.6	2.6
Government	1.3	1.4	1.5	1.5	1.9	1.5	0.9	0.8	1.1	1.1	1.3
Public enterprises	1.4	1.5	1.6	1.9	1.4	1.6	1.3	1.2	1.3	1.4	1.6
Private corporate	1.7	1.8	1.8	1.8	1.5	1.5	1.4	1.2	1.2	1.3	1.3
Private household	8.4	7.5	8.5	8.2	7.8	9.9	11.6	9.9	9.3	11.1	11.3
Financial	2.8	2.9	2.7	3.5	2.9	4.1	2.9	2.5	2.2	2.3	3.2
Physical	5.6	4.6	5.8	4.7	4.9	5.8	8.7	7.4	7.1	8.8	8.1
Foreign savings	3.0	2.0	2.4	2.1	2.4	2.3	3.1	2.4	1.1	0.6	0.9

Source: Government of India, CSO (1989a).

Table 4.14 Real Gross Fixed Capital Formation, 1960/61 to 1970/71
(1980/81 prices)

	1960/61	1961/62	1962/63	1963/64	1964/65	1965/66	1966/67	1967/68	1968/69	1969/70	1970/71
Annual percentage changes											
Real GDFCF	—	6.2	8.3	10.5	11.6	6.0	-4.7	4.0	2.2	3.2	0.5
Public	—	-1.0	15.1	12.6	12.1	5.2	-13.1	-8.0	1.2	-2.1	2.5
Private	—	13.0	2.7	8.6	11.2	6.8	3.4	13.7	2.8	6.6	-0.7
Corporate	—	48.9	-22.2	45.6	-12.3	-36.2	-8.0	9.2	-3.6	-16.9	27.8
Household	—	-2.9	19.6	-7.7	27.6	27.5	6.1	14.6	4.1	10.9	-4.6
Percentage of real GDP at market prices											
Real GDFCF	15.5	15.9	16.7	17.3	18.0	19.5	18.7	18.0	17.8	17.2	16.5
Public	7.6	7.2	8.1	8.5	8.9	9.6	8.4	7.2	7.0	6.4	6.3
Private	7.9	8.6	8.6	8.8	9.1	10.0	10.3	10.9	10.8	10.8	10.2
Corporate	2.4	3.5	2.6	3.6	3.0	1.9	1.8	1.8	1.7	1.3	1.6
Household	5.5	5.1	6.0	5.2	6.1	8.0	8.5	9.1	9.1	9.5	8.6

Note: The source below provides public and private fixed capital formation at current prices. Constant price estimates were arrived at by using construction and machinery deflators implied by figures given in the same source for fixed capital formation disaggregated into construction and machinery at both current and constant prices.

Source: Government of India, CSO (1989a).

Table 4.15 India's Balance of Payments, 1960/61 to 1970/71
(millions of dollars)

	1960/61	1961/62	1962/63	1963/64	1964/65	1965/66	1966/67	1967/68	1968/69	1969/70	1970/71
Exports	1,576	1,669	1,766	2,052	2,131	2,058	1,882	1,851	2,079	2,155	2,122
Merchandise	1,348	1,386	1,438	1,665	1,714	1,693	1,645	1,591	1,811	1,884	1,850
Nonfactor services	328	283	328	386	418	365	237	260	268	271	272
Imports	2,583	2,497	2,598	2,795	3,064	3,196	3,178	2,909	2,765	2,407	2,448
Merchandise	2,394	2,291	2,375	2,568	2,833	2,959	2,964	2,677	2,523	2,148	2,179
Nonfactor services	189	206	223	227	231	237	214	232	243	259	269
Trade balance	-1,046	-905	-937	-903	-1,119	-1,266	-1,319	-1,086	-712	-264	-329
Resource balance	-907	-827	-832	-743	-932	-1,138	-1,297	-1,059	-687	-252	-326
Net factor income, of which	-151	-206	-227	-235	-309	-344	-328	-344	-203	-214	-244
M/LT interest	0	-70	-68	-113	-107	-138	-136	-141	-164	-176	-189
Net current transfers	137	132	200	229	334	292	53	48	213	49	83
Current balance	-922	-901	-859	-750	-907	-1,191	-1,572	-1,355	-677	-437	-487
M/LT capital inflow	803	689	853	1,065	1,372	1,561	1,440	1,325	897	746	536
Official grant aid	62	46	31	34	42	72	139	81	87	237	206
Net M/LT loans	741	520	797	1,081	1,330	1,427	1,171	1,211	888	696	583
Disbursements	801	665	902	1,205	1,477	1,551	1,355	1,494	1,124	964	890
Repayments	60	145	105	124	147	124	184	283	236	268	307

(table continues on next page)

Table 4.15 (continued)

	1960/61	1961/62	1962/63	1963/64	1964/65	1965/66	1966/67	1967/68	1968/69	1969/70	1970/71
Net credit from IMF	0	123	25	-50	0	62	130	33	-78	-187	-253
Other capital flows	7	183	-11	-177	-481	-288	123	211	17	27	-76
Errors and omissions	-13	16	12	-115	-102	19	21	-100	-152	-19	-210
Change in reserves (minus = increase)	125	13	5	-23	118	-101	-12	-81	-51	-317	237
Memorandum items											
GDP at market prices	34,021	37,071	38,799	44,597	52,005	54,903	42,184	46,148	48,899	53,849	57,551
Current account deficit (percentage of GDP)	2.7	2.4	2.2	1.7	1.7	2.2	3.7	2.9	1.4	0.8	0.9
Current account deficit (percentage of exports)	55.0	54.0	48.6	36.6	42.6	57.9	83.5	73.2	32.6	20.3	23.0

Source: World Bank (various years), "India: Country Economic Memorandum." The World Bank's figures are based principally on those published by the Reserve Bank of India.

Chapter Five

The Crisis of 1973–75:
Causes and Resolution

Any precise dating of the beginning and end of a crisis is bound to be somewhat arbitrary, but there can be no doubt that 1973/74 and 1974/75 were crisis years. The crisis had a political component and a macroeconomic component, and the latter in turn had an inflation component as well as a balance of payments component. These different components interacted in a rather complex way.[1]

The balance of payments began to deteriorate in October 1973 as a consequence of the rise in the price of imported commodities, particularly oil. The terms of trade worsened by 40 percent between 1972/73 and 1975/76. The current account deficit increased from $455 million in 1972/73 to $951 million in 1974/75, representing 16 and 21 percent respectively of exports of goods and services.[2] This aspect of the crisis was mainly external in origin and was superimposed on a domestically-caused inflation. Inflation (as evidenced by the WPI) accelerated from 5.6 percent a year in 1971/72 to 10, 20.2, and 25.2 percent respectively in the following three years. It was caused mainly by internal factors, particularly the severe droughts of 1972 and 1974, combined with expansionist macroeconomic policies. The political situation became increasingly disturbed during 1973 and 1974, partly but not entirely as a result of inflation and food shortages, culminating in the imposition of a national emergency by Mrs. Gandhi in June 1975.

The resolution of the various components of the crisis was not exactly synchronized. The rates of inflation given above are financial-year averages; month-to-month changes tell a slightly different story. Inflation was at its height between mid-1973 and September 1974 when it was running at an annual rate of about 33 percent. It began to abate rather dramatically from October 1974, shortly after the tough anti-inflationary measures enacted by the government in July 1974. Prices actually fell for more than a year and, though they then began rising again, inflation remained very low until 1979/80. The balance of payments crisis was over during 1975/76 when the current account deficit fell to $91 million (1.6 percent of exports). Indeed, in the following two years India ran large current account surpluses. In one sense the political aspect of the crisis ended with the imposition of the emergency which put a stop to all political ferment. But in another sense the breakdown of democracy was itself a crisis that ended only with the defeat of Mrs. Gandhi in the elections of March 1977.

The Causes of the High Inflation of 1972/73 to 1974/75

This section examines the origins of the high-inflation episode and attempts to separate the roles of domestic and external shocks, real and monetary factors, and factors beyond the government's control as opposed to plain mismanagement.

Exogenous Shocks

From 1971 to 1974 there were a number of exogenous shocks over which the government either had little control or had to accept as given in its economic policy-making. These shocks are briefly described here, though their effects will be further discussed later in this chapter.

THE INFLUX OF REFUGEES FROM EAST BENGAL. After the agitation in the then-East Pakistan in March 1971, 10 million refugees poured into India over the following nine months. This created an enormous economic burden, and government expenditures rose sharply in 1971/72 and 1972/73 to feed and clothe the refugees.

THE INDO-PAKISTAN WAR OF 1971. Indo-Pakistani relations deteriorated sharply during 1971 as a consequence of the above events, and there were active preparations for war on both sides. Pakistan launched a preemptive strike against Indian airbases on 3 December 1971. India responded on all fronts against Pakistan while underscoring its lack of territorial ambition by formally recognizing the government of Bangladesh. Pakistan surrendered on 16 December. The preparation, conduct, and aftermath of the war resulted in a sharp increase in defense expenditure.

THE DROUGHTS OF 1972–74. In 1972/73 both the summer and the winter rains failed, and there was an 8 percent reduction in foodgrain and agricultural production. Though output recovered in the following year, it was still below trend. In 1974/75 there was another sharp drop in output. Table 5.1 gives the relevant facts. These sharp declines in foodgrain and agricultural production were mainly caused by the failure of the rains. Another factor was the unusually low temperatures in the Himalayas that led to insufficient water flowing into reservoirs. As a result, the amount of water available for irrigation was reduced and so was the hydroelectric power necessary to energize wells and run fertilizer plants. These supply shocks contributed to the generation of inflation by reducing marketable supplies of food,

Table 5.1   Annual Changes in Foodgrain and Agricultural Production, 1970/71 to 1978/79

(percent)

Year	Foodgrain production		Agricultural production	
	Annual change	*Deviation from trend*	*Annual change*	*Deviation from trend*
1970/71	8.6	9.2	7.4	6.7
1971/72	−1.3	4.8	−0.3	3.7
1972/73	−8.2	−6.3	−8.1	−7.1
1973/74	7.8	−1.6	10.0	−0.5
1974/75	−5.4	−9.5	−3.4	−6.3
1975/76	22.0	7.5	15.1	5.1
1976/77	−9.0	−4.9	−7.0	−4.8
1977/78	15.5	6.9	14.3	6.0
1978/79	4.3	8.5	3.8	7.2

Source: Government of India, Ministry of Finance (various years), *Economic Survey.*

increasing the prices of industrial raw materials, and putting upward pressure on government expenditure for drought relief.

THE SUSPENSION OF U.S. AID AND THE REDUCTION IN FOREIGN AID. Gross foreign aid declined after 1967/68 and net aid declined even more sharply. Relations between India and the United States had in any case been rather cool since 1965, but they cooled further before the war of 1971 when President Nixon and his secretary of state, Henry Kissinger, followed their policy of a "tilt toward Pakistan." American aid virtually ceased in 1972/73, and the United States also successfully opposed a proposal in 1971 for increased debt relief for India from the consortium. The figures for gross and net aid as a proportion of GDP are given in table 5.2.

Thus, while the government was faced with higher current expenditures due to drought and war, and felt the need to increase capital expenditures to compen-

Table 5.2   Aid Disbursements, 1961/62 to 1973/74

(percentage of GDP)

	III Plan 1961/62 to 1965/66	*"Plan Holiday"* 1966/67 to 1968/69	*IV Plan* 1969/70 to 1973/74
Gross aid	2.6	3.1	1.8
Net aid	2.1	2.2	0.8

Source: Government of India, Ministry of Finance (various years), *Economic Survey.*

sate for the stagnation in investment in the late 1960s, the budgetary support given by foreign aid was substantially reduced. Consequently, the government's dependence on borrowing from the Reserve Bank (that is, on printing money) increased.

THE RISE IN WORLD COMMODITY PRICES, INCLUDING OIL. The increase in world prices occurred mainly from 1973/74 onward; prior to that, import prices were fairly stable, though export prices did increase about 11 percent in 1972/73. In 1973/74 import prices increased across the board, those that mattered most being food, fertilizers, and oil. Oil prices started rising in October 1973 but the main effect came in 1974/75. The nature of India's trade regime has some implications for the connection between world prices and domestic prices. On the import side the presence of quantitative controls implies that the "law of one price" is clearly broken and that the effect of increased import prices on domestic prices of final goods comes through the rise in the cost of production. On the export side, however, the link is more direct since quantitative controls are less important (though in many cases, such as with sugar, the link is imperfect due to state trading). India's export and import unit value indices (UVI) in rupees are given in table 5.3.

The import unit value figures are easier to interpret because India is mainly a price-taker in imports. It can be seen that import costs increased approximately 150 percent from 1972/73 to 1974/75 (of which about 15 percent was because of the depreciation of the rupee). It has been estimated that the primary impact of a 1 percent increase in import costs on the WPI is about 0.1 percent. Thus, as an es-

Table 5.3   Export Prices, Import Prices, and the Terms of Trade, 1970/71 to 1978/79

(1978/79 = 100)

Year	Export unit value		Import unit value		Terms of trade	
	Index	Percentage change	Index	Percentage change	Index	Percentage change
1970/71	45.1	n.a.	35.3	n.a.	127.8	n.a.
1971/72	46.0	1.0	32.9	−7.0	139.8	9.4
1972/73	51.1	11.1	34.3	4.3	149.0	6.6
1973/74	62.1	21.5	48.8	42.3	127.3	−14.6
1974/75	77.9	25.4	84.5	73.2	92.2	−27.6
1975/76	83.9	7.7	99.1	17.3	84.7	−8.1
1976/77	89.4	6.6	96.3	−2.8	92.9	9.7
1977/78	100.3	12.2	88.0	−8.6	114.0	22.7
1978/79	100.0	−0.0	100.0	13.6	100.0	−12.3

Source: Government of India, Ministry of Finance (various years), *Economic Survey.*

timate, the increase in import prices increased the WPI in these two years by 15 percent (of which 1.5 percent could be attributed to rupee depreciation). If we treat India as a price-taker in export markets as well, the 50 percent increase in export prices during these two years would have increased the WPI by another 2.5 percent (since exports were about 5 percent of GDP). So, altogether about 16 percent of the increase in the WPI (of the 50 percent that occurred) may have been the result of the rise in world prices (excluding the effect of rupee depreciation).[3]

Having outlined the exogenous shocks that contributed to inflation, we now turn to the role played by government policies. In understanding these, it is useful to keep in mind the euphoria that was a feature of the politics of 1971/72 to 1973/74 (see chapter 3).

Supply Management

Management of food supplies is an important instrument of Indian macroeconomic policy. The government has an elaborate public distribution system (PDS) for foodgrains (see chapter 2). The PDS secures food through imports (which are a government monopoly) and domestic procurement. In a drought year the government can increase public distribution above its normal rate by importing more and disposing of stocks. This mechanism worked extremely badly in the crisis years of 1973 and 1974.

Inaccurate crop estimates must take part of the blame. For example, the government's *Economic Survey* of 1971/72 (which appeared in February 1972) estimated foodgrain output in 1971/72 as being 112 million tonnes—in fact it turned out to be 104 million tonnes. Similar overassessments occurred in the following two years. The Ministry of Agriculture, whose job it was to supply the information consistently, gave seriously overoptimistic estimates. The euphoria about the green revolution might have played a part.

Food imports were delayed. Even though 1972/73 was a disastrous year for grain output, there were no imports in that year. One reason for the delay was the government's reluctance to go back on the radical announcements made in earlier months concerning the achievement of self-sufficiency and the ending of food imports, particularly from the United States. In the autumn of 1972 grain prices in the United States appeared to be riding high and action was postponed. But the delay was costly. The world price of grain skyrocketed, and the market was so tight that it was difficult to secure grain even at the ruling price. As a result, in 1973 the import of grain was much less than the cabinet had authorized.

There is also evidence that the government's stock management policy had not been particularly skilful. Stocks were not built up sufficiently during the bumper crop year of 1970/71 (perhaps because elections were in the offing), and they were released too early in 1972 so that by the end of 1972 they were at their lowest levels since 1967. Apparently, at that time the government also released stocks by selling to the private sector (rather than through its own fair price shops). It was criticized for this by the left-wing press on the ground that the traders simply hoarded their purchases. It is possible that there is some truth in this criticism on the likely hypothesis that private traders knew the facts of the severe reduction in domestic supplies better than the government did.

Toward the end of 1972 the Congress party adopted the policy of nationalizing the grain trade, and this was tried initially for wheat in the spring of 1973. In making this decision, the left-radical group surrounding the prime minister had an important influence. The underlying belief was that inflation was caused by the speculative behavior of traders and also that if the government could circumvent the traders and procure from farmers on a large scale, fiscal risks could be taken in planning for growth that would otherwise be frustrated by inflationary tendencies. Elimination of the large number of retail traders was impossible, so the move was limited to an attempt to cut out the wholesale trade. Whatever chance of success this move might have had was destroyed by the decision not to increase the procurement price of wheat. The government can procure easily when the procurement price acts as a support price, but in a bad year this is not the case, and because of this the procurement effort in spring 1973 failed miserably. The fiasco of nationalization led to extremely low procurement in 1973 (in spite of some increase in procurement prices in the course of the year), and the government gave up the nationalization attempt toward the end of that year. In 1974 the government reinstated the wholesale traders with an agreement that they would transfer 50 percent of their purchases from farmers to the government at the procurement price. Monitoring and enforcement of this proved to be impossible.

The mess over food-stock management in these years was an example of a pervasive problem in Indian planning—the adoption of radical-sounding policies without political and organizational support. The confusion in government policy undoubtedly had a bad effect on expectations. After all, stocks were largely in private hands, and the mishandling of imports and procurement probably led to some destabilizing private speculative behavior. Figures on foodgrain availability are given in table 5.11.

Fiscal Policy

All indicators of fiscal policy in 1971/72 and 1972/73 show an expansionary tendency. Since there is a strong (though imperfect) link between fiscal deficits and high-powered money, fiscal expansion tends to spill over into monetary expansion. Nevertheless, at the cost of some artificial separation, monetary developments (and the fiscal-monetary connections) are discussed under the next heading. This portion of the chapter should be read with reference to table 5.4 and tables 5.13 and 5.14.

Current government expenditure accelerated rapidly in this period. This was particularly true in 1971/72 when there were big increases in defense expenditure (which grew by 27 percent) and refugee relief. Current expenditure in 1971/72 grew by 22.3 percent. Without the above two items the increase would have been

Table 5.4   Indicators of Expansion, 1967/68 to 1972/73
(period averages)

	1967/68 to 1969/70	*1970/71 to 1972/73*
Nominal percentage changes		
M1	8.7	11.5
M3	11.0	14.7
Reserve money	8.3	10.0
RBI credit to government	4.3	16.3
WPI	4.7	7.0
Consolidated government revenue	9.8	13.6
Consolidated government current expenditure	11.0	14.3
Consolidated government capital expenditure	–11.8	18.0
Consolidated government fiscal deficit	–10.6	20.1
Real percentage changes		
GDP	5.7	1.9
Agricultural GDP	8.0	-0.3
Manufacturing GDP	5.5	3.2
Public fixed investment	–3.0	10.6
Government consumption	5.8	6.7
Percentage of GDP		
Consolidated government fiscal deficit	4.6	5.0
Increase in RBI credit to government	0.4	1.4

Source: Tables 5.12, 5.13, 5.14, 5.15, and 5.16.

13.5 percent. Expenditure continued to grow rapidly in 1972/73 when drought relief was added to the burdens imposed by defense and refugees, and food subsidies also increased sharply. Many of these increases were inescapable, but euphoria also played a part in increasing expenditure across the board (see chapter 3). The government was correctly criticized for spending money on schemes that sounded worthy but that resulted in waste. Capital expenditure also grew rapidly—partly as a natural and desirable reversal of the post-1966 stagnation in investment. The turnaround in capital expenditure can be gauged from the fact that it fell at an average rate of 11.8 percent a year in the three years before 1970/71 and increased at an average rate of 18 percent a year from 1970/71 to 1972/73. National accounts estimates of public capital formation confirm this picture. Public real fixed investment fell by 3 percent a year from 1967/68 to 1969/70 and grew by 10.6 percent a year from 1970/71 to 1972/73.

On the revenue side, there was a sizable tax effort, particularly in 1971/72. In 1971 there was a supplementary budget in December in addition to the regular budget, and as always, the increases came principally from increased excise and customs duties. Revenue receipts rose from 14.6 percent of GDP in 1970/71 to 16.3 percent in 1972/73. But expenditure grew even faster, and the consolidated government's fiscal deficit increased by about 1.4 percent of GDP from 1969/70 to 1972/73. All the above numbers refer to the consolidated government. But both the central government and the state governments were expansionary.

Monetary Policy

The fiscal expansion of the early 1970s continued the monetary acceleration that, as was shown in chapter 4, had already begun at the turn of the decade as a result of the improvement in the balance of payments. In 1971/72 and 1972/73, however, reserve money grew primarily due to sharp increases in Reserve Bank credit to the government (23.2 and 17.1 percent respectively in these two years). This is not only because fiscal deficits rose significantly—they were also monetized to a significantly greater extent since foreign aid was dwindling. The Reserve Bank was slow to respond by offsetting changes in monetary policy. Growth of M1, which had averaged 8.7 percent from 1967/68 to 1969/70, increased to 11.5 percent from 1970/71 to 1972/73. In 1973/74 growth of M1 increased further to 17.4 percent. The government's fiscal stance had tightened by then, but Reserve Bank lending to the commercial sector (including commercial banks) exploded.[4]

The high inflation of 1973/74 and 1974/75 is consistent with the view that it was caused by supply shocks combined with the lagged effect of monetary growth.[5] Money growth exceeded real GDP growth by increasing amounts from 1970/71 to 1972/73. At first this was not fully reflected in prices. The velocity of circulation fell; that is, real balances increased. This corresponds with the view that if the money supply grows faster than the past trend (and is in that sense unanticipated), it is willingly held to a greater extent than is usual. This period lasted from 1970/71 to 1972/73, but in 1973/74 the crossover occurred. Inflationary expectations caught up with reality, and the velocity of circulation of money increased sharply and continued to do so in 1974/75. (Velocity figures are given in table 5.13.) As mentioned earlier, the annual averaging conceals some information. Prices peaked in September 1974 and fell thereafter. On a monthly basis the period of rising velocity of money probably extends from mid-1972/73 to mid-1974/75.

Questions naturally arise regarding the wisdom of monetary policy during this period. The Reserve Bank could not prevent government deficits, but it does have monetary instruments at its disposal to squeeze the nongovernment sector. Part of the problem arose because the Reserve Bank's informal, internal money supply targets were based on the assumption of 5 percent GDP growth that was built into the fourth plan. This projected growth rate of GDP was considerably higher than the erstwhile trend of 3.5 percent (though it might have seemed reasonable in light of the actual experience in the 1967–70 period and the promise of the green revolution). In fact, GDP grew at an average rate of less than 1 percent in 1971/72 and 1972/73, and agricultural production fell substantially. Unfortunately, this was not known in time, and the Reserve Bank apparently went along with the optimistic assessments originating from the Ministry of Agriculture. So there was what the textbooks would call a marked "recognition lag."

As a consequence, no measures were taken to moderate monetary growth between January 1971 and August 1972. At that point the statutory liquidity ratio was increased from 28 to 29 percent, and the net liquidity ratio (which specified the ratio of eligible assets to deposits below which Reserve Bank accommodation was available only at progressively higher rates) was raised in steps from 34 to 37 percent. This was thought to be adequate (although the banks were in a highly liquid state and had excess holdings of cash and government securities) because credit demand from the commercial sector was slack. The situation turned around with a vengeance in 1973 when bank credit to the commercial sector began to increase at an extremely rapid rate. The Reserve Bank was taken by surprise and finally began to respond in mid-1973 by progressively raising the cash reserve ratio from 3 to 8 percent, the net liquidity ratio in steps from 37 to 40 percent, and the statutory liquidity ratio from 30 to 32 percent. The interest rate charged on Reserve Bank accommodation was also raised, and in November 1973 the automaticity of accommodation was abandoned. The minimum lending rate on bank advances was increased from 10 to 11 percent. In spite of these fairly comprehensive measures, the Reserve Bank re-established monetary control only toward the end of 1973/74 because the banks found various ways of getting round the monetary measures.[6]

It seems clear that the Reserve Bank must bear part of the blame for the excessive monetary expansion of the period. It reacted too late and was at first unwilling to use the cash reserve ratio to regulate the growth of money, and it showed a touching faith in the efficacy of raising nominal interest rates when real interest rates were falling sharply.

The Causes of the Balance of Payments Deterioration of 1973/74 and 1974/75

Balance of payments and trade data are presented in tables 5.19 to 5.24. The balance of payments aspect of the crisis of 1973/74 and 1974/75 was caused largely by the sharp worsening of the external terms of trade. Domestic inflation did not have much to do with it—import controls prevented any significant rise in the volume of imports, and exports did not falter.

In 1972/73 the balance of payments had shown some improvement in spite of repayment of borrowings from the IMF and a reduction in inflows of aid. This can largely be traced to a better trade balance. Exports grew moderately in 1971/72 and 1972/73, helped by the world boom and a small real depreciation. Imports recovered in 1971/72 from the stagnation of the late 1960s but did not rise much in 1972/73 because no food was imported and import controls were tightened.

Consequent upon these developments, the current account deficit fell to $455 million (about 16 percent of exports and 0.7 percent of GDP). Foreign reserves were $1.3 billion in 1972/73 (five months of imports). A deliberate attempt had been made over several years to improve the reserve position in order to reduce the country's vulnerability to foreign pressure. Thus, the initial external position was not threatening.

By 1974/75 the current account had deteriorated to $951 million (about 21 percent of exports and 1.1 percent of GDP).[7] This development can be attributed almost entirely to import prices. Exports continued to perform well and increased by 64 percent in dollar value and 17 percent in volume from 1972/73 to 1974/75. (The role of exchange rate policy in achieving this will be discussed later.) Imports soared by 87 percent in dollar value, though almost all of this increase was on account of "bulk goods" (that is, food, fertilizers, oil and petroleum products, iron and steel, and nonferrous metals) that already constituted 40 percent of India's imports. The volume increase in imports was only 5 percent, concentrated in food and fertilizers. Oil and petroleum-product imports stayed level. All other imports fell in volume, held down by import controls (which were tightened), restraint of domestic expenditure, and economies in oil consumption engineered by passing on oil price increases. Of course, import prices rose sharply, particularly in the case of oil prices, which quadrupled, and fertilizers, which more than trebled in price. Other bulk goods also showed sharp price increases of 50 to 100 percent. The terms of trade deteriorated by 38 percent from 1972/73 to 1974/75, and by the end of 1974/75 bulk goods constituted 75 percent of India's imports. India's terms of trade declined by a further 8 percent in 1975/76, but by then the balance of payments had turned round.

The magnitude of the external shock can be summed up by saying that the terms of trade deteriorated by 43 percent from 1972/73 to 1975/76.[8] More informatively, the terms of trade shock can be expressed as a proportion of exports of goods and services or of GDP (see table 5.5).[9]

Thus the cumulative three-year shock was about 50 percent of exports and 2.4 percent of GDP, with about half the effect concentrated in 1974/75. This was a substantial shock, and the current account deterioration was moderate only because adjustment was so swift.

Table 5.5   Terms of Trade Shock, 1973/74 to 1975/76

	1973/74	*1974/75*	*1975/76*
Percentage of exports	−15.4	−30.7	−9.9
Percentage of GDP	−0.6	−1.3	−0.5

Source: The formula given in note 9 to chapter 5 has been applied to figures from tables 5.3 and 5.19.

Inflation: Resolution and Consequences

We have described above the largely separate causes of the inflation and balance of payments components of the 1973–75 crisis. We now discuss the resolution of these two aspects of the crisis.

The Timing and Manner of the Government's Response to Inflation

The government did not respond to inflation until 1973/74 though there were clear danger signs toward the end of 1972 when prices rose contraseasonally. Apart from slow recognition and mismanagement, there was probably some procrastination in the hope that 1973 would see a reversal of the decline in food output.

The price situation worsened in 1973/74 and the political situation deteriorated. As discussed earlier, food imports were slow to increase.[10] Public distribution of food from existing stocks was stepped up in 1972, but replenishment was hampered by the reduction in domestic procurement during the nationalization fiasco. As a result, from 1973 to 1975, overall food availability fell as much as food production; management of food supply made little contribution to the moderation of inflation.[11]

The main plank of the government's response was fiscal and monetary policy. There was little early action. But from the middle of 1973 the government began to respond to inflation in a firm but quiet manner, reducing its own expenditure and tightening monetary policy. Inflation raged on and the political situation deteriorated further. The end of 1973 saw another sharp contraseasonal increase in prices despite a moderately good *kharif* crop in 1973. The regular budget of 1974 featured some tax increases, but it was not particularly tough, perhaps in view of some crucial state elections and again hoping for a good *rabi* harvest in spring 1974. Meanwhile, the political situation took an explosive turn with a threatened rail strike by 2 million workers and near anarchy in some states. Following this, and the knowledge of a bad *rabi* harvest, the government responded in a highly visible manner in June 1974 by uncompromisingly breaking the rail strike, and in July 1974 by some extremely tough fiscal, monetary, and incomes-policy measures enacted through a supplementary budget and by presidential ordinances.[12] A summary list of the July measures is given below.

- Excise duties were increased on a wide range of goods, including petroleum products.
- Rail fares and other administered prices were increased.
- All wage and salary increases of workers in the organized sector were frozen; 50 percent of dearness allowance payments to the same group were also frozen.
- All income tax payers were required compulsorily to deposit between 4 and 10 percent of their taxable incomes with the Reserve Bank.

- Dividend distributions by companies were limited to 33 percent of profits.
- The statutory liquidity ratio of banks was increased from 32 to 33 percent.[13]
- The bank rate was raised from 7 to 9 percent.
- Minimum lending rates of commercial banks were increased from 11 to 12.5 percent.
- Lending rates and margin requirements on bank advances against stocks of commodities were increased sharply.
- A tax of 7 percent was imposed on the interest income of commercial banks. (This was expected to be passed on in higher lending rates.)

The fiscal and incomes policy components of the above measures were estimated to reduce disposable incomes by 2 percent in a full year.

The Speed of Reaction to Anti-Inflationary Policies

A striking and rather puzzling fact is that prices began to fall in October 1974, only two months after the tough anti-inflationary package. The WPI declined by 3 percent (and food prices by 4 percent) between September and December 1974, reasserting the usual seasonal pattern that had been broken in the two preceding years. After that, wholesale prices were stable, except for some minor blips, until October 1975 (food prices, however, fell by 13.5 percent). Wholesale prices fell again by 8 percent between October 1975 and March 1976 (food prices fell by 15 percent). On a financial year average basis the WPI fell by 1 percent in 1975/76.

It is difficult to believe that the package of July 1974 could have worked so fast. Nor can the price decline be adequately explained by the behavior of food output and availability. Although availability in 1974 was better than in 1973 (because of the moderate agricultural recovery in 1973/74 and higher imports) the monsoon had failed in 1974, and consequently the *kharif* harvest of 1974 was expected to be bad. In fact, both the *kharif* and *rabi* crops of 1974/75 turned out to be very bad. Closer examination reveals that it is the "quiet" fiscal and monetary tightening starting a year before September 1974 that must have had an effect on prices.

On the fiscal front, the correction in 1973/74 was mainly concerned with government expenditure. This was a mid-course correction undertaken in the middle of the financial year by the central government. Both current and capital expenditure was affected—the ratio of total government expenditure to GDP fell by 2 percent in that year. In spite of a fall in revenue receipts as a proportion of GDP, the fiscal deficit as a proportion of GDP fell by almost 1 percent. This picture of a fiscal squeeze is confirmed if we adjust the fiscal deficit in the usual manner for cyclical variations in GDP. The fiscal impulse was strongly deflationary in both 1972/73 and 1973/74 (see table 5.6).[14] It should also be noted that the rapid inflation of 1972/73 and 1973/74 resulted in a substantial erosion of the real value of domestically-held government debt with some unquantifiable deflationary effect.[15]

Table 5.6   Fiscal Deficits and Fiscal Impulse, 1970/71 to 1975/76
(percentage of GDP)

Year	Fiscal deficit	Fiscal impulse
1970/71	4.6	+1.1
1971/72	5.3	+0.5
1972/73	5.2	−0.9
1973/74	4.3	−0.9
1974/75	4.1	−0.6
1975/76	4.6	+1.4

Note: + indicates an expansionary impulse.
Source: Table 9.3.

On the monetary front, the annual figures conceal the timing of the measures. M1 growth accelerated from 12.3 percent in 1972/73 to 17.4 percent in 1973/74 before falling back to 11 percent in 1974/75. This conceals the fact that the Reserve Bank began to tighten monetary policy in mid-1973 and that there had been a substantial monetary tightening before September 1974. (Part of the tightening was due to the reduction in the foreign exchange component of reserve money. But this too was "policy" in the sense that the Reserve Bank did not sterilize this reduction.) This is shown in table 5.7, which gives second-quarter to second-quarter growth in money supply for relevant years.

In fact, the monetary squeeze in the second quarter of 1974/75 (that is, just before prices started falling) was very severe; M1 fell by 5.7 percent in that quarter. This shows that the July 1974 package came on top of an already very contractionary monetary-fiscal policy. Moreover, while this package itself could not have exerted much of its effect on disposable incomes by September, its announcement effects were important. From May to July there had been a series of

Table 5.7   Money and Reserve Money, 1971/72 to 1976/77
(second quarter to second quarter annual percentage changes)

	1971/72 to 1972/73	1972/73 to 1973/74	1973/74 to 1974/75	1974/75 to 1975/76	1975/76 to 1976/77
M1	11.70	18.59	13.97	4.10	11.21
M3	16.50	20.76	14.50	11.86	18.47
Reserve money	8.37	24.14	8.55	2.81	12.58
Net RBI credit to government	17.26	21.98	9.03	14.14	−9.04

Source: Quarterly data given in Singh, Shetty, and Venkatachalam (1982).

tough statements by Mrs. Gandhi refusing to countenance inflationary wage increases. The package showed that the government meant business. The government also made clear its intention to import grain in sufficient quantities to feed the public distribution system. There was also a series of well-publicized raids against "hoarders."

Fiscal policy in 1974/75 was strongly deflationary. The fiscal measures not only reduced government expenditure but disposable incomes as well (by an estimated 2 percent in a full year) and were undertaken in two stages, first in the regular budget and then in the July package. The fiscal deficit was brought down by 0.3 percent of GDP, but the deflationary fiscal impulse was 0.6 percent. In 1975/76 there was a considerable easing of the fiscal stance, but the growth rate of money continued to fall. M1 grew by only 5.9 percent.[16] The food supply situation (dependent on the previous year's crops) was extremely tight despite large imports. However, the rains were good, and the expectations regarding market arrivals were favorable. The severe deflationary fiscal policies of the previous two years, the continuing monetary tightness, and the reinforcement of the announcement effects by the imposition of the emergency resulted in declining inflation throughout 1975/76.

The Effect of the Anti-Inflationary Package on Capital Formation and Output

National accounts data show that public fixed capital formation grew rapidly in 1971/72 and 1972/73. This was followed by a small decline in 1973/74 and a decline of 14.5 percent in 1974/75. Thus, the tendency for public expenditure cuts to fall on fixed investment, observed in the mid-1960s, is seen again in this crisis. But this time the cut was much sharper at the state level.[17] Private gross fixed capital formation did not show such sharp movements and moved in contrary directions to public investment.

Cuts in public fixed capital formation in 1974/75 were particularly marked in public administration and defense though agriculture and electricity also suffered. It appears that cuts in infrastructure were less severe compared to those in the mid-1960s.

From 1975/76 there was a marked revival of fixed capital formation, particularly the public component. This contrasts with what happened in the late 1960s when public investment stagnated for much longer. Capital formation figures are contained in tables 5.16, 5.17, and 5.18.

We now turn to the effect of the anti-inflationary package on nonagricultural output. Total nonagricultural output growth was hardly affected in the crisis years, but there were sharp setbacks in some sectors. In 1973/74, construction and railway output fell; in the following two years the impact was mainly in registered manufacturing, which slowed down significantly (without actually falling).[18] From 1976/77 there was a recovery, although it would be wrong to attribute these sectoral slowdowns entirely (or even largely) to the anti-inflationary package. They were mainly caused by the agricultural decline. Other factors emphasized in the *Economic Survey* for 1974/75 were infrastructure bottlenecks (particularly transport and electricity) resulting from the stagnation of public investment in the late 1960s and shortages of imported inputs.[19] The anti-inflationary measures probably played only a small part. The cuts in public investment directly affected orders for some sectors (for example, heavy electrical, defense industries, and construction). More generally, the severe tightening of fiscal and monetary policy and the attendant squeeze on disposable incomes reduced aggregate demand.

A further question is why the recession was not more severe and why it was reversed relatively quickly. The contrast with the more severe prolonged recession of the mid-1960s is evident. But it must be remembered that the agricultural decline in the mid-1960s was far sharper than in this period. In addition, the deflationary policy was reversed very quickly, in contrast to the late 1960s. The government's fiscal stance became expansionary in 1975/76 and public investment was stepped up. Money and credit also eased significantly from 1976/77 onward.

Effect of Drought, Inflation, and the Anti-Inflationary Package on Absorption and Income Distribution

There is very little reliable information on changes in the functional or personal distribution of real income and expenditure during the crisis years. The following is a summary account of such information as exists.

- There is an unreliable series on the daily wages of agricultural workers. Real wages declined in three successive years after 1971/72, by 7, 11, and 11 percent respectively. To see a full picture one would need to know how many days in a year the typical agricultural laborer was employed. But it seems plausible to suggest that in these drought years there would have been a substantial decrease in the demand for labor.
- Average annual real earnings of workers in organized manufacturing declined from 1972/73 to 1974/75. The largest annual drop was 11.7 percent in 1974/75. Real product earnings also declined, though somewhat less (see table 5.8).
- The national accounts (old series) give annual data on factor incomes at current prices for the public and private organized sectors and for the unorganized sectors. These data, in conjunction with data on employment from other sources, and deflated appropriately, can yield a series for real incomes (see table 5.9). Some features of the data deserve comment. First, the drop in public sector organized workers' incomes is less pronounced than that of their private sector counterparts. This is plausible because indexation of wages is much more prevalent in the public than in the private sectors. (The rise of public sector wages in 1974/75 is suspicious—it is doubtful that the figures allow for the impounding of 50 percent of the dearness allowance introduced in the package of July 1974. By the same

Table 5.8   Real Wages in Agriculture and Organized Manufacturing, 1970/71 to 1979/80
(1960 prices)

Year	Agriculture real wage (rupees per day)	Organized manufacturing (rupees per year)	
		Real wage	Product wage
1970/71	1.58	1,387	1,520
1971/72	1.59	1,453 (4.8)	1,501 (–1.3)
1972/73	1.48	1,436 (–1.2)	1,494 (–0.5)
1973/74	1.32	1,426 (–0.7)	1,438 (–3.4)
1974/75	1.18	1,259 (–11.7)	1,351 (–6.1)
1975/76	1.49	1,426 (13.3)	1,589 (17.6)
1976/77	1.68	1,342 (–5.9)	1,351 (–15.0)
1977/78	1.62	1,424 (6.1)	1,519 (12.4)
1978/79	1.68	1,627 (14.3)	1,773 (16.7)
1979/80	1.52	1,682 (3.4)	1,623 (–8.5)

Note: Figures in parentheses are annual percentage changes.

Source: Lucas (1986a), Tulpule and Datta (1988), and Government of India, Ministry of Agriculture (various years), *Agricultural Wages in India.*

token, the private organized sector's fall in 1974/75 is understated, and both sectors' rise in 1975/76 is overstated.) Second, there is a clear and large drop in real per capita incomes of unorganized employees from 1972/73 to 1974/75. Third, mixed incomes of the self-employed appear to increase in 1973/74. This may be because rising food prices increased the real incomes of medium and large farmers in a year such as 1973/74 when agricultural production was bad but not disastrously so.

- The national accounts (old series) provide information on factor shares in the aggregate and by sector. These show that the share of wages in total GDP went down by 4 percent between 1972/73 and 1974/75 and that the relative gains were shared by profits and "mixed incomes of the self-employed." This overall tendency is also seen in the primary and secondary sectors, with some minor variations.
- Three consumer expenditure surveys were conducted by the National Sample Survey between July 1970 and June 1974. These show an increase of 3 percent in the proportion of the population below a defined poverty line.

On the basis of the above observations, it seems clear that from 1972/73 to 1974/75 there was a substantial drop in the real income of landless rural laborers

Table 5.9   Percentage Changes in Real Per Capita Incomes, 1972/73 to 1975/76

Year	Organized sector employees		Unorganized sector employees	Mixed incomes of self-employed
	Public	Private		
1972/73	−2	+4	−13	+0.7
1973/74	−4	−12	−8	+17.0
1974/75	+4	−5	−7	−5.0
1975/76	+18	+17	+17	0.0

Source: Sen (1986).

and unorganized employees generally. The real incomes of organized workers, particularly in the public sector, were better (though by no means fully) protected. Aggregate data do not bring out intraorganized sector changes. We know, for example, that in the public sector the lower-paid employees were substantially indexed, higher-paid employees far less so.

What the information presented above fails to detect, of course, is the extent to which the changes in real income were caused by drought and inflation on the one hand and by anti-inflationary policies on the other hand. Our guess would be that the movements in real earnings of landless agricultural workers were almost entirely the result of drought and inflation. The effects of anti-inflationary policies were felt principally on organized sector incomes and unorganized nonrural employees; the rural poor may well have benefited.

Resolution of the Balance of Payments Crisis

We saw that the current account of the balance of payments worsened in 1973/74 and in 1974/75, largely due to import prices. The terms of trade shock was large as a proportion of exports. However, the current account deficit fell from $951 million (21 percent of exports) in 1974/75 to $91 million in 1975/76 (1.6 percent of exports), a dramatic change (see table 5.19).

In the early stages the shock was financed partly by external aid and loans. India borrowed from the IMF's Compensatory Financing Facility (CFF) ($75 million in 1973/74), other low-conditionality facilities (about $350 million in 1974/75), and the IMF's Oil Facility (about $500 million spread over 1974/75 and 1975/76). In addition, there was a substantial increase in grants and official loans, both bilateral (including aid from OPEC countries) and multilateral. This increase cannot be regarded as the result of government policy, except insofar as international financial diplomacy counts as policy. (India made a considerable effort to persuade the international community that it was "severely affected" by the oil shock.)

Growing remittances from Indian workers abroad also eased the balance of payments pressures. Net current transfers grew from $97 million in 1972/73 to $470 in 1975/76. These were related to the boom in construction-related activities in the Middle East. This element of the balance of payments improvement was an unexpected byproduct of the oil price rise. But policy contributed by maintaining a competitive exchange rate that reduced the incentive to remit through illegal channels. The government also took some measures to attract remittances and nonresident deposits—for example, the introduction of a foreign currency nonresident account, with attractive interest rates, from which funds could be repatriated without restriction.

The resource balance also improved considerably, a change in which government policy played a critical part and that can clearly be described as "adjustment." As far as imports were concerned, overall volume growth was negative in 1974/75 and 1975/76, though food and fertilizer imports rose. There were three underlying reasons for this. First, import controls were tightened in 1973/74 and 1974/75. Second, measures were taken to restrain consumption of petroleum products. Prices of fuel oil, diesel, gasoline, and even kerosene were increased.[20] Third, imports were restrained as a byproduct of the restrictive macroeconomic policies during the crisis. The decline in public investment is particularly important in this context because it is much more import-intensive than private investment (which includes a large element of farm construction, for example).

Exports rose fast, and demand restraint helped in this respect by reducing the pull of the home market, but the role of exchange rate policy was crucial. As we saw in chapter 3 (see also chapter 11), from December 1971 to September 1975 the rupee was pegged to the pound sterling. This turned out to be a good move as sterling was weak during this period and the rupee depreciated with it. Overt depreciation would have been very difficult in the current Indian context. The fall in the nominal effective exchange rate from 1972 to mid-1975 more than compensated for the high domestic inflation, and the real exchange rate depreciated by about 10 percent (see table 5.24, but note that it only gives annual figures). In September 1975, India changed to a multicurrency peg with undisclosed weights, though sterling remained the currency in which the rupee was officially quoted. By then Indian inflation was negative, so keeping a constant nominal effective rate was enough to secure a depreciating real exchange rate.

Both India's sterling peg and the tailormade basket proved very useful because they enabled a few civil servants effectively to manage a downward float of the rupee without anyone, including the cabinet, having much of an idea what was going on. It was important that these civil servants were not panicked into preventing the depreciation (say by revaluing the rupee against sterling) by the usual argument that devaluation is inflationary. (As we shall see in chapter 11, in a large country like India, inflation is little affected by the exchange rate.)

Table 5.23 brings out an interesting fact. India's exports grew rapidly, even in the years 1974/75 and 1975/76, when industrial country GDP and world trade were static and other nonoil developing countries' exports suffered. The main reason was a competitive exchange rate, but the geographical spread of India's exports, buttressed by an active search for markets, also helped. India's exports to oil-exporting countries increased very rapidly.

The account given here explains why, in spite of suffering a large terms of trade shock, India's current account deficit did not deteriorate much and why such deterioration as existed was quickly corrected.

The Sequel to the Crisis: 1975/76 to 1978/79

Politically, these years saw dramatic upheavals. As described in chapter 3, Mrs. Gandhi declared an emergency in June 1975. The economic position had begun to improve before that, and even the Jayaprakash movement seemed to be losing ground. The emergency was Mrs. Gandhi's response to the challenge to her personal power, and it lasted almost two years. She declared an election in March 1977 to secure legitimacy, and she was comprehensively defeated. The anti-Gandhi coalition formed a government that broke down during 1979 as a result of fierce internal squabbles.

The above is an extremely bare description of a highly charged period in Indian politics. But in economic terms, these years were benign. Prices had already stabilized a few months before the emergency. Inflation, as measured by the wholesale price index, was negative in 1975/76. In the following three years it stayed low in spite of large increases in the money supply. GDP, including both its agricultural and manufacturing components, grew faster than the erstwhile trend.[21] The balance of payments improvement in 1975/76 was followed by large current account surpluses in 1976/77 and 1977/78. The current account went into deficit again in 1978/79, but the balance of payments position remained very comfortable. Availability of food rose, and NSS surveys show that the proportion of people below a defined poverty line fell substantially. Domestic savings increased sharply, and fixed capital formation recovered after the decline during the crisis years.[22] Some puzzles and questions concerning this period are commented on below.

Why Was Inflation Abnormally Low from 1975/76 to 1978/79?

The movement of the wholesale price index in the relevant calendar and financial years is recorded in table 5.10. Inflation was negative in 1975/76 in spite of the poor availability of foodgrains (largely determined by production in 1974/75). As already discussed, this was partly because of the severe monetary and fiscal restraint that operated from mid-1973/74 onward. (The complexities of timing in

Table 5.10   Wholesale Price Index, 1973/74 to 1978/79

(annual percentage changes)

Year	Calendar years	Financial years
1973, 1973/74	16.46	20.22
1974, 1974/75	28.57	25.20
1975, 1975/76	3.90	−1.09
1976, 1976/77	−1.93	2.08
1977, 1977/78	7.54	5.21
1978, 1978/79	−0.90	0.00

Source: Government of India, Ministry of Finance (various years), *Economic Survey*; and Chandok (1978).

this connection have already been mentioned.) The monetary squeeze became even tighter in 1975/76, although the fiscal stance became more relaxed. There was also a favorable expectations effect from the knowledge of the good monsoon rains in the summer of 1975. Inflation remained low in 1976/77, which makes sense because of the bumper crop of 1975/76 (7.5 percent above trend) and increased food imports. Inflation rose somewhat in 1977/78 because of poor foodgrain production in 1976/77 (5 percent below trend) and reduced food availability, despite greater distribution from government stocks and despite some offsetting effect from the knowledge of a good 1977 monsoon. Inflation fell again very sharply in 1978/79 because of the bumper crop of 1977/78 (7 percent above trend).

Thus, low inflation in the period 1975/76 to 1978/79 fits very well with what was happening to food supplies. Agricultural output was well above trend in three out of four years. Government food stocks were increased by the large imports of foodgrains in 1975/76 and 1976/77, and by large public procurement of grain. The government had drawn the appropriate lessons from the high inflation episode. Imports were used not only to augment stocks of foodgrains but to increase supplies of edible oils, cotton, and other commodities, with favorable effects on industrial raw material prices. In addition, import prices fell by 10 percent from 1975/76 to 1977/78. Nor must one forget the announcement effects of the tough package of 1974 and of the declared intention and manifest ability of the government (given the comfortable foreign exchange position) to augment supplies of foodgrains and industrial inputs. This must have affected private stockholding behavior in these commodities. It is also relevant that during the emergency, the power of trade unions to obtain money wage increases was greatly reduced.

Nevertheless, a puzzle remains because money supply (M1 and particularly M3) growth in this period was rapid and accelerating. In the four years from 1975/76 to 1978/79, M1 grew by 5.85, 12.97, 14.57, and 18 percent respectively, and M3 grew by 12.45, 19.77, 20.11, and 20.33 percent respectively. These rates of money supply increase are similar to those that prevailed in the high inflation years of 1972/73 to 1974/75. Indeed they are somewhat higher. Our econometric model (see the appendix to chapter 10), which attempts to explain prices by food and nonfood agricultural output, money supply, and import prices, overpredicts inflation in this period. How can the "missing inflation" be explained?

The fall in the velocity of circulation can be traced to factors at work that caused an abnormal increase in the demand for money.

- This was a period of very rapid increases in household financial saving.[23] Aggregate household saving was going up in any case, partly because GDP growth was considerably above trend (a "permanent income" explanation). Some of this would in any case be in monetary form, but the monetary component was also increasing because of the sharp increase in bank branch expansion in rural areas.
- As a result of the success of the drive to spread banking into rural areas, there was an increase in the proportion of rural deposits to total deposits (from 7 percent in 1970–74 to 10.6 percent by 1979).[24] This is relevant because rural deposits tend to be held for longer periods than other deposits.
- The sharp turnaround in inflation and the decline in the expected rate of inflation due to good harvests and high food stocks must have increased the demand for both M1 and M3. Nominal deposit rates on term deposits did increase, so there was also a shift toward term deposits (manifested in the more rapid increase in M3 compared to M1).
- Remittances by emigrant Indian workers constituted an important part of the increase in measured domestic financial saving. It is a reasonable presumption that "the suddenness of the emergence of these remittances resulted in delayed decisions by beneficiaries about their utilization."[25]
- To the above factors must be added the usual lags in the adjustment of money demand when growth of money supply accelerates in an unanticipated manner after a period of deceleration.

Was There Overadjustment of the Balance Of Payments?

From 1976/77 to 1978/79 the balance of payments position continued to strengthen and foreign exchange reserves increased by more than $5 billion. By the end of 1978/79 reserves had reached $7.4 billion, equal to more than nine months of imports. The current account showed large surpluses in 1976/77 and 1977/78 before going into a small deficit in 1978/79.[26]

Exports continued to grow fast. We believe the main reason was again the real exchange rate depreciation, though world demand conditions were also helpful.[27] In these three years the real exchange rate depreciated by 17 percent and export volume grew by about 30 percent. The nominal effective exchange rate was almost stationary in 1976/77 and 1977/78, so that the movements of the real exchange rate (large fall in 1976/77, small rise in 1977/78) can be explained almost entirely by domestic inflation (relative to foreign inflation). In 1978/79, however, the U.S. dollar weakened considerably. A rigid application of the basket would have led to a substantial nominal appreciation against the dollar. To avoid this, the nominal effective rate was devalued by about 5 percent.[28] This combined with stable prices to produce another large real depreciation.

In fact, from 1975/76 the competitiveness of exports improved more than the real effective rate would suggest because export incentives were increased substantially. In 1974/75 the average export subsidy was only 3 percent of export value, and by 1978/79 it had reached 9 percent.[29] These figures, moreover, refer only to measurable incentives. Less quantifiable but important incentives were also given from 1975/76 in the form of a relaxation of import licensing restrictions for exporters. These changes were easier to put into effect during the emergency, but it is also significant that the economic bureaucracy in the Finance Ministry was then headed by Manmohan Singh who believed in the importance of exports.

Remittances continued to increase and imports were stagnant until 1976/77. Inflows of medium- and long-term loans were high in 1976/77 but fell away after that. From 1977/78, imports grew strongly, and a current deficit re-emerged in 1978/79. But as a result of some unexplained capital inflows and errors and omissions, the balance of payments continued to be in surplus.

The behavior of the balance of payments in this period raises the question— was there "overadjustment" and overaccumulation of reserves? The rapid growth in exports was surely to be welcomed, as was the depreciation of the real exchange rate that produced this result. The question, therefore, comes down to whether import growth was too low and, more generally, whether macroeconomic policy was too cautious, given the extraordinarily comfortable position as regards accumulated stocks of food and foreign exchange.

There was contemporary concern that macroeconomic policy was not sufficiently expansionary.[30] Indeed the government's own *Economic Survey* for 1977/78 commented on "the paradoxical situation of a poor country lending abroad." Is there anything in this charge? The facts as regards fiscal expansion are not easy to summarize. The following features stand out in a rather complicated picture.[31]

- The consolidated government fiscal deficit increased from 4.6 percent in 1975/76 to 5.7 percent in 1978/79.[32] The public deficit (that is, the gap between public investment and saving), however, fell from 5.4 percent in 1975/76 to 4.9 percent in 1978/79.
- Cyclical adjustment of the consolidated government fiscal deficit reveals a sizable expansionary fiscal impulse in 1975/76 and 1978/79 but negligible expansion in 1976/77 and 1977/78 (see chapter 9).
- Budgetary data show the increase in government expenditure to be significantly biased toward current rather than capital expenditure.
- National accounts data show a strong increase in public fixed capital formation until 1976/77 and stagnation thereafter. Disaggregation shows that

the main impetus for the increase in capital formation came from the states. Capital formation by the central government grew slowly, and in 1978/79 capital formation by nondepartmental enterprises actually fell.

Thus, it would be incorrect to say that there was no fiscal expansion. But it is clear that there was no determined or sustained push.

There were some fairly obvious reasons for the cautious attitude of the authorities—they were caught in a trap. To begin with, they were afraid that both the agricultural recovery and the inflow of remittances might not last. Second, they were worried about expansion, given their inability to control current expenditures. Finally, money supply was growing quickly due to rising balance of payments surpluses.[33] As it happens, the demand for money was also rising abnormally fast, but that was not predicted. Against this background, the fear that greater fiscal expansion would be inflationary is not hard to understand.

In theory, the obvious solution would have been to step up the pace of public investment and liberalize imports at the same time. This would have been a way of expanding investment without pressure on the supply of money, since the balance of payments source of high-powered money would have declined at the same time as the governmental source increased. But the required trade liberalization did not accord with the policy of import control. This is an example of how macroeconomic flexibility is inhibited by the government's own microcontrol policies. Another possibility that was canvassed was a major rural public works program. This was, as usual, hampered by the absence of an existing shelf of projects and the lack of administrative capability.

The confused political atmosphere of 1977/78 and 1978/79 was not conducive to major changes. The Janata government got bogged down in internal strife. A great deal of time was wasted in the Planning Commission scrapping the existing outline of the plan and formulating a new one. Civil servants, particularly in the Finance Ministry, were left to get on with the job of managing the economy, and without clear political leadership they could not undertake the radical policies that would have been necessary to increase public investment in a noninflationary manner. They drew in their horns and regarded their main responsibility as preventing the growth of unproductive expenditures.

As a result of favorable harvests and the buoyancy of exports, all sectors of the economy grew rapidly. There were missed opportunities in relation to an ideal scenario in which the government could have expanded, liberalized, and even increased external borrowing moderately. But what actually happened was better than the more realistic counterfactual scenario of a wasteful squandering of food and foreign exchange reserves. We also know with the benefit of hindsight that there was a second oil crisis in 1979. So the food and foreign exchange reserves accumulated in this period in fact came in very handy.

Assessment of Macroeconomic Policy and Adjustment, 1971/72 to 1978/79

There clearly were some policy mistakes (for example, overexpansionary mone- tary policy and mismanagement of food supplies) in the lead up to the crisis of 1973–75, though it was principally caused by exogenous factors (droughts and a negative terms of trade shock). Luck did play some part in the satisfactory resolu- tion of the crisis, particularly as regards the growth of remittances from the Middle East, but the policy response was much more important. Several elements in the policy response were clearly appropriate, particularly the management of the nominal exchange rate and the economies in oil consumption. The role of defla- tionary policies is somewhat more controversial. Was the fiscal-monetary crack- down necessary? The counterfactual scenario would have involved the government riding out the droughts while simply waiting for food production to improve.

We incline to the view that once the crisis was under way, deflationary pol- icies *were* appropriate. They did exert downward pressure on food prices; thereby they also helped the agricultural poor. Doing so through higher imports (say through more foreign borrowing) faced the difficulty that world food pric- es were themselves very high. India was not creditworthy enough at that stage to borrow much on the commercial market. Greater IMF borrowing would have involved drawing on high-conditionality facilities, themselves requiring defla- tionary policies. Deflationary policies were probably also necessary for break- ing rampant inflationary expectations and as an adjunct to depreciation in improving the balance of payments. As in 1966, however, the question does arise whether the *form* of the deflation in 1974, through cuts in public invest- ment, was well judged. In retrospect it seems that it would have been better to have introduced the July 1974 measures to reduce disposable income in 1973. As it happens, unlike in 1966, the deflation did not last very long and was re- versed in 1975/76. Thus, it seems clear that the response to the crisis, though a bit late, was on the whole appropriate. Policy played a positive role in the adjustment.

In the sequel to the crisis, inflation remained moderate, and the balance of payments strengthened enormously. Luck played a large part in this. A run of good agricultural years, improving terms of trade, and rising demand for money as a byproduct of the spread of banking, helped to keep inflation low in spite of rapid growth of the money supply. The low inflation helped to keep the real exchange rate competitive without much nominal depreciation.[34] Remittances grew rapidly, and world trade grew at a satisfactory rate from 1976/77. It could indeed be argued that policy was deficient in allowing such a large balance of payments improve- ment to take place and that faster expansion would have been feasible and desir- able. We do not ourselves take this view, which we think is based on implausible assumptions regarding the political possibility of radical trade policy changes dur- ing this period.

Appendix

Appendix tables 5.11 to 5.24 follow.

Table 5.11   Foodgrain Availability, 1970–78

(millions of tonnes)

Year	Net production	Net imports	Public procure-ment	Public distri-bution	Net availability[a]
1970	87.06	3.55	6.71	8.84	89.49
1971	94.87	2.01	8.86	7.82	94.31
1972	92.02	–0.50	7.67	10.49	96.22
1973	84.90	3.59	8.42	11.41	88.79
1974	91.58	5.16	5.65	10.79	97.14
1975	87.35	7.54	9.56	11.25	89.33
1976	105.91	6.92	12.85	9.17	102.08
1977	97.27	0.10	9.97	11.73	98.99
1978	110.61	–0.60	11.10	10.18	110.25

a. Net availability = net production + net imports – change in government stocks.

Note: Production figures relate to the agricultural year just finished. Thus 1970 figures relate to 1969/70, and so on. Net production equals gross production minus a 12.5 percent allowance for seed requirements and waste. Figures for procurement and public distribution relate to calendar years.

Source: Government of India, Ministry of Finance (various years), *Economic Survey.*

Table 5.12 Output and Price Indicators, 1970/71 to 1978/79
(annual percentage changes)

	1970/71	1971/72	1972/73	1973/74	1974/75	1975/76	1976/77	1977/78	1978/79
Real GDP[a]	5.0	1.0	-0.3	4.6	1.2	9.0	1.3	7.5	5.5
Real GDP (agriculture)[a]	7.4	-2.7	-5.6	8.4	-2.8	14.2	-6.1	12.5	2.0
Real GDP (manufacturing)[a]	2.4	3.3	3.9	4.5	2.9	2.1	8.8	6.2	12.4
Real GDP (registered manufacturing)[a]	2.4	1.8	3.2	4.9	1.0	1.0	12.5	6.7	10.9
Real GDP (unregistered manufacturing)[a]	2.3	5.3	4.9	3.8	5.5	3.5	4.1	5.6	14.3
Food production	8.6	-1.3	-8.2	7.8	-5.4	22.0	-9.0	15.5	4.3
Agricultural production	7.4	-0.3	-8.1	10.0	-3.4	15.1	-7.0	14.3	3.8
Foodgrain availability	4.5	5.4	2.0	-7.7	9.4	-8.0	14.3	-3.0	11.4
WPI (overall index)	5.5	5.6	10.0	20.2	25.2	-1.1	2.1	5.2	0.0
WPI (foodgrains)	-0.7	3.4	15.6	18.7	38.0	-11.1	-12.3	11.1	1.8
WPI (food articles)	2.6	1.1	10.1	22.7	26.0	-4.9	-5.1	11.8	-0.7
WPI (nonfood agriculture)	7.6	-1.4	9.0	36.4	11.7	-14.6	19.7	6.3	-4.3
WPI (fuel, power, and light)	5.9	4.0	18.6	51.8	10.5	5.3	1.5	4.5	4.5
WPI (manufactured products)	7.4	9.5	11.3	14.4	21.0	1.4	2.3	2.3	0.1
CPI (industrial workers)	5.1	3.2	7.8	20.8	26.8	-1.3	-3.8	7.6	2.2

a. At factor cost.
Source: GDP: Government of India, CSO (1989a). Food and agriculture: Government of India, Ministry of Finance (various years), *Economic Survey.* Wholesale prices (Base 1970/71, average of weeks), and consumer prices (Base 1960, average of months), from Government of India, Ministry of Finance (various years), *Economic Survey;* and Chandok (1978).

Table 5.13 Monetary Indicators, 1970/71 to 1979/80

	1970/71	1971/72	1972/73	1973/74	1974/75	1975/76	1976/77	1977/78	1978/79	1979/80
Annual percentage changes										
M1[a]	11.8	10.5	12.3	17.4	11.0	5.9	13.0	14.6	18.0	19.0
M3[a]	13.3	14.5	16.4	19.8	13.6	12.5	19.8	20.1	20.3	20.3
Reserve money[a]	10.3	10.4	9.5	22.5	6.9	3.3	14.7	19.2	20.5	23.1
RBI credit to government[b]	8.8	23.2	17.1	13.6	5.4	1.9	3.4	6.7	16.0	34.6
RBI credit to commercial sector[b]	30.1	–1.5	–2.3	73.1	27.3	26.4	18.3	–19.7	25.1	17.9
RBI net foreign exchange assets[b]	–6.9	13.0	–7.4	19.4	–42.0	276.5	135.8	78.3	21.5	–0.2
Absolute values										
Velocity of M1	7.27	7.04	6.92	7.17	7.63	7.75	7.39	7.30	6.71	6.19
Velocity of M3	4.18	3.92	3.71	3.76	3.91	3.74	3.37	3.17	2.86	2.61
Money multiplier (M1) (unadjusted)	1.30	1.30	1.33	1.28	1.33	1.36	1.34	1.28	1.26	1.22
Money multiplier (M1) (adjusted)	—	—	—	1.34	1.36	1.38	1.39	1.42	1.44	1.45
Money multiplier (M3) (unadjusted)	2.26	2.40	2.49	2.43	2.58	2.82	2.93	2.96	2.95	2.88
Money multiplier (M3) (adjusted)	—	—	—	2.54	2.65	2.86	3.04	3.26	3.39	3.39
Percentage of GDP										
Change in RBI credit to government	0.7	1.9	1.6	1.2	0.5	0.2	0.3	0.6	1.2	2.6

a. Monthly average.
b. Last Friday of financial year.
Source: Reserve Bank of India (various years), *Report on Currency and Finance;* table 10.1 in this book; and Singh, Shetty, and Venkatachalam (1982).

Table 5.14   Fiscal Indicators: Consolidated Government, 1970/71 to 1978/79

	1970/71	1971/72	1972/73	1973/74	1974/75	1975/76	1976/77	1977/78	1978/79
Annual percentage changes									
Current expenditure	8.4	22.3	12.3	10.5	14.0	19.9	17.0	8.1	15.8
Capital expenditure	33.4	11.5	9.1	8.4	48.1	31.1	9.3	3.1	20.7
Total expenditure	14.2	19.4	11.5	10.0	22.3	23.2	14.6	6.6	17.2
Revenue	10.0	17.7	13.0	12.7	25.7	24.0	11.5	7.7	14.2
Fiscal deficit	29.0	24.2	7.2	1.7	11.3	21.0	26.1	2.9	27.5
Percentage of GDP at market prices									
Current expenditure	13.3	15.1	15.4	14.0	13.5	15.0	16.3	15.6	16.7
Capital expenditure	4.9	5.1	5.1	4.5	5.7	6.9	7.0	6.4	7.1
Total expenditure	18.2	20.2	20.5	18.5	19.2	22.0	23.3	22.0	23.8
Revenue	13.6	14.9	15.3	14.2	15.1	17.4	18.0	17.1	18.0
Fiscal deficit	4.6	5.3	5.2	4.3	4.1	4.6	5.4	4.9	5.7
Primary fiscal deficit	4.3	4.8	4.8	3.8	3.5	3.8	4.7	4.5	5.0

Source: Government of India, Ministry of Finance (various years), *Indian Economic Statistics—Public Finance.*

Table 5.15 Investment and Saving, 1970/71 to 1978/79
(percentage of GDP at market prices)

	1970/71	1971/72	1972/73	1973/74	1974/75	1975/76	1976/77	1977/78	1978/79
Gross domestic capital formation (adjusted)	16.6	17.3	15.9	19.1	18.3	18.8	19.7	19.5	23.3
Gross domestic capital formation (unadjusted)	17.1	18.5	17.1	18.3	19.8	20.8	20.9	19.8	22.3
Public	6.5	7.1	7.3	7.7	7.6	9.6	10.1	8.2	9.5
Private corporate	2.4	2.8	2.6	2.6	3.7	2.7	1.5	2.4	2.2
Private household	8.2	8.6	7.2	8.0	8.5	8.5	9.3	9.2	10.6
Gross domestic savings	15.7	16.2	15.4	18.4	17.4	19.0	21.2	21.1	23.2
Public	2.9	2.8	2.6	2.9	3.7	4.2	4.9	4.3	4.6
Government	1.3	1.2	1.0	1.5	2.0	2.7	2.5	2.2	2.4
Public enterprises	1.6	1.6	1.6	1.4	1.6	1.6	2.4	2.2	2.2
Private corporate	1.5	1.6	1.5	1.7	2.0	1.3	1.4	1.4	1.6
Private household	11.3	11.8	11.2	13.8	11.8	13.4	15.0	15.3	17.0
Financial	3.2	3.4	4.2	5.8	3.2	5.0	5.7	6.1	6.4
Physical	8.1	8.5	7.0	8.0	8.5	8.4	9.2	9.2	10.6
Foreign savings	0.9	1.0	0.6	0.6	0.9	-0.2	-1.5	-1.5	0.1

Source: Government of India, CSO (1989a).

Table 5.16 Real Gross Fixed Capital Formation, 1970/71 to 1978/79

(1980/81 prices)

	1970/71	1971/72	1972/73	1973/74	1974/75	1975/76	1976/77	1977/78	1978/79
Annual percentage changes									
Real GFCF	0.5	6.2	5.2	-1.0	-3.1	9.7	12.6	9.6	0.9
Public	2.5	10.6	18.7	-2.2	-14.5	17.9	23.7	6.5	0.3
Private	-0.7	3.5	-3.7	-0.1	6.0	4.4	4.6	12.2	1.4
Corporate	27.8	21.2	-4.9	17.0	-15.3	34.9	-36.9	35.6	-31.3
Household	-4.6	0.2	-3.4	-3.8	11.6	-1.8	16.2	8.7	7.6
Percentage of GDP at market prices									
Real GFCF	16.5	17.2	18.2	17.5	16.7	16.8	18.6	19.0	18.1
Public	6.3	6.8	8.1	7.7	6.5	7.0	8.5	8.5	8.1
Private	10.2	10.4	10.1	9.8	10.2	9.8	10.0	10.5	10.1
Corporate	1.6	1.9	1.8	2.1	1.7	2.1	1.3	1.7	1.1
Household	8.6	8.5	8.2	7.7	8.5	7.6	8.7	8.8	9.0

Note: The source listed below provides public and private fixed capital formation at current prices. Constant price estimates were obtained by using construction and machinery deflators implied in figures given in the same source for fixed capital formation disaggregated into construction and machinery at both current and constant prices.

Source: Government of India, CSO (1989a).

Table 5.17 Real Public Gross Fixed Capital Formation, 1970/71 to 1979/80

(Rs crores, 1980/81 prices)

	1970/71	1971/72	1972/73	1973/74	1974/75	1975/76	1976/77	1977/78	1978/79	1979/80
Public GFCF	6,335	7,005	8,316	8,137	6,957	8,200	10,144	10,806	10,843	11,142
Center	1,255	1,525	1,544	1,547	1,415	1,422	1,552	1,572	1,661	1,640
States	2,479	2,900	3,513	3,572	2,567	2,683	3,378	3,753	4,264	4,467
Nondepartmental enterprises	2,590	2,580	3,259	3,018	2,975	4,095	5,214	5,481	4,918	5,035

Source: The figure for the total comes from table 5.15. The division into center, state, and nondepartmental enterprises is arrived at by using the same proportions as obtained for public fixed capital formation in the old series of national accounts (see note to table 4.5).

135

Table 5.18 Gross Fixed Capital Formation in the Public Sector, by Industry, 1970/71 to 1979/80
(Rs crores, at 1970/71 prices)

	1970/71	1971/72	1972/73	1973/74	1974/75	1975/76	1976/77	1977/78	1978/79	1979/80
Total	2,391	2,610	3,137	3,117	2,658	3,256	4,072	4,301	4,345	4,515
Agriculture	327	342	435	409	338	393	563	635	661	671
Mining	76	79	112	130	109	196	336	389	294	301
Manufacturing	315	340	428	444	434	549	891	791	645	698
Electricity, gas, and water	586	581	588	613	569	851	903	994	1,028	1,052
Construction	-4	10	2	28	37	20	19	9	11	39
Railways	224	235	271	274	240	244	247	456	272	293
Other transport	187	168	262	228	260	249	279	244	277	242
Communication	55	79	92	84	97	115	125	139	138	134
Public administration and defense	495	627	764	769	455	477	538	562	719	806
Other services	67	84	114	98	92	109	149	188	177	176

Source: Government of India, CSO (1983).

Table 5.19 India's Balance of Payments, 1970/71 to 1979/80
(millions of dollars)

	1970/71	1971/72	1972/73	1973/74	1974/75	1975/76	1976/77	1977/78	1978/79	1979/80
Merchandise imports	2,294	2,678	2,785	3,503	5,212	5,483	5,389	6,471	9,015	11,857
Merchandise exports	1,870	2,089	2,460	3,017	3,987	4,828	5,742	6,345	6,769	7,679
Trade balance	-424	-589	-325	-486	-1,225	-655	353	-126	-2,246	-4,178
Balance nonfactor services	3	9	57	61	210	311	366	691	716	1,042
Resource balance	-431	-580	-268	-425	-1,011	-344	719	565	-1,529	-3,136
Net current transfers	83	112	97	159	258	470	692	1,077	1,181	1,852
Net factor income	-244	-200	-284	-259	-190	-217	-161	-89	2	287
Current balance	-592	-748	-455	-525	-951	-91	1,249	1,553	-347	-997
Official grants	206	400	109	91	118	327	275	304	333	377
M/LT loans (net)	583	613	473	563	961	1,290	1,032	694	587	644
IMF credit (net)	-253	0	0	75	522	242	-337	-330	-158	0
Other capital flows	-76	-140	-40	10	-331	-697	-291	-155	345	187
Errors and omissions	-105	-86	-42	-264	-368	-255	-362	-18	715	13
Change in reserves	287	-39	-5	-106	49	-816	-1,556	-2,048	-1,475	-224
Memorandum items										
GDP at market prices	57,551	61,676	67,200	80,112	90,432	93,987	94,798	109,916	127,216	141,600
Current account deficit (% GDP)	1.03	1.21	0.68	0.66	1.05	0.10	-1.32	-1.41	0.27	0.70
Current account deficit (% exports)	27.60	31.40	16.30	15.40	20.80	1.60	-18.40	-20.10	4.10	10.00

Note: The World Bank's balance of payments figures are based principally on information published by the Reserve Bank of India.
Source: World Bank (annual), "India: Country Economic Memorandum."

Table 5.20 Value of Merchandise Imports, 1970/71 to 1979/80
(millions of dollars)

	1970/71	1971/72	1972/73	1973/74	1974/75	1975/76	1976/77	1977/78	1978/79
Bulk goods	1,018	1,126	1,067	2,261	4,129	4,495	3,635	4,198	4,961
Food	284	176	105	607	958	1,552	971	143	106
Edible oils	—	—	—	—	15	16	112	829	649
POL	181	261	265	719	1,450	1,417	1,581	1,811	2,044
Fertilizers	134	153	188	279	885	937	347	498	706
Iron and steel	196	319	293	320	531	360	246	307	572
Nonferrous metals	159	138	142	180	224	116	176	224	302
Gems	—	—	—	—	66	97	202	386	583
Capital goods	527	632	691	836	873	1,080	1,172	1,297	1,497
Other imports	634	693	665	696	663	510	869	1,535	1,841
Total imports	2,179	2,451	2,423	3,793	5,665	6,085	5,676	7,030	8,300

Note: The World Bank's trade figures are based on those published by the Government of India, DGCIS, *Monthly Statistics of the Foreign Trade of India*. They differ from Reserve Bank of India figures used in table 5.19.

Source: World Bank (various years), "India: Country Economic Memorandum."

Table 5.21 Merchandise Imports at Constant Prices, 1970/71 to 1978/79

(millions of dollars at 1978/79 prices)

	1970/71	1971/72	1972/73	1973/74	1974/75	1975/76	1976/77	1977/78	1978/79
Bulk goods	2,941	3,462	3,321	4,032	4,180	4,078	4,016	4,346	4,961
Food	601	380	168	680	883	1272	866	124	106
Edible oils	—	—	—	—	19	21	117	865	649
POL	1,317	1,620	1,717	1,900	1,793	1,695	1,807	1,893	2,044
Fertilizers	312	400	449	482	625	558	583	514	706
Iron and steel	349	676	614	509	595	290	202	280	572
Nonferrous metals	232	232	230	200	170	117	187	226	302
Gems	—	—	—	—	94	124	255	444	583
Capital goods	1,216	1,383	1,391	1,450	1,244	1,384	1,481	1,492	1,497
Other imports	1,461	1,516	1,338	1,208	944	653	1,098	1,765	1,841
Total imports	5,618	6,360	6,050	6,691	6,388	6,115	6,595	7,603	8,300

Source: World Bank (various years), "India: Country Economic Memorandum." (See also note to table 5.20.)

Table 5.22 Merchandise Exports, 1971/72 to 1978/79
(annual growth rates)

	1971/72	1972/73	1973/74	1974/75	1975/76	1976/77	1977/78	1978/79
Primary exports								
Value	0.0	6.92	38.0	34.0	15.59	-0.72	17.96	-3.8
Volume	0.0	3.31	8.89	-0.46	11.11	2.5	-14.8	7.5
Manufactured exports								
Value	17.98	25.13	20.96	25.94	9.72	38.3	6.03	17.8
Volume	9.08	19.11	2.66	8.20	10.25	38.9	-5.1	1.7
Total exports								
Value	16.76	18.43	26.23	29.27	11.93	23.1	9.77	10.5
Volume	5.22	12.65	5.00	4.81	10.55	25.4	-8.0	3.3
Volume[a]	-1.9	15.4	4.1	6.5	10.6	18.4	-3.5	7.2

a. Alternative estimate.
Source: All value data from Government of India, DGCIS (various years). All volume data from World Bank data files except the last row, which comes from Government of India, DGCIS (various years).

Table 5.23 India's Exports in a Broader Perspective, 1970/71 to 1979/80
(annual percentage changes)

	1970/71	1971/72	1972/73	1973/74	1974/75	1975/76	1976/77	1977/78	1978/79	1979/80
India's export volume[a]	5.4	-1.9	15.4	4.1	6.5	10.6	18.4	-3.5	7.2	6.2
India's export volume to convertible currency areas[b]	3.9	-2.3	12.1	8.2	8.3	12.2	22.5	-3.6	10.7	6.6
Industrial countries' real GDP[c]	2.8	3.3	4.9	5.7	0.9	-0.5	4.6	3.6	4.2	3.3
World trade (volume)[d]		—	8.0	12.5	5.0	-4.0	11.0	5.0	5.5	6.5
Nonoil developing countries' export volume[e]	4.9	5.0	16.9	8.1	0.2	0.0	14.6	5.2	6.3	9.3
Export volume of "exporters of manufactures"[f]	10.5	11.8	6.0	17.9	13.2	-2.0	4.7	7.6	11.7	6.9

Sources:

a. Government of India, DGCIS (various years).
b. Government of India, DGCIS (various years).
c. IMF (annual), *International Financial Statstics Yearbook.*
d. IMF (biannual), *World Economic Outlook.*
e. IMF (1988) *International Financial Statistics Yearbook: Supplement on Trade Statistics.*
f. IMF (1988) *International Financial Statistics Yearbook: Supplement on Trade Statistics.*

Table 5.24   Effective Exchange Rate Indexes, 1970/71 to 1978/79
(1978/79 = 100)

Year	NER	RER	RERsa
1970/71	137.02	138.35	149.63
1971/72	134.33	137.03	147.76
1972/73	124.18	132.61	141.83
1973/74	113.28	125.98	135.01
1974/75	110.77	130.64	140.15
1975/76	106.15	120.70	127.62
1976/77	105.07	108.71	112.42
1977/78	104.89	109.19	113.64
1978/79	100.00	100.00	100.00

NER is the nominal effective exchange rate.
RER is the real effective exchange rate.
RERsa is the real effective exchange rate adjusted for export subsidies.
   Source: Table 11.3.

Chapter Six

The Crisis of 1979–81 and Its Aftermath

The 1979–81 crisis was caused by the simultaneous occurrence of a disastrous harvest and a jump in the price of imported oil, which led to both high inflation and a large current account deficit. Prices were almost stationary in 1978/79 but increased by 17 and 18 percent in the following two years respectively. The current account of the balance of payments was in surplus in 1978/79 but went into a deficit of about 26 percent of exports in 1979/80 and 30 percent of exports in 1980/81.

Thus, the origin of the crisis was remarkably similar to that of 1973. However, the outcome was quite different. The government was much less restrictive in its response and attempted to bring about an "expansionary adjustment." Inflation came down during 1981/82, but the current account deficit remained about 25 percent of exports until 1984/85, and the public finances deteriorated. This was a prelude to even bigger current account and fiscal deficits in the second half of the 1980s.

The Causes of the High Inflation of 1979/80 to 1980/81

From February 1979, prices rose rapidly for $2^1/_2$ years. Inflation stopped in August 1981 when prices fell for a few months before rising moderately in 1982. Two facts about this high-inflation episode are worth noting. First, prices started rising rapidly some months before the drought of 1979; second, food prices, in general, played a smaller role than they did in 1973–75, mostly due to the government's comfortable food-stock position, which enabled it to step up public distribution sharply. The main contribution to the inflation came from manufactured goods and fuel.

Exogenous Shocks and their Consequences

The principal exogenous shock was the exceptionally severe drought of 1979/80 that affected both the *kharif* and the *rabi* crops. This resulted in a drop of 17.6 percent in

Table 6.1   Annual Changes in Foodgrain and Agricultural Production, 1977/78 to 1984/85

(percent)

Year	Foodgrain production		Agricultural production	
	Annual change	*Deviation from trend*	*Annual change*	*Deviation from trend*
1977/78	15.5	8.6	14.3	6.0
1978/79	4.3	8.5	3.8	7.2
1979/80	–17.6	–13.0	–15.2	–11.4
1980/81	19.8	1.5	15.6	–0.2
1981/82	2.2	0.9	5.6	2.7
1982/83	–3.4	–6.0	–4.0	–4.0
1983/84	18.6	9.6	14.2	6.8
1984/85	–4.2	2.7	–0.9	3.1

Source: Government of India, Ministry of Finance (various years), *Economic Survey.*

foodgrain production and 15 percent in agricultural production (13 and 11 percent below trend respectively. See table 6.1). The supply of industrial raw materials was severely affected by the drought, and their prices rose steeply (see table 8.2).

But the drought was not the only exogenous shock. Import prices rose by about 50 percent between 1977/78 and 1980/81 (see table 6.2) of which the most dramatic rise was in the price of imported crude petroleum, which more than doubled. Most of the oil price rise took place in 1979 and 1980. Apart from that, the most significant price increases were in fertilizers and nonferrous metals; in both these cases, import prices in dollars rose by about 50 percent in two years. Domestic fuel costs were raised not only by the oil price shock but also by the disruption to domestic oil production resulting from the agitation in Assam. Shortage of water and the disruption of fuel supplies led to power shortages that in turn led to shortages of coal and transport facilities. Though wage data in India are unreliable, it seems clear that money wages in organized industry grew rapidly in 1977 and 1978, considerably faster than the CPI. This probably reflects the increased strength of trade unions in the heady post-emergency atmosphere.

Supply-Side Mismanagement

The government's supply-management policies were sensible as far as foodgrains were concerned. Lessons had been learned from previous crises, and there were large releases from the stocks of foodgrains. Even so, there were some delays because the severity of the reduction in food supplies was underestimated (for exam-

Table 6.2   Import Prices, Export Prices, and the Terms of Trade, 1977/78 to 1984/85

(1978/79 = 100)

Year	Import unit value		Export unit value		Terms of trade	
	Index	*Percent change*	*Index*	*Percent change*	*Index*	*Percent change*
1977/78	88.0	n.a.	100.3	n.a.	114.0	n.a.
1978/79	100.0	13.6	100.0	–0.0	100.0	12.3
1979/80	114.1	14.1	105.4	5.4	92.4	–7.6
1980/81	134.2	17.6	108.5	2.9	80.8	–12.6
1981/82	133.1	–0.8	124.1	14.4	93.2	15.4
1982/83	136.3	2.4	132.0	6.4	96.8	3.9
1983/84	125.8	–7.7	151.0	14.4	120.0	24.0
1984/85	161.7	28.5	169.8	12.5	105.0	–12.5

Source: Government of India, Ministry of Finance (various years), *Economic Survey.*

ple, the *Economic Survey* for 1979/80 estimated a fall of about 10 percent in both foodgrain and agricultural output; in fact they fell by 17 and 15 percent respectively). More seriously, when the prices of edible oils, sugar, and industrial raw materials began rising in early 1979, the government did not increase imports quickly even though foreign exchange reserves were ample.

As regards infrastructure, the government's supply-side failure had a chronic and long-term element related to the neglect of nontradable output in Indian planning. Lack of adequate investment was one problem, but there were others. A familiar litany was repeated year after year in the *Economic Surveys*. There were growing shortages of power in spite of additions to installed capacity; capacity was increasingly underutilized because of an inadequate supply of coal and a decline in its quality; coal production was stagnant because of labor problems; railways could not move coal because of power shortages; and so on. Thus, the infrastructure was already fragile; the drought made it creak even more.

A further point concerns the government's handling of increases in administered prices, which was less than ideal. There has been a tendency for increases in administered prices in India to be guided by overall macroeconomic considerations. Thus, increases are postponed during periods of fiscal expansion and imposed during periods of fiscal contraction. Since the government is likely to adopt a contractionary stance when it is worried about inflation, this means that increases in administered prices tend to occur precisely when their cost-push effect is likely to worsen inflation in the short run. A number of such increases occurred in 1979. Prices of a wide range of key commodities such as coal, iron, steel, and aluminum were increased. While such increases were unavoidable, they occurred in a jump and were, therefore, large enough to have cost-push effects.

Fiscal Policy

The supply constraints outlined above operated in the context of a highly liquid economy and expansionist policies. Both fiscal and monetary policies were on a loose rein, particularly the latter. The relevant figures are given in tables 6.11, 6.12, and 6.13.

As we saw in chapter 5, from 1975/76 to 1978/79 fiscal policy was relaxed, though not aggressively so. The consolidated government fiscal deficit increased from 4.1 percent in 1974/75 to 5.7 percent in 1978/79. In 1979/80 it widened further to 6.5 percent.

The fiscal relaxation in the second half of the 1970s was characterized by a rapid growth of consolidated government current expenditure, which rose from 15 percent of GDP in 1975/76 to 17.8 percent in 1979/80. The most important component of the rise in current expenditure was the increase in subsidies, the political economy of which is discussed in chapter 3. Food subsidies doubled from Rs 250 crores in 1975/76 to Rs 500 crores in 1976/77; fertilizer subsidies increased from Rs 60 crores in 1976/77 to Rs 603 crores in 1979/80. Export subsidies increased from Rs 80 crores in 1974/75 to Rs 375 crores in 1978/79. All visible subsidies together increased by nearly 1 percent of GDP from 1975/76 to 1979/80.

Though government current expenditure increased rapidly from 1975/76, the overall balance of the budget was not unduly expansionary until the end of 1977/78.[1] But in 1978 and 1979 there was a noticeable change. In both years, fiscal deficits turned out to be much greater than had been planned at the beginning of the fiscal year. In 1979 this was partly the result of unanticipated drought-related expenditure.[2] But that was not the only reason. These two years saw increases in procurement prices for foodgrains unmatched by issue prices, tax reductions on a wide range of agricultural inputs, and increased transfers to loss-making public sector units at both the central and the state level.[3] State government finances should have improved because the Seventh Finance Commission increased their share of central taxes. Nevertheless, state overdrafts from the Reserve Bank increased. These fiscal developments had monetary consequences. From 1978/79 the fiscal laxity ensured that high-powered money continued to expand rapidly even though the balance of payments surplus had begun to dwindle.

Monetary Policy

As we saw in chapter 5, both reserve money and total money supply grew very rapidly from 1976/77 to 1979/80. Until 1977/78 these increases were fueled by balance of payments surpluses and thereafter by government borrowing from the Reserve Bank.

The relationship between reserve money and total money can be varied by monetary policy, and some attention must therefore be paid to the role of the Reserve Bank in the process. There is evidence that in each of these years the increase in money supply exceeded the informal, internal targets of the Reserve Bank.[4] This was partly because its projections were faulty; the balance of payments adjustment was unexpectedly favorable. Growth in exports and remittances was underestimated, and imports (1975/76 to 1977/78) were overestimated. Budget deficits (1978/79 and 1979/80) were underestimated. But in addition, the Reserve Bank's policies lacked force. There was some skepticism within the Reserve Bank on the link between high-powered and total money and an undue faith in "macrocredit planning"—the idea that total credit could be controlled by laying down credit ceilings for individual banks. During these years, such ceilings were consistently exceeded.

There were some restrictive monetary measures. The cash reserve ratio was raised from 4 to 6 percent in 1976, and a further cash ratio of 10 percent on incremental deposits was imposed in January 1977. The statutory liquidity ratio was raised from 33 to 34 percent in December 1978.[5] Not only were these measures mild, given the large increase in reserve money, but they failed to bite because the banks defaulted on the required reserve ratios (the financial penalties for doing so were not tough enough) and continued to increase lending by exploiting a major loophole in the system.[6]

The consequence of all this was that money supply growth was very rapid from 1976/77 to 1979/80, on average about 16 percent a year for M1 and 20 percent a year for M3. Until 1978/79 this was accompanied by low inflation, an apparently puzzling phenomenon discussed in chapter 5. The velocity of circulation fell sharply for various reasons, but it was in the nature of this exceptional decline that it would be reversed in the normal course of events and all the more so if there were negative shocks to output. The timing of the upsurge of inflation is noteworthy. Prices started rising in February 1979, well before the failure of the monsoon became evident around August. In fact, the major part of the price rise in 1979/80 in both food and manufactured goods took place from April to September.[7] Rising import prices played a role in this, but it seems clear also that previous monetary expansion was beginning to be reflected in prices.

As in the 1973–75 crisis, the Reserve Bank reacted rather late to events. It was probably itself the victim of some complacency induced by the run of good harvests. It was only in the middle of 1979, after prices had risen strongly for a few months, that monetary policy turned firmly toward restraint.

Causes of Balance of Payments Deterioration

As in the first oil crisis, the sharp deterioration of the balance of payments in 1979 and 1980 was caused mainly by a terms of trade shock, but two points of difference may be noted. First, the worsening of the terms of trade was itself principally caused by the rise in the price of oil; unlike in 1973, there was only a moderate increase in other import prices. Second, unlike in 1973, imports had been growing rapidly for two years before the oil price rise.

In 1976/77 there was a modest trade surplus ($350 million) and a large current account surplus ($1,250 million). The trade balance deteriorated by about $2.5 billion in the next two years. The export growth of the previous years slowed down, and imports rose substantially, mainly due to economic recovery and partly due to import liberalization. But remittances continued to grow strongly, so while the current account worsened there was only a moderate deficit in 1978/79 ($347 million). Balance of payments figures are given in table 6.16.

The import liberalization that took place was very gradual. By the middle of the 1970s the disadvantages of the rigid import control system were begining to be appreciated, and the easing of the foreign exchange situation made it possible to contemplate a change. The first steps were taken in 1976, and a more systematic overhaul took place in 1978. Consumer goods imports continued to be banned, but the rigors of licensing were softened for the import of intermediate and capital goods. Policy was most liberal with respect to goods that did not compete with domestic production. But even with competitive imports, two important changes were made. First, items that were manufactured in India but that previously had been imported were still subject to licensing, but the licenses now allowed for some automatic growth and supplementation over past levels. Second, a "global tender" policy was introduced with respect to capital goods so that Indian suppliers had to compete with worldwide tenders (prices of the latter were of course landed prices—that is, the cost in freight price plus tariffs). These changes, though pursued with varying degrees of consistency, contributed toward sizable increases in imports of intermediate and capital goods. Significantly, these policies were not reversed (except marginally in 1980/81) in response to the second oil price shock.

In 1979/80 and 1980/81 the trade balance deteriorated by more than $5 billion. The price of a barrel of oil rose from $13 in 1978 to $34 by March 1981. The terms of trade deterioration was only 20 percent, since prices of nonoil imports did not rise much and export prices rose to some extent. Oil imports in these two years increased by 30 percent in volume but more than trebled in value from $2 billion to $6.6 billion. The value of nonoil imports went up by 50 percent (from $6.2 billion to $9.3 billion), about half of which was a volume increase. Thus, growth of nonoil imports, particularly intermediate and capital goods, as a result of increased import-intensive public investment and import liberalization, did play some part in the worsening trade account. Remittances continued to grow rapidly (from $1.2 billion in 1978/79 to $2.7 billion in 1980/81), cushioning the rise in the trade deficit; even so, the current account deficit grew to $997 million (10 percent of exports) in 1979/80 and $2.7 billion (26 percent of exports) in 1980/81. The deficit was financed by an increase in grants and loans, particularly from the International Bank for Reconstruction and Development (IBRD), the International Development

Association (IDA), and the IMF Trust Fund. Foreign exchange reserves, therefore, fell only slightly.

The magnitude of the 1980/81 shock can be gauged from the following. The current account changed from a deficit of 0.3 percent of GDP (4 percent of exports) in 1978/79 to a deficit of 2 percent of GDP (31 percent of exports) in 1981/82. The terms of trade deteriorated by about 30 percent from 1977/78 to 1980/81 (see table 6.2). The resulting terms of trade shock (computed by using the same method and sources as in chapter 5) is shown in table 6.3.

Thus, the cumulative negative shock in these two years was about 20 percent of exports and 1.5 percent of GDP, a slightly smaller shock than in 1973–75. Note also that many developing countries that were heavily indebted also suffered from an "interest rate shock." This was of negligible importance for India, which had a low ratio of external debt (and particularly of variable-rate commercial debt) to exports at that time.

The Course of the Crisis and the Policy Reaction, 1979/80 to 1981/82

The division of the years 1979/80 to 1984/85 into "crisis" and "aftermath" is easy as far as inflation is concerned. But it is much less straightforward for the balance of payments since there was hardly any current account adjustment over the entire period. In this section we somewhat arbitrarily divide the period at 1981/82 to mark the end of the crisis, on the grounds that inflation was extinguished by August 1981 and the sense of crisis in the balance of payments was dispelled by the large loan from the IMF in November 1981. We describe briefly the course of the crisis and the policy reaction from 1979/80 to 1981/82, and end with an account of the IMF loan. More extended discussion of both the crisis and the aftermath can be found later in this chapter.

Undoubtedly 1979/80 and 1980/81 were crisis years manifesting both high inflation and large current account deficits. The government's reaction to inflation, as compared to previous crises, emphasized management of food supplies far more than conventional monetary and fiscal policies. These were, on balance, non-accommodating but not severe. This response arose partly from the comfortable food-stock position and partly from a reaction against the conservative financial

Table 6.3   Magnitude of the Terms of Trade Shock, 1979/80 and 1980/81

	1979/80	*1980/81*
Percentage of exports	−8.4	−13.4
Percentage of GDP	−0.6	−0.9

Source: Authors' calculations. The formula given in note 9 of chapter 5 has been applied to figures from tables 6.2 and 6.16.

policies adopted in reaction to the previous oil shock. In 1981/82, however, both monetary and fiscal policy moved decisively toward restraint in preparation for the approach to the IMF. In August 1981, inflation stopped in its tracks; indeed, prices fell for several months. Note, however, that real public investment was increased throughout the crisis.

The large accumulation of foreign exchange reserves at the start of the crisis enabled the authorities to avoid a tightening of import controls in response to the current account deficits. Moreover, as India borrowed about $1 billion from the soft windows of the IMF, there was only a negligible loss of reserves in 1979/80 and 1980/81. In 1981/82, however, reserves fell more than $2 billion, and the year ended with reserves down to 3.5 months of imports. The nominal effective exchange rate was held steady; so given the high inflation, the competitiveness of exports declined. As a consequence of this and the world recession, export growth slowed down. There were, however, adjustment measures as regards oil. Preparations were made to accelerate the extraction of offshore oil, and oil consumption was reduced by raising taxes on oil products. In 1981/82 the current account deficit was 31 percent of exports, higher than in the previous two years.

The IMF Loan

The external and internal politics of the IMF loan negotiations were discussed in chapter 3. The loan of SDR 5 billion was formally approved in November 1981, payable in three installments—SDR 900 million by the end of June 1982, SDR 1,800 million by the end of June 1983, and the balance by November 1984. The performance criteria for the full payment of the first installment specified ceilings effective at the end of March 1982 for net bank credit to the government (20 percent above end-March 1981) and total domestic credit (19.4 percent above end-March 1981).[8] Other significant performance criteria were a limit on total foreign non-IMF borrowing of SDR 1.4 billion in the first year of the program and a prohibition against intensification of import restrictions. Accompanying the performance criteria was the government's "statement of economic policies," which set out the general agreement between the government and the IMF on the policies the government would pursue.

Apart from the observance of the performance criteria, the only concrete aspects of the agreement related to limiting the growth of M3 to 15.7 percent in 1981/82 and increasing public investment in domestic oil production and infrastructure. The rest consisted of vague declarations by the government, with little operational force, promising many things, including export promotion, a "realistic" exchange rate, and policies to strengthen public finances and encourage private saving and investment. We shall see later that the outcome fell short of the announced intentions in several respects.

The program was little altered during periodic reviews. Ceilings on the growth of net bank credit to government, domestic credit, and foreign borrowing were broadly similar in 1982/83 and 1983/84. The target for M3, present in the program for 1981/82, was dropped thereafter.

Inflation: Resolution and Aftermath

Monetary policy was tightened in July 1979 by making defaulting banks fall in line, closing the loopholes in the reserve-ratio regulations, and cutting banks' overdraft limits across the board. This tightening could not reduce the inflationary momentum, but it doubtless helped to prevent its getting worse. But toward the end of 1980 the authorities were concerned about recession and so banks were exempted from the incremental cash ratio of 10 percent that had been imposed in 1977. This resulted, however, in such an explosion of borrowing and credit that a severe monetary squeeze was instituted from the middle of 1981. The CRR was raised in steps, from 6.5 percent in July 1981 to 7.75 percent in January 1982, and the SLR from 34 to 35 percent in July 1981. Reserve money also began falling sharply because of the drain on the reserves.[9] As a result, growth of M1 fell sharply from mid-1981 to mid-1982 (see table 6.12). There seems to have been some overkill in the monetary contraction, and the Reserve Bank had to step in with accommodating finance to cushion the abnormally severe squeeze on banks.

Fiscal policy also seesawed in terms of toughness. The consolidated government fiscal deficit went up from 5.7 percent of GDP in 1978/79 to 6.5 percent in 1979/80 and 8.1 percent in 1980/81 (see table 6.13). The expansion in 1979/80 is somewhat illusory since the downturn had its usual effects on revenue and expenditure. Our calculations in chapter 9 show a contractionary fiscal impulse (−1.6 percent of GDP). But in 1980/81 there was a significantly worse revenue performance by both the center and the states and consequently a large expansionary fiscal impulse (2.1 percent of GDP). The budget of 1981, however, was very tough, partly because of worries about continuing inflation and partly in anticipation of the IMF program. Excise and customs duties and rail fares were raised, and there were major increases in the administered prices of key goods such as iron and steel, aluminum, fertilizers, and cement. The fiscal deficit came down to 6.7 percent of GDP; this is confirmed by a fiscal impulse that was contractionary (−1 percent of GDP). Thus, fiscal and monetary policies were, on balance, nonaccommodating but far from draconian.

In 1979/80 the WPI rose by 17 percent. Food prices, however, rose by only 8 percent (in fact only 4 percent in 1979) while prices of manufactures went up by 20 percent. The moderate increase in food prices is explained by the fact that food availability remained satisfactory in spite of the drought. The government increased public distribution from the large stocks it had built up during the run of good harvests. In 1980/81 food prices went up by 12 percent (15 percent in 1980) as the effect of the 1979 drought came through on marketed output, softened though it was by a massive 25 percent increase in public distribution (see table

6.9). Prices of manufactures again increased by 20 percent, driven by rising prices of oil and industrial raw materials and other cost-push forces. Food production in 1980/81 more than made up the shortfall in 1979/80 and continued to be satisfactory in 1981/82. Public distribution continued at a high level. Prices of industrial raw materials eased after the agricultural recovery of 1980, and import prices were also stationary.

Overall inflation came down from 18 percent in 1980/81 to 9 percent in 1981/82. But monthly data show a more dramatic movement. Prices fell from August 1981 to March 1982 and then rose moderately for a year (2.6 percent in 1982/83). Although the bursting of the inflationary bubble was mainly due to the agricultural recovery, the virtual price stability for almost two years from August 1981 owed something to monetary and fiscal policy, both of which had become tight by the middle of 1981.

In 1983/84 and 1984/85 there was a resurgence of inflation, though it did not reach dangerous levels. There was a drought in 1982/83 (although not a very severe one) that reduced food availability in 1983 in spite of increased imports and public distribution of foodgrains and edible oils. Food prices rose by 10 percent and the prices of manufactures by 9 percent in 1983/84. The critical element in the return of inflation was fiscal and monetary relaxation. After the liquidity crunch of 1982 there were fears of an industrial recession, and monetary policy was eased. The cash reserve ratio was reduced to 7 percent, and there were several relaxations of credit. Reserve money grew rapidly, both because the balance of payments improved due to larger capital inflows and inflows of nonresident deposits, and because fiscal deficits widened. Underlying the latter was a very rapid growth of government expenditure, which increased the borrowing requirement by 2.4 percent of GDP in the two years from 1982/83. Monetary policy was again tightened in 1983/84, and the cash reserve ratio was increased in successive steps from 7 to 9 percent. Nevertheless, M1 and M3 accelerated due to the rapid expansion of reserve money. These tendencies continued in 1984/85 in spite of further tightening in the form of an increase in SLR from 35 to 36 percent. Overall inflation moderated to 7 percent, however, as a result of the bumper harvest of 1983/84.[10]

The above review of the inflation experience from 1979/80 to 1984/85 makes a rather complex story. But we should not lose sight of the following general points concerning the moderation of inflation in 1981/82 and 1982/83.

- Inflation came down in these two years as a result of a combination of agricultural recovery, falling import prices, and relatively tight financial policies.
- Though financial policies were generally tight for two years, they were so only relative to an underlying trend of greater laxity. Fiscal deficits were above those of the 1970s. Monetary tightening was neither as consistent nor as draconian as between 1973 and 1975.
- Having to meet IMF ceilings helped in the tightening of financial policies in these two years. It is significant that in 1984/85, after the termination of

the IMF program, fiscal and monetary policies were very lax. The fact that it was an election year also contributed to this outcome.

Capital Formation during and after the Crisis

Though there was some tightening of monetary policy in response to the inflation of 1979, there was deliberately no cutback in public investment. Indeed, there was a considerable boom in real public fixed capital formation, which began in the crisis years and continued thereafter. As table 6.15 shows, real public fixed investment grew by 3 and 5 percent respectively in 1979/80 and 1980/81. This increase was considerably more rapid than in the two precrisis years, and it may be recalled that in earlier crisis episodes public investment actually fell. Real public investment grew even more strongly in 1981/82 and 1982/83 (an average of 14 percent a year) before falling back to a more moderate pace in 1983/84 and 1984/85. The average ratio of real public fixed investment to real GDP increased by about 2 percent in the period 1980/81 to 1984/85 over the previous five-year period. The most pronounced increases in public investment were in the energy and infrastructure sectors (coal, petroleum, electricity, and railways) and to a lesser extent in manufacturing. Public investment in agriculture, however, declined markedly, which may be one reason among others for the decline in agricultural growth rates in this period.[11]

Private fixed investment fluctuated more than public fixed investment in this period and was rather stagnant. It is illuminating, however, to break down private investment into its "private-corporate" and "household" components, bearing in mind that the "household" sector includes unincorporated enterprises. Private investment in registered manufacturing fell in 1979/80, as might be expected in a drought year. But from 1980/81 there was a strong revival in private corporate investment. In contrast, real household investment fell sharply. The reasons for this are not entirely clear, but the following two may be adduced, the second of which is somewhat speculative.

- The rising relative price of construction had a particular effect on household sector investment, which is construction-intensive. Possible reasons for the rising price of construction include the decontrol of construction materials such as steel and cement and the emigration of skilled labor to the Middle East.[12] These developments, however, are independent of macroeconomic policy.
- The above factor only exacerbated a tendency that was already there, in the sense that the current-price ratio of household fixed investment to GDP also fell sharply. It is possible that this reflects a "crowding out" effect in reaction to the growing public deficits and the public and private corporate investment boom.

The contrary tendencies in private corporate and household investment added up to a rather stagnant course for private fixed investment as a whole. Total real fixed investment (that is, public and private sectors together) therefore rose more moderately after 1980/81 than did public investment alone.

The Behavior of Output during and after the Crisis

Accompanying the crisis was a recession in manufacturing industry. Output in registered manufacturing fell in both 1979/80 and 1980/81 (see table 6.10). In 1979/80 output also fell in construction, transport, and trade. It should be noted, however, that all these falls were in the private sector. Output in the public sector continued growing, presumably because of the deliberate attempt to increase public investment and the interrelated nature of many public sector activities.

The industrial recession of 1979/80 and 1980/81 was quite severe, more so than in the 1973 crisis, but that is not difficult to explain. The drought of 1979 was more severe than that of 1973 and so were the cumulative infrastructure shortages. Wage costs rose faster and the government was more prompt in passing on increased prices of petroleum products. The fact that the government did not tighten import controls may also have been a small contributory factor. It is doubtful if anti-inflationary policies had a major role to play in the 1979 recession. As already noted, anti-inflationary policies were not as tough as in the 1973 crisis.

From 1981/82 to 1984/85, manufacturing production, and registered manufacturing in particular, grew strongly. The growth rate of value added in registered manufacturing was about 10 percent a year. Unregistered manufacturing grew at the more subdued rate of 4.5 percent, which is perhaps not surprising in view of the squeeze on capital formation in the household sector. There is some evidence of an increase in the trend growth of manufacturing from 1981/82. While the maintenance of public investment and the creeping liberalization of controls were contributory factors, the main reason was probably a high pressure of demand (see chapter 13).

Effects on Absorption and Income Distribution

The effects of the crisis on absorption and income distribution were somewhat different from those during the first oil crisis. Aggregate consumption and fixed investment fell only in 1979/80, the year of the big drought. Moreover, public consumption and public fixed investment grew in that year, so the fall was entirely in private consumption and investment. In 1980/81, both consumption and investment grew considerably faster than gross domestic income. These facts are a reflection of the expansionary character of the response.

Table 6.4   Real Wages in Selected Sectors
(1960 prices)

Year	Agriculture real wage[a]	Organized manufacturing		Public sector real wage[a]
		Real wage[b]	Product wage[b]	
1977/78	1.62	1,424	1,519	10.4
1978/79	1.68	1,627	1,773	11.4
	(3.7)	(14.3)	(16.7)	(9.6)
1979/80	1.52	1,682	1,623	11.9
	(–9.5)	(3.4)	(–8.5)	(4.4)
1980/81	1.39	1,672	1,447	12.2
	(–8.6)	(–0.6)	(–10.8)	(2.5)
1981/82	—	1,632	1,585	12.2
		(–2.4)	(9.5)	(0.0)
1982/83	—	1,717	1,784	12.7
		(5.2)	(12.6)	(4.1)
1983/84	—	1,807	1,938	13.5
		(5.2)	(8.6)	(6.3)

Note: Figures in parentheses are annual percentage changes.
a. Rupees per day.
b. Rupees per year.
Source: Agriculture from Lucas (1986); organized manufacturing from Tulpule and Datta (1988); public sector from CMIE (1984).

Even so, agricultural real wages fell in both 1979/80 and 1980/81, about 17 percent over the two years (see table 6.4). It is interesting that agricultural real wages fell in 1980/81 when agricultural production rose strongly, illustrating the fact that agricultural laborers are net buyers of food—food-price inflation was quite rapid in 1980/81. Real wages in organized manufacturing fell only about 3 percent in 1980 and 1981 and public sector real wages did not fall at all. This confirms impressionistic evidence that the extent of indexation in the organized sector had increased between the two oil crises. (Note, however, that there was a large fall in the product wage as a result of the rising price of energy.) Thus, the fall in real wages that did occur affected mainly agricultural laborers and probably unorganized employees generally, and was related to drought and inflation rather than to stabilization policy. Table 6.4 gives some real wage data.

Non-Adjustment of the Balance of Payments after the Second Oil Crisis

In 1980/81, mainly as a result of the oil price increase, the current account deficit reached a level of 1.7 percent of GDP and 26 percent of exports. Unlike the adjustment after the first oil shock, there was no turnaround in the current account deficit in the ensuing years. This remained virtually unchanged as a proportion of GDP and exports until 1984/85 (see table 6.16). The trade deficit (and the resource deficit) did fall but not sufficiently to affect the current account deficit. We now examine the reasons underlying this performance. One feature of the story stands out immediately—the current account failed to improve despite a highly successful import-substitution program in oil.

Import-Substitution in Oil

In one sense, India was reasonably well positioned to adapt to the oil crises of the 1970s. The Oil and Natural Gas Commission (ONGC) and Oil India Ltd (OIL) had been set up in the 1950s, and some experience had been acquired over the years in both exploration and drilling. By 1973/74 India was producing 7 million tonnes of crude oil. Imports of oil and petroleum products were 17 million tonnes, constituting about three-quarters of domestic consumption.

Offshore exploration had begun before 1973. When the first oil shock came, India had a lucky break in the form of the discovery of the Bombay High Field. Extraction of oil in the Bombay High Field began in 1976 and domestic production of oil increased gradually. Expenditure on exploration was also stepped up sharply and by 1980 several new fields had been discovered in the Bombay offshore region. Nevertheless, in 1980/81 after the second oil price rise, the situation looked serious. Domestic production was 10.5 million tonnes but oil and oil-product imports were 20.6 million tonnes. The oil import bill took up three-quarters of export earnings.

The sixth Five-Year Plan had originally fixed a target of 21 million tonnes of crude oil for 1984/85. However, after the second oil price increase and the troubles in Assam, it was decided to implement an "accelerated program" for extraction of oil from the Bombay High Field. A new target of 29 million tonnes was set and achieved. Expenditure on oil exploration and production was almost doubled in real terms. The IMF loan clearly helped. By 1984/85 net imports of oil and oil products were down to 13 million tonnes, less than one-third of domestic consumption, and the oil import bill was also down to one-third of export earnings. Unquestionably, India's import-substitution program in oil was a great success. The program benefited from dynamic management of the oil sector, but this would not have been possible without a substantial delegation of authority from the government and freedom from the normal bureaucratic restraints.[13]

Import substitution in oil was achieved not only by expanding domestic supply but also by restraining domestic consumption. Domestic prices of oil products were maintained substantially above cif prices, as in the previous oil crisis. The margin above cif prices tended to slip somewhat between the two oil crises but was restored by further increased taxation in 1982 and 1983. There were some exceptions to the policy of keeping oil-product prices high, notably kerosene (for social reasons) and naphtha (to reduce the cost of fertilizer production).

The value of oil imports fell from $6.6 billion in 1980/81 to $3.2 billion in 1984/85. Half of this fall was accounted for by a decline in volume related to the factors discussed above, the other half was due to reduced world oil prices.

The Behavior of Imports

Bulk imports increased sharply both in value and in volume in 1979/80 and 1980/81, not only because of oil, but because infrastructure problems caused production difficulties in fertilizers, iron and steel, and nonferrous metals. From 1981/82 this increase was reversed. This was mainly the result of import-substitution in oil; other bulk imports benefited from higher domestic capacity utilization. Foodgrains and edible oils were, however, imported in large quantities after the drought of 1982.

Nonbulk imports increased rapidly in contrast to the first oil shock period. This was closely connected with the character of the government's response to the crisis, namely the increase in import-intensive public investment and the continuation of import liberalization. The volume of capital goods and "other imports" (largely intermediate goods) grew at 12.7 and 6.3 percent a year respectively between 1980/81 and 1984/85.

Total imports stayed level in volume and fell in value after 1980/81. To understand the persistence of the current account deficit, therefore, one has to focus on the stagnation of exports.

Appreciation of the Real Exchange Rate and Stagnation of Exports

In marked contrast to the first oil shock period, export volume stagnated (see table 6.5). Aggregate exports increased in volume by about 2 percent a year, but that includes the effect of crude oil exports. Nonoil exports were virtually stationary between 1979/80 and 1984/85, and nonoil exports to convertible currency areas actually fell. The volume of exports of manufactured goods fell from 1978/79 to 1982/83; the volume of exports of engineering goods fell from 1978/79 to 1984/85. Export earnings in dollars also stagnated because export prices rose very slowly and in some years fell in absolute terms (see table 6.16). The value of exports of manufactures fell between 1980/81 and 1982/83; the value of engineering goods' exports fell from 1980/81 to 1985/86. Since this dismal performance of exports largely accounts for the higher current account deficit, it is important to explore its causes.

The factor that has most commonly been emphasized in explaining the export outcome is the slowdown in world trade and industrial countries' GDP during part of this period (1980–82). There undoubtedly was such a slowdown as table 6.17 shows. Note, however, that industrial countries' GDP and world trade actually fell in only one year, 1982. The dollar value of nonoil imports by industrial countries (but not the volume) fell in two years, 1981 and 1982. The dollar value of imports

Table 6.5   Index Numbers of Export Volume
(1978/79 = 100)

Year	Total exports	Nonoil exports	Nonoil exports[a]
1977/78	93.3	93.3	90.3
1978/79	100.0	100.0	100.0
1979/80	106.2	106.2	106.6
1980/81	108.0	108.0	98.3
1981/82	110.1	108.7	99.9
1982/83	116.7	104.6	98.7
1983/84	113.0	104.5	98.6
1984/85	120.8	110.9	104.3

a. Refers to nonoil exports to convertible currency areas only.
Source: Government of India, Ministry of Finance (various years), *Economic Survey*; and World Bank (various years), "India: Country Economic Memorandum."

of manufactures by industrial countries did not fall in any year. (Data on trade in manufactures are not given in table 6.17, but are available in the United Nations Trade Data System.)

India's performance was unusually bad. Such slowdown as there was in industrial countries and in world trade occurred during 1980–82, but Indian exports stagnated from 1979/80 to 1985/86. Moreover, while there was a slowdown in aggregate world trade, exports of various relevant developing-country groupings such as "nonfuel exporters," "nonoil developing countries," and "exporters of manufactures" continued growing strongly during this period (see table 6.17). This was true not only of dynamic exporters such as the Republic of Korea, but of many others. (For example in 1982/83, when India's export value of manufactured goods fell by 3 percent, all the following countries showed an increase—Argentina, Brazil, Mexico, Indonesia, Pakistan, Korea, Sri Lanka, and Turkey.)

Thus, India's export performance was considerably worse than that of other relevant developing countries. While there is something in the explanation of a world trade slowdown, it is clearly far short of being the whole story. It seems that two other explanations are much more important—the appreciation of the real exchange rate and the stagnation of domestic savings. A devaluation of the real exchange rate was called for in view of the deterioration in the terms of trade and the need to increase the competitiveness of nonoil exports. In fact, the real effective exchange rate appreciated by about 15 percent between 1979 and 1981 and then stayed roughly level until 1984. The behavior of the real effective exchange rate index adjusted for export incentives is roughly similar (see table 6.6.).

How can one account for this rather perverse behavior? From 1979/80 to 1981/82, domestic inflation was considerably higher than that of India's trading partners. To even stop the real exchange rate appreciating would have required a

Table 6.6   Exchange Rate Indexes
(1978 = 100)

Year	NER	RER	RERsa
1977	104.9	109.2	113.6
1978	100.0	100.0	100.0
1979	97.8	99.8	101.4
1980	100.3	109.5	109.7
1981	100.5	114.5	112.5
1982	101.0	112.2	109.6
1983	98.9	115.6	114.4
1984	93.7	114.7	114.6

NER is the nominal effective exchange rate.
RER is the real effective exchange rate.
RERsa is the real effective exchange rate adjusted for export incentives.
   Source: Table 11.3.

devaluation of the nominal exchange rate. This presented certain problems in contrast to the earlier period of high inflation (1972/73 to 1974/75) when the rupee was formally pegged to the pound sterling and depreciated automatically with it. Beginning in September 1975 the rupee was pegged to an undisclosed basket of currencies. In formal terms this was an adjustable peg regime. An effective nominal devaluation would have therefore required either an explicit change of peg or a devaluation by stealth within the context of the basket peg, making use of the smoke screen provided by the secret weights.

Day-to-day exchange rate management was in the hands of top officials in the Ministry of Finance and the Reserve Bank of India. But a change of peg would have certainly required cabinet approval and so would any large devaluation by stealth. A devaluation was still regarded as politically highly sensitive. Moreover, Mrs. Gandhi returned to power in 1980, and she was known to be extremely wary of devaluation after the experience of 1966. The policy of devaluation by stealth was eventually pursued, but only after 1982.

This account suggests that the relevant bureaucrats would have liked to devalue but could not because of political constraints. This is not quite correct. There was at this stage no clear policy as regards targeting or even monitoring the real exchange rate. Exchange rate policy was made on an ad hoc basis depending on two considerations: maintaining the nominal effective exchange rate within the band and not allowing too big a movement in terms of the U.S. dollar. In the interests of the latter, the bands around the peg were widened from 2.5 to 5 percent in January 1979 at a time when the dollar was falling sharply. The nominal effective exchange rate did fall by about 2 percent in 1979, but this was reversed in 1980 when there was a sharp sterling appreciation. Thus, there was an appreciation of the nominal effective exchange rate in 1980—a very odd move indeed.

There are two common objections to nominal exchange rate devaluation and they have both influenced the thinking of the Indian bureaucracy. The first is that devaluation is inflationary—a curious objection given the small share of foreign trade in GDP and the small size of the indexed sector. The second is that demand and supply elasticities are low. These objections, both of which, in our opinion, are false (see chapter 11), played their part in preventing a sensible exchange rate policy. A technical point should also be mentioned. India's policymakers monitored the nominal effective exchange rate on the basis of a four-country index (Germany, Japan, the United Kingdom, and the United States). This index was too narrow given the diversity of India's trade. In a period in which, first sterling and then the dollar appreciated strongly with respect to all other currencies, this narrow index overstated the depreciation of the rupee and did not give the right signals (see Joshi 1984).

Some of these problems were ironed out in 1983 when the management of the exchange rate became more sophisticated. The real exchange rate became a focus of interest, and the nominal exchange rate became less politicized. Nevertheless, all that was done in 1983 and 1984 was to prevent a worsening of the competitive position. The damage done in 1980 and 1981 remained. It should be noted that developing countries whose exports grew rapidly in this period did not allow their real exchange rates to appreciate.

Invisibles on Current Account

The three main items that make up net invisibles on current account stagnated or deteriorated after 1980/81, as listed below.

- *Balance of Nonfactor Services.* In this case, the stagnation is related to the decline in net earnings from transportation and tourism. As in the case of visible exports, this outcome probably resulted more from the appreciation of the real exchange rate than from the world recession.
- *Net Factor Income.* After 1980/81, as foreign exchange reserves declined, so did investment income. From 1982/83, interest payments increased due to increasing external borrowing from the IMF and commercial sources.
- *Current Transfers.* These flattened out after 1980/81 because of the end of the boom in the Gulf countries and their tighter immigration policies. It is possible, moreover, that exports of labor were also adversely affected by appreciation of the real exchange rate against competitor countries.

Saving, Investment, and the Current Account Deficit

Another perspective on the current account deficit is gained by considering the macroeconomic identity that the current account deficit is equal to the difference between domestic investment and national saving. (Note here that the Indian national accounts concept of "gross domestic saving" is a misnomer and, in fact, corresponds to gross national saving. Thus, the figures for gross domestic saving in the tables in this book in fact refer to gross national saving.) This overall investment-savings gap is itself identically equal to the sum of the investment-savings gaps of the public, corporate, and household sectors. Of course, these identities can be used to make causal statements only by the exercise of informed judgment.

We saw above that the period 1979/80 to 1984/85 can usefully be broken at 1981/82 to separate crisis and aftermath. The average current account deficit widened by 2 percent of GDP between 1975/76 to 1978/79 and 1979/80 to 1981/82. As table 6.7 shows, the counterpart of this increase was a widening of both the public and the corporate sector deficits by about 1 percent of GDP; the household sector surplus was unchanged. The increased public sector deficit can be attributed

Table 6.7   Investment-Saving Balances, 1975/76 to 1984/85
(percentage of GDP)

	1975/76 to 1978/79	*1979/80 to 1981/82*	*1982/83 to 1984/85*
Public investment	9.4	9.8	10.6
Public saving	4.6	4.1	3.5
Public gap	4.8	5.7	7.1
Corporate investment	2.2	3.6	4.5
Corporate saving	1.4	1.8	1.6
Corporate gap	0.8	1.8	2.9
Household investment[a] (adjusted)	8.8	9.0	4.9
Household saving	15.2	15.4	13.6
Financial	5.8	5.9	7.1
Physical	9.4	9.5	6.5
Household gap	-6.4	-6.3	-8.6
Current account deficit[b]	-0.8	1.2	1.4

a. Errors and omissions in investment (that is, the difference between adjusted and unadjusted capital formation in table 6.14) are attributed entirely to household investment.

b. Current account deficit = Public gap + Corporate gap + Household gap.

Source: Table 6.14.

roughly equally to increased public investment and reduced public saving. The increased corporate deficit was entirely caused by a sharp increase in investment. Common sense suggests that the increased current account deficit during the crisis was largely exogenously driven (by the higher price of imported oil). This deficit and the counterpart changes in the public and private sectors were not inappropriate in the short run, given the ample food and foreign exchange reserves.

But a similar judgment cannot apply from 1982/83 onward. There was no adjustment of the current account deficit, which remained roughly unchanged as a proportion of GDP. The counterpart changes were as follows. Public and corporate investment continued to rise strongly. Public savings continued to fall and corporate savings to stagnate. Hence, both public and corporate deficits increased by more than 1 percent of GDP. These increases were almost fully financed by an increase in the household surplus. The latter arose from continued growth in financial savings combined with a substantial crowding out of household investment. Indeed, but for the severe squeeze on household investment, the current account deficit would have increased even more. In making a judgment about cause and effect in this phase, we must remember that there were, on balance, no adverse exogenous shocks. (As seen above, oil prices fell, and the slowdown in industrial countries was not especially serious.) Current account adjustment was evidently necessary. So mistakes in demand management must take part of the blame for the persistent current account deficit. If we further take the view that the public investment boom was an appropriate response to the oil shock and the cumulative infrastructure shortages, permitting a decline in public savings can be isolated as a crucial policy error in addition to mistakes in exchange rate policy. This is compatible with the view that these policy errors were themselves encouraged by the IMF loan, which made it possible to finance continued current account deficits.[14]

Financing the Current Account Deficit: The Increase in External Commercial Borrowing

Official grant aid, which had averaged about $400 million a year from 1975/76 to 1978/79, increased to about $600 million a year in 1979/80 and 1980/81 in response to the oil crisis but then fell away back to precrisis levels from 1981/82 to 1984/85. This fall reflected both "aid-weariness" and the redirection of aid toward China and Africa. Disbursements of concessional loans, of which more than half came from IDA, were about $1,400 million a year between 1981/82 and 1984/85, a slight increase in nominal terms over 1975/76 to 1978/79 but a fall in real terms. (IDA commitments began to fall sharply from 1984/85, but the effects of that were not felt until the end of the 1980s.)

Thus, aid and concessional inflows were not much higher than during the period when India was running current account surpluses. The current account deficit was financed principally by borrowing from the IMF and from other nonconcessional borrowing. The IMF loan was disbursed over the years 1981–83. There was an increase in borrowing from the IBRD as well, from about $100 million a year during 1975/76 to 1978/79 to $300 million a year during 1979/80 to 1984/85. But the main increase came in the form of borrowing from commercial sources, both bank and nonbank, publicly guaranteed and nonguaranteed. Included in this was a steady increase in nonresident deposits attracted to India by generous schemes that paid interest rates 2 percentage points above international rates. Disbursements of commercial loans, which averaged about $150 million a year from 1975 to 1979, rose to $660 million in 1980/81 and then grew steadily to $2.1 billion in 1984/85.

There was thus a big change in the composition of borrowing toward nonconcessional sources. The grant element in official multilateral borrowing also decreased, and there was an overall hardening in the terms of borrowing. India's debt service therefore increased from about $1.2 billion in 1980/81 to $2.1 billion in 1984/85, and the ratio of debt service to exports of goods and services went up from about 9.2 percent in 1980/81 to 18.2 percent in 1984/85. The level was not yet dangerous, but the trend was, and the situation was to get much worse in the later 1980s. In the short term, however, the problem was masked by continuing foreign borrowing. Foreign exchange reserves in 1984/85 were comfortable enough (about $6 billion), representing about 4.5 months of import cover.

Deterioration in the Public Finances

In retrospect, perhaps the most striking feature of the period 1979/80 to 1984/85 was a deterioration in the public finances. The continuation of this trend in the second half of the 1980s was to cause a crisis at the end of the decade.

Underlying this phenomenon were a number of political-economy changes that came to a head during this period. These have already been discussed in chapter 3. Briefly, "political awakening" had over the years increased the demands of various groups (for example, the middle-level farmers who, with the coming to power of the Janata coalition, were directly represented in New Delhi) while "political decay" had led to the advent of populist policies and the erosion of both the "agencies of constraint" and the institutions of conflict resolution. To these were added a change in the fiscal style of the policymaking elite as a reaction to what was felt to have been a too conservative reaction to the first oil shock. There was, therefore, a quite conscious decision to increase public investment financed by external borrowing. (The satisfactory position with respect to food and foreign exchange reserves was seen as reducing the risk.) But expansionist public investment policies as regards investment were not accompanied by adequate restraint of current expenditures of the government.

The timing of the fiscal deterioration is striking and can be seen in all the components of government and public finances, as discussed in greater detail below. It began in the second year of the Janata government (1978/89) and continued during the first two years of the crisis (1979/80 and 1980/81). (Of course the crisis itself played a part in worsening the government's financial position, but it is notable that the government acted passively.) In 1981/82 there was considerable tightening, partly to lay the groundwork for the IMF loan negotiations and perhaps as insurance in case they did not succeed. In 1982/83 the deterioration recommenced despite the IMF program, continued in 1983/84, and became significantly worse in 1984/85—an election year—after the program was terminated. The IMF program (and other external borrowing) enabled the fiscal worsening to continue by postponing the necessity of adjustment.

The evolution of the fiscal position can be examined on the basis of two different sets of data that unfortunately are not entirely consistent with each other. We look first at government budget figures and then at national accounts figures for the public sector as a whole.

The Budgetary Position

The most obvious change from 1978/79 is the explosion of government expenditure. The budget figures show this to be concentrated mainly in current expenditure, which grew as a proportion of GDP by almost 4 percentage points between 1977/78 and 1984/85 (see table 6.13).[15] Subsidies grew rapidly, particularly on food, fertilizers, and exports. The growth of the first two is clearly related to the increasing strength of the farm lobby combined with the desire of politicians to prevent unrest in the cities.[16] Food subsidies doubled in the year 1976/77 and doubled again by 1984/85. The large increase in fertilizer subsidies can be quite precisely dated to the period of the Janata government. Fertilizer subsidies increased from Rs 60 crores to Rs 600 crores from 1976/77 to 1979/80; they continued at that level until 1982/83 after which there was another large rise to Rs 1,800 crores over the next two years. Export subsidies grew steadily from Rs 149 crores in 1975/76 to Rs 500 crores in 1984/85. But subsidies are only a part of the picture. Other elements of current expenditure also grew strongly, some of which can be clearly identified, for example, public employment and wages. But most of them are difficult to pin down because they are spread across all categories of expenditure. Another part of increased expenditure that is clearly visible is the very large increase in interest payments due largely to the higher primary deficits and partly to the increasing cost of government borrowing.

Government revenue, however, grew very slowly. Between 1978/79 and 1984/85 there was a negligible increase in government revenue as a proportion of GDP. The central budget of 1981 was tough, and budgets in succeeding years also raised indirect taxes and rail fares. Nevertheless, they did no more than prevent a worsening of revenue as a proportion of GDP.[17]

The consolidated government fiscal deficit almost doubled from an average of 5 percent in 1975/76 to 1977/78 to 9.7 percent in 1984/85. (The primary fiscal deficit also shows a similar order of increase.) The domestic financing of the fiscal deficit increased even more sharply, particularly borrowing from the Reserve Bank and from nonbank sources. Reflecting these changes, the government's domestic debt (inclusive of debt to the Reserve Bank) grew from an average of 34 percent of GDP in 1975/76 to 46 percent in 1984/85.

Part of the reason for the overall fiscal deterioration was the changing financial relationship between the center and the states. A particular form that "political awakening" had taken over the years was the growing feeling that financial powers were excessively concentrated in the center. During the Janata regime, the general mood in favor of decentralization was reflected in the Report of the Seventh Finance Commission, which greatly increased the share for the states of the taxes collected by the center. (The states' share in central excise taxes went up from 20 to 40 percent and of income taxes from 80 to 85 percent.) At the same time, grants and loans from the center to the states were also on an upward trend. These changes increased central deficits. But there were no compensating surpluses at the state level. (The states can run deficits, though their power to do so is heavily circumscribed; but they cannot be forced to run surpluses.) Consequently, overall government deficits increased.

It should be noted, however, that the center's fiscal deficit worsened by more than the increase in center-state transfers. Similarly, the states' fiscal deficit increased in spite of increased tax devolution and grants from the center. The fiscal deterioration was thus quite pervasive (see table 6.8).

The Public Sector Financial Position

Public investment went up as a proportion of GDP during and after the crisis as a matter of deliberate policy, but public savings went down. Government savings fell by 2.5 percent of GDP from 1978/79 to 1984/85, reaching a negative level in the latter year.[18] (More than half of this deterioration took place from 1982/83, that is, after the IMF program was introduced.) Subsidies grew by 1 percent of GDP. Public enterprise savings grew moderately but largely because of the profitable oil sector.[19] Nonoil public enterprises continued, in general, to show a very low rate of return. The public deficit (that is, the gap between investment and saving) rose from 4.9 percent of GDP in 1978/79 to 8 percent in 1984/85. Table 6.14 shows the relevant figures.

The Effects of Fiscal Deterioration

An apparently puzzling question is why the fiscal deterioration documented above did not produce any marked untoward effects in terms of inflation. This is because increased governments deficits were only partly financed by borrowing from the Reserve Bank. Also, their effects on the supply of money were partially offset by the reduction in the RBI's foreign exchange assets and by increases in the cash reserve ratio. The increase in public borrowing was absorbed partly by crowding out of the private sector and partly by the persistent deficit on the current account of the balance of payments. This was itself covered by increased external borrowing

Table 6.8 Central and State Governments: Deficits and Transfers, 1975/76 to 1984/85
(percentage of GDP)

	1975/76 to 1977/78	1978/79	1979/80	1980/81	1981/82	1982/83	1983/84	1984/85
Central government fiscal deficit	4.1	5.0	5.6	6.5	5.4	6.1	6.6	7.7
State governments fiscal deficit	1.8	2.6	2.6	3.2	2.7	2.9	3.1	3.6
Net fiscal transfer from center to states	4.2	5.6	6.3	5.8	5.3	5.7	5.5	5.7
Consolidated government fiscal deficit	4.9	5.7	6.5	8.1	6.7	7.3	8.2	9.7

Source: Government of India, Ministry of Finance (various years), *Indian Economic Statistics—Public Finance.*

from the IMF and from commercial sources. Thus, the increasing fiscal deficits were reflected in the growth of internal and external debt rather than in monetization. In the short term there were no untoward effects, but problems were stored up for the future.

An Assessment of the IMF Loan

The conventional view of the IMF program in India is that it was highly successful.[20] In one sense this is true. The principal aim of the loan from India's point of view was to secure the balance of payments while a large public investment program in energy and infrastructure was put into effect. This aim was achieved. In 1981/82 reserves had fallen to 3.5 months of imports; in the ensuing years, reserves increased in spite of increasing public investment. (Note, however, that India was also borrowing from other sources, multilateral and commercial.) Another sense in which the IMF program was successful was that the credit targets were met throughout. Nonetheless, the success of the program was far short of what it was supposed to be. Indeed it could plausibly be argued that IMF financing goes some way toward explaining the lack of adjustment.

While the only performance criteria in the IMF program related to ceilings on domestic credit and bank credit to government, there were several other objectives to the program, and in these respects success was mixed at best. The following points are relevant.

- The current account projection of the program was roughly correct, but it was achieved fortuitously. The program envisaged a growth of export volume of 8 percent a year over three years from 1982/83. In fact, as we saw, export growth was negligible, due mainly to the behavior of the real exchange rate. It is clear that in this respect there was no attempt to influence the Indian government. The program itself was extremely vague on the topic and spoke merely of a realistic exchange rate policy. No doubt one reason for this was that it was a highly sensitive issue and the IMF wished to avoid it. Another reason was that there had been a substantial real depreciation of the rupee from 1975 to 1979, and not all of it had been nullified by the real appreciation from 1979 to 1981. It does not seem to have been appreciated by the IMF that the earlier real depreciation was a necessary response to the first oil shock and that the second oil shock needed another real depreciation (or at least constancy of the real exchange rate). The IMF's current account projections worked out reasonably well only because imports grew much more slowly than projected—because oil prices fell—and because other bulk imports also grew very slowly.
- The program target of net bank credit to government was met. But it is notable that while government savings and public savings behaved as envis-

aged by the IMF program in 1981/82 and 1982/83, they fell sharply below projections in 1983/84. In 1983/84, net bank credit to government was kept under control, but "other" domestic borrowing by the government expanded substantially, as did the fiscal deficit. In 1984/85 the public finances deteriorated sharply, perhaps because it was an election year. So even the moderate amount of financial discipline that was maintained during the IMF program evaporated. It is possible that the expectation that IMF targets were going to be difficult to meet was one of the reasons for the termination of the program by the government.

- There was very little of the "structural adjustment" that was one of the stated objectives of the program. Liberalization was cautious, patchy, and slow. There was no public sector reform.
- The fears of the domestic left-wing critics of the IMF loan proved to be almost wholly wrong. They had expected a deflationary outcome with subsidies being cut. Precisely the opposite happened. This is not to say that the United States was right to oppose the IMF loan. The United States was basically against structural adjustment loans and wanted India to approach commercial banks rather than the IMF. It could be argued that the loan should have had *more* conditionality on the issues of the exchange rate, liberalization, and government expenditure. But an attempt to impose such conditionality would probably have scuppered the loan altogether.

General Assessment of Macroeconomic Policy during and after the Shocks of 1979 and 1980

The crisis of 1979–80 was similar in its origins to the crisis of 1973–74. In both cases the crisis was caused by a severe drought combined with a sharp deterioration in the terms of trade impinging upon a highly liquid economy. The effects of the drought in 1979/80 were more severe than in 1973/74 while the external shock was of roughly the same size. The position as regards food and foreign exchange reserves was extremely favorable in 1979/80.

The response to the crisis of 1979 was, however, quite different from that of 1973. In some ways it was better but in other respects considerably worse. We summarize below the positive and negative features.

Positive Features

- As far as the immediate response to inflation was concerned, many lessons had been learned from previous crisis episodes. This time, food stocks were unloaded on a substantial scale to keep food-price inflation in check. Food imports were also stepped up well in time to deal with the minor drought of 1982.
- Another lesson learned from previous episodes was that it was counterproductive to fight inflation by cutting public investment. It may be recalled

that in 1974/75 public real investment fell by 14 percent. This time, public investment was quite consciously stepped up, particularly in the energy and infrastructure sectors. Financial policies were moderately tightened but in the main the policy toward inflation consisted of waiting for an agricultural recovery.

- Rather than having a deflationary adjustment to domestic inflation and the oil price increase, there was an attempt at securing an expansionary adjustment financed in part by a loan from the IMF. In some respects this worked extremely well. There was massive and efficient import substitution in oil and some other sectors, and infrastructure constraints were greatly eased. Moreover, all this was achieved with some import liberalization and liberalization of other controls affecting industry.

- The aftermath of the crisis (1982/83 to 1984/85) showed rapid growth of GDP in manufacturing by Indian historical standards. The manufacturing sector grew at 7.7 percent a year (registered manufacturing grew by almost 11 percent a year). The reasons for this rapid growth are discussed in chapter 13. It seems probable that it was mainly demand-led. But high and stable public investment especially in infrastructure, and the tilt toward liberalization were also partly responsible.

Negative Features

- The principal defect of the macroeconomic response was the deterioration of the public finances. Government and public deficits increased sharply, not only during the crisis but well beyond. The main cause of this deterioration was not the increase in public investment but the fall in government and public savings, itself principally caused by the explosive growth of government current expenditure. The deterioration in the public finances was reflected mainly in the persistence of current account deficits after the second oil shock. The escape valve of the current account deficit prevented the fiscal deficits being reflected in increased inflation or crowding out in any major way. But problems were being stored up for the future in that both internal and external public debt rose rapidly.

- The persistence of current account deficits was caused by macroeconomic mismanagement in another major respect. Exchange rate policy during the crisis was bad. We have argued above that the appreciation of the real exchange rate was the main reason for the near-stagnation of nonoil exports in the first half of the 1980s.

- There was little structural adjustment or supply-side reform. In that sense, foreign borrowing was wasted.

Appendix

Appendix tables 6.9 to 6.17 follow.

Table 6.9 Foodgrain Availability, 1977 to 1984
(millions of tonnes)

Year	Net production	Net imports	Public procurement	Public distribution	Net availability[a]
1977	97.27	0.10	9.97	11.73	98.99
1978	110.61	-0.60	11.10	10.18	110.25
1979	115.41	-0.20	13.85	11.66	114.86
1980	95.99	-0.34	11.18	14.99	101.83
1981	113.89	0.66	12.98	13.01	114.29
1982	116.83	1.58	15.42	14.76	116.88
1983	113.33	4.07	15.67	16.21	114.74
1984	133.33	2.37	18.72	13.33	128.63

a. Net availability = net production + net imports − change in government stocks.
Note: Production figures relate to the agricultural year just finished. Thus 1979 figures relate to 1978/79, for example. Net production equals gross production minus a 12.5 percent allowance for seed requirements and waste. Figures for procurement and public distribution relate to calendar years.
Source: Government of India, Ministry of Finance (various years), *Economic Survey.*

Table 6.10 Output and Price Indicators, 1977/78 to 1984/85

(annual percentage changes)

	1977/78	1978/79	1979/80	1980/81	1981/82	1982/83	1983/84	1984/85
Real GDP[a]	7.5	5.5	-5.2	7.2	6.1	3.1	8.2	3.9
Real GDP (agriculture)[a]	12.5	2.0	-13.4	14.4	6.3	-1.3	11.6	-0.1
Real GDP (manufacturing)[a]	6.2	12.4	3.2	0.2	8.0	6.5	9.9	6.5
Real GDP (registered manufacturing)[a]	6.7	10.9	-2.1	-1.6	7.7	9.6	14.7	8.4
Real GDP (unregistered manufacturing)[a]	5.6	14.3	-4.7	2.7	8.5	2.5	3.3	3.5
Real GDP (public manufacturing)[a]	9.9	2.7	1.6	9.4	-2.0	11.9	10.2	5.3
WPI (overall index)	5.2	0.0	17.1	18.2	9.3	2.6	9.5	7.1
WPI (foodgrains)	11.1	1.8	6.9	17.3	9.2	5.1	10.0	0.7
WPI (nonfood agriculture)	6.3	-4.3	14.2	11.6	10.8	1.9	15.5	13.1
WPI (fuel, power, and light)	1.5	4.5	15.5	25.1	20.9	7.5	7.6	4.7
WPI (manufactured goods)	2.3	0.1	20.0	19.0	5.5	0.4	8.8	8.1
CPI (industrial workers)	7.6	2.2	8.8	11.4	12.5	7.8	12.6	6.4

a. At factor cost.

Source: GDP: Table 5.12 and Government of India, CSO (1991), *National Accounts Statistics.* Wholesale prices: (Base 1970/71, average of weeks), and consumer prices (Base 1960, average of months), from Government of India, Ministry of Finance (various years), *Economic Survey.*

Table 6.11 Monetary Indicators, 1977/78 to 1984/85

	1977/78	1978/79	1979/80	1980/81	1981/82	1982/83	1983/84	1984/85
Annual percentage changes								
Narrow money (M1)[a]	14.6	18.0	19.0	12.9	14.6	11.1	14.6	18.3
Broad money (M3)[a]	20.1	20.3	20.3	16.3	17.4	14.3	17.4	18.2
Reserve money[a]	19.2	20.5	23.1	13.3	13.7	11.1	15.7	19.6
RBI credit to government[b]	6.7	16.0	34.6	32.1	29.1	13.5	19.3	11.8
RBI credit to commercial sector[b]	-19.7	25.1	17.9	7.02	2.4	8.8	25.6	12.2
Net foreign exchange assets of RBI[b]	78.3	21.5	-0.2	-14.3	-44.3	-34.1	-6.1	87.4
Net bank credit to government[b]	22.2	14.3	24.9	28.6	21.9	15.3	16.6	20.9
Bank credit to commercial sector[b]	14.7	19.4	20.9	18.3	18.4	19.2	17.3	18.0
Absolute values								
Velocity of M1	7.3	6.7	6.2	6.5	6.7	6.7	6.4	6.4
Velocity of M3	3.2	2.9	2.6	2.7	2.7	2.6	2.6	2.4
Money multiplier (M1) (unadjusted)	1.28	1.26	1.22	1.21	1.22	1.22	1.21	1.20
Money multiplier (M1) (adjusted)	1.42	1.45	1.44	1.47	1.49	1.48	1.51	1.57
Money multiplier (M3) (unadjusted)	2.96	2.95	2.88	2.96	3.06	3.15	3.19	3.15
Money multiplier (M3) (adjusted)	3.26	3.39	3.42	3.58	3.73	3.80	3.96	4.13
Percentage of GDP at market prices								
Change in RBI credit to government	0.48	1.13	2.59	2.72	2.78	1.49	2.08	2.60

a. Average of months.
b. Last Friday of financial year.
Source: Reserve Bank of India (various years), *Report on Currency and Finance;* table 10.1 in this book; and Singh, Shetty, and Venkatachalam (1982).

Table 6.12 Money and Reserve Money, 1978/79 to 1984/85

(second quarter to second quarter annual percentage changes)

	1978/79 to 1979/80	1979/80 to 1980/81	1980/81 to 1981/82	1981/82 to 1982/83	1982/83 to 1983/84	1983/84 to 1984/85
M1	22.5	8.7	18.0	9.7	14.7	17.6
M3	22.7	14.3	19.4	13.4	17.4	17.7
Reserve money	26.7	11.0	19.0	8.3	14.1	20.4
RBI credit to government	18.9	38.4	35.3	23.0	11.0	—

Source: Quarterly data given in Singh, Shetty, and Venkatachalam (1982); and Reserve Bank of India (various years), *Report on Currency and Finance.*

173

Table 6.13   Fiscal Indicators: Consolidated Government, 1977/78 to 1984/85

	1977/78	1978/79	1979/80	1980/81	1981/82	1982/83	1983/84	1984/85
Annual percentage changes								
Current revenue	7.7	14.2	13.0	12.4	21.2	14.6	11.7	16.2
Current expenditure	8.1	15.8	17.3	16.5	17.5	20.1	17.0	20.9
Capital expenditure	3.1	20.7	11.6	34.8	5.8	7.4	16.4	22.1
Total expenditure	6.6	17.2	15.6	21.8	13.8	16.3	16.8	21.3
Fiscal deficit	2.9	27.5	23.9	48.7	-2.3	20.9	29.9	32.4
Percentage of GDP at market prices								
Current revenue	17.1	18.0	18.6	17.5	18.1	18.6	17.8	18.6
Current expenditure	15.6	16.7	17.8	17.4	17.4	18.8	18.9	20.5
Balance on current revenue	1.5	1.4	0.8	0.1	0.6	-0.2	-1.1	-1.9
Capital expenditure	6.4	7.1	7.2	8.2	7.4	7.1	7.1	7.8
Total expenditure	22.0	23.8	25.0	25.6	24.8	25.9	25.9	28.2
Fiscal deficit	4.9	5.7	6.5	8.1	6.7	7.3	8.2	9.7
Primary fiscal deficit	4.5	5.0	5.5	7.2	5.7	6.3	6.7	8.3

Source: Government of India, Ministry of Finance (various years), Indian Economic Statistics—Public Finance.

Table 6.14 Investment and Saving, 1977/78 to 1984/85
(percentage of GDP at market prices)

	1977/78	1978/79	1979/80	1980/81	1981/82	1982/83	1983/84	1984/85
Gross domestic capital formation (adjusted)	19.5	23.3	22.1	22.7	22.6	20.6	20.0	19.6
Gross domestic capital formation (unadjusted)	19.8	22.3	22.9	20.9	25.1	22.9	20.7	21.1
Public	8.2	9.5	10.3	8.7	10.5	11.3	9.8	10.8
Private corporate	2.4	2.2	2.7	2.5	5.7	5.7	3.4	4.4
Private household	9.2	10.6	9.9	9.7	8.8	6.0	7.6	6.0
Gross domestic savings	21.1	23.2	21.6	21.2	21.0	19.1	18.8	18.2
Public	4.3	4.6	4.3	3.4	4.6	4.4	3.3	2.8
Government	2.2	2.4	2.3	1.9	2.4	1.6	0.6	-0.1
Public enterprises	2.2	2.2	2.1	1.5	2.2	2.8	2.7	3.0
Corporate	1.4	1.6	2.1	1.7	1.6	1.6	1.5	1.7
Household	15.3	17.0	15.2	16.1	14.9	13.1	14.0	13.7
Financial	6.1	6.4	5.3	6.3	6.0	7.2	6.4	7.7
Physical	9.2	10.6	9.9	9.8	8.9	5.9	7.6	6.0
Foreign savings	-1.5	0.1	0.5	1.5	1.6	1.5	1.2	1.4
Memorandum item								
Public deficit	3.9	4.9	6.0	5.3	6.0	6.9	6.5	8.0

Source: Table 5.15 and Government of India, CSO (1991), *National Accounts Statistics.*

175

Table 6.15 Gross Domestic Fixed Capital Formation (GFCF), 1977/78 to 1984/85

	1977/78	1978/79	1979/80	1980/81	1981/82	1982/83	1983/84	1984/85
Percentage of nominal GDP at market prices								
Nominal GFCF	17.9	18.1	18.6	19.3	19.7	20.1	19.3	19.7
Public	8.0	8.0	8.7	8.6	9.1	10.4	9.9	10.1
Private	9.9	10.1	9.9	10.7	10.6	9.7	9.4	9.6
Corporate	1.6	1.1	1.6	2.6	3.7	4.2	3.2	3.6
Household	8.3	9.0	8.3	8.1	6.9	5.5	6.2	6.0
Percentage of real GDP at market prices								
Real GFCF	19.0	18.1	18.6	19.3	19.4	19.5	18.3	18.4
Public	8.5	8.1	8.7	8.6	9.1	10.1	9.6	9.8
Private	10.5	10.1	9.8	10.7	10.3	9.4	8.7	8.6
Corporate	1.7	1.1	1.6	2.6	3.7	4.4	3.3	3.7
Household	8.8	9.0	8.3	8.1	6.6	5.0	5.4	4.9
Annual percentage changes								
Real GFCF	9.6	0.9	-2.9	10.9	6.9	4.3	1.2	3.9
Public	6.5	0.3	2.8	4.9	12.5	15.9	2.0	5.7
Private	12.2	1.4	-7.4	16.2	2.4	-5.9	0.2	1.9
Corporate	35.6	-31.3	38.9	74.6	51.6	22.3	-18.4	15.4
Household	8.7	7.6	-13.0	4.9	-13.4	-21.7	16.5	-6.4

Source: Tables 5.15 and 5.16 for 1977/78 and 1978/79. For rest of table, Government of India, CSO (1991), *National Accounts Statistics.*

Table 6.16 Balance of Payments

(millions of dollars)

	1977/78	1978/79	1979/80	1980/81	1981/82	1982/83	1983/84	1984/85
Exports	7,729	8,376	9,983	11,281	11,394	11,276	12,370	13,216
Merchandise	6,345	6,769	7,679	8,332	8,697	8,389	9,090	9,769
Nonfactor services	1,384	1,607	2,304	2,949	2,697	2,887	3,280	3,447
Imports	7,164	9,905	13,119	17,408	17,248	16,271	16,974	17,774
Merchandise	6,471	9,015	11,857	15,892	15,552	14,387	14,782	15,424
Nonfactor services	693	890	1,262	1,516	1,696	1,884	2,192	2,350
Resource balance	565	−1,529	−3,136	−6,127	−5,854	−4,995	−4,605	−4,558
Net factor income	−89	2	287	356	53	−677	−1,094	−1,449
Factor receipts	311	478	796	1,083	912	525	449	493
Factor payments	400	476	509	727	859	1,202	1,543	1,942
Net current transfers	1,077	1,180	1,852	2,860	2,314	2,625	2,691	2,496
Current balance	1,553	−347	−997	−2,911	−3,487	−3,047	−3,007	−3,511
Direct investment	0	0	0	8	10	65	63	62
Official grant aid	304	333	377	643	497	399	367	453
Net M and LT loans	694	587	644	1,425	1,630	1,966	1,907	2,697
Disbursements	1,221	1,190	1,290	2,180	2,376	2,899	2,992	3,787
Repayments	527	603	646	755	746	933	1,085	1,090
Net credit from IMF	−230	−158	0	1,014	652	1,968	1,306	67
Disbursements	0	0	0	1,023	692	1,968	1,376	201

(table continues on next page)

Table 6.16 (continued)

	1977/78	1978/79	1979/80	1980/81	1981/82	1982/83	1983/84	1984/85
Repayments	527	603	646	9	40	0	70	134
Other capital flows	-155	345	187	-325	-1,258	-1,056	721	222
Nonresident deposits	—	—	—	339	364	671	937	814
Net short-term capital	—	—	—	228	278	687	745	220
Others	—	—	—	-891	-1,900	-2,114	-961	-812
Errors and omissions	-18	715	13	-200	-441	210	-475	273
Change in reserves[a]	-2,048	-1,75	94	346	2,397	-505	-882	-263
End-of-year reserves[b]	5,823	7,298	7,204	6,858	4,461	4,965	5,847	6,110
(Number of months of imports)	(9.0)	(9.4)	(6.9)	(5.2)	(3.4)	(4.1)	(4.7)	(4.8)
Memorandum items								
GDP at market prices	109,916	127,216	141,600	172,328	178,915	185,009	201,306	194,658
Current account deficit[c]	-1.4	0.3	0.7	1.7	2.0	1.7	1.5	1.8
Current account deficit (percentage of exports)	-20.1	4.1	10.0	25.8	30.6	27.0	24.3	26.6
Trade deficit[c]	0.1	1.8	3.0	4.4	3.8	3.2	2.8	2.9
Resource deficit[c]	-0.5	1.2	2.2	3.6	3.3	2.7	2.3	2.3

a. Minus indicates increase.
b. Excluding gold.
c. Percentage of GDP.
Source: World Bank (various years), "India: Country Economic Memorandum." World Bank figures are based largely on those published by the Reserve Bank of India.

Table 6.17 India's Exports in a Broader Perspective, 1977/78 to 1984/85

(annual percentage change)

	1977/78	1978/79	1979/80	1980/81	1981/82	1982/83	1983/84	1984/85
India's nonoil merchandise export volume (value)[a]	−3.5 (10.5)	7.2 (6.7)	6.2 (13.4)	1.7 (8.5)	0.7 (4.4)	−3.8 (−3.5)	0.0 (8.4)	6.1 (7.5)
India's nonoil export volume (value) to convertible currency areas[b]	−3.6	10.7 (13.5)	6.6 (10.4)	−7.8 (−2.8)	1.6 (−0.7)	−1.2 (−3.8)	0.0 (19.1)	5.9 (3.3)
Real GDP of industrial countries[c]	3.6	4.2	3.3	1.3	1.5	−0.2	2.7	4.9
Nonoil import volume (value) of industrial countries[d]	4.1 (14.4)	8.0 (19.4)	10.4 (25.1)	2.5 (14.5)	0.2 (−5.4)	1.1 (−3.4)	5.9 (1.6)	13.9 (11.9)
World trade (volume)[e]	4.7	5.4	6.6	1.5	0.7	−2.3	2.1	8.8
Nonoil developing countries export volume (value)[f]	5.2 (17.7)	6.3 (14.0)	9.3 (28.6)	2.1 (24.7)	3.4 (2.4)	0.9 (−4.2)	6.3 (2.4)	9.2 (9.4)
Export volume (value) of developing country "exporters of manufactures"[g]	7.2 (15.5)	9.1 (20.6)	8.4 (24.0)	4.5 (19.7)	5.6 (9.7)	3.6 (0.1)	10.9 (4.4)	13.2 (14.6)

Source:

a. Government of India, DGCIS (various years), *Monthly Statistics of the Foreign Trade of India.*
b. Government of India, DGCIS (various years), *Monthly Statistics of the Foreign Trade of India.*
c. IMF (annual), *International Financial Statistics.*
d. IMF (biannual), *World Economic Outlook,* April 1985. table 20.
e. IMF (biannual), *World Economic Outlook,* April 1985.
f. IMF (1988).
g. IMF (1988).

Chapter Seven

The Road to Crisis, 1985/86 to 1990/91

As with previous crises, the two overt manifestations of the crisis that began in late 1990 were a rise in the rate of inflation above 10 percent and a widening of the current account deficit. The latter followed the oil price increases associated with the Iraqi invasion of Kuwait in August 1990. Since India was by then a substantial borrower in world capital markets, the external crisis took the form of a sharp downgrading of the country's credit rating and a cutoff of foreign loans. But notwithstanding these dramatic events, exogenous factors were of minor importance in causing this crisis. Unlike previous crises, it was largely policy-induced. The invasion of Kuwait and the Gulf War should not have produced any significant adverse effects in the normal course of events. They did so because macroeconomic policy mistakes over a long period had left the economy in a fundamentally unsound state.[1] Explaining the crisis of 1990 therefore requires close examination of macroeconomic policies and performance earlier in the decade.

Public Finances

We saw in chapter 6 that the deterioration of government finances, which began in the late 1970s, was arrested during the early part of the IMF program but was resumed in 1983/84. In the second half of the 1980s the deterioration continued. In table 7.1 we compare the average position in the first and second halves of the decade with respect to various indicators of the consolidated government's financial position. Tables 7.5 and 7.6 are also relevant.

Government revenue rose by 1.9 percent of GDP. This rise was not the result of the much vaunted income and corporation tax reductions undertaken by the Rajiv Gandhi government in 1985/86. In fact, direct tax revenue fell slightly as a proportion of GDP. But customs revenue rose as tariff rates were increased sharply (along with some liberalization of import quotas). Current expenditure rose by no

Table 7.1   Consolidated Government Fiscal Indicators, 1980/81 to 1989/90
(percentage of GDP)

	Average 1980/81 to 1984/85	Average 1985/86 to 1989/90
Revenue	18.1	20.0
Current expenditure	18.6	23.0
Interest	2.6	3.9
Defense	2.7	3.0
Subsidies	2.6	3.6
Capital expenditure	7.5	7.1
Fiscal deficit	8.0	10.1
Memorandum items		
Net interest	1.2	2.5
Primary fiscal deficit	6.8	7.5
Net center to state transfer	5.6	6.4
Domestic debt	43.5	54.8

Source: Table 7.5.

less than 4.4 percent of GDP. The increase affected both the center and the states. At the central government level, the main increases were in interest (1 percent) and subsidies (0.8 percent) but defense, grants to states, and wages (raised in line with the recommendations of the Fourth Pay Commission) also contributed. A similar story was repeated at the state level.

Capital expenditure fell slightly as a proportion of GDP. A substantial increase in 1986/87 was followed by a squeeze in 1987/88 in response to inflationary pressures arising from two successive minor droughts. The squeeze was continued in succeeding years—this was the only way the government found to respond to fiscal pressures. The pattern is confirmed by national accounts figures. Public real fixed capital formation fell from 10.4 percent in 1986/87 to 9.6 percent of GDP in 1987/88 and to 9.1 percent of GDP thereafter (see table 7.9).

Both the current (revenue) deficit and the fiscal deficit of the government increased sharply, the former from 0.5 to 3 percent of GDP and the latter from 8 to 10 percent of GDP. The rise in the primary deficit was smaller, from 6.8 to 7.5 percent of GDP. Thus, more than half the increase in the fiscal deficit was on account of interest payments. The government's domestic debt rose from 43.5 to 54.8 percent. There was also a sizable increase in external debt, as outlined below.

The national accounts also show a marked worsening of overall public finances. The finances of public enterprises continued to be weak, particularly nonoil enterprises and state enterprises. There was, nevertheless, a slight improvement in public enterprise savings mainly attributed to central government enterprises (especially the oil companies). But this was outweighed by the large fall in government saving. The public sector deficit increased from 6.5 to 8.4 percent in spite of the squeeze on public investment after 1986/87.

Thus, the fiscal record of the government was poor. It is true that fiscal pressures were growing as a result of various political forces (see chapter 3), but the government cannot be absolved of responsibility for the crisis. A number of questions arise. Did the top civil servants in the Finance Ministry appreciate the seriousness of the problem? Did they fight hard to persuade the cabinet? Did the cabinet and the civil service make any serious effort to reduce fiscal deficits? Only an examination of unavailable internal papers would tell us the whole truth.

Formed on the basis of interviews, our impression is that faulty analysis, lack of prudence, and weakness in the face of pressure all played a part. Unlike some developing countries, fiscal decisions were centralized in the Finance Ministry. None of the domestic or foreign borrowing happened in an unknown way. The government itself issued a White Paper in 1985 emphasizing the need for fiscal discipline. But it is not clear that civil servants realized the seriousness of the situation even though the simplest intertemporal analysis (see chapter 9) would have sufficed to show the unsustainability of the fiscal track.[2] Much energy seems to have been spent on trying to find novel ways of increasing domestic and foreign borrowing rather than on reducing such borrowing.

The V. P. Singh government took office at the end of 1989, having added to the problem by its pre-election promise of writing off debts of small farmers. It was then blindingly obvious that the fiscal problem was of the utmost gravity. Even so, the attempt to brazen it out continued. In the latter half of 1990/91 political instability made major policy changes very difficult. It was then just a question of waiting in hope for the return of a stable government.

Balance of Payments and External Debt

We saw in chapter 6 that from 1982/83 to 1984/85 there was little current account adjustment. The trade gap did improve because of import substitution of oil and falling oil prices. But the improvement fell far short of what was achievable because exports stagnated. Thus, when the Rajiv Gandhi government came in, the balance of payments was already unsatisfactory. From 1985/86 to the end of the decade, the current account deficit as a proportion of GDP increased sharply. Moreover, this happened in spite of two favorable developments—exports grew rapidly and oil prices fell further. Balance of payments figures are presented in tables 7.10 and 7.11.

Exports and the Real Exchange Rate

Export performance from 1985/86 to 1989/90 was very good. The dollar value of exports increased by about 14 percent a year. The volume of exports grew by about 12 percent a year and that of manufactured exports by almost 15 percent a year. In contrast, real nonoil exports had grown only about 1 percent a year from 1980/81 to 1984/85. Part of the reason for this change was the faster growth of world trade and GDP of industrial countries in the later period. As table 6.17 shows, from 1980/81 to 1984/85 Indian exports grew more slowly than world trade and GDP of industrial countries, and grew far more slowly than the exports of other developing country exporters of manufactured goods. In contrast, from 1986/87 onward, Indian exports grew considerably faster than world trade and GDP of industrial countries, and about as fast as the exports of other comparable countries. The real exchange rate was again a critical factor as it depreciated by about 30 percent from 1985/86 to 1989/90. Since Indian inflation in this period rose faster than that of its trading partners, a devaluation of the nominal effective exchange rate of about 45 percent was required and achieved (see table 11.3). This reflects a considerable change in the official attitude toward exchange rate depreciation. The change had already begun in 1983, but during 1983 and 1984 action was restricted to keeping the real effective exchange rate constant. From 1985 onward exchange rate policy became more active though the fiction of a fixed basket-peg was still maintained. From a presentational point of view, the sharp devaluation of the U.S. dollar, which began in 1985, helped a great deal. A devaluation of the real effective exchange rate could be secured by keeping the exchange rate or the rupee against the dollar constant, and in fact there was a mild depreciation in terms of the dollar as well. Cabinet approval was sought and obtained to achieve the real effective exchange rate prevailing in 1979 (thus offsetting the competitive disadvantage that had been suffered since then). When that objective had been reached, cabinet approval was again obtained to devalue the rupee further to maintain the competitive relationship vis-à-vis a narrower range of developing-country "competitor countries," many of whom depreciated in real terms along with the U.S. dollar in 1986. This was a sensible exchange rate policy. Policymakers recognized that a real exchange rate devaluation was necessary though the terms of trade were modestly improving, because the debt-service burden had increased and a faster growth of imports was to be expected in the wake of industrial and import liberalization.

In fact, the incentive to export increased more than the movement of the real exchange rate would suggest since various other export incentives were stepped up sharply from 1985. The traditional export subsidies (cash assistance, premium on import replenishment licenses, and duty drawbacks) increased from 9 to 13 percent of total exports during this period. We estimate that the real exchange rate, adjusted for measurable export incentives, depreciated by about 40 percent (see table 11.3). Indeed, export incentives increased even more than this because of other measures, some of them very difficult to quantify. The major nonquantifiable changes that took place between 1985/86 and 1989/90 are listed below.

- There was a substantial widening of the coverage of products available to exporters against replenishment and advance licenses.
- In the 1985 budget 50 percent of business profits attributable to exports were made income tax deductible; in the 1988 budget this concession was extended to 100 percent of export profits.
- The interest rate on export credit was reduced from 12 to 9 percent.
- In October 1986 duty-free imports of capital goods were allowed in selected "thrust" export industries. In April 1988 access for exporters to imported capital goods was increased by widening the list of those available on OGL and by making some capital goods available selectively to exporters without going through "indigenous clearance."
- Exporters were given an assurance that the incentives announced in the export-import policy would not be reduced for a period of three years.

There is no doubt that the above "quasi-Southeast Asian style" reforms increased export incentives substantially, particularly for manufactured goods. There was a strong response in leather manufactures, gems and jewelry, chemicals, engineering goods, and other manufactures—the potentially dynamic exports that had stagnated in the previous five years.

The Behavior of Imports and the Trade Deficit

From 1980/81 to 1984/85 imports fell in value and volume (see tables 6.16, 7.10, and 7.11). From 1985/86 to 1989/90 the dollar value of imports increased by about 10 percent a year and import volume by about 8 percent a year (see table 7.11). The volume of oil imports grew rapidly as Indian oil production leveled; so the dollar value of oil imports remained constant even though oil prices fell. The main import growth came from capital goods, gems, intermediate goods, and components. This was partly the result of the continuation and extension of import liberalization. But there was little liberalization of imports that competed with domestic production (except to some extent for exporting firms). Liberalization of noncompetitive imports was somewhat greater, particularly for inputs in industries such as computers, electronics, and chemicals. Since quantitative import restrictions were retained on the final products, effective protection of these activities increased substantially. This led to strong growth in these industries but also to large imports of components. Nevertheless, we do not believe that liberalization was the sole or main reason for the rapid import growth overall; rising fiscal deficits were more important, as discussed further below.

There was a growing discrepancy between the customs and RBI figures for imports. This discrepancy was between $2 billion and $4 billion after 1987/88—it used to be only about $0.5 billion in the early 1980s. The balance of payments figures show a faster growth of imports than customs figures, presumably to be accounted for by imports such as offshore oil rigs, and military imports that do not pass through the customs.

The trade deficit widened after 1984/85. Exports grew slightly faster than imports in dollar value, but there was a substantial trade deficit to begin with.

The Current Account Deficit

Historically, India has had a small surplus in nonfactor services. This fell slightly in the second half of the 1980s. Changes also took place in other invisibles. Transfer receipts were stagnant and thus fell as a proportion of GDP. There was a substantial worsening after 1984/85 in net factor income, largely because of interest payments on the increased external borrowing from the IMF and other sources, official and commercial. In 1984/85 there was a deficit on net factor income of about $1.5 billion; by 1989/90 this had increased to more than $3 billion. As a consequence, the current account deficit widened absolutely, and as a proportion of GDP. In the first half of the 1980s the average current account deficit was about $3 billion or 1.7 percent of GDP; in the second half of the 1980s the average current account deficit was more than $7 billion, about 3 percent of GDP (inclusive of accrued interest).

Table 7.2 decomposes the change in the current account deficit as a percentage of GDP from 1982/83 to 1984/85 and from 1985/86 to 1989/90 into its various constituents.

Table 7.2   Components of the Balance of Payments on Current Account, 1982/83 to 1989/90

(percentage of GDP)

	Average 1982/83 to 1984/85	*Average 1985/86 to 1989/90*	*Change*
Merchandise exports (customs)	4.3	4.9	0.6
Merchandise imports (customs)	7.0	7.2	0.2
Trade balance (customs)	−2.7	−2.3	0.4
Merchandise exports (RBI)	4.7	5.1	0.4
Merchandise imports (RBI)	7.7	8.3	0.6
Trade balance (RBI)	−3.0	−3.2	−0.2
Net nonfactor services	0.5	0.3	−0.2
Resource balance	−2.4	−2.8	−0.4
Net factor income	−0.5	−1.0	−0.5
Net interest payments	−0.8	−1.2	−0.4
Net current transfers	1.3	1.0	−0.3
Current account balance	−1.7	−2.9	−1.2
Non-interest current account	−0.8	−1.7	−0.9

Source: Tables 6.16 and 7.10; and Government of India, DGCIS (annual).

The current account worsened by 1.2 percent of GDP, of which interest payments accounted for 0.4 percent. The rest can be attributed roughly equally to a worsening in the trade deficit, net nonfactor services, and net current transfers. It is worth noting that the balance of trade moved in different directions as measured by customs and the RBI, the discrepancy between the two being 0.6 percent of GDP.

Foreign Borrowing and the Deterioration in the External Debt Position

The financing of the current account deficit shows some changes. There was no change in official grant aid, which was about $400 a year throughout the decade. Direct investment increased, but only marginally. In the first half of the decade the current account deficit was financed by medium- and long-term borrowing, and loans from the IMF. In the second half of the decade IMF borrowing was replaced by IMF repayments. Concessional long-term borrowing from IDA fell, but there was a big increase in nonconcessional borrowing from the IBRD and private commercial sources (including nonresident deposits).[3] Even so, *net* long-term borrowing rose only from an average of $1.9 billion in 1980/81 to 1984/85, to $3.5 billion in 1985/86 to 1989/90 because the increase in nonconcessional borrowing in the first half of the decade was already taking its toll in the form of sharply increased repayments. Note also that "other" capital flows, and errors and omissions, were a large negative figure in the first half of the decade and a large positive figure in the second half. This indicates an increase in short-term borrowing in the later period.

By the end of the decade there had been large changes in the country's external debt position. According to the *World Debt Tables* (World Bank 1992), external debt increased from about $20.6 billion in 1980/81 to $64.4 billion in 1989/90. The general story is one of a continuation of the deterioration that began in the first half of the decade. Between 1984/85 and 1989/90 the following changes occurred.

- The total debt-to-GNP ratio increased from 17.7 to 24.5 percent and the debt-to-exports ratio from 210 to 265 percent. The debt service ratio rose from 18 to 27 percent. Such high ratios had not been seen in India since the end of the 1960s.
- The share of private debt in long-term debt increased from 28 to 41 percent, and the share of nonconcessional debt from 42 to 54 percent. Variable-interest debt increased from 11 to 19 percent of long-term debt. The average maturity of debt fell from 27 to 20 years. Thus in addition to the increase in the debt burden there was also a worsening of the debt profile. The composition of debt changed toward private sources of a rather unstable variety. By the end of the decade, the stock of non-resident deposits was $10 billion and short-term debt was $4 billion.

Import Liberalization, Fiscal Deficits, and the Current Account

That the current account deficit worsened is beyond dispute. The question remains whether this is to be attributed to import liberalization. It is not surprising that import liberalization led to increases in imports in some categories—that is what was intended in the interests of efficiency and growth—but it cannot be held responsible for the evolution of the current account. We saw above that the worsening of the trade gap accounted for only a small part of the increase in the current account deficit. Indeed, the "customs trade deficit," which is directly relevant to import liberalization, actually improved. Imports rose more than indicated by customs figures as a result of public imports such as military equipment but these have little to do with import liberalization (and quite a lot to do with the overall level of government expenditure).

One can turn the question the other way round and ask what would have happened if imports had not been liberalized. Would the trade deficit have been reduced substantially? Two arguments are directly relevant. First, exports would not have risen so fast, having been denied the benefit of easier availability of imported inputs. Second, industrial production would have been lower, but with the same monetary and fiscal stance the pressure of demand on home resources would have been higher, leading either directly or through higher inflation to lower exports as well as to higher imports in the permitted categories.

Similar issues arise in considering why the current account did not improve despite substantial exchange rate depreciation. Elementary balance of payments theory tells us that a devaluation can be no more than a necessary condition for improving the trade account, not a sufficient condition. It cannot succeed without a reduction in the gap between investment and saving, and this reduction normally requires appropriate macroeconomic measures.

We must remind the reader at this point that "domestic savings" in India's national accounts are measured inclusive of net current transfers and net factor income from abroad; in other words, Indian "domestic savings" represent what are conventionally called national savings. Hence the sum of the public and private investment-saving gaps is identically equal to the current account deficit, not as in conventional accounting to the resource deficit, that is the deficit on goods and nonfactor services.

We saw in chapter 6 that there was no current account improvement in the aftermath of the second oil shock from 1982/83 to 1984/85 in spite of the large rise in the household sector surplus. We attributed this outcome to the rise in the public sector deficit and pointed out that the current account deficit would have been even worse but for the severe squeeze on household investment. We can now compare saving-investment balances in 1982/83 to 1984/85 and in the second half of the decade (table 7.3 refers).[4]

Table 7.3 should be read in conjunction with table 6.7. The public deficit went up by 1.3 percent of GDP and the corporate sector deficit fell slightly. Household financial savings continued to rise, though at a slower pace. Household investment

Table 7.3   Investment-Saving Balances, 1982/83 to 1989/90
(percentage of GDP)

	Average 1982/83 to 1984/85	*Average* 1985/86 to 1989/90
Public investment	10.6	10.8
Public saving	3.5	2.4
Public gap	7.1	8.4
Corporate investment	4.5	4.5
Corporate saving	1.6	1.9
Corporate gap	2.9	2.6
Household investment (adjusted)[a]	4.9	7.4
Household saving	13.6	16.0
Financial	7.1	7.8
Physical	6.5	8.2
Household gap	–8.6	–8.6
Current account deficit[b]	1.4	2.4

a. Errors and omissions in investment (that is, the difference between adjusted and unadjusted capital formation in table 6.14) are attributed entirely to household investment.

b. Current account deficit = Public gap + Corporate gap + Household gap.

Source: Tables 6.7 and 7.8.

recovered from its abnormally low level and it can hardly be argued that this was undesirable. The current account deficit increased by 1 percent of GDP. Reducing it instead by, say, 1 percent, without reducing the public deficit would have required a rise in private financial savings to 9.8 percent of GDP. Given the slowdown in the spread of banking, this rise could not have occurred naturally and there was no obvious way of achieving it in the relevant time span. Thus, the current account adjustment could not have been engineered without a reduction in the public deficit. Since a large fall in public investment would have been undesirable, this in turn implies that it was the failure of the government to use tax and expenditure policy to increase public savings that was the main reason for the lack of current account adjustment.[5] Another possible line of argument is that the causality ran from the current account deficit to the public deficit, and not the other way round. But there were no unexpected adverse external shocks between 1985/86 and 1989/90. (Interest payments were of course rising, but only in an expected fashion.) We have also checked that the above arguments and conclusion continue to hold if Indian savings figures are doctored to conform to conventional concepts of domestic savings and the focus is on the resource deficit rather than on the current account deficit.

The events surrounding the Gulf war in 1990 constituted a moderate external shock of about 1 percent of GDP. But the shock turned out to be temporary. If the economy had been in a sounder position, it could have weathered the shock by the use of reserves or by borrowing. But in the event, foreign lending dried up and the government had to resort to draconian import curbs (see chapter 3).

Inflation

Overall inflation was moderate from 1985/86 to 1989/90, about 7 percent a year (see table 7.4). This was a slightly lower rate than in the first half of the decade despite a slightly higher growth of M1 and M3 (see table 7.5). The poor rains in 1986/87 and 1987/88 did, however, lead to a faster increase in foodgrain prices (averaging 12 percent a year) in 1987/88 and 1988/89. The droughts were not too severe and were mainly handled by increased public distribution and income-support policies (see chapter 3). There was also a slight tightening of fiscal and monetary policy. The fiscal retrenchment fell mainly on public capital formation (see table 7.9). Monetary policy measures took the usual form of small increases in the cash reserve ratio (CRR) and the statutory liquidity ratio (SLR). In 1988/89 food production rebounded; inflation of foodgrain prices fell sharply in 1989/90. Food production continued to grow satisfactorily in 1989/90 and 1990/91. Two factors should be kept in mind in interpreting the low overall rate of inflation from 1985/86 to 1989/90. First, import prices fell and the terms of trade improved; and second, the widening of the current account deficit siphoned off demand from the home market.

In 1990/91, the crisis year, overall inflation accelerated to more than 10 percent and prices of "food articles" rose more than 12 percent, despite satisfactory harvests.[6] Part of the reason was the lagged effect of the increase in monetary growth in 1989/90. That was an election year and a large rise in the fiscal deficit spilled over into money creation. In addition, 1990/91 witnessed a large increase in import prices, and also in many domestically administered prices, including food procurement. It is probable also that the government's mounting fiscal difficulties added to inflationary expectations and arrested the rising trend in the demand for money. The inflation of 1990/91 was more worrying than India's periodic inflationary bubbles because it was not triggered by a drought. Increased indexation in the economy also promised to make it more difficult to resolve.

Growth

GDP grew at 5.6 percent a year between 1985/86 and 1989/90, continuing the relatively fast growth of the first half of the decade (see table 7.4). Growth was concentrated mainly in manufacturing and services, both of which grew at 7 percent a year. Within manufacturing, the main impetus came from capital goods (10 percent a year) and consumer durables (12 percent a year).

The causes of the fast growth are discussed in some depth in chapter 13. Here it will suffice to make a few key points.

- The rapid growth cannot be accounted for by a rise in the investment ratio. Neither real fixed capital formation nor any of its components (public, corporate, or household) increased as a proportion of GDP between 1980/81 to 1984/85 and 1985/86 to 1989/90 (see table 7.9).
- Fast industrial growth took place in spite of moderate trade liberalization. It appears that the supply-side effects of industrial deregulation and import liberalization outweighed any dampening effect from import competition. In fact, much of the import liberalization had no dampening effect since, as noted earlier, it was lopsided and increased the effective protection of industry (particularly consumer durables).
- It appears that "Keynesian" expansion, reflected in large fiscal deficits, was a major cause of fast growth. In that sense, given the macroeconomic policy mix, the growth was unsustainable.

Overall Assessment

The crisis of 1990 had its roots in the policy stance taken in the aftermath of the second oil shock. At that stage, exports stagnated due to real exchange rate appreciation. There was little current account adjustment. The fiscal position deteriorated. Both domestic and foreign debt increased rapidly. As a result, the underlying macroeconomic situation in 1985/86 was unsatisfactory.

There were some good policy decisions in the second half of the decade. The exchange rate was managed more flexibly and exports grew rapidly in response. There were moves toward industrial deregulation and trade liberalization, which contributed to rapid industrial growth. The policy environment was also benign. The terms of trade improved and world trade was buoyant. There were no major droughts, and from 1988/89 food production grew strongly.

The major mistake of macroeconomic policy lay in neglecting the danger signs evident in 1985/86 on the fiscal front. Fiscal deterioration was allowed to proceed apace. As a consequence, the current account deficit continued to worsen and domestic and foreign debt continued to increase at a dangerous rate. By the end of the decade, the macroeconomic fundamentals were out of joint. Even a strictly temporary shock like the Gulf War was enough to trigger a full-scale crisis.

Appendix

Appendix tables 7.4 to 7.11 follow.

Table 7.4 Output and Price Indicators, 1980/81 to 1990/91
(annual percentage change)

	Average 1980/81 to 1984/85	1985/86	1986/87	1987/88	1988/89	1989/90	1990/91	Average 1985/86 to 1989/90
Real GDP[a]	5.7	4.1	3.9	4.5	10.4	5.2	5.6	5.6
Real GDP (agriculture)[a]	5.6	0.3	-1.7	0.7	16.3	2.3	4.3	3.6
Real GDP (manufacturing)[a]	6.2	4.0	7.0	7.3	8.4	7.4	7.3	6.8
Real GDP (registerd manufacturing)[a]	7.8	2.3	5.8	7.3	9.5	6.9	7.6	6.4
Real GDP (unregistered manufacturing)[a]	4.1	6.7	8.9	7.2	6.7	8.1	6.8	7.5
Real GDP (tertiary sector)[a]	5.3	7.4	6.8	6.5	8.1	6.3	5.9	7.0
Real GDP (public admin. and defense)[a]	6.6	7.7	9.9	10.2	6.2	6.9	3.8	8.2
Foodgrain production	6.6	4.9	-4.9	-2.7	21.8	0.4	3.0	3.9
WPI								
New series[b]	9.3	4.4	5.8	8.2	7.5	7.4	10.3	6.7
Old series[c]	9.3	5.7	5.3	7.6	7.4	(7.4)	(10.3)	6.7
WPI (food)								
New series[b]	10.4	6.8	3.2	9.3	14.9	1.9	8.5	7.2
Old series[c]	8.5	7.3	1.0	11.0	17.5	(1.9)	(8.5)	7.7
Foodgrain availability	2.7	-3.3	7.6	0.9	-2.7	12.3	-3.0	3.0

a. At factor cost.
b. 1981/82 =100.
c. 1970/71=100.

Source: Government of India, CSO (1991, 1992), *National Accounts Statistics;* Government of India, CSO (1991), *Quick Estimates of National Income 1989–90;* Government of India, Ministry of Finance (various years), *Economic Survey.*

Table 7.5 Consolidated Government Fiscal Indicators, 1980/81 to 1990/91
(percentage of GDP)

	Average 1980/81 to 1984/85	1985/86	1986/87	1987/88	1988/89	1989/90	1990/91	Average 1985/86 to 1989/90
Revenue	18.1	19.5	20.0	20.1	19.6	20.9	19.5	20.0
Current expenditure	18.6	21.4	22.6	23.1	22.7	24.8	23.9	23.0
Defense	2.7	3.3	3.8	4.0	3.8	3.6	—	3.0
Interest	2.6	3.3	3.6	4.0	4.2	4.6	4.8	3.9
Subsidies[a]	2.6	3.3	3.4	3.5	3.6	4.2	—	3.6
Capital expenditure	7.5	7.4	8.3	7.0	6.3	6.5	6.0	7.1
Total expenditure	26.1	28.8	30.9	30.1	29.0	31.3	29.9	30.1
Fiscal deficit	8.0	9.3	10.9	10.0	9.4	10.4	10.4	10.1
Memorandum items								
Net interest	1.2	1.7	2.2	2.5	2.8	3.2	3.5	2.5
Primary fiscal deficit	6.8	7.6	8.8	7.5	6.6	7.2	6.9	7.5
Net center to state transfer	5.6	7.5	6.2	6.4	6.0	5.7	6.0	6.4

a. CSO estimates.
Source: Government of India, Ministry of Finance (various years), *Indian Economic Statistics—Public Finance,* except figures for subsidies, which come from the National Accounts.

193

Table 7.6 Central and State Governments: Fiscal Indicators, 1980/81 to 1990/91
(percentage of GDP)

	Average 1980/81 to 1984/85	1985/86	1986/87	1987/88	1988/89	1989/90	1990/91	Average 1985/86 to 1989/90
Central government								
Revenue	9.7	10.7	11.3	11.1	11.0	11.8	10.8	11.2
Current expenditure	10.5	12.8	14.0	13.9	13.8	14.6	14.2	13.8
Capital expenditure	5.6	6.4	6.8	5.8	5.4	5.8	5.1	6.0
Fiscal deficit	6.4	8.5	9.5	8.6	8.2	8.4	8.5	8.6
Primary fiscal deficit	5.7	7.4	8.1	6.9	6.4	6.2	6.2	7.0
State governments								
Revenue	11.2	12.2	12.3	12.7	12.1	12.2	12.2	12.3
Current expenditure	10.8	12.0	12.3	13.0	12.6	13.2	13.3	12.6
Capital expenditure	3.4	3.2	3.2	3.0	2.5	2.6	2.7	2.9
Fiscal deficit	3.1	3.0	3.2	3.3	3.0	3.6	3.8	3.2
Primary fiscal deficit	2.7	2.4	2.4	2.4	2.1	2.6	2.6	2.4

Source: Government of India, Ministry of Finance (various years), *Indian Economic Statistics—Public Finance.*

Table 7.7 Monetary Indicators, 1980/81 to 1990/91
(annual percentage changes)

	Average 1980/81 to 1984/85	1985/86	1986/87	1987/88	1988/89	1989/90	1990/91	Average 1985/86 to 1989/90
Narrow money (M1)[a]	14.3	11.4	17.3	14.5	15.1	19.9	17.4[b]	15.7
Broad money (M3)[a]	16.7	17.1	17.6	17.0	17.4	19.6	16.6[b]	17.7
Reserve money[a]	14.0	20.3	18.2	18.9	16.7	20.0	16.0[b]	18.8
Net RBI credit to government[c]	21.2	30.7	17.7	15.3	13.7	21.7	20.6[b]	19.8

a. Monthly average.
b. Provisional.
c. Last Friday of financial year.
Source: Reserve Bank of India (various years), *Report on Currency and Finance*; and table 10.1 of this book.

Table 7.8   Investment and Saving, 1980/81 to 1989/90
(percentage of GDP)

	Average 1980/81 to 1984/85	1985/86	1986/87	1987/88	1988/89	1989/90	Average 1985/86 to 1989/90
Gross domestic capital formation[a]	21.1	22.1	20.6	22.4	23.9	24.1	22.6
Errors and omissions	1.0	1.9	2.4	0.3	0.0	-0.5	0.8
Gross domestic capital formation[b]	22.1	24.0	23.0	22.7	23.9	23.6	23.4
Public	10.2	11.1	11.7	10.4	9.9	10.7	10.8
Corporate	4.3	5.5	5.3	3.6	4.2	3.9	4.5
Household	7.6	7.4	6.1	8.6	9.8	8.9	8.2
Gross domestic saving	19.7	19.7	18.4	20.3	21.0	21.7	20.2
Public	3.7	3.2	2.7	2.2	2.0	1.7	2.4
Government	1.3	-0.2	-0.8	-1.6	-2.1	—	-1.2
Public enterprises	2.4	3.4	3.6	3.8	4.1	—	3.7
Corporate	1.6	2.0	1.7	1.7	2.1	2.1	1.9
Household	14.3	14.5	13.9	16.5	17.1	17.8	16.0
Financial	6.7	7.1	7.9	7.8	7.3	8.9	7.8
Physical	7.6	7.4	6.1	8.6	9.8	8.9	8.2
Foreign saving	1.5	2.4	2.2	2.1	2.8	2.4	2.4
Memorandum item							
Public deficit	6.5	7.9	9.0	8.2	7.9	9.0	8.4

a. Adjusted.
b. Unadjusted.
Source: Government of India, CSO (1991), *National Accounts Statistics.* Government of India, CSO (1991), *Quick Estimates of National Income 1989/90;* and Government of India, CSO (1992), *National Accounts Statistics.*

Table 7.9   Gross Domestic Fixed Capital Formation, 1980/81 to 1989/90

	Average 1980/81 to 1984/85	1985/86	1986/87	1987/88	1988/89	1989/90	Average 1985/86 to 1989/90
Percentage of nominal GDP at market prices							
Nominal GFCF	19.6	20.7	21.0	21.3	21.1	21.4	21.1
Public	9.6	10.5	11.4	10.4	10.0	10.4	10.5
Private	10.0	10.2	9.6	10.9	11.1	11.0	10.6
Corporate	3.4	3.8	4.2	3.1	3.1	3.2	3.5
Household	6.6	6.4	5.4	7.8	8.0	7.9	7.1
Percentage of real GDP at market prices							
Real GFCF	19.0	18.7	18.6	19.4	19.0	18.9	18.9
Public	9.5	9.7	10.4	9.6	9.1	9.1	9.6
Private	9.5	9.0	8.1	9.7	9.9	9.9	9.3
Corporate	3.5	3.9	4.2	3.2	3.2	3.1	3.5
Household	6.0	5.1	3.9	6.5	6.7	6.8	5.8

Source: Government of India, CSO (1991), *National Accounts Statistics*; Government of India, CSO (1991), *Quick Estimates of National Income 1989/90*; and Government of India, CSO (1992), *National Accounts Statistics*.

Table 7.10 India's Balance of Payments, 1980/81 to 1990/91

(millions of dollars)

	1980/81	1984/85	1985/86	1986/87	1987/88	1988/89	1989/90	1990/91
Imports	17,408	17,774	19,419	19,950	22,839	26,851	28,123	30,269
Merchandise	15,892	15,424	17,295	17,728	19,812	23,626	24,785	27,052
Nonfactor services	1,516	2,350	2,124	2,222	3,027	3,225	3,338	3,577
Exports	11,281	13,216	12,771	13,677	16,215	18,218	20,913	22,664
Merchandise	8,332	9,769	9,461	10,460	12,644	14,262	16,850	18,392
Nonfactor services	2,949	3,447	3,310	3,217	3,571	3,956	4,063	4,272
Trade balance	-7,560	-5,655	-7,834	-7,268	-7,168	-9,364	-7,935	-8,660
Balance on nonfactor services	1,433	1,097	1,186	995	544	731	725	695
Resource balance	-6,127	-4,558	-6,648	-6,273	-6,624	-8,633	-7,210	-7,965
Net current transfers	2,860	2,496	2,207	2,327	2,698	2,654	2,256	2,055
Net factor income	356	-1,449	-1,552	-2,045	-2,471	-2,985	-3,305	-4,023
Current account balance	-2,911	-3,511	-5,993	-5,991	-6,397	-8,964	-8,259	-9,933
Official grants	643	453	359	403	410	406	500	524
M/LT loans (net)	1,425	2,697	2,544	2,911	3,791	4,369	4,245	4,142
Disbursements	2,180	3,787	3,853	5,200	5,683	6,319	6,167	6,502
Repayments	755	1,090	1,309	2,289	1,892	1,949	1,921	2,360
IMF credit (net)	1,014	67	-264	-648	-1,082	-1,210	-1,008	1,117
Nonresident deposits	339	814	1,579	1,825	1,992	2,650	2,341	1314

Other capital flows (net)	−655	−529	1,848	1,594	1,678	1,176	1,330	1,066
Errors and omissions	−200	272	474	−101	−731	141	—	—
Change in reserves[a]	346	−263	−547	−73	339	1,432	851	1,770
Memorandum items								
End of year reserves	6,858	6,610	6,657	6,730	6,391	4,959	4,108	2,338
(Number of months of imports)	(5.2)	(4.6)	(4.6)	(4.6)	(3.9)	(2.5)	(2.0)	(1.0)
GDP at market prices	172,328	194,658	214,032	228,346	256,480	278,248	265,720	283,800
Trade balance (percentage of GDP)	−4.4	−2.9	−3.7	−3.2	−2.8	−3.4	−3.0	−3.1
Resource balance (percentage of GDP)	−3.6	−2.3	−3.1	−2.8	−2.6	−3.2	−2.7	−2.8
Current account balance (percentage of GDP)	−1.7	−1.8	−2.8	−2.6	−2.5	−3.3	−3.1	−3.5
Current account balance (percentage of exports)	−25.8	−26.6	−46.9	−43.8	−39.5	−49.2	−39.5	−43.8

Note: The World Bank's balance of payments figures are based principally on those published by the Reserve Bank of India.
a. Minus indicates an increase.
Source: World Bank (1991), "India: Country Economic Memorandum."

Table 7.11 Foreign Trade, 1981/82 to 1990/91

(annual percentage changes)

	Average 1981/82 to 1984/85	1985/86	1986/87	1987/88	1988/89	1989/90	1990/91	Average 1985/86 to 1989/90
Merchandise exports (volume)[a]	0.8	3.5	11.4	13.6	14.1	15.9	4.4	11.7
Merchandise exports (value)[b]	4.2	-3.2	10.6	20.9	12.8	18.2	9.2	11.9
Merchandise imports (volume)[a]	-1.2	25.4	4.3	-6.2	12.4	3.3	3.8	7.8
Merchandise imports (value)[b]	-0.6	12.1	2.5	11.8	19.3	4.9	9.2	10.1

a. Customs figures.
b. Balance of payments figures.
Source: Customs figures are taken from Government of India, DGCIS (various years). Balance of payments figures are from Reserve Bank of India (various years), *Report on Currency and Finance.*

Chapter Eight

Crisis and Short-Term Macroeconomic Policy: An Appraisal

In this chapter we appraise the role of short-run macroeconomic policy in relation to the four crises that have been analyzed in chapters 4 to 7, and consider what lessons can be drawn. Hereafter, the crises are referred to as first crisis (1965–67), second crisis (1973–75), third crisis (1979–81), and fourth crisis (1990 and beyond). The first three crises were principally caused by exogenous shocks while the fourth was largely policy induced.[1] We shall mostly be concerned with the first three crises because it is too early to appraise the policy response to the fourth crisis, which is still continuing. But we will discuss the policy mistakes that caused the fourth crisis. Data relevant to the text are given in tables 8.1 and 8.2.

We are concerned in this chapter with policy in relation to crises, not with a connected account of specific policies over the whole period. Further, we consider mainly short-term policy; that is, those aspects of policy that can be varied fairly quickly (within, say, two years). We ignore the effects of the general "style" of macroeconomic policy. Of course, even short-run policy should be formulated in the light of long-run constraints (for example, the intertemporal budget constraint) and long-run objectives (such as the rate of growth). Some reference is made to these issues in this chapter, but detailed analysis is left to later chapters.

We begin with a brief comparison of the symptoms and causes of the first three crises. In all these crises the government was primarily concerned about two developments—high inflation and a marked deterioration of the balance of payments. Of course, symptoms of the crises were also manifested in other ways. For example, in each case there was an industrial recession caused partly by the supply shocks themselves. Though important, this problem was of less pressing concern to the government than inflation and the balance of payments, and it was in fact willing to undertake stabilization policies that increased the severity of the recessions. While the government was also concerned about declines in the real incomes of vulnerable groups, it saw fighting inflation as its major weapon in alleviating increased poverty.

In all three crises inflation was above 10 percent for two years in succession; in the first two crises, food price inflation was more than 15 percent for two successive years. In a poor, largely unindexed economy, these are high rates, bearing in mind that they are averages for the whole country, concealing much higher rates in food-deficient states. In the first two crises, food prices rose faster than the prices of manufactures but this tendency was reversed in the third crisis.

The balance of payments deteriorated severely during each of the three crises. Since India is a large economy that was also inward-looking, foreign trade was a small proportion of GDP and so were current account deficits. For such an economy, the ratio of the current account deficit to exports is a more relevant measure of pressure on the balance of payments. In the second and third crises, this ratio increased to 20 percent or more.[2] The first crisis was even more serious; the ratio was high to begin with (about 40 percent) and went up to 84 percent.

The points of similarity and difference in the origin of the first three crises can be summarized as follows.

- A drought-induced reduction in food and agricultural output was involved in each crisis. The supply shock was largest in the first crisis when there were very severe droughts for two years in succession. In the third crisis there was one very severe drought year. In the second crisis there were two years of fairly severe drought interspersed by a reasonably normal year.
- In the run up to the first two crises, but not to the third, wars and border conflicts played a part in increasing government expenditure.
- In the first crisis the shock was wholly internal in origin (apart from the war with Pakistan). In the second and third crises there was in addition a severe external shock, namely, a sharp deterioration in the terms of trade due to a rise in the price of imported oil. This resulted in large current account deficits. In the first crisis the current account deficit was even larger. But this arose from the drought itself, combined with an extremely weak balance of payments position prior to the crisis.
- In each crisis the inflation component was triggered primarily by agricultural failure. Oil price increases and/or world inflation also played a part, but they were secondary in importance.
- In each crisis the shocks impinged on an already overheated economy. In the first two crises the overheating was partly caused by rising defense expenditure, though rapid increases in public investment or nondefense current expenditures were also in evidence. Fiscal deficits or money supply growth, or both, show an increase in the run up to each crisis (particularly the second crisis).
- Though overheating of the economy was present in each case, there were some differences in initial conditions. Before the first crisis the economy was in a weak state due to stagnation in agriculture and "import starvation." There was no spare margin in food or foreign exchange reserves.

Before the second crisis the foreign exchange situation was better but food stocks were again inadequate. In the third crisis, however, the economy was in a strong defensive position in both respects.

Thus the first three crises were caused primarily by severe exogenous shocks, but government policies also contributed to converting shocks into crises. The fourth crisis is different, though the usual symptoms of crisis were again in evidence—inflation above 10 percent and a widening of the current account deficit. But the widening was from a base of persistently high deficits (35 percent of exports or more for several years) and a heavy buildup of foreign debt. A new element, absent in previous crises, was a cutoff of private foreign lending that had become a significant element in the capital account of the balance of payments. But the main difference of the fourth crisis from the other crises is that it was largely induced by policy. Food production grew satisfactorily for two years prior to the crisis. There was an increase in oil prices for a few months after August 1990 but this was preceded by several years of falling, or low, oil prices. The mini oil shock of 1990 could have been absorbed quite easily by additional borrowing had the macroeconomic situation not been in a fragile state due to persistently overexpansionary fiscal policies. The cutoff of foreign lending and the collapse of international confidence was not an exogenous shock but mainly an endogenous reaction to these policies, though the absence of political stability also played a contributory role. The next three sections analyze the policy response to exogenous shocks, and are thus concerned with the first three crises. They are followed by a brief discussion of the origin of the policy-induced fourth crisis, and by an overview.

Appropriate Response to Exogenous Shocks: Some Theory

How should a government respond to exogenous macroeconomic shocks? Can basic economic principles throw light on the optimal response to the two negative shocks that have featured in Indian macroeconomic crises—a reduction in food output and a deterioration in the terms of trade caused by a rise in the price of imported oil?

Economic theory emphasizes the crucial distinction between temporary and permanent negative shocks to real income. A temporary shock is self-reversing and does not represent a reduction in permanent income. Current consumption should therefore be maintained above the temporarily low current income. But with a permanent negative shock, the presumption is in favor of an immediate cut in consumption since income has gone down permanently. We now consider the response to the above shocks in greater detail.

Drought-Induced Reduction in Food Output

In a monsoon economy, droughts occur irregularly but quite often. A drought is therefore a classic example of a temporary, reversible shock. The appropriate response to such a shock is to smooth the path of consumption. Perfect stabilization of consumption is not optimal because stabilization incurs the costs of stock-holding or borrowing. With the usual assumption of a diminishing marginal utility of income, the marginal benefit from extra stabilization falls as the amplitude of fluctuations in consumption is reduced. A balance has to be struck between the falling marginal benefit and the rising marginal cost of extra stabilization. There is thus an argument for state action to moderate the rise in food prices without stabilizing them completely.[3]

Stabilization of food prices (or commodity prices) can be carried out either by building up a buffer stock ahead of time (from domestic procurement or imports) or by importing as and when necessary. The latter in turn can be done either by building up foreign exchange reserves ahead of time or by borrowing abroad as and when necessary.[4] In theory, each of these methods should be pursued until their marginal costs are brought into equality with one another (and with the marginal benefit).

Accumulating stocks of food or foreign exchange spreads the cost of stabilization backward in time, while borrowing spreads it forward. The cost of a buffer stock consists of the cost of storage, the inevitable loss due to rotting and wastage, and the interest cost of holding the stock. Foreign exchange reserves do not involve the cost of storage and physical deterioration, only the opportunity cost of tying up resources in that form represented by their rate of return in alternative uses *minus* the interest earned on the reserves. Contemporaneous external borrowing involves only the cost of servicing the loan.

This suggests that the use of foreign exchange reserves or loans is clearly a cheaper method of stabilization than buffer stocks.[5] But there are other considerations involved. Arranging international loans may involve delays and can be done easily and cheaply only if the country is judged to be creditworthy. (Sometimes aid is available but there may be political strings attached.) Moreover, spreading the cost forward has an element of risk attached to it. Delivering imported food (whether on the basis of reserves or borrowing) may also be subject to delays and large internal transport costs. There is also the risk that international prices of foodgrains can themselves fluctuate significantly. (Indeed, it has been claimed that there are times when rice is unavailable on the international market at any price.) Domestic buffer stocks have the advantage of greater speed and certainty of delivery, which helps to prevent any destabilizing private speculation that might be engendered by uncertainty and delay. Arguably, therefore, buffer stocks have a favorable effect on price expectations. In India, as argued below, lack of an adequate buffer stock of food had adverse consequences in the first two crises.[6]

Stabilizing consumption of particular vulnerable groups during droughts may well require redistributive measures in addition to price stabilization. These could take the form of price subsidies to poor consumers while maintaining high producer prices for incentive reasons (and also to sustain the incomes of poor farmers in a drought). But price subsidies may not be sufficient because droughts can lead to a collapse of income and employment (for example, in the case of landless agricultural laborers). There is, therefore, a case for income support during droughts (either in cash or in kind, and either unrequited or in exchange for work).

An agricultural supply shock reduces not only food but output of industrial raw materials. Given some downward money wage inflexibility in industry, a rise in raw material prices contributes to both recession and cost push inflation. Again, if the shock is temporary, it may be sensible to stabilize raw material prices by imports (or domestic buffer stocks).[7] Finally, a word about investment. When faced with a temporary shock, there is no particular reason why investment should be altered since there is *ex hypothesi* no change in long-term investment possibilities or time preference. Fluctuations in investment would produce unnecessary fluctuations in income and output in the presence of wage and price inflexibility in industry.

The upshot of this discussion is that a temporary and reversible agricultural supply shock is best handled by maintaining investment and running down previously accumulated food and foreign exchange reserves to stabilize food prices, food consumption, and prices and availability of industrial raw materials. The argument thus suggests no obvious role for demand management policy of the conventional kind. But complications are introduced if the economy suffering an agricultural supply shock is also suffering from overheating and excess liquidity and if there are mechanisms that translate an increase in the relative price of agricultural products into an overall inflationary spiral. As we shall see, this was the perception of the Indian government.

A Permanent Rise in the Price of Imported Oil

A rise in the world price of oil and the consequent deterioration in the terms of trade could, in principle, be temporary or permanent. In fact, both the oil shocks of the 1970s were thought to be permanent by most informed observers and institutions. That being so, a rise in the price of imported oil would reduce the country's real income permanently below its previous trend. Though it may be optimal to postpone some of the necessary cuts in consumption (if income is growing), the presumption must be that a large part of the income loss should fall on consumption fairly quickly and that external borrowing for consumption should be used sparingly.

The optimum path of investment is more ambiguous. The profitability of investment in domestic oil production and oil substitutes will rise. There may also be a good case for a general increase in investment if the world rate of interest falls (as happened in the 1970s due to the shift in world income to high-saving, oil-producing countries). However, in some activities profitability will fall as a consequence of the oil price increase. On balance, in a country with significant domestic oil production possibilities, optimum investment may well increase, though no general argument can be adduced in favor of such a proposition.

Given the short-run inelastic nature of oil demand, the current account deficit can be expected to widen by nearly the full extent of the rise in the value of a constant quantity of oil imports immediately after an oil price increase. But the above considerations suggest that the government should seek to achieve fairly rapidly some reduction in the current account deficit below this level (since it is very unlikely that the increase in optimal current investment would exceed the reduction in optimal current consumption), and further reductions in the ratio of the current account deficit to exports should be achieved over time. This generally requires mobility of resources and a depreciation of the real exchange rate to shift production toward tradable goods and consumption away from them (switching). This in turn may require a depreciation of the nominal exchange rate. Internal balance must also be achieved if both excess demand and a loss of output are to be avoided. Given that a permanent fall in real income is expected to result from the oil price rise, the increased expenditure on oil imports may be offset, or even more than offset by reduced private expenditure elsewhere. If, therefore, private savings do not fall, resources will be available to reduce the current account deficit. There may thus be no call for fiscal and monetary retrenchment. Indeed, some monetary relaxation may be appropriate, assuming that savings in the public sector are not allowed to fall as a consequence of the public sector oil bill. But qualifications to this account should be kept in mind. First, if the private sector responds inappropriately and reduces its saving in response to a negative oil shock, current account adjustment may require public savings to be increased by contractionary policies. Second, the case for contractionary policies would be reinforced if the economy were suffering from excess demand and rapid inflation before the impact of the oil shock. Third, it may be difficult to avoid some transitional fall in employment and output in the course of current account adjustment because of "friction" in the movement of resources and inflexibility of real factor prices.

Comparison of Indian policy responses to the 'ideal' responses discussed above is complicated by the fact that macroeconomic crises in India were not pure cases of one kind of shock. In the second and third crises, both droughts and oil price increases played a role. Even in the first crisis, which is apparently a pure case of drought, the pre-existing import starvation clearly influenced the measures taken. In addition, in all crises there was some prior overheating of the economy and the possibility of an inflation spiral had to be taken into account.

Since in each crisis there was a mixture of shocks, we have thought it best to compare the crises by comparing policy reactions to the principal manifestations of crisis; that is, inflation and balance of payments deterioration. It is necessary to bear in mind that inflation in all three crises was mainly due to the droughts; that the balance of payments deterioration in the second and third crises was mainly due to the oil shocks; and that there are some common elements in policies required to combat inflation and balance of payments deterioration.

Policy Response to Inflation

In all three crises inflation was primarily triggered by droughts. The policy response to this can be grouped under three headings—supply management, income support, and demand management.

Supply Management

In all three crises there was an attempt to stabilize food prices, partly to stabilize food consumption and partly because of their critical contribution to inflation. It is notable that food availability fell less sharply than food production in the first and third crises, but almost as much as food production in the second crisis (see table 8.1). The underlying reason is that in the first and third crises, public distribution was stepped up massively (with the help of aid-financed imports in the first case and domestic destocking in the third). In the second crisis food stocks were low and imports were inadequate because, in addition to foreign exchange scarcity, world prices of food had themselves risen to very high levels by the time the decision to import was made; consequently, public distribution could not be increased very much.

Aggregate food availability may not be as good an indicator of the effect of the drought on poor consumers as food prices themselves. Food prices rose more sharply in the first two crises than in the third. Leaving monetary factors aside, there were some reasons specific to the food market for these differences in price behavior. The difference between the first and the third crises is particularly instructive because food prices rose much more sharply in the former despite large increases in public distribution in both cases. We suggest that part of the reason lies in the uncertainty of increased food supply in the first crisis when the increase in supply came from imports, the process being marred by delays and political uncertainty about whether food would be shipped by the United States. In addition, the food market in India was clogged up by the existence of food zones. It is hardly surprising if in these circumstances there was destabilizing private speculation in food. In the third crisis, in contrast, food zones had been abolished and there was a substantial domestic buffer stock. In the second crisis there was the worst of all worlds—imports were inadequate, delayed, and for a time quite uncertain; domestic procurement had been disrupted by the temporary nationalization of the wholesale trade in cereals; and food zones were still in existence. These were of course ideal breeding grounds for speculative activity, particularly in the context of a highly liquid economy. Food prices rose more sharply in the second crisis than in the other two crises (see table 8.1).

Table 8.1 Some Macroeconomic Indicators Before, During, and After Crises
(annual percentage increases, unless otherwise indicated)

Period	Food production	Food availability	GDP (factor cost)	GDP (registered manufacturing)	Prices (wholesale)	Food prices (wholesale)	Prices of manufactures (wholesale)
1961/62 to 1964/65	2.4	1.1	4.5	9.6	5.3	8.3	4.1
First crisis							
1965/66	-19.6	8.3	-3.7	3.3	7.7	8.4	6.3
1966/67	1.7	-13.1	1.0	0.1	13.9	16.3	12.1
1967/68	28.0	0.5	8.1	-3.3	11.6	18.3	11.2
1968/69 to 1971/72	4.1	6.5	3.8	7.1	3.5	0.9	3.3
Second crisis							
1972/73	-8.2	2.1	-0.3	3.2	10.0	10.1	11.3
1973/74	7.8	-7.7	4.6	4.9	20.2	22.7	14.4
1974/75	-5.4	9.4	1.2	1.0	25.2	26.0	21.0
1975/76	22.0	-8.0	9.0	1.0	-1.1	-4.9	1.4
1976/77 to 1978/79	3.6	7.6	4.8	10.0	2.4	2.0	1.6
Third crisis							
1979/80	-17.9	4.2	-5.0	-2.1	17.1	8.2	20.1
1980/81	19.8	-11.7	7.2	-1.6	18.2	11.4	19.2
1981/82	2.2	12.9	6.1	7.7	9.3	13.1	5.2
1982/83 to 1984/85	3.7	4.2	5.1	10.9	6.4	8.2	5.6
1985/86 to 1989/90	3.9	3.0	5.6	6.4	6.7	6.9	7.5
Fourth crisis							
1990/91	3.0	-3.0	5.6	7.6	10.3	12.3	8.3

Table 8.1 (continued)

(annual percentage increases, unless otherwise indicated)

Period	Money supply (narrow)	Real public fixed investment	Fiscal deficit (percentage of GDP)	Export volume	Real exchange rate	Current account deficit (percentage of exports)	Real public fixed investment (percentage of GDP)
1961/62 to 1964/65	7.5	9.7	5.7	5.2	3.6	45.5	8.2
First crisis							
19656/6	8.8	5.2	6.7	-8.3	6.0	57.9	9.6
1966/67	8.2	-13.1	7.3	-4.9	-18.4	83.5	8.4
1967/68	7.3	-8.0	5.5	6.7	-3.5	73.2	7.2
1968/69 to 1971/72	10.5	3.1	4.5	3.4	0.0	28.0	6.6
Second crisis							
1972/73	12.3	18.7	5.2	12.1	-3.2	16.3	8.1
1973/74	17.4	-2.2	4.3	8.2	-5.0	15.4	7.7
1974/75	11.0	-14.5	4.1	8.3	3.7	20.8	6.5
1975/76	5.9	17.9	4.6	12.2	-7.6	1.6	7.0
1976/77 to 1978/79	15.2	10.2	5.3	9.9	-5.7	-11.5	8.5
Third crisis							
1979/80	19.0	2.8	6.5	6.6	0.0	10.0	8.7
1980/81	12.9	4.9	8.1	-7.8	9.4	25.8	8.6
1981/82	14.6	12.5	6.7	1.6	4.5	30.6	9.1
1982/83 to 1984/85	14.4	7.9	8.4	1.5	0.0	26.0	9.8
1985/86 to 1989/90	15.7	4.4	10.0	10.5	-5.0	43.8	9.6
Fourth crisis							
1990/91	14.4	6.5	10.4	4.4	-7.1	43.8	8.9

Source: Tables 4.9, 4.10, 4.12, 4.14, 4.15, 5.11, 5.12, 5.14, 5.16, 5.19, 6.9, 6.10, 6.13, 6.15, 6.16, 7.4, 7.5, 7.9, 7.10, and 11.3.

Income Support

Another policy response in each of the three crises, particularly in rural areas where serious famine conditions were prevalent (for example, Bihar in 1967 and Maharashtra in 1973), was to distribute food directly or to start public works programs in which workers were paid in cash.[8] These redistributive schemes were additional to India's permanent food price subsidy scheme that operates through "fair price shops" but whose coverage is mainly in urban areas. The scope of these schemes was limited by budgetary and management considerations.

Demand Management

In all three crises, and particularly in the first two, the response to inflation went beyond direct action in the food market and extended to a tightening of fiscal and monetary policy. The first question that arises is why deflationary policy played any part in the government's response. As we saw above, it can be argued that the optimal response to a drought-induced inflation is to stabilize food prices by supply management. On this view, aggregate demand restriction is a particularly unsuitable measure. A drought causes a rise in the relative price of food, to be corrected in due course when food production rebounds. A fiscal-monetary restriction would be positively harmful. Since the income elasticity of demand for food is very low, the pressure on food prices would be little reduced, while the reduction in demand for manufactured products would cause a recession in industry.

The above view is too extreme. The following arguments can be made in favor of some demand restriction, and probably constituted the explicit or implicit reasoning of the government.

- The assumption made above was that the demand for foodgrains is very income-inelastic. In fact, available evidence indicates that the income and expenditure elasticities of demand for foodgrains are quite large—in the region of 0.4 at all income and expenditure levels.[9] Demand restriction by fiscal means has its primary impact on the incomes of the not-so-poor.[10] This would reduce the demand for foodgrains and moderate the rise in food prices, thereby benefiting poor consumers, particularly in rural areas (who are insulated from the direct income effects of fiscal restriction and may, in any case, receive some income support from employment programs). Reduced food demand in combination with increased public distribution and rising interest rates can also reduce food prices by causing private stocks to be sold. Some indirect evidence in favor of the sensitivity of food prices to fiscal and monetary restriction comes from the fact that in 1974 (and to some extent in 1967 as well) the decline in food prices started *before* any sign of a good harvest.[11] The moderation of food price increases also has favorable effects on inflation even in the organized sector. In parts of this sector, rising food prices are a marker for trade union activity and an important source of wage push.

- There is evidence that prices in manufacturing industry are set on the basis of costs (wages, agricultural raw materials, domestic and imported components) plus a variable markup (which depends on the pressure of demand).[12] It should be noted that in each of the three inflations under consideration, manufactured goods prices rose by more than 10 percent a year. (Thus none of the inflationary episodes could be described purely in terms of an increase in the relative price of food.) Demand restriction can moderate manufactured goods prices by reducing profit margins, by moderating price increases of agricultural raw materials, and by reducing pressure for increased wages.

- In each crisis there was overheating and/or excess liquidity to begin with, combined with some procrastination in implementing restrictive policies. It seems clear that governments acted because there was a danger that the trend rate of inflation might increase even after the supply situation improved or, even worse, that a serious inflationary spiral would develop. The deflationary packages constituted attempts to buy credibility and to signal government determination to maintain a low trend rate of inflation.[13]

- Finally, it should be noted that the deflationary packages were in part motivated by balance of payments considerations (as discussed in the next section).

The Timing, Magnitude, and Nature of Demand Management

While some deflationary action was thus justified, that still left a lot of choice as to the timing, magnitude, and content of a policy package. If there is to be a restrictive policy it should obviously be timely; that is, it should begin early in a crisis and not continue beyond the point when the cycle has naturally turned round. As far as possible it should not be directed at expenditure on capital formation since it is not wise to slow down growth of productive capacity in reaction to a temporary decline in agricultural output. Each crisis has been extensively discussed in earlier chapters, so we give below only a brief summary of the salient points concerning the character of stabilization policy.

First Crisis

The first crisis began in 1965/66, but fiscal restriction did not come until 1966/67. (The measured fiscal deficit, however, widened slightly in the latter year.) The fiscal contraction continued in 1967/68, the year in which agricultural recovery took place, and in fact the measured fiscal deficit as a proportion of GDP declined continuously from 1967/68 to 1969/70. Calculations of the "fiscal impulse" (which is the change in the fiscal deficit adjusted for the revenue and expenditure effects of cyclical changes in GDP) are even more striking. They show that the fiscal impulse was continuously negative from 1965/66 to 1969/70, though only mildly so in the first two years.[14] As for the character of the fiscal restriction, it was heavily weighted toward cuts in government and public sector expenditure on capital formation in all sectors including infrastructure.[15] While these cuts were not responsible for long-run deficiencies in infrastructure, the instability of public investment probably contributed to low growth of output for many years by reducing the productivity of investment in general (see chapter 13). Growth of manufacturing industry suffered. There was a severe recession in 1966/67 and 1967/68. From 1968/69 to 1970/71, when the agricultural situation was satisfactory, manufacturing output recovered, but the growth rate was lower than in the first half of the 1960s. In the capital goods industries, production was almost stationary in 1968/69 and 1969/70. Fiscal restriction by the government surely played a part in this industrial stagnation. Inflation came down sharply in 1968/69 and continued at the low average rate of 3.4 percent from 1968/69 to 1970/71. Monetary policy was nonaccommodating during the crisis itself but was somewhat expansionary from 1968/69.

In retrospect, therefore, demand management policy in the first crisis had several shortcomings. It was instituted rather late, it went on long after the agricultural recovery, and it was concentrated on cuts in public investment. This was not very efficient in reducing the demand for food during the crisis (for that purpose reductions in disposable incomes would have been better), and the persistence of the cuts had adverse effects on growth.

Second Crisis

In the second crisis the fiscal reaction came in two stages. In 1973/74, the second year of crisis, fiscal policy was tightened.[16] This took the form mainly of a slowdown in expenditure, both current and capital. Monetary policy was also tightened in 1973 but only after the acceleration of inflation had been firmly established, and the tightening was inadequate. In 1974, when inflation showed no sign of abating, the second stage of demand restriction was put into effect. This was fierce. There were increases in taxation, a partial freeze of wages, dearness allowances and dividends, and forced savings through a compulsory deposit scheme. In addition, there were sharp cuts in public investment in manufacturing and infrastructure. Monetary policy was also significantly tightened. Unlike the first crisis, however, public investment cuts were reversed after the agricultural recovery of 1975/76. The growth of manufacturing output fell sharply in 1974/75 and 1975/76 (without becoming negative). However, it bounced back, and in the three years 1976/77 to 1978/79 proceeded at the very healthy rate of 8 percent a year. Inflation became negative in 1975/76 and remained very low until 1978/79 (an average annual rate of only 1.4 percent) in spite of rapid monetary growth. This was because of an exceptionally large increase in the demand for money for reasons that had little to do with short-term macroeconomic policy.

The response to inflation in the second crisis shared some of the defects of the response in the first crisis, but on balance was rather better. Fiscal restriction was a bit late, but not unduly so. In the first stage, it took the form of expenditure cuts (though this time the cuts were less heavily directed toward capital formation). There was monetary restriction as well, but it was clearly late given the lags in its operation. In the second stage, there was some overkill. The disposable income-reducing measures taken at this stage should have come in the first stage. There were again avoidable cuts in expenditure on capital formation. But, unlike the first crisis, they were quickly reversed when the agricultural supply situation improved. Public fixed investment grew rapidly (see table 8.1), as did industrial production. Even so, it has been claimed that fiscal policy in the aftermath of the crisis was not expansionary enough.[17] There is some plausibility in this line of argument in view of the large accumulation of food and foreign exchange reserves after 1976/77. We take the view that the caution of the authorities was understandable given the overall policy framework (see chapter 5). It should also be noted (with the benefit of hindsight) that the caution paid off as the accumulated reserves proved to be invaluable during the third crisis, which broke in 1979/80.

Third Crisis

This time there was no fiscal tightening in the first two years of the crisis (1979/80 and 1980/81) taken as a whole. The fiscal deficit worsened for the two years in succession. The "fiscal impulse" was negative in 1979/80 but was strongly positive in 1980/81. There was some monetary tightening in 1979 (after several years of rapid monetary growth) which was reflected in a reduction in money supply growth in 1980/81. Fiscal and monetary tightening came in 1981/82 along with the IMF program, and was quite severe for a short period. By this time the crisis had ended, and the tightening did not last very long. There were no cuts in public investment, unlike during the first two crises. Indeed, real public investment increased even during the crisis years. There was a sharp industrial recession during 1979/80 and 1980/81, but this must largely be attributed to the drought, as there was little fiscal restriction. After 1980/81 the industrial growth rate was very satisfactory, probably because of the absence of cuts in investment and some easing of industrial and import-licensing policies. Inflation came down but the average rate from 1981–84 was 8.6 percent, higher than in the aftermath of the two earlier crises.

Thus, in some ways the response to inflation in the third crisis was much better. Inflation was not accommodated but there was no crackdown either. This was wise, particularly in view of the strong position with regard to food and foreign exchange reserves. The problem with the policy response this time did not arise during the crisis but in the aftermath when the deterioration in the fiscal balance continued. This is examined below.

Policy Response to Balance of Payments Deterioration

Balance of payments problems during the second and third crises cry out for comparison because they were both caused by an external terms of trade deterioration. The first crisis stands apart from the other two.

The First Crisis

In this crisis the balance of payments deteriorated because of two severe droughts that led to an increase in food imports and a reduction in primary product exports. If this were a complete description of the balance of payments problem, it could be classified as wholly "temporary," to be dealt with by the use of reserves or foreign borrowing until the agricultural situation improved. But the balance of payments position was extremely weak even before the droughts, due to agricultural stagnation and slow export growth. The current account deficit was large, and would have been considerably larger had it not been suppressed by severe import controls that were hampering industrial production.

The government's devaluation-liberalization package was designed principally to address this long-term problem (a "structural adjustment package" in recent jargon). In addition, the government instituted a fiscal squeeze that, while primarily motivated by anti-inflationary considerations, had the secondary objective of strengthening the balance of payments. The course of the crisis has been discussed at length in chapter 4. To make a long story short, any favorable effects of the devaluation-liberalization package were swamped by the drought, and the balance of payments deteriorated in 1966/67 and 1967/68. It did improve later, but mainly because of the agricultural recovery and the industrial recession; the liberalization itself was progressively reversed over the period.

In appraising the policy response to the first crisis it has to be borne in mind that it is almost impossible to consider the actions of the authorities in isolation from those of the aid donors; and that the policy actions were motivated by a mixture of short-term and long-term considerations. The most obvious lesson to be drawn from the first crisis concerns not the policy response but the initial condition of the economy. While the droughts were undoubtedly severe, their effects on the economy were compounded by the lack of adequate stocks of food and foreign exchange. This condition was the result of inappropriate *past* macroeconomic policies. Droughts must clearly be expected and guarded against. However, inappropriate resource allocation policies must also share the blame. The weak state of the economy and the balance of payments had much to do with neglect of agriculture and exports and the pervasive control of imports that had reduced them to bare essentials.[18]

Taking the initial condition of the economy as given, a devaluation-liberalization package was an obviously correct long-run measure. But the timing of the package was bad; it was determined by the momentum of the negotiations, not by the objective economic situation. The vulnerable state of the economy gave the donors tremendous leverage. The donors wanted to use this leverage to secure desirable reforms. In the event, the package was instituted long before the effects of the drought of 1965 had worked themselves through, and just before the drought of 1966.[19] The effect of the droughts on exports and inflation interfered seriously with the working of the package and made it even more unpopular than it otherwise would have been. It would have been better to finance the balance of payments during the drought years (perhaps with some rationalization of export subsidies and tariffs but without a large explicit devaluation) and to have devalued after the agricultural recovery in 1967.

The composition of the aid part of the package was also less than ideal. It seems clear, in retrospect, that the volume of aid was not sufficiently generous to support a liberalization program undertaken during a drought. If food aid had been larger in volume and speedier in delivery, the moderation of food price inflation and the support to the balance of payments would have obviated the need for severely deflationary policies. More generous project and nonproject aid might have prevented the persistent squeeze on public investment after the agricultural recovery, and the reimposition of import controls.[20]

Second and Third Crises

In both these crises there was thought to be a permanent shock in the form of a sharp increase in the price of oil imports. The immediate effect in both cases was a large widening of the current account deficit. As already argued, the general presumption is that in the face of a negative oil shock there should be a fairly rapid adjustment of the current account deficit as a proportion of GDP, followed by further reductions in that ratio over time. The difficult task for macroeconomic policy is to achieve this adjustment without loss of output. In India the task was made more complicated by the fact that in each case there was both an agricultural supply failure and an overheated economy. This meant that the current account adjustment to the oil shock had to be achieved while simultaneously dealing with domestic inflation.

There are several points of similarity and contrast in the policy responses to balance of payments deterioration in the two crises. In the short run, increased concessional financing played a major role in both crises. In the second crisis there was substantial borrowing from the various "soft" facilities of the IMF (the Compensatory Financing Facility, low-conditionality credit borrowing, and the Oil Facility) and from bilateral donors. There was no borrowing from commercial sources. In the third crisis as well, in spite of the good reserve position, there was substantial concessional borrowing from the IMF Trust Fund, IDA, and the consortium countries. The policy response to the current account deficit was similar and appropriate in one respect. Measures were taken in both crises to stimulate oil production and to restrain oil consumption. But in other respects the response was very different.

- In the second crisis import controls were tightened; in the third crisis the cautious import liberalization of the intervening years was largely preserved.
- In both crises current account adjustment required a real depreciation. In the second crisis policy was compatible with this requirement. The nominal exchange rate was pegged to sterling and depreciated with it. Consequently, in spite of the high domestic inflation, the real exchange rate changed little. In contrast, in the third crisis the nominal exchange rate was allowed to appreciate slightly in the face of rapid domestic inflation, so that there was a large real exchange rate appreciation (see tables 8.1 and 11.3).
- The fiscal and monetary stance was also different. In the second crisis, there was a strongly restrictionist fiscal policy and (after initial procrastination) a very tight monetary policy. In the third crisis both fiscal and monetary policies were far less severe.

The differences in fiscal, monetary, and exchange rate policies go a long way toward explaining the larger current account deterioration in the third crisis in contrast to the second. Allowing the real exchange rate to appreciate was clearly a mistake. At the same time, it must not be forgotten that the avoidance of tighter import controls and cuts in investment were positive features of the third crisis. A sizable but temporary widening of the current account deficit (and the associated fall in reserves and increase in external borrowing) was not necessarily a mistake. Unfortunately, the macroeconomic stance continued to be expansionary for a prolonged period, as emphasized below.

Second and Third Crises: Aftermath

The current account turned around very quickly after the second crisis and then went into massive surplus for two years. After the third crisis, however, the current account as a proportion of GDP showed no improvement. This difference in outcome can be attributed to three policy differences during and after the crises.

First, in the second crisis foreign borrowing was used mainly in the early stages of the crisis. As seen above, it was concessional and accompanied by adjustment measures. In the third crisis, in addition to such borrowing, there was heavy medium-term borrowing from the IMF and commercial sources, at nonconcessional rates. This borrowing came two years after the crisis broke, by which time inflation had already collapsed. Its stated objective was to cushion the reserves while structural adjustment was carried out. But it seems clear, with the benefit of hindsight, that it led to complacency and impeded adjustment. The failures related particularly to two crucial areas—exchange rate policy and public savings.

Second, exports soared after the second crisis and stagnated after the third. World demand conditions were partly responsible, but another reason was exchange rate policy. After the second crisis, the real exchange rate depreciated substantially. Of course the behavior of the real exchange rate after the second crisis cannot be attributed entirely to policy. It was mainly the result of India's low rate of inflation, which resulted from a mixture of factors. But one can at least say that policymakers did not fight the real depreciation. After the third crisis, although the real appreciation that took place during the crisis was arrested by some nominal depreciation, it was not reversed. More generally, the heavy borrowing of the period was not used to boost exports, for example by promoting export-oriented investment.

Third, the stance of fiscal policy was very different in the aftermath of the second and third crises and partly accounts for the different current account outcomes. Revenues after the second crisis were buoyant because the higher tax rates and compulsory deposit schemes instituted during the crisis were maintained. But more importantly, there was firm control of the government's current expenditure. Private savings also grew rapidly and while this was not directly the result of macroeconomic policies, they helped to produce low inflation and hence positive real interest rates. In contrast, after the third crisis the public finances deteriorated and the growth of private savings slowed significantly. The latter can be attributed to the slowing down of the spread of banking. The former was caused by explosive growth of government current expenditure and excessive foreign borrowing. In effect, foreign borrowing was used to finance public consumption. These unwise policies had serious long-run implications and played a large part in the buildup to the crisis of 1990.

Saving and Investment Balances and Macroeconomic Crises

A useful perspective on the relationship between macroeconomic policies and current account adjustment is provided in table 8.2, which shows public and private saving-investment balances and the corresponding current account deficits before, during, and after the three crises. Since the current account deficit is identically equal to the sum of the public sector deficit and private sector surplus, causal statements inevitably involve informed judgment rather than exact proofs.

It can be seen that the first crisis was preceded by a rapid increase in public capital formation over several years. Though public saving also rose in the first half of the 1960s, there were large current account deficits and heavy external borrowing for almost a decade before the crisis. This partly accounts for the vulnerable state of the economy before the droughts of the mid-1960s occurred. The adjustment to the crisis took place mainly by a fall in the public deficit rather than a rise in the private surplus; and the fall in the public deficit was engineered through a fall in public investment rather than a rise in public saving.

There was an increase in the public deficit at the beginning of the second crisis but steps were taken to bring it down during the crisis itself. After the crisis public investment revived, but the current account nevertheless turned round dramatically. Exchange rate depreciation played a critical role, but it would not have worked without a strong rise in public and private savings. The former was direct-

Table 8.2 Saving/Investment Balances Before, During, and After Crises
(percentage of GDP at market prices)

Period	Public investment	Public saving	Public gap	Private investment	Private saving	Private gap	Foreign saving
1950/51 to 1954/55	3.1	1.7	1.4	6.7	7.9	-1.2	0.3
1955/56 to 1959/60	5.8	1.7	4.1	8.4	10.1	-1.8	2.3
1960/61 to 1964/65	7.5	3.0	4.4	7.8	9.8	-2.1	2.4
First crisis							
1965/66	8.5	3.1	5.4	8.3	11.4	-3.1	2.3
1966/67	7.2	2.3	5.0	11.2	13.0	-1.8	3.1
1967/68	6.8	1.9	4.8	8.7	11.1	-2.4	2.4
1968/9 to 1971/72	6.3	2.6	3.6	7.7	10.5	-2.7	0.9
Second crisis							
1972/73	7.3	2.6	4.7	8.6	12.7	-4.1	0.6
1973/74	7.7	2.9	4.8	1.4	15.5	-4.1	0.6
1974/75	7.6	3.7	3.9	10.7	13.7	-3.1	0.9
1975/76 to 1978/79	9.4	4.6	4.8	11.0	16.6	-5.6	-0.8
Third crisis							
1979/80	10.3	4.3	6.0	11.8	17.3	-5.5	0.5
1980/81	8.7	3.4	5.2	14.1	17.7	-3.7	1.5
1981/82	10.5	4.5	6.0	12.1	16.4	-4.3	1.6
1982/83 to 1984/85	10.6	3.5	7.1	9.4	15.2	-5.8	1.4
1985/86 to 1989/90	10.8	2.4	8.4	11.8	17.9	-6.0	2.4
Fourth crisis							
1990/91	9.7	0.9	8.8	14.9	21.0	-6.1	2.7

Note: Saving is defined in this table as in the national accounts. It includes net transfers and net factor income from abroad. Foreign saving is thus the current account deficit not the "resource deficit." "Errors and omissions" in investment are attributed entirely to private investment.

Source: Government of India, CSO (1989a); Government of India, CSO (1991), *National Accounts Statistics*; Government of India, CSO (1991), *Quick Estimates of National Income 1989/90*; Government of India, CSO (1992), *National Accounts Statistics*; and tables 4.13, 5.15, 6.14, and 7.8.

ly the result of policy, the latter only indirectly so. (The growth of private saving is discussed more fully in chapters 5 and 12.)

During the third crisis, both public investment and the public deficit rose and the private surplus fell, partly because of the strong growth of corporate investment. After the crisis there was no fiscal adjustment, in sharp contrast to the first two crises. The public deficit went up even further, mainly due to a fall in public savings. The counterpart of this was a lack of current account adjustment in spite of some rise in the private surplus. These tendencies continued apace in the second half of the 1980s.

Policy-Induced Crises

Bad policies almost invariably make some contribution to creating or exacerbating crises, even when the latter are mainly exogenous in origin. Several examples of this have been given. But a crisis that is primarily policy induced can arise only from unsustainable policies over a number of years. The policy element was important in creating the first crisis. But it is the fourth crisis that was a policy-induced crisis par excellence. We focus on it next without embarking on a general discussion of the various ways in which mistaken policies might lead to crisis.

We saw above and in chapter 7 that the origin of the fourth crisis can be traced back to policy mistakes during and after the third crisis. (In particular, the heavy foreign borrowing of that period created a large debt service burden in the second half of the 1980s.) But there need not have been a crisis if some of these mistakes had not persisted for a long time. Danger signals of macroeconomic trouble that were already flashing in 1985 in the form of large and persistent fiscal and current account deficits continued to become more ominous over the next five years. Some good policy measures were undertaken. For example, the policy of active exchange rate depreciation and export promotion was correct and helped to achieve rapid growth of exports. The dilution of industrial controls was long overdue and helped to maintain rapid industrial growth. The policy environment was also favorable—world trade grew rapidly, oil prices fell until the mini-shock of late 1990, and food production was satisfactory from 1988 onward. But policymakers neglected the crux of the macroeconomic problem.

The main problem needing attention was the growing fiscal deficit, as was evident from the fact that the current account deficit continued to worsen despite exchange rate depreciation.[21] Table 8.2 is illuminating. It can be seen that in the second half of the 1980s the private sector surplus was roughly constant. The current account deficit could have been reduced without cutting public investment only by raising public (and in particular government) saving.[22] A different and competing hypothesis is that the current account deficit determined the public deficit rather than the other way round. But until August 1990 there were no unexpected adverse external shocks driving current account deficits. Fiscal complacency was doubtless partly induced by the ease of foreign borrowing, which made it possible to finance large current account deficits. But that surely counts as a policy mistake. De facto, the public deficit may have been the passive element but in appraising policy the right conclusion to draw must be that it should not have been passive.[23] Policymakers were taken in by the apparent ease of commercial foreign borrowing despite the obvious lessons to be drawn from the experience of countries in Latin America. Of course, reducing the fiscal deficit would have presented some delicate problems of pace and timing. But that was no excuse for virtual inaction over half a decade.

Thus, the fourth crisis was fundamentally the result of a neglect of fiscal dynamics. A more thorough examination of the fiscal sustainability issue is made in chapter 9.

Conclusions

The main lessons arising from India's experience of macroeconomic crises can be summarized as follows.

- Anticipatory policy is important. Macroeconomic stability requires devoting adequate resources to build up buffer stocks of food and/or foreign exchange reserves, and to maintain on average some unused international borrowing capacity. This lesson clearly applies to expected temporary shocks such as droughts. But it is also important to insure to some extent against unexpected permanent shocks. The policy response to droughts was clearly defective in the above respect in the first two crises but has been much better since then.
- Contractionary demand management policies should be used with caution in combating inflationary bubbles arising from droughts. They may sometimes have a useful role to play but their timing and content is critical. If used, they should be directed at the disposable incomes of the relatively well-off. Income support policies have a vital role to play in cushioning the poor. Cuts in public investment should be avoided as far as possible. In the first crisis cuts in public investment were too severe and lasted too long. In the second crisis as well, there was some overkill. In the third crisis these features were corrected.
- Notwithstanding the above point, the policy response to inflationary bubbles that arise from exogenous shocks should be nonaccommodating so that inflation does not get built into the system. In this respect, India's policies have, on the whole, been good.
- Although financing an adverse, permanent external shock may be sensible for a time, particularly in the interests of maintaining investment, adjustment should begin early. Two specific aspects of adjustment policies are

especially noteworthy. First, the behavior of the real exchange rate is critical for achieving satisfactory adjustment. A negative external shock will, in general, require a real exchange rate depreciation and that in turn is best achieved in India's circumstances by a depreciation of the nominal exchange rate (for further discussion see chapter 11). In this respect, there is a glaring contrast between the good policy response in the second crisis and the bad response in the third crisis. Second, current account adjustment will require not only exchange rate depreciation but supporting fiscal and monetary policies. Again, in this respect the policy response in the third crisis was unsatisfactory. While it was sensible to maintain public investment during the crisis, allowing public savings to fall in the aftermath of the crisis was inappropriate.

- Excessive foreign borrowing should be avoided, both in response to negative external shocks and as a general rule. Foreign borrowing should not, except for a brief period, be used to finance consumption. It must be justified by its expected returns in convertible foreign exchange and that, in general, requires projects and policies to promote rapid growth of exports. Ease of foreign borrowing should not be used as an excuse to postpone adjustment because sentiment in capital markets can turn round very rapidly if the debt burden is high. In this respect, policy was prudent in the second crisis and imprudent in the aftermath of the third crisis and beyond.
- Fiscal policy should be cautious. Continuously growing fiscal deficits should be avoided. This lesson was neglected from 1983 onward for the rest of the decade, and inevitably led to the fourth crisis. India's experience confirms that neglect of fiscal dynamics is a recipe for disaster.

We have concentrated above on short-term policy. Some long-term issues are alluded to but they are given greater precision in the later chapters. Finally, we must not forget that the overall framework of macroeconomic policy—not least the microeconomic control system—can over time make the economy more vulnerable to crisis. This issue too is addressed in later chapters.

Part Three

Policy Trends and Long-Run Growth

Chapter Nine

Fiscal Policy

In its macroeconomic aspect, fiscal policy comprises the deliberate use of budgets (of central and state governments and, on a broader interpretation, of public sector enterprises as well) to achieve macroeconomic objectives, in particular stabilization and growth. In this chapter we examine fiscal policy and performance over the entire period 1960/61 to 1989/90.

Overview of Public Finances

We begin with an overview of India's public finances.

Deficits and Borrowing

Table 9.1 shows the course of consolidated government revenue, expenditure, and borrowing (and selected components of each) over the period 1960/61 to 1989/90, divided into five-year averages and expressed as percentages of GDP.

Revenue rose steadily from 12.7 to 20.2 percent of GDP. The rise was more than accounted for by the rise in indirect taxes, which consist mainly of excise and customs. In the 1980s customs duties increased greatly in importance. Direct taxes (mainly corporation and income tax) have not kept pace with GDP, and in the last quinquennium accounted for only about 12 percent of total revenue. This reflects the absence of agricultural income taxation, the low direct tax base more generally, and probably growing tax evasion as well. Nontax revenues (mainly from public sector enterprises) have been stagnant as a proportion of GDP.

Current expenditure has also risen from 11.8 to 23.0 percent of GDP, outstripping the rise in the revenue. Over time the rise has accelerated. Table 9.1 shows that the rise in the succeeding quinquennia was 1.1, 1.3, 2.1, 2.3, and 4.4 percent-

Table 9.1 Consolidated Finances of Central and State Governments, 1960/61 to 1989/90
(percentage of GDP at market prices)

	1960/61 to 1964/65	1965/66 to 1969/70	1970/71 to 1974/75	1975/76 to 1979/80	1980/81 to 1984/85	1985/86 to 1989/90
Revenue	12.7	13.4	14.6	17.8	18.1	20.0
Direct taxes	2.9	2.5	2.5	2.9	2.4	2.4
Indirect taxes	6.9	8.1	9.5	11.7	12.7	14.6
Nontax revenue	2.9	2.8	2.6	3.2	3.0	3.0
Current expenditure	11.8	12.9	14.2	16.3	18.6	23.0
Defense	2.6	3.0	3.0	2.9	3.0	3.7
Explicit subsidies	0.7	0.9	1.1	1.9	2.6	3.6
Net interest payments	0.4	0.4	0.5	0.7	1.2	2.5
Current revenue balance	0.9	0.5	0.4	1.5	−0.5	−2.9
Capital expenditure	6.6	6.0	5.1	6.9	7.5	7.1
Total expenditure	18.4	18.9	19.3	23.2	26.1	30.0
Fiscal deficit	5.7	5.5	4.7	5.4	8.0	10.0
Domestic borrowing	3.4	3.0	2.7	3.6	5.6	7.3
External borrowing	1.9	1.8	0.7	0.9	0.7	0.7
"Budgetary deficit"	0.4	0.8	1.2	0.9	1.7	2.0
Primary fiscal deficit	5.3	5.2	4.2	4.7	6.8	7.5

Note: The "budgetary deficit" is a peculiarly misleading Indian concept, and is by definition virtually equal to sales of treasury bills. Unfortunately, therefore, it does not equate to borrowing from the RBI. It overstates such borrowing insofar as treasury bills may be sold to other lenders, and understates it insofar as the government may sell longer-dated securities to the RBI. Domestic borrowing in this table includes long-dated borrowing from the RBI.

Source: Government of India, Ministry of Finance (various years), *Indian Economic Statistics—Public Finance.*

age points of GDP. More than half of this runaway rise in current expenditure is accounted for by the three components shown; that is, defense, subsidies, and interest. The rise in subsidies and interest is notably large. The rise in subsidies is explicable largely in terms of the growing political power of interest groups (see chapter 3).[1] The rise in interest payments is partly due to higher interest rates, but is mainly due to the rise in the debt (see table 9.2). The current revenue balance—that is the savings of government—has deteriorated fairly steadily, except for the quinquennium 1975/76 to 1979/80, moving from a positive 0.9 percent to a negative 2.9 percent of GDP. For more detail on government savings see chapter 12.

Government capital expenditure does not show a clear trend, averaging about 6.5 percent of GDP. It dipped from the first half of the 1960s to the first half of the 1970s, but then rose to a peak in the first half of the 1980s, when it fell again to about 6.5 percent of GDP in 1989/90.

The bottom line of the above account is the consolidated government fiscal deficit (or total borrowing requirement inclusive of borrowing from the Reserve Bank).[2] This fell from 5.7 percent of GDP in the first half of the 1960s to 4.7 percent in the first half of the 1970s. Since then it has risen almost continuously to 10.0 percent of GDP in the second half of the 1980s.

Table 9.1 also records the "primary" deficit, that is the fiscal deficit less net interest payments. This is of interest in that it is the balance of revenues and expenditure that are in principle under control. Interest payments, in contrast, are the result of past transactions, and can in principle be reduced only by default or by the grace of creditors (though as a proportion of GDP their domestic component may be reduced by inflation). The primary deficit has followed the same pattern as the fiscal deficit, but has not risen as fast because interest payments have come to form a higher proportion of expenditure. In 1974/75 it was at a low point of about 3.5 percent of GDP; since then it has risen to about 7.5 percent in the second half of the 1980s.

We turn to the financing of the consolidated government fiscal deficits, that is to the sources of borrowing. External borrowing more than halved in the first half of the 1970s, largely reflecting a fall in concessional finance. Since then the figures show little change, and thus do not reflect the large rise in India's use of foreign savings in the 1980s (the two concepts diverge on account of public enterprise and private sector foreign borrowing, and changes in the reserves). As a counterpart of the reduced fiscal importance of foreign borrowing, the very rapid rise in domestic borrowing (including the "budgetary deficit," which is essentially treasury bill sales (see note to table 9.1) is notable—it rises from 3.8 percent of GDP in the early 1960s to 9.3 percent in the second half of the 1980s. The significance of this is brought out later when we discuss the growth of government indebtedness and its sustainability.

The mid-1970s marks a turning point in some important respects. Government savings peaked in 1975/76, at 2.3 percent of GDP. Thereafter the deterioration was almost uninterrupted, dissavings running at well over 3 percent of GDP in the late 1980s. The fiscal deficit was at a low of 4.1 percent of GDP in 1974/75, rising almost continuously (with a brief retrenchment in 1981/82 and 1982/83) to over 10 percent in the late 1980s.

The above account derives from budgetary sources; a similar story can be told for the public sector as a whole, using the national income accounts. This story is told at some length in chapter 12 (see table 12.1). We note, very briefly at this point, that public sector savings were on a rising trend until the mid-1970s, reaching over 4.5 percent of GDP, and then fell away to little more than 2 percent in the late 1980s. Public investment, in contrast, was on a rising trend throughout, albeit with quite large variations. Therefore the public sector deficit (investment minus savings) showed no marked trend until the mid-1970s, after which it rose from about 5 percent of GDP to about 9 percent in the late 1980s. This rise in the public sector deficit or borrowing requirement was mainly the result of a fall in savings as public investment rose only by about 1 percent of GDP.

The Debt

Indebtedness rises with borrowing, unless debts are forgiven. The story of the rise in debt therefore closely parallels the above discussion of deficits. As before, we consider first the debt of the government (including state governments), that is the fiscal aspect; and then the overall indebtedness of the Indian economy, that is the balance of payments aspect. All figures are percentages of GDP at market prices. It should be noted in this connection that a government may reduce the domestic debt as a percentage of GDP by permitting or inducing inflation (provided the debt is not indexed, and in India it never was). Foreign debt cannot be reduced in this way as it is expressed in foreign currency, but it will be reduced by world inflation.

The first part of table 9.2 shows the government's debt for selected years, together with its division between various creditors. The division between RBI and non-RBI debt is of particular importance. Only borrowing from the RBI raises the quantity of base money, which in turn influences the quantity of money however defined.

In the 1960s domestic debt fell as a percentage of GDP. As we have seen, the fiscal deficit was modest (about 5.5 percent of GDP) and external borrowing was quite high, with a resultant rise in total external debt from 6.1 percent of GDP to 16.7 percent. In addition to this, the ratio of debt to GNP was reduced by inflation (the price level rose by about 80 percent over the decade).

In the 1970s these movements went into reverse. While the domestic debt continued to fall until 1974/75 (as a result of the heightened inflation of the early 1970s), there was a large rise in the second half of the 1970s. This reflected a rise in the fiscal deficit together with a fall in external borrowing as aid was reduced. This resulted in an actual fall in external debt as a percentage of GDP. Inflation also was very low, so that there was almost no reduction of the "burden" of debt on that score.

In the 1980s the debt engine was firing on all cylinders, though the rise in domestic debt from 40.4 to 54.6 percent was much larger than the external gov-

Table 9.2 **Consolidated Government Debt, Domestic and Foreign, 1960/61 to 1989/90**
(*percentage of GDP*)

	1960/61	1970/71	1974/75	1979/80	1984/85	1989/90
Government of India						
Domestic banking system	15.4	12.6	13.7	17.5	21.8	26.7
RBI	11.7	9.3	9.7	10.8	14.9	16.6
Commercial	3.6	3.4	3.9	6.7	6.9	10.0
Nonbank private sector	23.4	19.7	18.1	22.9	23.9	27.9
Small savings	6.0	5.0	4.4	6.0	7.4	9.2
Other	17.4	14.7	13.7	16.9	16.4	18.8
Total domestic	38.8	32.4	31.8	40.4	45.7	54.6
Non-RBI	27.0	23.1	22.1	29.5	30.8	37.9
External (net of PL 480)	3.8	11.9	8.8	8.7	9.3	12.2
PL 480	2.3	4.8	n.a.	n.a.	n.a.	n.a.
Total (net of PL 480)	42.6	44.3	40.6	49.1	55.0	66.8
India's foreign debt (percentages)						
Debt/GNP net of PL 480	5.0E	15.1	13.4	12.6	17.6	23.9
Debt/exports	100.0E	360.0	253.9	142.0	208.3	258.4
Debt service/exports	7.3E	23.0	16.5	10.2	18.1	26.3
Debt interest/exports	—	8.7	5.6	3.7	10.5	14.2
Concessional debt/total debt	90E	87.2	86.4	82.2	51.0	42.0

Note: E indicates authors' estimate. Before 1979/80 India's external debt figures are for long-term debt only. PL 480 debt was subject to very special terms under which it was not a significant burden. The U.S. Government was persuaded by Ambassador Moynihan to write off the debt in 1973.

Source: Government of India figures are from Government of India, Ministry of Finance (various years), *Indian Economic Statistics—Public Finance.* Figures for India's foreign debt are from World Bank (annual), *World Debt Tables,* and World Bank (various years), "India: Country Economic Memorandum."

ernment debt rise from 8.7 to 12.2 percent. These rises reflect primarily the increase in the fiscal deficit, which was discussed earlier. The total government debt-to-GDP percentage (about 67 percent) was still not extravagantly or exceptionally high—many OECD country governments are comparably indebted. But the rate of increase of the debt was alarming and could not continue. This issue of the sustainability of government and public sector deficits is examined later in this chapter.

India's total external debt-to-GNP ratio follows much the same course as the government's external debt, except that nongovernment foreign debt has come to account for a larger proportion of the total debt than was the case in earlier years. Nongovernment foreign debt includes borrowing by public sector entities other than the government, private sector debt guaranteed by the government, and a small amount of private sector unguaranteed debt. Thus, even excluding PL 480, government debt was almost 80 percent of the total in 1970/71, but only about 50 percent in 1989/90. Both government and total external debt were at a low point in 1979/80; 8.7 and 12.6 percent of GNP respectively. But by 1989/90 government external debt had reached 12.2 percent and total external debt 23.9 percent.

By the standards of other developing countries a figure of 23.9 percent for total external debt is quite low. The figure for all developing countries taken together was 41.8 percent in 1990. But the debt-to-exports percentage of 265.1 is high and compares with a figure of 176.8 for all developing countries. As shown by India's experience of 1990 and 1991 it is a level at which commercial borrowing becomes difficult, or even impossible. It should, however, be noted that the start of the decade of the 1990s was not the first time that India's debt-to-exports ratio had reached a very high figure. This was also true of the start of the 1970s, after heavy foreign borrowing in the 1960s. Then, also, India had low reserves and no unused borrowing capability, so that the balance of payments became a serious short-term constraint. The problem went away after 1974/75 as exports boomed and current account surpluses were achieved. This was to recur again at the end of the 1980s.

The deterioration of the public finances that began in the mid-1970s and accelerated at the end of the decade is closely related to political and institutional developments. This relationship is analyzed in chapter 3, and here we briefly summarize what seem to have been the main features. Unlike many developing countries, government expenditure (including that of the nationalized industries and the states) has always been under strict central treasury control. In the 1950s and 1960s this control and the political dominance of the Congress party, together with the relative weakness of interest groups, permitted the still austere Congress leaders to maintain a policy of reasonable fiscal discipline, though the attempt to maintain high levels of public investment in the face of increased defense expenditure, occasioned by wars with China and Pakistan, did result in large deficits in the mid 1960s.

The seeds of the erosion of fiscal discipline can be traced back to the victory of Mrs. Gandhi's Congress (R) party in 1971. Thereafter the power of the Congress party to manage the growing demands and strength of interest groups was weakened, both by Mrs. Gandhi's populist policies and by her "presidential" style (also termed "deinstitutionalization"). For several years this weakening was masked by the fiscal crackdown that seemed essential in the face of the inflation caused by drought and the first oil price rise. Deficits grew again during the Emergency (1975/76 to 1976/77), and the succeeding Janata government (despite the brief return to power of that arch-disciplinarian Morarji Desai). But all the while the political power of new interest groups, and the weakening of the Congress, made it difficult not to use government expenditure to try to manage their demands. Subsidies grew apace, as we have seen. Corruption was also growing rapidly, with a decay of public morality. The year of Mrs. Gandhi's return to power—1980/81—marked a rise in the consolidated government fiscal deficit to a level of 8.1 percent of GDP, never previously experienced. With a brief improvement at the time of the IMF loan, the deficit continued to mount through the 1980s, with ever-growing subsidies. The basic political conditions—weakening government, the strengthening of nongovernment organizations, and increasing ethnic and religious conflict—were not favorable.

Fiscal Policy: Stabilization and Adjustment

Within the long-run trends already described in this book there have been important changes in the government's budgetary dispositions in response to exogenous shocks, and also some changes that were needed in order to correct past fiscal errors. These are described in detail in chapters 4 to 7, while the appropriateness of fiscal policy in the context of four shocks is assessed in chapter 8. It was seen that the fiscal response answered to (and to some extent *had* to answer to) inflation and the state of the balance of payments, as well as to the objective of stabilizing output. Stabilizing output, or more precisely, avoiding both excesses and deficiencies of demand, is the traditional role ascribed to fiscal (as well as monetary) policy in Keynesian economics. There would have been more room for fiscal policy to be devoted mainly to this function if the economy had possessed greater stocks of foreign exchange reserves and commodities, especially foodgrains, the use of which would have reduced inflation by increasing supplies, and would have either ameliorated or financed a deterioration in the balance of payments.

We now try to determine whether fiscal policy was nevertheless, on balance, output-stabilizing, despite the complications of inflation and balance of payments problems caused by supply-side failures.

The Measurement of Fiscal Stance

A problem in appraising fiscal policy is how to judge whether it is tight or loose, expansionary or contractionary. The government deficit cannot itself be taken as an indicator of the fiscal stance since it is itself endogenous. A fall in output and income widens the deficit since tax revenues fall (and "committed expenditures" rise) and vice versa. In measuring the fiscal stance, that is the discretionary element in fiscal policy, it is therefore necessary to adjust the deficit for the cyclical position of the economy. These arguments apply to supply-side cycles as well as to demand-side cycles.

In measuring the fiscal stance of the Indian government we follow some standard procedures.[3] The critical assumption is that in the absence of discretionary policy, government revenue is unit-elastic with respect to actual nominal GDP, while government expenditure is unit-elastic with respect to the trend value of real GDP valued at current prices. The difference between the two gives the cyclically neutral fiscal deficit (CNFD). The difference between the actual fiscal deficit and the cyclically neutral fiscal deficit is the fiscal stance (FIS). Thus

$$(9\text{-}1) \qquad \text{CNFD} \equiv g\,\text{GDP*} - t\,\text{GDP}$$

where g is the expenditure-to-nominal GDP ratio, and t is the revenue-to-nominal GDP ratio, both in a given base period. GDP* is the trend value of GDP, and

$$(9\text{-}2) \qquad \text{FIS} \equiv X - \text{CNFD}$$

where X is the actual fiscal deficit. A positive FIS indicates an expansionary stance.

Finally the *fiscal impulse* is the change in the fiscal stance from year to year (ΔFIS). Note that both a contractionary fiscal stance that becomes less so, and an expansionary stance that becomes more so, yield a positive fiscal impulse. Table 9.3 gives the variables of equation 9-2 together with ΔFIS as percentages of GDP.

To correct for inflation, a further adjustment to fiscal deficits is sometimes made, because inflation reduces the real value of government debt. With free capital markets, interest rates and interest payments on the debt would rise with inflation. But this compensation for inflation would supposedly be used by holders of the debt to buy more government bills or bonds so as to restore the real value of their holdings of the debt. Therefore only changes in the inflation-adjusted, or "operational" deficit (that is, the noninterest deficit plus real interest payments) are thought to be relevant in gauging changes in demand in the goods markets. However, in India interest rates were administered and did not move in line with inflation. Moreover, bonds were held mainly by banks and other financial institutions that were compelled to hold them, and they were not required to increase their holdings in line with inflation. The result of inflation for these nationalized institutions was a fall in profits. In these circumstances use of the "operational" deficit would seem to have no merit.

Fiscal Stance in India

In calculating the fiscal stance (FIS) from equations 9-1 and 9-2 above, the period was broken into two subperiods at 1975/76 since there is evidence of a change of

Table 9.3   Consolidated Government: Fiscal Stance and Fiscal Impulse, 1960/61 to 1989/90

(percentage of GDP)

Year	X	CNFD	FIS	ΔFIS	GDP/ GDP*	WPI/ WPI*
1960/61	5.6	4.7	0.9	—	B	B
1961/62	5.1	4.6	0.6	–0.4	B	B
1962/63	5.8	4.6	1.2	0.6	B	B
1963/64	6.0	4.2	1.8	0.6	A	A
1964/65	6.0	3.5	2.5	0.7	A	A
1965/66	6.7	4.5	2.2	–0.3	B	A
1966/67	7.3	5.2	2.1	–0.1	B	A
1967/68	5.5	4.5	1.0	–1.1	B	A
1968/69	4.4	4.5	–0.1	–1.1	B	B
1969/70	3.8	4.0	–0.2	–0.1	A	B
1970/71	4.6	3.7	0.9	1.1	A	B
1971/72	5.3	3.9	1.4	0.5	A	B
1972/73	5.2	4.6	0.5	–0.9	B	A
1973/74	4.3	4.7	–0.4	–0.9	B	A
1974/75	4.1	5.1	–1.0	–0.6	B	A
1975/76	4.6	4.2	0.4	1.4	A	B
1976/77	5.4	5.2	0.3	0.2	A	B
1977/78	4.9	4.6	0.3	–0.0	A	B
1978/79	5.7	4.4	1.3	1.1	A	B
1979/80	6.5	6.8	–0.3	–1.6	B	A
1980/81	8.1	6.3	1.8	2.1	B	A
1981/82	6.7	5.9	0.8	–1.0	B	A
1982/83	7.3	6.1	1.2	0.4	B	B
1983/84	8.1	5.5	2.6	1.5	A	A
1984/85	9.7	5.7	3.9	1.3	B	B
1985/86	9.3	5.6	3.8	–0.2	B	B
1986/87	10.9	5.6	5.3	1.6	B	B
1987/88	10.0	5.6	4.5	–0.8	B	B
1988/89	9.4	4.5	4.9	0.5	A	B
1989/90	10.4	4.4	5.9	1.0	A	B

Definitions:
X = actual fiscal deficit of consolidated government
CNFD = cyclically neutral fiscal deficit
FIS = fiscal stance
ΔFIS = fiscal impulse (that is, the change in FIS)
GDP* = trend value of GDP
WPI* = trend value of WPI
   Note: In the fifth column, *A* means that GDP was above trend, and *B* below trend. GDP trends were calculated separately for 1960/61 to 1975/76 and 1975/76 to 1989/90. In the sixth column, *A* means that actual inflation of the WPI was above trend, and *B* below trend. Inflation trends were calculated separately for 1961/62 to 1970/71 and 1971/72 to 1989/90.
   Source: Authors' calculations, except for first column, which is from Government of India, Ministry of Finance (various years), *Indian Economic Statistics—Public Finance.*

trend in the GDP growth at that date. For the two subperiods the years 1968/69 and 1976/77 were taken as base periods for the calculations of g and t, because output in those years was close to trend. The resulting calculations are recorded in table 9.3.

If fiscal policy is to be output-stabilizing then the fiscal impulse (table 9.3, column 4) should be positive when output is below trend, that is when there is a B in column 5, and negative where there is an A in column 5.[4] Prima facie fiscal policy was destabilizing in no less than twenty-two of the twenty-nine years. In some of these years when output was below trend the fiscal authorities were inhibited from adopting an expansionary fiscal policy either by inflation or by balance of payments difficulties. This applies particularly to the three years surrounding the first and second crises, 1965/66 to 1967/68 and 1972/73 to 1974/75; and also to two of the three years of the third crisis, 1979/80 and 1981/82. Of the mere five cases in which we find a coincidence of low output and positive fiscal impulse, four occurred in the 1980s when the actual fiscal deficit had become very high. In 1984/85 and 1986/87, in particular, it cannot be said that fiscal expansion was appropriate, given government fiscal deficits of 8.1 and 9.3 percent in the previous years. Chronically large deficits may make an expansionary fiscal policy inadvisable, even when output is sluggish. Of the twelve cases when output was above trend, the fiscal impulse was expansionary in no less than ten; and in the two cases where it was contractionary, it was negligibly so. Fiscal policy was clearly inappropriate in these cases.

Comparing the fiscal impulse with whether inflation was above or below trend (column 6) produces a very different story. There was a clear tendency for fiscal *contraction* when inflation was above trend, and fiscal *expansion* when inflation was below trend (nineteen out of twenty-nine cases). We believe this provides the key to understanding Indian fiscal policy. Inflation was taken as the main guide. This is very understandable. Changes in most important prices are known immediately; changes in output are known for sure only with quite long delays. Nevertheless, reacting mainly to prices can lead to serious mistakes. For instance, inflation may be low during a boom for special reasons, such as rising balance of payments deficits financed by external borrowing. In such circumstances an expansionary fiscal policy can be destabilizing both cyclically and, as we shall see, in a long-run structural sense.

Longer-Run Fiscal Policy and Growth

The section above was concerned with short-term fiscal reactions, but the longer-term optimal adjustment of an economy to a change in circumstances that is expected to be long-lasting will usually require some fiscal change. The oil price shocks are obvious examples. The immediate result was a widening of the current account deficit. If the deficit was at an optimal level before, then it had become excessive and should have been reduced. Recall that the current account deficit is equal to the public sector deficit (or investment/savings gap) plus the private sector deficit (or less the private sector surplus). Both deficits will normally be increased by an import price rise. The private sector may adjust sufficiently, increasing its saving or reducing its investment. But the public sector should also adjust, and this will require some fiscal action. It is also possible that the public sector may need to take stronger action (reducing its deficit rather than preventing it rising) if the private sector does not adjust sufficiently. We saw that in fact the government's deficits (relative to GDP) were reduced after the first oil price shock. But after the second oil price shock they were allowed to increase, with a corresponding and persistent increase in the current account deficit, which led to severe problems later.

Indeed the crisis of 1990/91 and 1991/92 is wholly attributable to the lax fiscal policy of preceding years. The rapid growth of the debt, both domestic and external, and the high level of the latter relative to export earnings, together with the political instability that delayed effective response to the gathering storm, made it impossible to finance the balance of payments deficit without the emergency measures described in chapter 7. In short there was a full-blown crisis.

Thus fiscal policy itself, quite apart from any exogenous event to which it should react, may cause crises and damage the prospects of continuing growth. This has been the experience of many developing countries. India, like them, has thought of public sector expenditure, especially public sector investment, as an engine of growth and development. Since revenue is hard to come by (for administrative, political, and economic reasons) there is always an urge to spend more than is received, and hence, to run a deficit. We need, therefore, to examine the limits to deficit spending or, what comes to the same thing, the limits to borrowing (money creation can be regarded as a form of borrowing). We shall first examine these limits in a general theoretical way, and then relate this discussion to recent Indian history and the current situation.

The Sustainability of Public Deficits and Current Account Deficits

So far in this chapter we have concentrated mainly on consolidated government fiscal deficits and their financing. But we now lay out the theory of deficit financing in terms of the public sector as a whole, that is including nondepartmental enterprises. Figures for public sector deficits, that is public gross capital formation less public savings, are to be found in chapter 12, which deals with savings and investment in the public, corporate, and household sectors of the economy (see in particular table 12.2). The financing of public deficits as between domestic and foreign sources is to be found in table 12.4.

The Theory

First we make the point that part of the public deficit can be financed by base money creation. Some money creation is noninflationary, since the demand for money will increase with GDP. We call this pure seignorage. Beyond this, money creation results in inflation, giving rise to the inflation tax.[5] Some inflation may be regarded as acceptable. It follows that some part of the deficit can safely be financed by money creation.

Second, it is helpful to separate out net interest payments on the existing debt. The rest is called the primary deficit (or surplus). Suppose that the primary deficit, less that part of it financed by money creation, is and remains, zero. Then the inherited debt will grow with the rate of interest paid, because the government is simply borrowing to pay the interest. It follows that if the rate of interest exceeds the rate of growth of GDP, then the debt-to-GDP ratio will grow, and continue to grow so long as these conditions hold.[6] The level of borrowing is not then forever sustainable.

The rate of interest may exceed the rate of growth. But this does not necessarily imply that the government should not borrow. Indeed, it should borrow to invest if the return on new investment exceeds the interest rate, provided that the debt-to-GDP ratio is not dangerously high, for a marginal investment may earn more than the interest rate, though the economy as a whole is growing at a slower pace than the interest rate. (There may, however, still be a fiscal problem if the government cannot capture the returns in order to service the debt.) Thus the problem of sustainability arises only if the debt approaches a dangerous level.

If the interest rate equals the rate of growth of GDP, and there is no primary deficit, then the debt grows at the same rate as GDP and the debt-to-GDP ratio is stationary. If the interest rate is less than the rate of growth, a primary deficit is sustainable. But this "sustainability" may be purely theoretical. If the primary deficit is higher than a critical level the debt ratio will rise and its terminal value may be so high at to be unsustainable in practice (that is, the rate of interest would rise or the rate of growth would fall). In the appendix to this chapter we derive the following equation

$$(9\text{-}3) \qquad \Delta b = (x - s) + b\,(r - \tilde{Y})$$

where b is the debt-to-GDP ratio; x is the primary deficit-to-GDP ratio; s is that part of the deficit that can be safely financed by an increase in base money; $\tilde{Y}$ is the real growth rate of GDP; and r is the real interest rate.

This equation formalizes the argument in the text. It also shows that b may reach a limit if the rate of growth exceeds the real interest rate. This limit, if it exists, will be

$$(9\text{-}4) \qquad b = \frac{x - s}{\tilde{Y} - r}$$

So far we have made no distinction between borrowing at home or abroad. If markets were perfect no distinction would be needed, but this is not the case. In order to bring the argument down to earth it is necessary to consider foreign and domestic borrowing separately. Interest rates may differ between the markets. More importantly, different criteria determine what is a safe level of foreign debt and what is a safe level of domestic debt.

But making the distinction is to some degree arbitrary. As far as domestic debt goes, we are concerned only with the public sector. But a safe level of foreign borrowing must include at least public and publicly guaranteed borrowing, some of which is borrowing by the private sector for which we have no precise figures. We shall therefore proceed to establish safe and sustainable levels for total foreign borrowing. Public sector and, *a fortiori*, government borrowing must be less than this.

Total foreign borrowing by the nation is equal to the current account deficit less grants and equity investments. We call this the debt-creating current account deficit. The limiting size of the debt is determined not so much by the debt-to-GDP ratio as by the debt-to-exports ratio.[7]

Analogous with equation 9-3, we can write

$$(9\text{-}5) \qquad \Delta d = z - d\,(g - i^*)$$

where z is the noninterest debt-creating current account deficit-to-exports ratio, d is the external debt-to-exports ratio, g is the growth rate of the dollar value of exports, and i^* is the nominal dollar interest rate.

Assuming that $g > i^*$, the limiting value of the external debt-to-exports ratio is given by

$$(9\text{-}6) \qquad d = \frac{z}{g - i^*}$$

If the terms of trade are constant, one can further write

$$(9\text{-}7) \qquad \Delta d = z - d\,(g.\text{volex} - r^*)$$

where $g.$volex is the growth rate of the volume of exports, and r^* is the real interest rate on foreign borrowing.

The external debt-to-exports ratio grows without limit if the real interest rate exceeds the real growth rate of exports. If it is less, then the debt will stabilize at a value of

$$(9\text{-}8) \qquad d = \frac{z}{g.\text{volex} - r^*}$$

But this value may be higher than is consistent with the real rate of interest assumed. Indeed it is likely to become very difficult if not impossible to borrow commercially if the debt-to-exports ratio goes above 3.

Application to India

In the 1960s the domestic debt ratio was falling, although there was a primary government deficit of around 5 percent of GDP. This was possible partly because over 2 percent was financed by foreign borrowing, and partly because real interest rates were very low or even negative, and thus on average below the growth rate of GNP. These low rates were maintained by coercion of the banks and exploitation of the public. But the external debt (net of PL 480) rose, and became extremely high relative to exports (360 percent in 1970/71). This was not extremely serious only because almost all the debt was on highly concessionary terms. But India could not have borrowed commercially and was in this sense dependent on aid.

In the 1970s the external debt problem went away. Reliance on aid was reduced to less than 0.5 percent of GDP on average, and exports boomed, so that the debt-to-exports ratio was reduced to 142 percent. As the debt was still predominantly concessionary the debt service ratio was reduced to the low figure of about 10 percent. India had become eminently creditworthy. But the domestic debt was building up due to a continuing governmental primary fiscal deficit of about 4.5 percent of GDP, and a public sector deficit of about the same magnitude.

In the 1980s the government's primary deficits rose to about 7 percent while the public sector deficit reached about 9 percent. We proceed to show that public sector deficits of even half this magnitude are unsustainable. This is done by putting some prudent values on the variables of the equations that were derived in the previous section. Real GDP has grown at about 5.3 percent a year in the 1980s, compared with the earlier "Hindu rate of growth" of 3.7 percent. We do not consider it prudent to suppose that 5.3 percent can be indefinitely maintained, and take 4.5 percent as a prudent figure.[8]

Assuming that an average rate of inflation of 6 percent is acceptable, we have a growth rate of nominal GDP of 10.5 percent. The ratio of base money to income seems to be rather stable at 11 percent, and consistent with the low inflation rate assumed. Base money is here taken to be currency plus the noninterest-bearing component of the required cash reserves of banks. This implies that 10.5 percent $\times$ 0.11 = approximately 1.2 percent of GDP accrues to the government as seignorage and inflation tax. The primary deficit of the nonfinancial public sector in 1989/90 was probably about 6.7 percent.[9] Thus, the primary borrowing requirement was 5.5 percent (that is $x - s$ in equation 9-4 equals 0.055).

We turn now to the real interest rate. The current rate on government bonds is about 10 percent, but higher rates are paid on small savings. The average rate of inflation in the 1980s has been 7 percent. It may be somewhat optimistic to assume that the government can continue to borrow at a 3 percent real interest rate, which in any case understates the marginal rate (this is implied by the higher rate on small savings). Thus the assumed sustainable rate of growth of GDP (4.5 percent) less the real rate of interest is probably about 1 percent ($\bar{Y} - r$ in equation 9-4 = 0.01).

The existing ratio of non-monetized domestic debt to GDP, b, is taken to be 0.40; 0.38 is actually the ratio of consolidated government nonmonetized debt to GDP. We do not have firm figures for the debt of the nonfinancial public sector as a whole, but it is surely higher. With these figures and assuming no foreign borrowing we have from equation 9-3.

(9-9) $\Delta b = 0.055 - 0.40\,(0.01) = 0.05$

That is, the domestic debt ratio would be growing at about 5 percent a year. The ultimate level of the ratio is given by equation 9-4.

(9-10) $b = \dfrac{0.055}{0.01}$

That is, the debt ratio approaches 5.5 times GDP, with interest payments of about half of GDP. This is absurdly high, so let us see to what extent it can be reduced by foreign borrowing.

First we note that the external debt-to-exports ratio, d, is more than 2.5, the level beyond which the cost of borrowing is likely to rise sharply. It follows that d should not be allowed to rise. Reference to equation 9-7 shows that the noninterest, debt-creating current account deficit relative to exports, z, must not then exceed $d\,(g.\text{volex} - r^*)$.

The real growth rate of exports in the 1980s was about 5 percent, though it rose to about 10 percent in the second half of the decade. We think it would be imprudent to assume that more than 7 percent will be achieved over any long period. What is the likely real rate of interest on foreign borrowing, r^*? We suggest that India cannot bank on a lower rate than 4.5 percent.[10] This results in a figure for ($g.\text{volex} - r^*$) of 0.025. If d is not to rise beyond 3, the maximum prudent figure for z becomes 0.075. Exports are about 8 percent of GDP. This then implies a prudent figure for the noninterest current account deficit of about 0.6 percent of GDP or, being very generous, about 1 percent of GDP. We estimate that in 1988/89 to 1989/90 it was on average more than 2 percent.

If national foreign borrowing should not exceed 1 percent of GDP, this is *a fortiori* so for public foreign borrowing. We therefore next subtract 0.01 from the domestic borrowing requirement in equations 9-9 and 9-10. This reduces the growth rate of domestic debt to 4.0 percent, and the ultimate debt level to 4.5 percent times GDP—still far too high. It is impossible to imagine that the public would ever save enough, and want to hold enough of their savings in government bonds, for such a volume of domestic debt relative to GDP to be possible. Indeed, well before the domestic debt approached 100 percent of GDP it is likely that interest rates would have to rise. Already in 1989/90 household financial savings were no more than approximately equal to the public deficit. A rise in interest rates would compound the problem of financing the deficit, and would tend to crowd out private investment and reduce the rate of growth. The rate of interest could then exceed the rate of growth, and a primary surplus would be needed.

There is no longer an escape route by forcing the banks to buy public debt at existing interest rates. Even if it were compulsory that all increases in bank deposits were invested in government securities, they would be barely enough to cover the deficit (since private financial savings are roughly equal to the public sector deficit). Moreover, such a policy would result in acute financial repression. In order to remain viable, the banks would have to reduce deposit rates and raise lending rates. This would very probably reduce private savings, and private investment would certainly be crowded out. The upshot is that the debt has reached such levels that India cannot afford to run primary deficits at the level prevalent even in the 1960s and 1970s—4 to 5 percent of GDP. Indeed, the figures suggest that the primary deficit should be virtually eliminated. There would then still be a public sector deficit of about 4 percent of GDP.

Whatever the precise figures, there is no doubt that a very large reduction is required. We realize that this presents difficult economic and political problems. This book is not the place, nor are the authors well-placed to propose any detailed short- or medium-term plan to bring it about. However, the main lines of the adjustment required if long-term growth is not to suffer are clear. Whatever contributions may be achievable from the revenue side, and from improved performance of public enterprises, it is government current expenditure—especially on subsidies but also on employment and pay—that must bear the brunt of reduction and restraint.[11]

Fiscal Policy and Long-Run Growth

Raising Resources

In India central fiscal policy has been conducted within the framework of a high level of public investment. This was thought to be essential for rapid and reasonably egalitarian economic development. The more a country relies on a high level of public investment to promote and sustain a satisfactory long-run growth rate, the more important it is that the public sector itself achieves a high level of savings. In India it was presumed that public investment would be adequately supported by public savings, a presumption that has not been realized, as will be shown in more detail in chapter 12.

The reasons for disappointing public savings may lie, of course, both on the expenditure and the revenue sides of the balance. The reasons for the recent rapid growth of current public expenditure are largely of a political economy nature, and these are discussed elsewhere, particularly in chapter 3. Here we consider reasons of a more structural kind for the poor performance of public savings.

Total revenue as a proportion of GDP has in fact risen rapidly. But there are weaknesses which suggest that future rises cannot be relied on in the absence of some reform of the system. As table 9.1 shows, the rise in revenue is more than accounted for by indirect taxes. Direct tax has actually fallen as a percentage of GDP. This reflects the growth of the black economy in the 1980s, as well as increased tax allowances and offsets.[12] Nontax revenues have been flat, in part as a result of the poor performance of public enterprises that is discussed in chapters 12 and 13.

The structure of taxes is affected by relations between the center and the states. Since independence the tax collection by the center has risen more rapidly than that of the states. This is largely because the states feel unable, or are unwilling, to tax agriculture; and under the constitution it is only they who can do so. There is thus no central tax on agricultural income, which is levied in only a few states. Land tax was once the mainstay of the revenue in India; now it is only a tiny proportion even of the states' own revenue collection.

In recent years tax collection by the center has been about double that of the states. However, the states are entitled to parts of the personal income taxes and excise duties levied by the center. These parts are determined quinquennially by an autonomous Finance Commission appointed by the president. They have been raised several times and currently stand at 85 and 42.5 percent. The result is that the states' tax revenue is roughly equal to the net tax income of the center. It should be noted that the states do not share in customs revenue, corporation tax, or income tax surcharges levied by the center. The center has been accused of concentrating on these taxes, and it is indeed notable that during the 1980s customs revenue rose 6.0 times and excise revenue 3.8 times.

Certain distortions are evident. As the increasing share of central revenues accruing to the states suggests, the Finance Commissions tend to call on the center to plug the states' impending deficits. This decreases the states' incentives to raise tax revenue, reduce the losses of their departmental enterprises, and generally restrain current expenditure. The center in turn has little incentive to try to raise the revenue from income taxes and it cannot broaden the tax base by including agricultural incomes. As for indirect taxes, it has a strong incentive to concentrate on tariffs rather than on excise taxes, thus increasing the degree of protection. Overall, the very high reliance on indirect taxes, which are highly distortionary, is unfortunate and suggests that stricter control of expenditure is more desirable for growth than further attempts to raise revenue in the absence of difficult structural reforms.

Stabilization

Apart from considerations of equity, the main objective of fiscal policy is to stabilize the growth of output while also maintaining reasonable price stability. Stability and long-run growth are positively related, provided that price stability is not achieved by destabilizing investment. India's fiscal policy can be criticized in this respect. Price stabilization took precedence, and fiscal policy tended to destabilize industrial output. In particular, public investment in the 1960s and 1970s was less stable than it might have been. Price stabilization would have been better achieved by building higher reserves of foreign exchange and food stocks to be used when the harvest failed. This would have obviated the need to counter inflation by cutting investment.

In the 1980s fiscal policy became highly expansionary with large increases in current expenditure. As we shall see in chapter 13, this contributed to the achievement of an enhanced rate of growth of output. But this effect could not be sustained for very long since it required an excessive rate of growth of the public debt, which ended in crisis and recession in the early 1990s.

Appendix

This appendix is concerned with simple debt theory, and looks at overall debt and external debt.

Overall Debt

The budget identity for the nonfinancial public sector can be written

$$(9\text{-}11) \qquad X + iB \equiv \Delta S + \Delta B$$

where X is defined as the primary deficit, and iB is the sum of interest payments on the existing debt, B. ΔS is the increase in the monetary base (on which no interest is paid), which is termed "seignorage," and ΔB is the increase in the interest-bearing debt.

Using lowercase letters for proportions of GDP and writing GDP $= PY$ (real product $\times$ the price level), we have

$$(9\text{-}12) \qquad x + ib \equiv s + \frac{\Delta B}{PY}$$

Since $B = bPY$, and writing $\tilde{P} \equiv \Delta P/P$ and $\tilde{Y} \equiv \Delta Y/Y$, it follows that

$$\Delta B = PY\,\Delta b + bPY\,(\tilde{P} + \tilde{Y})$$

or

$$\frac{\Delta B}{PY} = \Delta b + b\,(\tilde{P} + \tilde{Y})$$

Therefore from equation 9-12 we derive

$$\Delta b = x + ib - s - b\,(\tilde{P} + \tilde{Y})$$

Defining r (the real interest rate) as $i - \tilde{P}$ we finally have

(9-13) $\Delta b = x - s + b\,(r - \tilde{Y}\,)$

where $\tilde{Y}$ is the real rate of growth.

External Debt

We express external debt relative to exports, rather than to GDP. For simplicity the external debt is assumed to be in dollars. Analogous to equation 9-13, we write

(9-14) $\Delta d = (i^* - g)\,d + z$

where d is the external debt-to-exports ratio, i^* is the dollar interest rate, g is the growth rate of export value, and z is the ratio of the noninterest current account deficit to exports (or the primary external deficit, or inward resource transfer).

If $i^* > g$, the debt-to-exports ratio grows without limit for any non-negative primary deficit. For any z, if $g > i^*$ the debt ratio will stabilize at the level $d = z/(g - i^*)$.

If the terms of trade are assumed to be constant, the real dollar interest rate and the volume of exports may be substituted in equation 9-14.

Chapter Ten

Monetary Policy

Monetary policy in India is not wholly subsidiary to fiscal policy nor is it heavily constrained by the balance of payments. Though there is a link between fiscal deficits and the supply of money, this can be weakened by instruments at the disposal of the authorities. The exchange rate is managed (and has sometimes been fixed for long periods) but exchange controls on capital movements have been effective enough to permit substantial monetary independence.

In this chapter we assess monetary policy in India from 1960–90. Figures relevant to the text can be found in tables 10.1, 10.2, and 10.3.

Monetary Policy—Objectives and Instruments

Monetary policy has several aims, but the focus of this chapter is on its contribution to stabilization and growth. Stabilization means smooth adjustment to exogenous shocks and avoidance of policy-induced shocks, but as with fiscal policy the variables of interest are not only output and employment but also consumption, investment, prices, and the balance of payments. Of these, monetary policy is especially concerned with the control of inflation. The use of monetary policy to promote growth involves many microeconomic issues such as the development of an efficient banking and financial system. We ignore these issues except insofar as they interact with the macroeconomic aspects of monetary policy.

India does not have an independent central bank. Responsibility for major decisions on monetary policy rests with the Finance Ministry, although the Reserve Bank is closely involved. (This should be borne in mind when we refer below to various operations of the Reserve Bank.) For some years after independence the Reserve Bank had a lot of de facto power and influence, but this was severely eroded after bank nationalization. Moreover, the Reserve Bank did not escape the politicization of institutions during the Emergency.

Table 10.1 Monetary Indicators, 1960/61 to 1990/91

Year	M1	M1g	M3	M3g	RM	RMa	V1	V3	m1	m3	m1a	m3a
1960/61	2,669	—	4,048	—	2,126	—	6.07	4.00	1.26	1.90	—	—
1961/62	2,756	3.3	4,123	1.9	2,234	—	6.23	4.17	1.23	1.84	—	—
1962/63	2,985	8.3	4,529	9.9	2,388	—	6.19	4.08	1.25	1.90	—	—
1963/64	3,274	9.7	4,928	8.8	2,611	—	6.49	4.31	1.25	1.89	—	—
1964/65	3,561	8.8	5,433	10.3	2,827	—	6.95	4.56	1.26	1.92	—	—
1965/66	3,853	8.2	5,989	10.2	3,043	—	6.79	4.37	1.27	1.97	—	—
1966/67	4,135	7.3	6,661	11.2	3,273	—	7.15	4.44	1.26	2.04	—	—
1967/68	4,402	6.5	7,275	9.2	3,472	—	7.86	4.76	1.27	2.10	—	—
1968/69	4,770	8.4	8,053	10.7	3,767	—	7.69	4.55	1.27	2.14	—	—
1969/70	5,312	11.4	9,113	13.2	4,151	—	7.60	4.43	1.28	2.20	—	—
1970/71	5,941	11.8	10,321	13.3	4,577	—	7.27	4.18	1.30	2.26	—	—
1971/72	6,567	10.5	11,813	14.5	5,051	—	7.04	3.92	1.30	2.40	—	—
1972/73	7,372	12.3	13,747	16.4	5,532	—	6.92	3.71	1.33	2.49	—	—
1973/74	8,651	17.4	16,470	19.8	6,777	6,473	7.17	3.76	1.28	2.43	1.34	2.54
1974/75	9,604	11.0	18,707	13.6	7,244	7,051	7.63	3.91	1.33	2.58	1.36	2.65
1975/76	10,166	5.9	21,036	12.5	7,486	7,346	7.75	3.74	1.36	2.82	1.38	2.86
1976/77	11,485	13.0	25,195	19.8	8,589	8,290	7.39	3.37	1.34	2.93	1.39	3.04
1977/78	13,158	14.6	30,262	20.1	10,237	9,282	7.30	3.17	1.28	2.96	1.42	3.26
1978/79	15,526	18.0	36,414	20.3	12,337	10,733	6.71	2.86	1.26	2.95	1.45	3.39
1979/80	18,475	19.0	43,789	20.3	15,182	12,807	6.19	2.61	1.22	2.88	1.44	3.42
1980/81	20,865	12.9	50,931	16.3	17,198	14,238	6.52	2.67	1.21	2.96	1.47	3.58

(table continues on next page)

245

Table 10.1 (continued)

Year	M1	M1g	M3	M3g	RM	RMa	V1	V3	m1	m3	m1a	m3a
1981/82	23,919	14.6	59,766	17.4	19,547	16,044	6.68	2.67	1.22	3.06	1.49	3.73
1982/83	26,563	11.1	68,326	14.3	21,706	17,959	6.71	2.61	1.22	3.15	1.48	3.80
1983/84	30,449	14.6	80,186	17.4	25,115	2,0231	6.82	2.59	1.21	3.19	1.51	3.96
1984/85	36,034	18.3	94,758	18.2	30,041	22,950	6.42	2.44	1.20	3.15	1.57	4.13
1985/86	40,143	11.4	110,971	17.1	35,288	26,310	6.52	2.36	1.14	3.15	1.53	4.22
1986/87	47,102	17.3	130,523	17.6	41,372	30,736	6.20	2.24	1.14	3.15	1.53	4.25
1987/88	53,954	14.5	152,669	17.0	49,953	—	6.16	2.18	1.08	3.06	—	—
1988/89	62,123	15.1	179,248	17.4	58,311	—	6.36	2.20	1.07	3.07	—	—
1989/90	74,485	19.9	214,292	19.6	69,967	—	5.94	2.08	1.06	3.06	—	—
1990/91	87,406	17.4	249,770	16.6	81,176	—	6.06	2.12	1.08	3.08	—	—

M1 = Narrow Money Supply (average of months) in Rupees Crores
M1g = Annual percentage increase in M1
M3 = Broad Money Supply (average of months) in Rupees Crores
M3g = Annual percentage increase in M3
RM = Reserve Money (average of months)
RMa = Adjusted Reserve Money. The "adjustment" allows for variations in the cash reserve ratio. See section in chapter 10 entitled "Stability of Money Multiplier."
V1 = Velocity of circulation of M1. Defined as GDP at current market prices divided by M1
V3 = Velocity of circulation of M3. Defined as GDP at current market prices divided by M3
m1 = Money Multiplier (narrow money). Defined as M1 divided by RM
m3 = Money Multiplier (broad money). Defined as M3 divided by RM
m1a = Adjusted m1. Defined as M1 divided by RMa
m3a = Adjusted m3. Defined as M3 divided by RMa.

Source: M1, M3, and RM figures come from Singh, Shetty, and Venkatachalam (1982) and Reserve Bank of India (various years), *Report on Currency and Finance*. The above series incorporate the corrections made by Singh, Shetty, and Venkatachalam to take account of certain problems of coverge, definition, and classification. See appendix 1 of Singh, Shetty, and Venkatachalam (1982). The GDP figures for the velocity calculations are from Government of India, CSO (1989a). RMa figures come from Rangarajan and Singh (1984), extended with data provided to the authors by the Reserve Bank of India.

Table 10.2 Monetary Indicators, Period Averages

Period	M1g	M3g	WPIg	V1	V3
1960/61 to 1964/65	7.5	7.7	5.3	6.39	4.22
1965/66 to 1969/70	8.3	10.9	7.2	7.42	4.51
1970/71 to 1974/75	12.6	15.5	13.3	7.21	3.90
1975/76 to 1979/80	14.1	18.6	4.7	7.07	3.15
1980/81 to 1984/85	14.3	16.7	9.4	6.63	2.60
1985/86 to 1989/90	15.7	17.7	6.6	6.24	2.21

M1g = Average annual percentage growth of narrow money
M3g = Average annual percentage growth of broad money
WPIg = Average annual wholesale price inflation
V1 = Velocity of M1
V3 = Velocity of M3
  Source: M1g, M3g, V1, and V3 from table 10.1. WPIg from Government of India, Ministry of Finance (various years), *Economic Survey*.

The range of monetary policy instruments in India is wide, embracing both direct (quantity) and indirect (price) approaches. The main direct instruments are reserve ratios, quantitative controls on Reserve Bank lending to banks and the commercial sector ("refinance"), and quantitative credit controls.[1] The indirect instruments operate through the administrative setting of various interest rates, for example on Reserve Bank lending, commercial bank lending, and deposits. While all these instruments have been available since 1960, the emphasis has varied. In the 1960s the emphasis was on indirect measures and there was hardly any variation in reserve ratios. In the 1970s the emphasis shifted to direct approaches, and this has persisted since then. Among the direct instruments the importance of variation in reserve ratios has increased considerably compared with variation in Reserve Bank refinance to the commercial sector and quantitative credit controls.

From the viewpoint of monetary control, the shift away from indirect to direct approaches in the early 1970s was a sensible move, given the rapid increase in fiscal deficits and the presence of various inflationary pressures. Administratively determined interest rates had too many conflicting objectives and were too inflexible to be used for macroeconomic control. This shift to a quantity approach did not initially involve adherence to a money-multiplier theory. The Reserve Bank tended to take an "accounting" view of money supply determination and thought in terms of controlling "net bank credit to government" and "bank credit to the commercial sector" without distinguishing clearly between Reserve Bank credit, which is a component of high-powered money, and commercial bank credit, which is not.[2] There was, consequently, a tendency to give as much importance to credit controls on banks as to reserve ratios. It was not surprising (given the cash-credit system and the ability of banks to mobilize nondeposit resources) that credit ceilings were overshot and reserve ratios were undershot. This confusion was gradually dispelled and by the beginning of the 1980s the Reserve Bank moved more definitely to a money-multiplier approach. As a result, penalties on nonobservance of the reserve ratios became very tough and quantitative credit controls became less important in practice, though they still remained in operation on paper. Again, this evolution of policy seems perfectly sensible.

It should be noted that all the monetary instruments in India, both direct and indirect, operate through administrative controls or fiat. The question has been raised in recent years whether the country should not move to a more market-oriented system, particularly as regards the financing of the budget. Interest rates would then be determined by the market, and open-market operations could become a genuine instrument of policy. This issue is discussed further below.

Monetary Policy and Macroeconomic Crises

In assessing the performance of monetary policy with respect to stabilization, we first consider crisis episodes and then some broader issues.

The first three crises were primarily caused by exogenous real shocks. But monetary policy played a contributory role. In each crisis, and particularly in the second and third crises, the exogenous shocks impinged on an excessively liquid economy. The crises were preceded by an acceleration of monetary growth. This can be attributed to fiscal deficits or to balance of payments surpluses (as in the prelude to the crisis of 1979–81). Early offsetting action by the Reserve Bank could have moderated monetary expansion.

Several related points are suggested by the evidence. There has been some tendency for excessive monetary growth following a good agricultural year and, *a fortiori*, following two or more good years, for example at the end of the 1960s and again from 1975–78.[3] The "inside lag" of monetary policy seems to have been quite large in reacting to inflationary pressures. This was evident in the second crisis when there was little or no monetary restriction until the middle of 1973 though inflation was well under way. Again, in the third crisis there was little restriction until the middle of 1979. Prices were stable until the end of 1978, but the inflationary potential of the monetary build up in the previous three years should have been recognized and acted upon. Lack of timely information has been a problem. In the second crisis the Reserve Bank was clearly acting on grossly overoptimistic estimates of agricultural output. Before the second and the third crises underestimation of government borrowing from the Reserve Bank or of balance of payments surpluses played a part in the Reserve Bank overshooting its own internal money supply targets. Another problem with money supply control was the ability of commercial banks to avoid the Reserve Bank's measures either by defaulting on reserve requirements or by exploiting loopholes in the definitions of deposits or credit. This was partly because until the end of the 1970s the Reserve Bank's analytical framework was confused. Too much reliance was placed on moral suasion to achieve quantitative credit targets, and on interest rates to restrict the demand for credit. It was not realized that these measures were unlikely to work in the context of strong reserve-money growth.[4]

Once the crises became evident and the procrastination was over, monetary policy became either nonaccommodating (as in the first and third crises) or actively contractionary (as in the second crisis). This response needs some explanation since in all three cases the main inflationary shock was a drought. The rationale for macroeconomic restriction has already been discussed in chapter 8 so we can be brief concerning the monetary aspect. It could be argued that if food output falls no special steps are needed to contract domestic credit. This is because maintaining consumption by running down food stocks or foreign exchange reserves would reduce undesired money balances and moderate the price increase. Some increase in prices and involuntary increase in velocity is unavoidable but would cease as output recovered. However, this argument hinges on the reserves position being comfortable and on previous monetary growth having been moderate. If these conditions are not met, there is a strong argument for nonaccommodation or even contraction to prevent an inflationary spiral. These arguments for tight money apply *a fortiori* if, in addition to a drought, there is a permanent negative shock such as a rise in the price of imported oil.

One or more of the above conditions favorable to monetary ease were not met in the three crises. Governments were therefore concerned to curb speculation, damp down organized sector wage demands, and prevent inflation expectations from taking a firm hold.[5] It seems likely also that they were buying credibility for dealing with future crises (in modern jargon they were acting in a "dynamically consistent" fashion), even at the cost of exacerbating an industrial recession. This interpretation would not make sense if the actions of the authorities were guided by purely electoral considerations, but we do not think that was the case.

An overall assessment of Indian monetary policy in the context of crises must surely be positive. There were lags in the implementation of policy and various loopholes diluting its effectiveness, but these problems are not unknown in other countries. Indian governments have on the whole been guided by the sensible idea that control of money matters for control of inflation. But they can be criticized for an element of stop and go in the implementation of policies that were inspired by this idea.

Monetary Policy and Stabilization

We now turn to an assessment of monetary policy in relation to stabilization over the period as a whole, keeping in mind the previous discussion about crises. Since monetary policy has operated mainly through direct (quantity) measures, its effectiveness clearly depends on favorable answers to the following three questions. First, is the demand for money stable? Second, is the money multiplier stable? And third, is reserve money controllable?

Stability of Money Demand

Even if the money supply could be controlled in line with the wishes of the authorities, it would not be a suitable intermediate target if the demand for money were highly unstable. The simple quantity theory of money hypothesizes a constant velocity of circulation. This is of course a very special assumption implying both a unit income-elasticity and a zero interest-elasticity of demand for money. In India the velocity of circulation of M1 has been virtually trendless while the velocity of M3 has shown a marked downward trend. However, both velocities show a good deal of year-to-year variation in relation to trend.[6] Prima facie this argues against the use of monetary policy as a reliable short-run instrument.

Constant velocity of money is a stronger condition than is required for the successful application of monetary policy. But it is generally considered necessary to have at least a stable demand function for money. Evidence from India is encouraging in this respect. There have been a number of studies showing stable demand both for aggregate money and for the components of money.[7] Typically, these studies relate the real demand for money to real income, interest rates, and expected inflation in a multiple linear regression. A rough summary of the results follows.

- The income elasticity of demand for M1 is about 0.4 in the short run and 1.01 in the long run, that of M3 is about 0.7 in the short run and 1.9 in the long run if estimated over the whole period. The income elasticities of deposits (particularly time deposits) are considerably higher than the income elasticity of demand for currency; the latter is somewhat less than 1.0 even in the long run.
- The reason for the high-income elasticity of demand for broad money is probably the increase in monetization of the economy and the spread of the banking habit, which has increased financial savings. It is also interesting to examine the demand for money estimated over the subperiods 1960/61 to 1970/71 and 1970/71 onward. The latter period shows considerably higher income elasticity for both M1 and M3 than in the earlier period. This is not surprising in view of the fact that there was a rapid spread of banking in the latter period, which begins with the nationalization of banking.[8]
- The interest rate coefficient has the right sign in the demand for money equation but it is not statistically significant. This is not surprising in view of the fact that the interest rate has been administered and infrequently varied. Some studies of the demand functions for the components of money have found statistically significant results for the interest rate variable with a negative relationship between the interest rate on time deposits and both currency and demand deposits; and a positive relationship of time deposits to their own rate of interest.
- Current inflation as a proxy for expected inflation is significantly negatively related to the demand for money.

There are major methodological difficulties in inferring a stable relationship between money and prices by inverting a demand for money function.[9] We have therefore tested the relationship between money and prices directly (see the appendix to this chapter) and find that it is stable and that it satisfies powerful econometric tests.

The evidence thus suggests that there is a stable demand for money in the long run and a stable long-run relationship between money, production, and prices,[10] and that there is quite a lot of short-run variation in the above relationships, as revealed by high equation standard errors notwithstanding various parameter stability tests being satisfied. Given the above and the problems of information and lags in policy formulation, there is a presumption in favor of monetary targeting and against fine-tuning. However, we would not go so far as to conclude in favor of a Friedmanesque rigid monetary target. In an economy that is subject to identifiable real shocks, policymakers can make sensible judgments regarding the direction of monetary policy changes. This is all the more so if shocks impinge on an economy that has already been destabilized by previous policy errors. The recommendation of a flexible money target (or a "money target with feedback") made by the Chakravarty Committee therefore seems appropriate.[11]

Stability of the Money Multiplier

Monetary control requires that reserve money should be controllable and that there should be a stable relationship between reserve money and the money stock. In this section we consider the latter issue. A conceptual point is worth making here. Conventionally, changes in the cash reserve ratio are regarded as affecting the money multiplier. But in measuring the stability of the money multiplier, it is clearly useful to separate changes in the multiplier that are deliberately brought about by changes in policy from changes that occur due to other factors. Some studies of the multiplier therefore adjust reserve money for changes in the cash reserve ratio. (For example, an increase in bank reserves brought about by an increase in the cash reserve ratio would be subtracted from reserve money.)

With reserve money adjusted in this way, a money supply equation can be estimated relating the money stock to reserve money. In India such a formulation has yielded a stable function for M1 and M3.[12] What this implies is that the relationship between reserve money and reserve ratios on the one hand, and the money stock on the other hand, is not rendered unstable by changes in the public's preference for currency or changes in banks' holdings of cash brought about by nonpolicy factors (for example, changes in the demand for credit). Of course, there is a certain amount of noise in the relationship but the above results explain why the Reserve Bank is able to control monetary growth by aggressive use of the cash reserve ratio. In contrast, controlling the exogenous elements of reserve money is beset by serious difficulties.

Controllability of Reserve Money

It is in this area that many of the problems of monetary policy lie. The growth of reserve money arises from (a) increased Reserve Bank lending to the government, (b) increased Reserve Bank lending to commercial banks and the commercial sector generally, and (c) growth of net foreign exchange assets of the Reserve Bank (that is balance of payments surpluses). The Reserve Bank has direct control only over component (b) but it can offset the effects of (a) and (c) on reserve money (that is, it can change "adjusted reserve money") by altering reserve ratios.

The main component of reserve money growth has been government borrowing from the Reserve Bank, which is associated with fiscal deficits that are not met by borrowing from commercial bank and nonbank sources (see table 10.3). The Reserve Bank has no control over this component other than by upward revisions in the statutory liquidity ratio (SLR), which prescribes banks' investment in government securities. Of course, it can advise and warn the government, and in recent years a convention has evolved of a continuous dialogue between the two institutions as to the manner in which the fiscal deficit is to be financed. Reserve money changes arising out of balance of payments surpluses and deficits are of course outside the control of the Reserve Bank.

Table 10.3   Changes in Components of Reserve Money as a Percentage of Changes in Reserve Money, 1960/61 to 1989/90

Period	Δ RBICG	Δ RBICC	Δ NFA	Δ GCL	Δ NMLL	Δ RM
1960/61 to 1964/65	94.6	20.5	–12.2	9.4	12.3	100.0
1965/66 to 1969/70	63.9	17.4	33.7	6.2	20.5	100.0
1970/71 to 1974/75	102.4	32.5	–6.3	5.6	34.6	100.0
1975/76 to 1979/80	54.7	13.3	56.2	0.7	24.9	100.0
1980/81 to 1984/85	121.5	18.6	–16.3	1.2	25.0	100.0
1985/86 to 1989/90	105.5	13.6	7.6	2.0	28.7	100.0

RBICG = RBI credit to government
RBICC = RBI credit to commercial sector, including commercial banks
NFA = RBI's net foreign exchange assets
GCL = Government currency liabilities to the public
NMLL = Net nonmonetary liabilities of RBI
RM = Reserve money
   Definitionally, Δ RM = Δ RBICG + Δ RBICC + Δ NFA + Δ GCL − Δ NMLL
   Source: Reserve Bank of India (various years), *Report on Currency and Finance*.

Thus, the only way to counter the expansion of reserve money arising from the above components is by offsetting changes in Reserve Bank lending to the commercial sector or by changes in the cash reserve ratio (CRR). Changes in Reserve Bank lending to the commercial sector can be brought about either by varying the price of refinance (which was the technique favored in the 1960s) or, more reliably, by combining it with discretionary changes. This technique did acquire some importance in the late 1970s in reaction to the years 1973–76 when Reserve Bank lending to the commercial sector constituted an important component of growth in reserve money. More recently, however, after several years of high fiscal deficits, the importance of this component of reserve money has declined sharply; moreover, Reserve Bank lending has become increasingly concentrated on the activities of banks in "priority" sectors such as food procurement and exports, which cannot be easily varied. For both these reasons, variations in Reserve Bank lending to the commercial sector have lost much of their effectiveness as a macroeconomic policy instrument.

The upshot of this is that the principal instruments in the hands of the Reserve Bank are the two reserve ratios CRR and SLR. Of these the former affects "adjusted" reserve money directly by immobilizing banks' cash holdings, while the latter affects reserve money indirectly by reducing the monetization of fiscal deficits. These have both been powerful and reliable instruments and they have been frequently used to insulate the growth of the total money stock from the influence of growing fiscal deficits. (Note, however, that while these instruments are powerful, they are also blunt and can dislocate money markets, as was threatened for example in the credit famine of 1982.). Even so, the Reserve Bank has at times been unwilling to stick to rigid targets for money growth in the face of rapid increases in reserve money because of the fear of crowding out credit to the private sector and causing a recession. (This was a relevant consideration in 1976–78 for example, though in this instance reserve money growth was largely due to balance of payments surpluses.)

Monetary control has been reasonably successful in spite of rising fiscal deficits because of the aggressive use of the reserve ratios. But in the last few years such changes have been almost entirely unidirectional (upward). So, in a sense, reserve ratios have not been genuine monetary policy instruments but fiscal policy instruments raising resources for the government. There are serious potential difficulties as the reserve ratios approach their legal limits. (In fact, the CRR is now at its legal limit of 15 percent and the SLR is 38.5 percent against a legal limit of 40 percent.) The law could be amended but that does not answer the deeper problem. The era of cheap government borrowing and controlled lending rates for priority sectors has reduced bank profitability to dangerously low levels. If interest rates on bank reserves and on government borrowing continue to be kept below market rates, the maintenance of bank viability would require a rise in interest rates on "nonpriority" commercial lending or a fall in deposit rates, a recipe for both increased financial repression and for crowding out.

Monetary Policy and Long-Run Inflation

India has been a low-inflation country and a large part of the credit must go to her conservative monetary and fiscal policies. (The political economy of low inflation has been discussed in chapters 1 and 3. There has been a dilution of fiscal conservatism in recent years, but fiscal deficits have not so far spilled over into excessive money creation or significantly eroded the commitment to low inflation.) There have been various exogenous shocks (principally droughts and terms of trade declines) that have led to inflationary bubbles, but these have always collapsed fairly quickly. In other words, shocks have made inflation more volatile without affecting the low long-run trend. Inflationary expectations have never been able to take a firm hold because of the low coverage of indexation and the nonaccommodating stance of policy.

Our views on this matter derive not only from the detailed examination of macroeconomic crises in earlier chapters, but from the econometric model of inflation in the appendix to this chapter. The model is supportive of two conclusions. First, while inflation is affected by exogenous shocks such as changes in food production, nonfood agricultural production (as a proxy for exogenous changes in costs of domestically produced raw materials), and import prices, it also clearly responds to monetary and fiscal policies. Second, the authorities are quick to react to changes in the rate of inflation.

Monetary Policy and Growth

Three questions suggest themselves. The first question is whether monetary tightening during crises has affected long-term growth adversely. No such connection can be discerned. A relationship has been alleged between public investment cutbacks and long-term growth, but public investment is not sensitive to monetary policy. Private investment, which *is* sensitive to monetary policy, has been far less volatile than public investment (see chapter 13). The second question is whether greater monetary ease (and therefore higher inflation) over the whole period would have increased the rate of growth by permitting higher public investment (financed by the inflation tax) or higher private investment (less crowding out). The inflation tax is a highly uncertain method of increasing growth. In India, given the trade and payments regime, such a strategy would have rapidly foundered against a balance of payments constraint. In any case, it would have been socially and politically unacceptable and was rightly eschewed. As for private investment, we find little evidence for crowding out except perhaps in the 1980s when growth of output was in any case unsustainably high. The third question is whether the philosophy and overall framework of monetary policy affects the long-term rate of growth adversely. A priori considerations would certainly suggest such a relationship. India's monetary system is characterized by high cash reserve ratios with below-market interest rates on bank reserves, by forced government borrowing from commercial banks at low interest rates, by controlled interest rates on bank deposits and loans, and by low interest rates on lending to favored activities. In this setting one should expect slow growth of private financial savings and inefficient investment. The consequence would be a reduction in long-term growth.

Many studies have confirmed the inefficient nature of Indian investment (see chapter 13), but private savings in India have actually grown fast. We attribute this to the fact that inflation was low. Financial repression was therefore mild and any deleterious effects on savings were offset by the rapid spread of banking (see chapter 12). However, the spread of banking has now slowed down, so financial repression may cause problems in the future. The growth of private savings showed signs of leveling off in the 1980s. Thus, liberalization of the financial system—like liberalization generally—would almost certainly be favorable to long-run growth if the transition could be successfully carried out. We discuss financial liberalization below but only as it pertains to government finance and monetary policy.

Government Finance, Financial Liberalization, and Monetary Policy

In recent years the framework of monetary policy in India has come under criticism and there has been growing support for a move away from directed credit and administered interest rates, including interest rates on government borrowing. It has also been felt that the present relationship between the government and the Reserve Bank creates a bias in favor of excessive monetary expansion. The Chakravarty Committee suggested moving toward a system in which the government would meet its financing needs from the market at market-related interest rates rather than from the Reserve Bank.[13] In the committee's view this would improve monetary control and reduce monetary expansion without crowding out the private sector.

This argument needs qualification. Consider first the long-run equilibrium after liberalization, setting aside the problems of transition. Ignoring foreign borrowing, any given fiscal deficit has to be financed by printing money or by domestic borrowing. This choice cannot be avoided by forcing the government to borrow from the market in the first instance. A decision would still have to be made on whether to avoid a rise in interest rates (that is, to print money by the back door through Reserve Bank lending to commercial banks rather than to the government) or to adhere to a monetary target thereby allowing interest rates to rise. This decision would have to be made either by an independent central bank or, as in India, by the government itself.

But liberalization also involves a transition from the present system to a new system where government paper is *voluntarily* held. If money supply growth is to be held constant, any given primary fiscal deficit then implies a larger gross fiscal deficit (since the interest cost of government borrowing would rise) and therefore some extra government borrowing and crowding out compared with the present equilibrium.[14] It is probably too much to hope that forcing the government to compete in the market for funds and the ensuing transparency of the true cost of borrowing would itself cause the government to reduce its primary fiscal deficit, choose projects more carefully, and take steps to improve the efficiency of public sector enterprises. In other words, financial liberalization cannot itself solve the problem of growing fiscal deficits, and if deficits are not contained then financial liberalization may well exacerbate the fiscal problem. The conclusion, however, is not that financial liberalization is undesirable but that fiscal deficits have to be reduced to make it possible.

There is no painless road to financial liberalization.[15] But if it is successfully completed, there would be benefits for monetary policy, quite apart from efficiency benefits. The development of a treasury bill and bond market would make open-market operations a genuine instrument of policy.[16]

Overall Assessment

- Indian monetary policy has, on the whole, been conservative. The authorities have been quick to impose monetary restriction whenever inflation has threatened to get out of hand.[17] Similar remarks apply to fiscal policy (but with substantial qualifications for recent years). As a result, the trend rate of inflation has remained fairly low in spite of various exogenous shocks.
- Monetary growth has been higher in the 1970s and 1980s compared with the 1960s, and this is reflected in somewhat higher inflation. But it is notable that though fiscal deficits have more than doubled as a proportion of GDP since the mid-1970s, money supply growth has not shown a large increase (see table 10.2). This is a testimony to the efficacy of monetary policy instruments.
- The instruments of policy have been impressive in their range but they have all operated in a command-control manner rather than through the market. The cash reserve ratio has been the principal instrument of control. Consequently, monetary policy has tended to be rather blunt and jerky.
- The long-run stability of money demand and of the "adjusted" money multiplier, combined with significant short-run variability in these relationships, and the presence of information and implementation lags, leads to a presumption in favor of money targeting (though not of a completely rigid variety). From this perspective, Indian policy has been overactive. (This is of course compatible with maintaining that aggressive moves to prevent accelerating inflation were entirely appropriate.)

- The government has been able to capture private savings by forcing the banks to acquire government securities at low interest rates. This increased monetary control in the short run, but in the long run it has probably contributed to complacency about fiscal deficits and thus complicated the operation of monetary policy.
- Financial liberalization would be good for efficiency and growth but only if the transition can be made smoothly. This requires fiscal deficits to be curbed. Liberalization itself cannot help in that respect except by making the effects of fiscal deficits more transparent. In the short run liberalization would raise the cost of government borrowing and thus tend to increase fiscal deficits. Fiscal consolidation is, therefore, a precondition for successful financial liberalization.

Appendix: A Model of Inflation

Indian inflation is explained using a four-equation model that distinguishes between movements in food prices (and all other prices), and that includes government reaction functions on the money supply and the consolidated government fiscal deficit. These equations are of the form

(10-1) $P_F = f_1(\text{M, GFD, FPROD})$

(10-2) $M = f_2(P_F)$

(10-3) $\text{GFD} = f_3(P_F)$

(10-4) $P_{NF} = f_4(P_Z, \text{M, GFD, NFPROD})$

where P_F denotes food prices, M denotes the money supply (taken to be either narrow money, M1, or broad money, M3, in the equations reported below), GFD is the consolidated government fiscal deficit as a proportion of GDP at current market prices, FPROD denotes food production, P_{NF} denotes nonfood prices, P_Z denotes import prices, and NFPROD denotes nonfood agricultural production.

All equations are dynamic and include lagged values of the regressors in initial estimation, following the "general → specific" modeling methodology associated with Hendry (see, for example, Hendry 1986). The form of the unknown dynamic responses is determined by the data. All the equations are estimated in logarithmic form with annual data.

Food Prices

A number of models of food prices are presented in table 10.4. All equations have food price inflation (or, strictly, the change in the logarithm, which is a close approximation) as the dependent variable. Initial general models that did not impose a unit coefficient on the lagged value of P_F (when the dependent variable was simply the level of food prices) yielded the result that the estimated coefficient was, indeed, not significantly different from unity. In all subsequent equations, this restriction was imposed.

Model *(i)* in table 10.4 suggests that increases in M1 increase the price of food with a lag, and that food production has a negative (lagged) effect on food prices. All the regressors are signed as we would expect a priori and are statistically significant. There is no evidence of autocorrelation, or of non-normal residuals. Given this fact, it is valid to condition on lagged values of variables, and hence estimation is through ordinary least squares—*t*-statistics are presented in paren-

Table 10.4   Food Price Models

| Regressor | Dependent variable: ΔP_F | | | |
	(i)	*(ii)*	*(iii)*	*(iv)*
$\Delta M1_{t-1}$	1.29		1.27	
	(2.81)		(3.03)	
$\Delta M3_{t-1}$		1.09		1.31
		(2.29)		(3.14)
$FPROD_{t-1}$	–0.20	–0.20	–0.27	–0.31
	(2.70)	(2.40)	(3.67)	(3.87)
GFD_{t-1}			0.11	0.14
			(2.42)	(3.03)
Constant	0.88	0.87	1.00	1.13
	(2.76)	(2.49)	(3.40)	(3.61)
Time period	1962/63– 1988/89	1962/63– 1988/89	1962/63– 1988/89	1962/63– 1988/89
DW	2.03	1.71	2.28	2.07
Normality $\chi^1(2)$	0.96	1.09	0.39	0.60
Chow	0.45	0.40	0.65	0.15
Percent s.e.	6.53	6.81	5.95	5.88
Heteroscedasticity	0.98	0.79	0.77	0.74

Source: Authors' calculations.

theses. There is also no evidence of heteroscedasticity as judged by the standard White test (distributed as an F-test).

The Chow test reported shows the effect of excluding the last four observations from the sample to check for parameter constancy. This is distributed as an F-test and indicates that there is no evidence that the parameter values are changing over time.

The same basic equation was estimated using M3 rather than M1 as the monetary aggregate in model *(ii)*. The only major (but predictable) difference is that the coefficient on the monetary variable has fallen in model *(ii)*, reflecting the fact that it is a larger aggregate in absolute terms than M1. Otherwise, all the previous comments apply.

In models *(iii)* and *(iv)* a measure of fiscal demand is also included in the equations, in addition to the monetary variables. The variable GFD measures the fiscal deficit as a proportion of GDP, and would be expected, a priori, to enter with a positive sign. As can be seen, this variable adds significantly to the explanatory power of the model, reducing the standard error of the equations by 9 and 14 percent respectively. There is no multicollinearity problem encountered by including both a fiscal and a monetary measure: the correlation between GFD_{t-1} and ΔM1_{t-1} is only 0.34 and the correlation between GFD_{t-1} and ΔM3_{t-1} is even lower, at 0.25.

An alternative measure of food production was also tried. When total agricultural production was substituted for food production the results were very similar. For example, in the equivalent of model *(i)*, (lagged) agricultural production entered with an estimated coefficient of -0.21 (*t*-statistic 2.16). All the other estimated coefficients were very similar and, hence, are not reported here. Similarly, rather than using food prices, it is possible to run the models with the more general definition of agricultural prices. Again the results are very similar. For example, the equivalent model to model *(i)* was estimated as

$$\Delta Pag_t = 0.79 + 1.07\ \Delta\text{M1}_{t-1} - 0.18\ \text{APROD}_{t-1}$$
$$(2.26)\ (2.26) \qquad\quad (2.17)$$

where *Pag* denotes agricultural prices and APROD denotes agricultural production.

Money Supply and Fiscal Deficit Reaction Functions

The model for the money supply reaction function that was suggested by the data was a simple partial adjustment model as reported in models *(i)* and *(ii)* in table 10.5. Since the series for the monetary aggregates were individually highly autoregressive in nature, they were transformed into first differences that approximate the percentage growth rates in M1 and M3.

While the reaction functions for M1 and M3 produce rather similar parameter estimates, the model for M3 performs better on most criteria. The equation standard error is only 1.77 percent—compared with 2.65 percent for model *(i)*—and there is some evidence of autocorrelated residuals in equation *(i)*, although the

Table 10.5   Reaction Functions for Money Supply and Fiscal Deficit

Dependent variables: $\Delta M1$, $\Delta M3$, and ΔGFD respectively in equations (i), (ii), and (iii)

Regressor	(i)	(ii)	(iii)
$\Delta M1_{t-1}$	0.53		
	(3.72)		
$\Delta M3_{t-1}$		0.64	
		(7.36)	
$\Delta P_{F_{t-1}}$	−0.17	−0.17	
	(2.45)	(3.71)	
ΔP_F			−0.73
			(2.06)
Constant	0.06	0.07	0.09
	(3.72)	(5.27)	(2.25)
Time period	1962/63–1987/88	1962/63–1987/88	1962/63–1987/88
Autocorrelation	4.05	1.51	0.70
Normality χ^2	1.87	0.92	2.04
Chow	2.32	0.09	0.78
Percent s.e.	2.65	1.77	1.34
Heteroscedasticity	1.19	0.63	0.41

Source: Authors' calculations.

critical value for this $F(1,22)$ test is 4.3, indicating that we still just accept the null of no autocorrelation (this test is valid in the presence of a lagged dependent variable, unlike the Durbin-Watson test). The money supply reaction functions suggest that a 1 percent rise in food price inflation reduces money supply growth by 0.19 and 0.17 percent in the short run, rising to between 0.36 and 0.47 percent in the long run, for equations *(i)* and *(ii)* respectively.

Equation *(iii)* is also well determined and clearly suggests the negative reaction of the fiscal deficit (as a proportion of GDP) to higher food price inflation. Again, there is no sign of autocorrelation, non-normality, or heteroscedasticity, and the model comfortably passes the Chow test for parameter stability.

Nonfood Prices

Nonfood prices, which include manufactured goods, are assumed to be a function of import prices, nonfood agricultural production, money supply, and the fiscal deficit (as a proportion of GDP). All equations have nonfood price inflation as the dependent variable.

In table 10.6 a variety of models is presented. Import prices and the money supply (both M1 and M3) have a positive relationship with nonfood prices, as would be expected, and the term for nonfood agricultural production (which is defined as the average of current and one-year lagged production) enters negatively. Attempts to include money wages as an explanatory variable were not successful—the coefficient on the money wages was statistically insignificant.

The models including M1 as an explanatory variable, for example models *(i)* and *(iii)*, appear to fit slightly better than those including M3, as shown by the equation standard errors. However, there is somewhat less evidence of first-order autocorrelation in the M3 equations (although none of the models would actually

Table 10.6 Nonfood Price Models

| Regressor | Dependent variable: ΔP_{NF} | | | |
	(i)	*(ii)*	*(iii)*	*(iv)*
$\Delta M1_{t-1}$	1.05		0.84	
	(2.91)		(2.36)	
$\Delta M3_{t-1}$		0.83		0.64
		(2.27)		(1.84)
ΔP_Z	0.15	0.17	0.19	0.21
	(2.52)	(2.85)	(3.20)	(3.59)
NFPROD	−0.16	−0.15	−0.15	−0.14
	(2.50)	(2.05)	(2.46)	(2.06)
ΔGFD_{t-1}			0.12	0.13
			(2.04)	(2.21)
Constant	0.72	0.66	0.68	0.63
	(2.56)	(2.12)	(2.58)	(2.20)
Time period	1962/63– 1988/89	1962/63– 1988/89	1962/63– 1988/89	1962/63– 1988/89
Autocorrelation	2.55	2.14	2.56	2.19
Normality χ^2	0.54	1.38	0.65	0.55
Chow	0.30	0.01	0.78	0.14
Percent s.e.	4.06	4.30	3.81	3.97
Heteroscedasticity	1.26	1.95	0.74	1.27

Source: Authors' calculations.

fail this test). Again, there is no evidence of non-normal residuals or parameter nonconstancy over time.

As in the food price models, a fiscal demand indicator was also included in models *(iii)* and *(iv)*. It appears to add to the explanatory power of the model. The data suggest that it should appear in lagged form.

Rather similar results were obtained when nonagricultural prices were used as the dependent variable instead of nonfood prices. For example, the equivalent of equation *(i)* is

$$\Delta Pnag_t = 0.80 + 0.14\ \Delta P_{Zt} + 1.25\ \Delta M1_{t-1} - 0.18\ \text{NFPROD}$$
$$\quad\ \ (2.85)\ (2.28) \qquad (3.45) \qquad\qquad (2.83)$$

where *Pnag* denotes nonagricultural prices.

Overall Inflation

A prediction of the overall inflation rate can be obtained by taking the predictions generated by the food price and nonfood price models. Using the weights for food and nonfood prices in the overall wholesale price index, a series for predicted overall inflation is presented in figure 10.1. The figure uses table 10.4 equation

Figure 10.1
Actual and Fitted Inflation

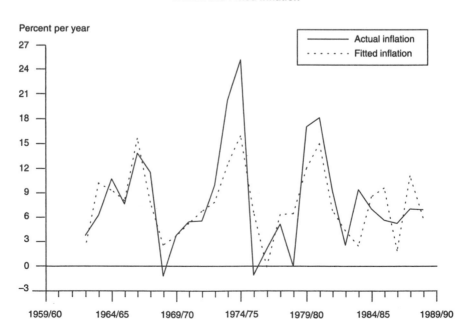

(iii), and table 10.6 equation *(iii)* as the relevant models for prediction. The reaction functions have been omitted in the overall prediction as they are temporally distinct; since money and government borrowing enter into the P_F and P_{NF} equations with a lag, it is best to use their actual values, which are known, rather than the fitted values. In other words the system is not simultaneous but follows a sequential pattern. The overall explanatory power of the model is high over what was a volatile period.

Data Sources for the Inflation Model

M1   Average of months. Table 10.1.

M3   Average of months. Table 10.1.

P_F Index of wholesale prices of "food articles." Base 1970/71 = 100, average of weeks. Government of India, Ministry of Finance, *Economic Survey.*

P_{NF} Index of nonfood prices, namely the index of wholesale prices of all commodities excluding "food articles." Base 1970/71 = 100, average of weeks. Source as for P_F.

FPROD   Base: Triennium ending 1969/70 = 100. Source as for P_F.

NFPROD Base: Triennium ending 1969/70 = 100. Source as for P_F.

GFD   Consolidated government fiscal deficit from Government of India, Ministry of Finance, *Indian Economic Statistics—Public Finance*, divided by GDP at current market prices (National Accounts old series, extended to include recent years).

P_Z Unit Value Index for imports. Base 1978/79 = 100. Source as for P_F.

Chapter Eleven

Trade and Payments Policy

In this chapter we review trade and payments policies over the period as a whole. These policies have significant effects on the efficiency of resource allocation but this aspect has been much studied by others and is here ignored.[1] Our focus is on the macroeconomic aspects of trade and payments policies.

The external objective of macroeconomic policy ("payments balance") can be characterized as the maintenance or achievement of a sustainable current account deficit (consistent with other objectives such as internal balance, low inflation, and high growth). We consider below the policy instruments (and combinations thereof) that are used in pursuing payments balance—aggregate demand management; use of reserves; official foreign borrowing; controls on private capital flows; trade intervention; and exchange rate policy. Of these, the first three are considered only indirectly or by implication. (They have also been examined earlier, in chapters 8 and 9.) The centerpiece of this chapter is an extensive discussion of exchange rate policy. Exchange rate and related data referred to in the chapter are given in table 11.3. In the appendix to the chapter we present our econometric work on export equations.

Some Terminological Preliminaries

We begin by defining terms.[2] The *nominal exchange rate* is the price of domestic currency in terms of foreign currency, that is so many units of foreign currency per unit of domestic currency. (Thus, we follow the British convention not the American convention. The latter defines the nominal exchange rate as so many units of domestic currency per unit of foreign currency. So for us, a fall in the exchange rate means a devaluation of the currency, and a rise means an appreciation.) The *real exchange rate* is not an exchange rate in the ordinary sense but a proxy for the competitiveness of tradable goods and it can be defined in different ways depending on the relative price that is the focus of interest. Two principal definitions have been used in the literature. It can be defined either as an index of the relative price of domestic and foreign tradable goods, or as an index of the relative price of domestic nontradable and tradable goods. The standard proxy for the real exchange rate is an index of relative domestic and foreign consumer prices (or wholesale prices) multiplied by an index of the nominal exchange rate. On reasonable assumptions this is a good measure of the first concept mentioned above, and behaves monotonically with respect to the second concept above. It should be noted that real exchange rates are pure numbers and express only changes relative to some base year.

Another important concept is that of effective exchange rates. In a world in which the nominal exchange rates of many countries are changing frequently, the nominal and the real exchange rate can be defined only against an average of other currencies. The average nominal and real exchange rate are referred to in current usage as the *nominal effective exchange rate* (NER) and the *real effective exchange rate* (RER), respectively. What the weights in these averages should be is a complicated question but in practice the only feasible weighting scheme is to use trade weights (perhaps modified to some extent to allow for third-country competition). In our study we have used a bilateral export-weighted index, the weights being the shares of the ten most important industrial countries in India's exports. This is because we use the RER principally to measure changes in export competitiveness. Note that the RER is a descriptive measure. What the RER should be is a different question. The appropriate (or equilibrium) real effective exchange rate is that RER which is required to produce internal and external balance (along with the accompanying macroeconomic and trade policies).

The RER as a measure of international or domestic competitiveness of tradables is well defined only if the latter can be meaningfully aggregated. Strictly speaking the aggregation requires that the economy should be small and that trade should be free or subject to constant tariffs. If these conditions are not met, it is necessary to look separately at the competitiveness of importables and exportables. As a measure of the latter we have constructed an index of the subsidy adjusted real effective exchange rate (RERsa). RERsa treats an increase in export subsidies (cash assistance, premia on import replenishment licenses, and duty drawbacks) as a devaluation of the RER (see table 11.3). It is almost impossible to allow for the effect on competitiveness of quantitative import restrictions of varying stringency. We do however give some qualitative judgments where relevant.

We now turn to terminology concerning exchange rate policy and regimes. The first point to make is that the real exchange rate is not a policy instrument. Exchange rate policy has to operate through the nominal exchange rate. Here one may distinguish between the *currency of designation*—the currency in which the exchange rate is announced (still sterling in India's case); the *currency of intervention*—the currency which the central bank buys and sells (in India's case, it used to be only sterling but now includes dollars as well); and the *peg-currency*—the currency in relation to which the exchange rate is held fixed (or within a certain range), if it is fixed. An exchange rate can be fixed to a *single-currency peg* or to a *multicurrency peg* (that is, a basket of currencies with fixed weights). In the latter case, it is the NER that is fixed. Fixing the NER would generally require that the nominal exchange rate in terms of the currency of designation should be continuously varied. With a single-currency peg, however, the home currency moves with the peg-currency against all other currencies. Pegging can be of various kinds in terms of timing and the underlying rules. Pegs can be permanent, adjustable (as under Bretton-Woods), or crawling. Under an *adjustable peg* the government retains the right to alter the peg to correct a "fundamental disequilibrium." With a *crawling peg*, the government retains the right to move the peg frequently in small steps either on the basis of a rule ("rule-based crawling") or in a discretionary manner ("discretionary crawling"). At the other end of the spectrum from a fixed exchange rate is a *floating exchange rate*. The float may be free or managed (by government intervention), but in either case the exchange rate is determined by the market.

Overview of Trade and Payments Policies and the Underlying Political Economy

1947–55

When India became independent in August 1947, the prewar exchange rate arrangements continued. The rupee was pegged to the British pound sterling (and formally to gold) at the prewar parity of Rupee 1 = 1sh 6d. When the pound was devalued in 1949 the rupee-sterling parity was kept unchanged. In the first half of the 1950s inflation in India was low (and in some years negative), so the real exchange rate depreciated modestly. "Export pessimism," however, led to high export taxes and neglect of investment and modernization in the export sector; consequently, exports stagnated. Though the wartime machinery for administering import controls was still in place, the import regime was in practice quite liberal. Capital controls were more restrictive than import controls but not particularly fierce.

1956–60

The second Five-Year Plan inaugurated in 1956 was based on an ambitious heavy-industry strategy. This was followed by a severe balance of payments crisis in 1957, to which the authorities responded by reactivating and intensifying import controls. In the next few years India moved to a system of comprehensive import licensing, one of whose crucial features was the "indigenous clearance" hurdle. This gave automatic quota protection to any imports for which there were domestic substitutes. Controls on private capital movements were also strengthened and have remained extremely stringent ever since. Formally, the exchange rate regime was an adjustable peg Bretton-Woods-style regime. But in practice it was operated as a fixed nominal exchange rate buttressed first by reserve losses, then by import and capital controls, and foreign aid. As reserves fell, foreign aid and official foreign borrowing increased substantially from 0.5 percent of GDP in 1956 to 3 percent of GDP in 1960. Inflation in India was faster than inflation abroad so the real exchange rate appreciated substantially and exports stagnated.

1960–65

The nominal exchange rate was fixed to the pound sterling and, given the nature of the Bretton Woods regime, the NER stayed constant. But Indian prices continued to rise faster than foreign prices and the RER appreciated further. The appreciation was modest (about 5 percent) from 1960–63 but sharp in 1964 and 1965 (about 16 percent). Export subsidies were introduced and increased, so from 1960 to 1963 RERsa was roughly unchanged. Over the next two years, however, it appreciated by 13 percent despite increasing export incentives. The import control regime increased in severity to the point where domestic industry was starved of essential inputs. In 1965 war and drought brought about a crisis. Exports grew moderately from 1960 to 1963, stagnated in 1964, and collapsed in 1965.

1966–71

There was a large nominal devaluation (36.5 percent) in June 1966 (undertaken under foreign pressure) combined with some import delicensing and reductions in tariffs and export subsidies. In fact, export taxes were introduced. On the export side, Bhagwati and Srinivasan (1975) estimate the incentive-adjusted nominal devaluation as 17.8 percent. But this was a period of high inflation. We estimate that RERsa was devalued by only 7 percent. The true incentive to export probably went up somewhat more as a result of import delicensing, but any favorable effects on exports were swamped by the drought. Export volume fell from 1965 to 1967. The devaluation was popularly judged to be a complete failure.

After the maxidevaluation of 1966 the nominal exchange rate was kept constant until 1971 when the U.S. dollar was no longer tied to gold. Export taxes were abolished and subsidies reintroduced so RERsa depreciated by about 8 percent from 1967 to 1971. But at the same time the import liberalization was aborted and there was a return to a regime of tight import control. So some of the measured increase in export incentives was offset.[3] As might be expected, there was only a modest increase in exports (apart from the bumper agricultural year 1968/69).

Thus, during the period 1947–71 as a whole, India was on an adjustable peg that was operated like a fixed nominal exchange rate (except for the devaluation of 1966). As we shall see, the wisdom of this policy is open to question. But it is not surprising that for some years after independence India did what other countries were doing under Bretton-Woods arrangements. The move to controls in reaction to the crisis of 1957 also fitted in with the antimarket bias of Indian planning and the belief in the rationality of selective state intervention. Moreover, "export pessimism" was then a widely held belief that also had academic respectability, certainly in the 1950s. In fact, "export optimism" would have been rather unusual at the time. But policymakers were slow in drawing the right lessons in the 1960s, a decade when the exports of East Asian economies grew extremely fast. Unfortunately, the devaluation of 1966 did not help. It was unpopular ex ante because of prevalent antimarket attitudes and also because it was clearly undertaken under foreign pressure. It was also unpopular ex post because its favorable effects were swamped by other adverse factors. The belief that donors had reneged on their promise of aid also increased the feeling against devaluation. All this made a deep impression on Mrs. Gandhi and devaluation was a taboo subject for many years. Exchange rate depreciation, when it occurred in the 1970s, had to be stealthy.

1972–74

In August 1971 when the U.S. dollar went off gold, the rupee was pegged to the dollar with a minor change of parity, but this lasted only a few months and there was a switch back to a sterling peg in December 1971. The reversal had some symbolic political value, given the bad state of relations between the United States and India during the war with Pakistan at the end of 1971. More importantly, some bureaucrats perceived the importance of the exchange rate for export competitiveness and thought it prudent to peg the rupee to what was expected to be a weak currency.

The first oil crisis came in 1973 and there were severe droughts in 1972 and 1974, leading to high inflation. But the sterling peg led not only to a nominal effective devaluation, but also to a real effective devaluation. From 1972 through September 1975 the nominal effective and real effective depreciations were about 20 and 10 percent, respectively. (This is not fully revealed by table 11.3, which gives only annual data.) Import controls were tightened in response to the oil crisis but export incentives were also increasing, so the depreciation of the RER represented a genuine improvement in export competitiveness. The behavior of the RER helped exports to grow quite rapidly in spite of the high domestic inflation.

1975–79

In September 1975 the peg was altered from the pound sterling to a basket of currencies with undisclosed weights, though sterling continued to be the currency of designation and intervention. There were two reasons for this change. The first was to reduce the volatility of the nominal effective rate resulting from the generalized floating of major currencies. The second was to arrest the depreciation of the rupee in line with sterling. It was felt that sterling would continue to depreciate and might even collapse. By this time inflation in India had been brought down to zero. A link with a weak currency had, therefore, outlived its usefulness. For two years from September 1975 the NER was kept constant (this involved an appreciation against sterling), but was, however, allowed to fall in 1978 and 1979 because the dollar was weak at the time. Keeping the NER stable would have involved "too large" an appreciation against the dollar. (The width of the band around the peg was increased in January 1979 to accommodate this change.)

Since inflation in India was low in this period, the RER fell about 17 percent and RERsa fell about 21 percent since export subsidies continued to increase. These changes reflected genuine improvements in export competitiveness because the import control regime also underwent a change from 1975. The improvement in the foreign exchange position in 1975 (due to growth of exports and remittances) was followed by some liberalization of imports. The liberalization was extremely cautious and gradual and affected only noncompetitive imports and imported inputs for export production. Nevertheless, the change was important because from then on there has not been a major tightening of import controls even in the face of balance of payments difficulties (until the emergency measures of 1990/91). Thus, after a long lag, and very gradually, Indian policy began to be influenced by real world evidence and the results of academic work of the 1960s regarding the inefficiency of inward-looking trade policies.

From 1975 to 1979 there was an export boom. This was mainly the result of the above developments though a buoyant world economy also helped.

1980–82

Significantly, after the second oil price increase, import controls were not tightened. But there was no exchange rate depreciation either. The NER was kept fixed (indeed there was a small appreciation) and current account deficits were financed partly by running down reserves and partly by increased foreign borrowing. Fear of adding to inflation was probably a reason for the reversion to nominal exchange rate rigidity but political factors were equally important. Mrs. Gandhi was back in power and perhaps the then governor of the RBI, who had been appointed by the erstwhile Janata government was anxious not to rock the boat. Inflation in India was high and the RER appreciated about 12 percent and RERsa about 10 percent. Overall exports in real terms slowed down sharply and the volume of exports to convertible currency areas fell.

1983–85

During this period the attitude to nominal exchange rate management changed quite markedly in the direction of flexibility. The RER began to be watched as an indicator for exchange rate policy. The nominal effective exchange rate was managed in such a way as to keep the RER approximately at the 1982 level. (RERsa also stayed roughly constant.) While this policy helped to prevent a further real appreciation, it did nothing to reverse the competitive disadvantage created during 1980 and 1981. Exports stagnated. We think that inadequate competitiveness must take a large part of the blame although slow growth of world demand contributed to some extent.

There was some further import liberalization but of a very cautious variety and relating mainly to noncompetitive imports. Tariff rates started to increase sharply in 1983 with implications mainly for revenue, as explained below.

1986–90

Nominal exchange rate policy became much more active and produced a depreciation of the NER of 47 percent and the RER of 35 percent. Export incentives continued to increase, so the depreciation of RERsa was even larger. The motives behind the policy were clear enough. There had been inadequate current account adjustment to the second oil crisis and the debt service burden had increased substantially. It is significant that depreciation of such a magnitude was carried out without undue fuss. Tariff rates were also sharply increased, but this was largely a revenue measure and did not much increase protection of import substitutes. (Quotas were still the binding constraint on imports, and tariffs were just soaking up rents. By the end of the period, however, there was evidence of "water in the tariff" in some sectors.) In response to exchange rate depreciation exports grew fast but the current account did not improve because the government did not, or could not, control fiscal deficits. When a macroeconomic crisis erupted in late 1990 harsh import controls were put in place. But they were recognized to be temporary and the new government of June 1991 undertook to remove them as soon as possible.

In the period 1972–90 as a whole one can see a gradual change toward depoliticization of the exchange rate. At the beginning depreciation was heavily disguised under the cover of a sterling peg. Even the move to a multicurrency peg in 1975 helped. Although it was operated for a few years as a fixed nominal effective exchange rate, it helped to accustom the public and the politicians to frequent exchange rate changes against the intervention currency. In due course it began to be used as a smoke screen behind which the exchange rate could be devalued. But the taboo against explicit devaluation was still strong, as witnessed by the exchange rate rigidity in 1980 and 1981 in the face of the second oil shock. From 1983 there was a quite definite move in the direction of a crawling multicurrency peg though the fiction of a fixed peg was not abandoned. Until 1985 the crawl was "passive"—just enough to maintain the real exchange rate constant—but from 1986 it became active and produced a sharp real depreciation. Toward the end of the decade it had become a very open secret that India was operating a discretionary crawling peg .

Capital Controls

Controls on private capital flows have been stringent throughout the period, although assessing their effectiveness is difficult. Two methods are currently in vogue in the literature for estimating capital flight. One method is to measure it as the sum of two items in the published balance of payments accounts: net short-term private capital outflows and "errors and omissions." On this basis, capital flight from India from 1970 to 1988 was only about 4 percent of recorded external debt incurred during the period. Another method is to measure capital flight as that part of the increase in recorded external debt that cannot be accounted for by current account deficits and additions to reserves. (In using this method care must be taken to allow for exchange rate valuation effects on the stock of debt.) On this basis capital flight was of negligible importance in the 1970s. It was, however, a more serious problem between 1980–84 when it amounted to almost 40 percent of the increase in recorded external debt according to our calculations. It is noteworthy that this was also a period when the rupee was overvalued in real terms.[4]

The black market premium on foreign exchange was much lower in the 1970s as compared with the late 1960s (see table 11.3). This is consistent with the hypothesis that the demand for foreign exchange on the black market fell when the official exchange rate became less rigid.[5] It is possible to argue, however, that the fall in the premium also reflects an increase in the supply of foreign exchange on the black market (for example, remittances from Indian workers abroad).

Econometric evidence appears to support the proposition that international mobility of capital has been low in India.[6] Our own judgment is that while capital controls have been sufficiently porous to permit some wealth-owners to place their funds abroad, they have been effective enough to prevent sudden or large-scale exports of capital. But, with the greater integration of capital markets, capital is becoming more mobile in India as it is elsewhere.

Capital controls have thus been reasonably effective but have they been desirable? The case for capital controls is twofold. First, they help to ensure that domestic savings are invested at home rather than abroad. This helps growth on the reasonable presumption that the social productivity of domestic investment is higher than that of investment abroad. Second, capital controls give macroeconomic policymakers an extra degree of freedom. Mobile capital flow creates obvious difficulties for the management of an adjustable peg. Indeed, if capital is highly mobile it becomes impossible to separate monetary policy and exchange rate policy. But the above case rests on the crucial assumption that private movements of funds may be irrational while policymakers would on balance use their discretion wisely. The counterargument to the use of capital controls is precisely that they permit the government to follow inappropriate policies such as repressed interest rates and exchange rate overvaluation. If the capital market is on balance guided by fundamentals, it provides an essential discipline on policymakers.

This is an extremely difficult debate to resolve but we do not need to pronounce on it. With the attitudes underlying Indian planning, the abolition of capital controls was never part of the politically feasible range of options. Moreover, capital controls have to be considered as a sequencing issue. Given India's extensive controls on foreign trade and domestic labor, product and financial markets, the dismantling of capital controls ahead of general liberalization would have risked substantial capital flight and greatly complicated the operation of macroeconomic policy.

Trade Intervention

Trade intervention has been extensively used in India as an instrument of balance of payments adjustment. This has taken the form of quotas and tariffs on imports and various export incentives. On the whole, the binding constraint on imports has been quotas; tariffs have served primarily a revenue purpose. Export subsidies have mainly been a device to mitigate the effects of import controls. Our discussion, therefore, concentrates principally on import controls.

Using import restrictions as a balance of payments device implies varying their severity in response to changes in the balance of payments position, instead of using other measures such as exchange rate variations. In India this kind of management was evident principally between 1957 and 1974 (apart from the brief liberalization episode after the 1966 devaluation). Import controls continued after 1975 but they were no longer varied much in response to shocks.

Import restrictions reduce the level and growth of real income by distorting the allocation of resources away from the country's comparative advantage; by absorbing scarce resources in rent-seeking; and by reducing innovation, technical progress, and x-efficiency.[7] We do not dwell on this line of argument though we agree with it. But something needs to be said about import restrictions and macroeconomic performance. The argument in favor of import restrictions is their certainty of operation in improving the current account. This makes them attractive to policymakers as a way of reconciling internal and external balance if reserves are low and exchange rate devaluation is dismissed on the basis of "elasticity pessimism" or because of its presumed inflationary consequences. As we shall see, these objections to devaluation are largely inapplicable in the Indian context. Moreover, import restrictions have their own disadvantages as a macroeconomic instrument except in the very short run. They reduce the relative price of exportables and the incentive to export, so that in the medium run the current account improvement is eroded. They also remove the anti-inflationary anchor that a fixed exchange rate is supposed to provide. Severe import restrictions can result in a fall in domestic production for want of imported inputs ("import starvation"), which implies that beyond a point, current account improvements have to be secured by deflation or a maxidevaluation. They lead to delays and administrative bottlenecks that reduce the elasticity of supply of exports and more generally the speed and flexibility with which the economy can respond to unfavorable (and indeed even favorable) shocks. Finally, import restrictions, once imposed, tend to stay. Many developing countries have exhibited the typical cycle of balance of payments deficit and inflation → import restrictions → loss of competitiveness and efficiency → current account deficit → maxidevaluation followed by a repetition of the same cycle.

The Indian experience with import controls as a macroeconomic device bears out the above analysis. The import control regime from 1957 to 1966 led to discrimination against exports and poor export growth (in spite of the introduction of export subsidies after 1962); and to growing delays, inflexibilities, and dislocation of production due to lack of imported inputs. As for inflation, it was higher than in the early 1950s. While import controls cannot be blamed for that, it is clear that they tended to undermine the anti-inflationary influence of the then fixed nominal exchange rate. Though the crisis of 1965/66 was triggered by severe droughts, the import control regime played a significant part in creating the weak balance of payments situation and the inflexible economic structure that turned shock into crisis. After the failure of the maxidevaluation of 1966 (for reasons discussed elsewhere in this book), import controls were revived and tightened. Indeed, they were tightened further in immediate response to the first oil crisis, but this time India escaped the vicious cycle described above because from 1972 the RER depreciated substantially. Moreover, from 1975 onward the attitude to import controls changed. They continued to be important but they were never again significantly tightened to control the balance of payments. Correspondingly, this implied greater reliance on exchange rate variation (nominal or real), which paid off in faster export growth. The slowdown in exports in the early 1980s and the lack of current adjustment was due to real exchange rate appreciation. The persistence and increase of the current account deficit in the late 1980s was due to budgetary irresponsibility. Import controls were not tightened in either case and it is very doubtful that they would have helped in anything but the very short run.

An interesting commentary on the macroeconomic consequences of the persistence of import controls once they are imposed is provided by the experience of the 1975–78 period. The balance of payments improved dramatically and it would have been both anti-inflationary and growth-promoting to increase import-intensive investment. But this option was not considered because no radical change in the import control regime was on the agenda. Import controls must therefore take part of the responsibility both for the loss of momentum in public investment and the rapid money growth during these years and therefore for the inflation that followed in 1979–81. Thus, the Indian experience shows that import controls are not to be recommended as a macroeconomic instrument.

Export subsidies first made their appearance in the early 1960s and increased rapidly to 1965. Though they were too small to affect materially the import-bias of the regime, they partly offset the worsening competitiveness of exports. After the devaluation of 1966 they were eliminated but were back on the scene by 1969 and again helped to improve export competitiveness. Their magnitude was increased further after 1975. Quantitatively, they were not as important for competitiveness as the exchange rate (as shown by a comparison of RER and RERsa in table 11.3). But they did soften significantly the rigors of the import control regime for exporters and they had the advantage of doing so while appearing not to make others worse off.

Exchange Rate Policy

Economists sometimes distinguish between the exchange rate *regime* and exchange rate *policy*. Regime suggests a set of rules binding the government. What the rules are is clear enough in the case of a permanently fixed exchange rate or a fully floating exchange rate. Matters are not so clear in intermediate cases such as an "adjustable peg" or a "crawling peg" or "managed floating" because the government has discretion.[8] A further point to be borne in mind in recent years is that pegging can be with respect to a single currency or to a basket of currencies. One must also distinguish between the formal status of an exchange regime and its de facto nature—an important point in the Indian context, as explained below. Exchange rate policy can be construed narrowly or broadly. Narrowly construed, it means the way government uses its discretion within the context of a given regime. Broadly construed, it covers both the choice of regime and the way it is operated. We use the word here in its broad sense.

In appraising Indian exchange rate policy, we organize the discussion around four topics. These are separated only for convenience and the interconnections are explicitly recognized.

- *Elasticities and external balance*. Under this heading we discuss whether the current account responds to variations in the real exchange rate.
- *The relationship between the nominal and the real exchange rate*. Here we compare alternative methods of devaluing the real exchange rate. Does a nominal devaluation stick in real terms? Does a fixed nominal exchange rate serve as an inflation anchor?
- *Exchange rates and internal balance*. Is a devaluation of the nominal exchange rate expansionary or contractionary? What policies have to accompany nominal devaluation to achieve internal and external balance simultaneously?
- *The nominal exchange rate and the appropriate real exchange rate*. In this section, we make an overall assessment of exchange rate management in India.

Elasticities and External Balance

How responsive the current account is to the real exchange rate matters for nominal exchange rate policy. Both fixed and variable nominal exchange rates rely primarily on alterations in the real exchange rate to change the current account.[9] "Elasticity pessimists" proceed on the assumption of very low elasticities, and are naturally led in the direction of trade intervention to manage the balance of payments.[10]

Casual empiricism suggests that in India the relevant elasticities are high— periods of rapid export growth (for example, the 1970s and the late 1980s) were associated with real exchange rate depreciation while periods of slow export growth (for example, the 1960s and the early1980s) were associated with real exchange rate appreciation. However, since exports are also affected by other factors, we have examined the issue econometrically (see the appendix to this chapter). Our single-equation estimates relate the volume of exports to the RER, world income, and a proxy for domestic excess demand. All these variables turn out to be significant. The exchange rate elasticity of exports is around 0.75 in the short run and around 2 in the long run, and 80 percent of the long-run effect comes through within two years. A single-equation approach may, however, be misleading since it mixes up demand and supply factors; and it should be noted here that "elasticity pessimism" specifically took a pessimistic view of the price elasticity of foreign demand for exports. We have, therefore, estimated the demand and supply price elasticities for exports in a simultaneous equation framework. The demand equation relates the volume of India's exports to world income and the relative price of Indian and world exports. The supply equation relates the volume of India's exports to the relative price of Indian exports on the domestic market and a domestic excess demand term. The results show that the price elasticity of supply of exports is about 0.7 in the short run and 1.1 in the long run, with over 80 percent of the long-run effect coming through within one year. The price elasticity of demand for exports is about 1.1 in the short run and about 3 in the long run, 80 percent of the long-run effect coming through within two years. The domestic excess-demand term in the supply equation is significant but the world income term in the demand equation is not.

These results show that India is not an exception to the general presumption that the price-competitiveness of exports is an important determinant of the volume of exports, and that the relevant elasticities are more than adequate for a real depreciation to improve the current account even with a zero price elasticity of demand for imports. We have not estimated the price elasticity of demand for imports since the meaningfulness of such estimates is dubious given the importance of import controls.

Note also that the estimated export elasticities are almost certainly biased downward (see the appendix to this chapter). Moreover, they reflect a domestic environment that is characterized by pervasive controls. The adequacy of the measured elasticities is an answer to "sophisticated" elasticity pessimists who argue that a (real) devaluation would not work because the government's own control regime would weaken the supply response; that is, that a (real) devaluation makes sense only as part of a full liberalization package, which, however, is politically impossible. Our estimates show that a (real) devaluation works even in the existing environment, which is not to deny that it would work even better if the environment were different.

The Relationship Between the Nominal Exchange Rate and the Real Exchange Rate

Even if the current account is responsive to the real exchange rate, the question remains as to how alterations in the real exchange rate can be secured. Consider two common reasons why a depreciation of the RER may be called for. The RER may appreciate above its appropriate level due to high domestic inflation, or the appropriate level of the RER may itself fall due to a negative external shock (say an oil price increase). With a fixed nominal exchange rate, the required real depreciation is supposed to come about through a fall in the domestic price level or its rate of change. But this may not occur quickly and reliably enough (and without sacrifice of other objectives—see below). A nominal exchange rate depreciation is, of course, a much more direct way of achieving the real depreciation. But the problem is that the real depreciation may not endure because the fall in the nominal exchange rate may lead to a rise in the domestic price level or its rate of change.

One would expect a nominal devaluation to stick in India because it is a large country with a small traded sector. The ratio of exports and imports to GDP is currently 7 and 10 percent respectively, and has been even lower in previous years. On this basis a 10 percent nominal devaluation would lead to a 1 percent rise in the price level directly. A similar result can be reached by looking at the direct and indirect import content of production on the basis of an input-output table.[11] But some qualifications need to be made. The presence of quantitative restrictions implies that the above estimate is on the high side since in many sectors devaluation would squeeze rents. However, in some sectors administered prices can be expected to rise on a cost-plus basis. To the extent that the price level does rise, the increase could be compounded by indexation of wages in the organized sector. But wages are indexed to the CPI, which is largely made up of food and services whose prices are relatively insensitive to devaluation. Note also that our econometric work on inflation (see the appendix to chapter 10) does not show money wages to be a significant factor in explaining inflation, which is primarily driven by money supply and food production. (However, nonfood prices are sensitive to import costs with a coefficient of around 0.17.)

Table 11.1 summarizes the association between the nominal and the real exchange rate over the period of study.

A fixed nominal exchange rate did not prevent substantial real appreciations from 1960–65 and from 1980–82, and both these periods ended with devaluations undertaken to restore competitiveness. The periods 1968–71 and 1976–77 look more encouraging for a fixed exchange rate, but inflation was low for special reasons that had nothing to do with the exchange rate (buoyant agriculture and sharply rising money demand). In fact, when the NER was fixed in September 1975, prices had already been falling for a year. When considering exchange rate depreciations it is useful to isolate the periods when the authorities were explicitly in-

Table 11.1   Changes in NER and RER in Different Exchange Rate Regimes, 1960–90

(percent)

Period	Change in NER	Change in RER
Fixed NER		
1961–65	0	+21
1968–71	0	0
1976–77	–1	–9
1980–82	+3	+13
Depreciating NER		
1966–67	–36	–21
1972–75	–21	–13
1978–79	–7	–9
1983–85	–12	0
1986–90	–47	–35

Source: Table 11.3.

tending to produce a real depreciation and devalued sufficiently in nominal terms to produce that effect. This was explicitly so in 1966–67 and in 1986–90, and covertly so in 1972–75; in all these cases they were successful. (From 1983–85 the authorities were only devaluing enough ex post to keep the real exchange rate constant.) The upshot of this discussion is that a nominal depreciation in India does translate into a real depreciation; and that a fixed NER is not a reliable way of reducing inflation, and maintaining or devaluing the RER.[12]

The hypothesis that a fixed nominal exchange rate regime serves as an anchor against inflation can also be examined directly. We must bear in mind that India has not had a pure fixed exchange rate regime for any part of the period. A comparison is possible, however, between an adjustable peg (with very infrequent exchange rate changes) and a crawling peg. This is shown in table 11.2 for two different ways of classifying the period.

In comparison *(i)* the whole period 1960/61 to 1982/83 is classified as an adjustable peg. This includes the years 1972/73 to 1975/76 when the NER was depreciating. This is on the argument that people had not yet realized that the fixed sterling peg in fact implied a continuous depreciation in nominal terms. In comparison *(ii)* however, the period 1972/73 to 1975/76 is classified as a crawling peg. In comparison *(i)* inflation rates are roughly the same under the adjustable peg and the crawling peg. Comparison *(ii)* is somewhat less favorable to a crawling peg. But it must be remembered that in 1972/73 to 1975/76 high inflation was clearly

Table 11.2   Inflation in Different Exchange Rate Regimes, 1960/61 to 1990/91

Regime	Years	Average inflation (percent)
Comparison (i)		
Adjustable peg	1960/61 to 1982/83	7.9
Crawling peg	1983/84 to 1990/91	7.5
Comparison (ii)		
Adjustable peg	1960/61 to 1971/72	
	and 1976/77 to 1982/83	6.8
Crawling peg	1972/73 to 1975/76	
	and 1983/84 to 1990/91	9.5

Source: Tables 4.10, 5.12, 6.10, and 7.4.

the result of drought and rapid money growth, and also that in the period 1976/77 to 1978/79, inflation was low for quite special reasons.

The truth is that inflation in India has had little to do with exchange rates one way or the other. It is primarily related to money supply growth, fiscal deficits, and food production. Conversely, money supply growth is not related to the exchange rate but rather to past inflation of food prices as a result of government reaction. The near complete independence of the path of inflation and the path of the exchange rate implies that a variable NER can serve as an efficient instrument of external adjustment if appropriate domestic expenditure policies are followed—a caveat that is further elaborated below. By the same token, it implies that a fixed NER is unlikely to reduce inflation if that is required for external adjustment (say to a negative real shock).[13] Certainly no "automatic" mechanism can be relied on, and the government is more likely to borrow or restrict trade rather than reduce inflation below a politically acceptable level.[14]

The trend of inflation in India has been lower than in many developing countries because the government has clamped down whenever inflation has threatened to get out of hand. But low inflation has been the result of a commitment to low inflation, not a commitment to a fixed nominal exchange rate. It must be admitted that the financially conservative attitudes of the government have shown considerable dilution in recent years. But it is hard to discern any connection between this change and the move toward exchange rate variability. Deeper changes in political economy are responsible for the weakening of fiscal control.

Exchange Rates and Internal Balance

Standard economic theory tells us that favorable elasticities are not a sufficient condition for a successful nominal devaluation. If money wages and prices are sticky downward, nominal devaluation in an economy without unemployed resources will improve the current account only if it is accompanied by a reduction in domestic real expenditure. Failure to reduce expenditure may lead to inflation. But even if it does not lead to inflation, current account adjustment will be thwarted.

Some economists have emphasized that devaluation can itself induce a reduction in absorption and therefore may not need to be complemented by expenditure reduction. Indeed, an expenditure increase may be necessary to avoid deflation. It is possible for a devaluation to reduce the current account deficit in foreign currency but increase it in domestic currency, which would be deflationary. Other possible deflationary mechanisms are the real balance effect and a shift in income distribution toward high savers. Such effects are no doubt possible but if they are to be deflationary on balance, there must be no generalized excess demand before the devaluation. But major downward movements of the NER in India (for example in 1966/67, 1972–75, and 1986–90) have always occurred against a background of excess demand. The failure of NER depreciation to improve the current account from 1986–90 (in spite of rapid export growth) can be attributed mainly to inadequate control of excess demand fueled by growing fiscal deficits.

In some developing countries (and sometimes in India), finance ministers have worried that the direct effect of devaluation would be to worsen the public finances, making expenditure contraction more difficult. In fact, this point has not been important in India because (a) there has been a positive net transfer from abroad throughout the period, (b) high tariff rates have ensured that government revenue increases significantly if the rupee depreciates, and (c) public sector enterprise pricing has been on a cost-plus basis. Of course, reducing fiscal deficits is politically difficult in India and became more difficult in the late 1980s, but fiscal deficits have not directly worsened due to currency depreciation (as alleged for example in some Latin American countries in recent years).

Some structuralists have put forward the view that even if nominal depreciation sticks in real terms, it would reduce investment and therefore growth. The reduction in investment is alleged to happen because devaluation increases the real price of imported capital goods.[15] This is not the place for a discussion of the theoretical basis of the argument, but the evidence does not support it in the Indian context. The years 1960/61 to 1975/76 were a period of stop and go in investment and slow growth. While investment cutbacks were dictated mainly by inflation, the balance of payments position was also relevant. If the balance of payments had been stronger and reserves higher, it would have been possible to use imports to prevent food prices from rising, which would have reduced the need to cut investment. An important cause of balance of payments weakness was real exchange rate appreciation in the early 1960s. This point was important even in the 1973/74 crisis. The effective exchange rate was no longer fixed but the previous trade and payments regime was still casting its shadow in the form of low reserves.

Since 1975/76 growth has been faster, which can be attributed to higher investment, steadier investment, and cautious liberalization policies (see chapter 13). As seen above, this has also been a period (with some interruptions) of RER depreciation (which itself has required NER depreciation except in 1975–79). Exchange rate variability has contributed to higher growth by raising the growth of exports and permitting import liberalization. It falls short of being a success story, however. As we have seen, in the first half of the 1980s the RER appreciated. Investment and growth continued but the appreciation played its part in preventing current account adjustment and encouraging high external borrowing, thereby sowing the seeds of the macroeconomic problems of 1990.

Finally, we address an issue which we have ignored so far, that is the macroeconomic significance of the fact that while the exchange rate peg has sometimes been fixed and sometimes crawling, it has since 1975 always been a weighted average of currencies. Once the sterling peg from 1972–75 had outlived its usefulness, in terms of the downward trend of the sterling exchange rate, it was good policy to insulate the rupee from the impact of random fluctuations in major currencies. Such fluctuations, which change the nominal and real effective exchange rate in an undesired way, can themselves take on the character of macroeconomic shocks. Of course, a single-currency peg can in principle deal with this problem by frequent offsetting changes in the peg. But it was useful for policymakers to separate out the problem caused by short-term currency fluctuations from the problem of maintaining the appropriate level of competitiveness.

Nominal Exchange Rate Policy and the Appropriate Real Exchange Rate

A crucial question, which we have been leading up to, is whether the nominal exchange rate in India was managed in such a way as to produce the appropriate real exchange rate. The latter can be defined as that value of the RER which would produce a sustainable current account deficit consistently with internal balance and low inflation. In principle this is a very complicated problem but, in practice, at least the appropriate direction of movement of the RER is quite clear from applying the following principle. The principle is that, assuming a satisfactory starting position, the RER should be kept constant unless there are permanent real changes in the environment that call for a change in competitiveness.

A change in the NER is a direct way of changing the RER unless it tends to be eroded by inflation. It is because of fear of such an erosion that countries sometimes deliberately choose the slow and painful way of bringing the real exchange rate down while keeping the nominal exchange rate fixed. The proof of the pudding is in the eating. Such a policy can be said to have failed unless inflation comes down and the RER moves in the appropriate direction within a reasonable time before internal balance and real competitiveness have been devastated.

The highlights of Indian experience are as follows.

- From 1960–65 the RER rose, and this was clearly inappropriate. The increase in import propensity following the ambitious planning effort surely implied a lower equilibrium value of the RER. The policy of a fixed nominal exchange rate (and import controls) was clearly unsuitable. It did not bring down inflation and eventually ended in the maxidevaluation of 1966. The fall in the RER that followed was necessary—not as a response to the temporary shock of the drought but for strengthening the long-run competitive position—though the timing of the nominal devaluation was unwise.

- The first oil shock led to a permanent terms of trade loss that required a depreciation of the RER. This was brought about by a clever, covert nominal depreciation.[16] The move to a fixed NER in 1975 was made only after inflation had been extinguished. The low inflation brought about a further desirable depreciation of the RER.

- The appreciation of the RER after the second oil price shock was undesirable. As with the first oil shock, a depreciation rather than an appreciation of the RER was required. The decision to keep the NER fixed was a grave mistake. It was devalued later, in 1983, and then only by enough to prevent a further appreciation of the RER. More was needed to offset the competitive disadvantage created earlier. Consequently export growth was slow, the current account deficit persisted, and foreign debt grew rapidly.

- By 1986 oil prices had come down but servicing the rapidly increasing foreign debt continued to indicate a need to devalue the RER. The creeping import liberalization of the past few years also pointed in the same direction. The aggressive nominal devaluation of 1986–90 was therefore desirable. Export growth responded strongly but not the current account. This was because the required fiscal adjustment was not carried out.

Concluding Remarks

India's macroeconomic performance has been handicapped by a reluctance to vary the nominal exchange rate actively. The two periods when this reluctance was most in evidence were 1960–65 and 1980–85. In the former period payments balance was maintained by import restrictions and concessional borrowing. Consequently, export growth was slow, reserves were inadequate and imports were reduced to bare essentials. Therefore, when the severe droughts came, the economy could not ride through them by increasing imports; it became necessary to have a severe cutback of investment and growth. From 1980–85 the reluctance first to devalue at all and then to devalue sufficiently led to stagnation of exports and to persistent current account deficits. This time, import controls were not tightened nor was investment cut. Payments balance was maintained by a sharp increase in nonconcessional borrowing from the IMF and commercial sources. The buildup of external debt sowed the seeds of later trouble. Leaving aside 1980–85, however, the overall trend in the 1970s and 1980s has been toward a gradual depoliticization of and greater flexibility in the use of the exchange rate instrument. Macroeconomic adjustment would have been even less smooth and growth lower without this flexibility.

Table 11.3   Exchange Rate Indexes, 1960–90

Year	NR	NER	ERP	RER	SA	RERsa	t	BMP($)	QXc	QXcg
1960	4.76	213.84	67.35	144.02	0.020	155.61	0.14	—	40.40	n.a.
1961	4.76	212.35	68.26	144.95	0.023	156.14	0.18	—	42.00	4.0
1962	4.76	212.05	70.22	148.90	0.046	156.61	0.21	—	44.10	5.0
1963	4.76	212.05	71.62	151.86	0.088	152.70	0.27	—	48.70	10.4
1964	4.76	212.05	77.67	164.71	0.085	166.16	0.29	—	49.30	1.2
1965	4.76	212.05	82.27	174.45	0.104	172.34	0.38	—	45.20	-8.3
1966	6.36	158.79	89.49	142.09	-0.055	165.28	0.24	0.74	43.00	-4.9
1967	7.50	134.87	102.15	137.77	-0.056	160.40	0.19	—	45.90	6.7
1968	7.50	137.68	100.00	137.68	-0.011	153.47	0.19	—	53.00	15.5
1969	7.50	137.79	98.84	136.19	0.014	148.05	0.22	—	51.10	-3.6
1970	7.50	137.02	100.97	138.35	0.019	149.63	0.28	0.68	53.10	3.9
1971	7.50	134.33	102.01	137.03	0.022	147.76	0.34	0.71	51.90	-2.3
1972	7.59	124.18	106.79	132.61	0.030	141.83	0.41	0.41	58.20	12.1
1973	7.74	113.28	111.21	125.98	0.028	135.01	0.31	0.20	63.00	8.2
1974	8.10	110.77	117.94	130.64	0.027	140.15	0.28	0.15	68.20	8.3
1975	8.38	106.15	113.71	120.70	0.041	127.62	0.25	0.15	76.50	12.2
1976	8.96	105.07	103.46	108.71	0.062	112.42	0.28	0.16	93.70	22.5
1977	8.74	104.89	104.10	109.19	0.056	113.64	0.27	0.13	90.30	-3.6
1978	8.19	100.00	100.00	100.00	0.093	100.00	0.34	0.18	100.00	10.7
1979	8.13	97.76	102.12	99.83	0.079	101.37	0.31	0.20	106.60	6.6
1980	7.86	100.33	109.11	109.47	0.091	109.72	0.26	0.10	98.30	-7.8
1981	8.66	100.51	113.94	114.52	0.109	112.50	0.32	0.15	99.90	1.6

	NR	NER	ERP	RER	SA	RERsa	t	BMP	QXc	QXcg
1982	9.46	100.99	111.14	112.24	0.114	109.64	0.38	0.26	98.70	-1.2
1983	10.10	98.91	116.83	115.56	0.102	114.41	0.38	0.18	98.60	-0.1
1984	11.36	93.67	122.44	114.69	0.094	114.56	0.45	0.24	104.30	5.8
1985	12.37	88.40	127.31	112.54	0.107	111.55	0.48	0.17	105.90	1.5
1986	12.61	71.50	138.68	99.16	0.128	95.33	0.56	—	117.30	10.8
1987	12.96	62.18	146.76	91.26	0.138	86.73	0.60	—	134.10	14.3
1988	13.92	55.30	155.42	85.95	0.138	81.69	0.56	—	152.84	14.0
1989	16.23	52.53	150.52	79.07	—	—	0.51	—	176.36	15.4
1990	17.50	46.39	158.53	73.54	—	—	0.48	—	184.19	4.4

NR = Nominal rupee-to-dollar exchange rate (rupees per dollar)

NER = Index of nominal effective (export-weighted) exchange rate, 1978 = 100

ERP = Index of ratio of Indian and foreign wholesale prices (export-weighted)

RER = Index of real effective (export-weighted) exchange rate, 1978 = 100

SA = Export incentives as a proportion of the value of exports

RERsa = Incentive-adjusted RER, 1978 = 100. RERsa = RER $(1 + SA)$ in indexed form

t = Average tariff rate

BMP = Black market premium on the dollar

QXc = Index of volume of India's nonoil exports to the world, excluding the former Soviet Union and Eastern Europe, 1978/79 = 100

QXcg = Annual percentage growth in QXc

Note: All exchange rate data refer to calendar years. Tariff rates and export volume data refer to financial years. In constructing the NER and RER indexes, the exchange rate is defined as foreign currency units per rupee. RER = NER x ERP by definition.

Source: NR: IMF (annual), *International Financial Statistics Yearbook*. NER: Nominal exchange rates from IMF (annual), *International Financial Statistics Yearbook*, weighted by the export shares of the ten most important industrial countries in India's exports from 1979–81. ERP: Wholesale prices from IMF (annual), *International Financial Statistics Yearbook*, with weights as for NER. RER: calculated by using the formula RER = NER x ERP. SA: budget documents for cash subsidies and duty drawbacks; authors' estimates for the premium on import replenishment licences. RERsa: calculated by using the formula RERsa = RER $(1 + SA)$. t: tariff revenue from budget documents divided by the value of imports from Government of India, Ministry of Finance (various years), *Economic Survey*. BMP: Pick's Currency Yearbook. QXc: Government of India, DGCIS (various years), and Government of India, Ministry of Finance (various years), *Economic Survey*. Figures for exports to convertible currency areas are available only on a value basis. It is assumed that export volume to convertible currency areas bears the same relationship to total export volume as the corresponding value figures.

The evidence shows clearly both that inflation in India is not significantly related to the nominal exchange rate and that the current balance is responsive to the real exchange rate. Shocks have occurred and no doubt will occur from time to time. Hence, the correct policy assignment in India is to manage the nominal exchange rate to secure external competitiveness while anchoring inflation by domestic monetary and fiscal policies. In this context, India's conservative financial tradition is a valuable asset which it would be unwise to squander.

Appendix: Estimated Demand and Supply of Exports

In several places within this book, and particularly in this chapter, we have given our view that Indian exports are price-sensitive. In this appendix we test this hypothesis econometrically. Single-equation models are inappropriate for the purpose since exports are affected by both foreign demand and domestic supply. We estimate export demand and supply equations in a simultaneous equation framework.[17] For the sake of completeness, we also estimate single-equation export models even though we do not regard them as satisfactory.

Structural Equations

EXPORT DEMAND. In this section a model corresponding to the demand side of the export market is estimated, which takes the following form

(11-1) $XD = f(PX/PW, WY)$

where XD denotes export demand, PX is a measure of Indian export prices, and PW is a measure of the price of exports of competitor countries. Thus, PX/PW is a measure of the relative price of Indian exports, and WY is a measure of world income. A priori we would expect PX/PW to enter with a negative sign, since if the price of Indian exports falls relative to the price of competitors' exports, demand should rise. The a priori sign of WY is clearly positive.

There are various ways to measure all the variables in the basic function. Below we list the different definitions of the variables that were used in the empirical work.

- XD. We considered three measures of export volume: QXa, which is defined as India's total export volume; QXb, which is defined as India's nonoil export volume; and QXc, which measures the volume of India's nonoil exports to convertible currency areas (that is the world *minus* the former Soviet Union and Eastern Europe). Since oil exports are unlikely to be price-sensitive, the results presented concentrate on QXb and QXc.

- *PX*. Two measures of export prices were used: *PXa*, defined as Indian export unit values in rupees; and *PXb*, defined as Indian nonoil export unit values in rupees.
- *PW*. Two possible measures of export prices of competitor countries were employed: *PWa*, which denotes the unit value of exports from industrial countries in rupees, weighted by India's trade with industrial countries; and *PWb*, which denotes the unit value of exports from nonoil developing countries in rupees.
- *WY*. Three different measures of world income were used. *WYa* denotes the GDP of India's industrial-country trading partners (weighted by India's trade with them); *WYb* denotes world GDP (net of the former Soviet Union and Eastern Europe); *WYc* is defined as export volume from nonoil developing countries (as a proxy for world demand for exports from nonoil developing countries as a whole).

As our focus is on the demand and supply of nonoil exports, the results reported concentrate on the appropriately defined variables, such as *QXb*, *QXc*, and *PXb*. (Broadly consistent results were obtained using the other definitions of the independent and dependent variables. Not surprisingly, they were somewhat less satisfactory statistically.) All the models were estimated in logarithmic form with annual data and the structure of the dynamic adjustment processes was freely determined.

Since *PX/PW* is found to enter contemporaneously, it is clearly an endogenous variable. So estimation is via two-stage least squares. Table 11.4 presents a variety of models explaining *QXc*. Equation *(i)* implies that the short-run price elasticity of export demand is 1.22, which rises in the long run to just over 3.0. More than 80 percent of the long-run effect comes through within two years after the current year. This pattern of elasticities varies rather little between equations *(i)* to *(iii)*—which differ only in the proxies used for world income. Equation *(ii)* suggests short- and long-run elasticities of 1.06 and 3.03 respectively, while equation *(iii)* suggests a short-run elasticity of 0.87 rising to 2.6 in the long run. *WYa* and *WYb* are not quite significant at the 5 percent level, although each is signed as would be expected a priori. The relevant equations show no evidence of auto-correlated or non-normally distributed residuals. *WYc* enters strongly, although the χ^2 test for autocorrelation suggests that this equation does suffer from first-order autocorrelated residuals. It should be noted that, in all equations, *WY* enters in change form as this was dictated by the data, with unrestricted estimates of current and lagged world demand entering with opposite signs and being of very similar magnitude. Similar results were obtained using *PXb/PWb* as the relative price variable.

Table 11.5 gives estimates for models with *QXb* as the dependent variable. The results are quantitatively rather similar with the long-run price elasticities for equations *(iv)*, *(v)*, and *(vi)*, being 3.0, 3.0, and 2.6 respectively. In this case, all the proxies for world demand enter significantly and there is no evidence of non-normally distributed or autocorrelated errors in any of the equations.

Table 11.4   Export Demand: Estimated Equations

Independent variables	*Dependent variable QXc*		
	(i)	*(ii)*	*(iii)*
PXb/PWa	−1.22	−1.06	−0.87
	(2.63)	(2.60)	(2.84)
QXc_{t-1}	0.60	0.65	0.67
	(3.66)	(4.38)	(5.58)
ΔWYb	2.13		
	(1.63)		
ΔWYa		1.44	
		(1.47)	
ΔWYc			0.89
			(2.97)
Constant	1.75	1.55	1.44
	(2.53)	(2.41)	(2.72)
Time period	1963–87	1963–87	1963–87
Autocorrelation $\chi^2(1)$	2.33	1.50	6.01
Normality $\chi^2(2)$	0.19	0.21	0.25
Percent s.e.	6.96	6.83	5.82

Note: Additional instruments used: $(PXb/PWa)_{t-1}$, $(PXb/PWa)_{t-2}$, $exD3_t$, $exD3_{t-1}$, $exD3_{t-2}$. See the discussion of the supply equation below for definition of exD3.

Source: Authors' calculations.

EXPORT SUPPLY. Export supply is postulated to be related to the following factors

(11-2) $XS = g(PX/P, DD, \text{trend})$

where *XS* denotes export supply, *PX* denotes Indian export prices measured as in the demand equation, *P* is domestic wholesale prices, and *DD* is domestic excess demand, proxies for which are discussed below. A time trend term is also included to capture trended movements not modeled explicitly. Clearly we would expect *PX/P* to enter positively, reflecting the tendency to increase export supply when export prices rise relative to domestic prices and vice versa. *DD* can be expected to enter negatively since the pressure of demand on the home market diverts goods away from export markets.

In estimating export supply the measures of export volume are obviously the same as listed earlier. We have doctored *PX* to allow for the effect of export subsidies that have been important in India. The price received by an exporter is equal to *PX* (1 + *SA*) where *SA* is the rate of export subsidy. We write *PX*(1 + *SA*) as *PXsa*. The relative price thus is either *PXasa/P* or *PXbsa/P*.

Table 11.5   Export Demand: Estimated Equations

Independent variables	Dependent variable QXb		
	(iv)	*(v)*	*(vi)*
PXb/PWa	−1.29	−1.10	−0.93
	(3.28)	(3.12)	(3.64)
QXb_{t-1}	0.57	0.63	0.64
	(4.04)	(4.81)	(6.40)
ΔWYb	2.36		
	(2.30)		
ΔWYa		1.49	
		(1.90)	
ΔWYc			0.88
			(3.85)
Constant	1.89	1.66	1.59
	(3.09)	(2.88)	(3.56)
Time period	1963–87	1963–87	1963–87
Autocorrelation $\chi^2(1)$	0.20	0.38	2.97
Normality $\chi^2(2)$	0.90	1.07	0.87
Percent s.e.	5.65	5.57	4.41

Note: Additional instruments used: $(PXb/PWa)_{t-1}$, $(PXb/PWa)_{t-2}$, $exD3_t$, $exD3_{t-1}$, $exD3_{t-2}$. See the discussion of the supply equation for definition of exD3.

Source: Authors' calculations.

An important problem in the estimation of models such as equation 11-2 is how to measure the pressure of domestic demand. A number of possible proxies are used below, which concentrate on the excess of monetary growth (real or nominal) over the growth rate of real GDP. Thus, we define the following proxies for the pressure of domestic demand

$$ex\,D3_t = \Delta M3_t - \Delta Y_t$$
$$ex\,DI_t = \Delta M1_t - \Delta Y_t$$
$$ex\,RD3_t = \Delta(M3/P)_t - \Delta Y_t$$
$$ex\,RDI_t = \Delta(M1/P)_t - \Delta Y_t$$

where M3 and M1 denote broad and narrow money respectively, Y denotes real GDP, and P denotes the wholesale price index. One potential problem might be the correlation between the excess demand variables and the relative price variable. In actual fact this correlation is very small, being typically in the range 0.4 to 0.5, depending on the definition of excess demand. In some equations, we have also

Table 11.6   Export Supply: Estimated Equations

Independent variables	Dependent variable QXc					
	(i)	(ii)	(iii)	(iv)	(v)	(vi)
$QXc_{(t-1)}$	0.56	0.56	0.48	0.61	0.38	0.36
	(3.77)	(3.60)	(3.28)	(3.74)	(2.36)	(2.14)
$(PXbsa/P)_{(t-1)}$	0.53	0.51	0.78	0.49	0.70	0.72
	(2.45)	(2.28)	(3.28)	(2.20)	(3.10)	(3.08)
$exD3_{(t-1)}$	−0.52	−0.42		−0.50		
	(2.03)	(1.62)		(1.96)		
$exRD3_{(t-1)}$			−0.41			
			(2.11)			
GFD	−1.20		−0.95	−1.81		
	(1.64)		(1.84)	(1.95)		
TFE					−3.21	−4.08
					(1.88)	(2.10)
Trend	0.02	0.02	0.02	0.02	0.02	0.02
	(3.54)	(3.13)	(3.71)	(2.87)	(3.76)	(3.27)
Constant	2.11	2.06	2.57	1.94	2.85	2.96
	(3.21)	(3.02)	(3.85)	(2.77)	(3.87)	(3.86)
Time period	1962–87	1962–87	1962–87	1962–84	1962–87	1962–84
Autocorrelation $\chi^2(1)$	1.44	3.20	0.00	0.32	1.41	1.63
Normality $\chi^2(2)$	0.53	1.22	2.41	0.17	1.15	0.03
Percent s.e.	6.00	6.24	5.96	5.98	5.73	5.93

Note: Additional instruments used in equations (v) and (vi): GFD, $TFE_{(t-1)}$, $TFE_{(t-2)}$, exD3, WYb.
Source: Authors' calculations.

included *GFD*, defined as consolidated government fiscal deficit as a proportion of GDP at market prices, as another proxy for domestic demand.

In initial instrumental variables estimates it became clear that the effect of the *PX/P* term only started to have an impact on *XS* after around one year. Consequently, provided the errors are not autocorrelated, it is valid to condition on lags of *PX/P*. So, for the first four equations of table 11.6, our estimation method was ordinary least squares.

In table 11.6 some estimates for models of the form given in equation 11-2 above are presented for *QXc*. In practice all the excess money growth proxies gave very similar results and so we concentrate here on the broad money measure for nominal excess money (*exD3*) and excess real money (*exRD3*). In equations (*i*) and (*iii*) a measure of fiscal demand, *GFD*, is also included.

Equations *(i)* and *(iii)* give very similar results. The short-run elasticity of export supply with respect to the relative price of exports is between 0.53 and 0.78, rising in the long run to between 1.2 and 1.5. Typically, 80 percent of the long-run effect comes through within a year after the current year. The excess money terms are both significant and signed as expected a priori, while the fiscal demand term is not quite significant at normal significance levels. The monetary demand terms enter with a lag while the fiscal demand term enters contemporaneously. There is no evidence of first-order autocorrelation and the residuals seem to be normally distributed (thus enabling valid inference). There is also no evidence of multicollinearity between the proxies for monetary and fiscal excess demand. For example, the correlation between *GFD* and *exD3* is only 0.15.

In equation *(ii)* the fiscal demand term is excluded. As can be seen the estimated elasticities are very similar, although the effect of the remaining monetary demand term is somewhat reduced in both size and significance. Hence there seems to be a good case for including both effects in the regression.

Given the large increases in the fiscal deficit in more recent years, which may have caused the estimate on *GFD* to change over time, equation *(iv)* presents the same model as *(iii)* estimated over the shorter period 1962–84. The price elasticity of the model is still within the range stated above, but the significance and size of the fiscal excess demand term is increased.

Equations *(v)* and *(vi)* replace the monetary and fiscal demand terms with an alternative proxy for the pressure of domestic demand; that is *TFE* defined as total final expenditure as a proportion of GDP at market prices. Because this variable is endogenous, estimation of equations *(v)* and *(vi)* is by two-stage least squares. As can be seen, the elasticity estimates are similar to the equations *(i)* to *(iv)* with short-run elasticities of 0.7 rising to 1.1 in the long run. The equation standard error improves slightly relative to comparable equations such as *(i)* or *(iii)*. In equation *(vi)* the sample is again cut off at 1984 and a similar result obtains as before—the demand term becomes somewhat more significant but the estimated price elasticities are virtually unchanged.

Table 11.7 presents corresponding equations explaining the behavior of *QXb*, which measures total nonoil exports. The results differ from table 11.6 in that the range for the short- and long-run price elasticities is rather different and the statistical significance of some other terms is much lower. The short-run estimated price elasticities of supply vary from 0.32 to 0.48, thus being uniformly lower than the elasticities estimated for *QXc*. The long-run elasticities vary from 0.75 to 1.02—again uniformly lower than for *QXc*. This is to be expected, however, since *QXb* includes exports to the former Soviet Union and Eastern Europe, which are unlikely to be sensitive to price effects as exports to the convertible currency areas. The excess demand effects are less statistically significant for *QXb*, although *TFE* still enters significantly, especially up to 1984.

Table 11.7   Export Supply: Estimated Equations

Independent variables	Dependent variable QXb				
	(i)	(ii)	(iii)	(iv)	(v)
$QXb_{(t-1)}$	0.57	0.53	0.62	0.41	0.40
	(3.42)	(3.41)	(3.42)	(2.47)	(2.33)
$(PXbsa/P)_{(t-1)}$	0.34	0.48	0.32	0.44	0.45
	(1.84)	(2.38)	(1.74)	(2.60)	(2.59)
$exD3_{(t-1)}$	−0.33		−0.31		
	(1.35)		(1.26)		
$exRD3_{(t-1)}$		−0.30			
		(1.44)			
GFD	−0.73	−0.62	−1.36		
	(1.04)	(0.90)	(1.58)		
TFE				−3.08	−4.10
				(1.85)	(2.43)
Trend	0.02	0.02	0.02	0.02	0.02
	(2.76)	(2.89)	(2.28)	(3.51)	(2.91)
Constant	1.89	2.15	1.78	2.59	2.63
	(2.74)	(3.13)	(2.44)	(3.75)	(3.67)
Time period	1962–87	1962–87	1962–84	1962–87	1962–84
Autocorrelation $\chi^2(1)$	0.39	0.00	0.20	1.88	4.30
Normality $\chi^2(2)$	1.35	0.93	1.01	1.44	0.83
percent s.e	5.74	5.71	5.72	5.07	5.20

Note: Additional instruments used in equations (iv) and (v): GFD, $TFE_{(t-1)}$, $TFE_{(t-2)}$, exD3, WYb.
Source: Authors' calculations.

Single-Equation Models

Though we do not believe that single-equation models for exports are satisfactory, we have nevertheless estimated such equations for the sake of completeness. In all cases the equations take the form

(11-3) $X = f(RERsa, WY, DD)$

where X denotes nonoil exports (defined as either QXc or QXb), WY and DD as before denote world demand for Indian exports and the pressure of domestic demand, respectively. RERsa measures the real effective exchange rate, allowing for the impact of export subsidies. The weights in the exchange rate index are the shares of India's most important industrial-country trading partners in India's exports. A priori we would expect RERsa to enter with a negative sign. Domestic demand can also be expected to enter negatively and WY positively.

The proxies used for domestic demand are the same as those used in the supply equation above. The results of a selection of the estimated models are presented in table 11.8. In all regressions the demand effects proxied by monetary measures enter with a lag.

Equations *(i)* to *(iv)* differ according to the demand proxy used for monetary conditions. All include an estimate of fiscal demand pressure *GFD*. The equations yield rather similar results. They suggest that the short-run elasticity of exports

Table 11.8   Exports: Estimates of Single-Equation Models

Independent variables	*Dependent variable QXc*				
	(i)	*(ii)*	*(iii)*	*(iv)*	*(v)*
$QXc_{(t-1)}$	0.60	0.61	0.59	0.61	0.49
	(6.01)	(6.11)	(6.64)	(6.93)	(5.32)
RERsa	−0.69	−0.67	−0.85	−0.83	−0.72
	(4.45)	(4.29)	(6.19)	(6.26)	(5.59)
WYb	0.18	0.17	0.09	0.07	0.17
	(1.55)	(1.45)	(0.93)	(0.72)	(1.80)
$exD3_{(t-1)}$	−0.36				
	(1.64)				
$exD1_{(t-1)}$		−0.37			
		(1.75)			
$exRD3_{(t-1)}$			−0.42		
			(2.82)		
$ex\,RD1_{(t-1)}$				−0.45	
				(−3.05)	
GFD	−1.04	−0.89	−1.13	−0.95	
	(1.76)	(1.53)	(2.11)	(1.94)	
TFE					−2.49
					(2.66)
Constant	4.37	4.29	5.52	5.45	4.96
	(3.86)	(3.78)	(5.71)	(5.80)	(5.38)
Time period	1962–87	1962–87	1962–87	1962–87	1961–87
Autocorrelation $\chi^2(1)$	1.18	1.22	0.03	0.02	0.88
Normality $\chi^2(2)$	0.74	0.68	0.29	0.78	0.67
Percent s.e.	4.88	4.84	4.39	4.29	4.56

Source: Authors' calculations.

with respect to the real (subsidy adjusted) exchange rate is between 0.67 and 0.83 in the short run, rising to between 1.72 and 2.13 in the long run. About 80 percent of the long-run effect comes through within two years after the current year. The real-money excess demand variables are clearly significant, the nominal-money ones somewhat less so. The signs are as expected. The fiscal excess demand variable *GFD* is normally significant and enters with the expected sign. The effect of world demand is not statistically significant at the 5 percent level in any of the equations. This was also true when other proxies for world demand, such as *WYa* or *WYc* were used.

Equation *(v)* is slightly different insofar as the monetary and fiscal proxies for domestic demand are replaced by *TFE* defined as before. As can be seen this variable enters significantly but the standard error of the equation rises somewhat, to 4.56 percent. There is also some doubt as to the weak exogeneity of this variable (given the fact that exports are a part of the variable) and so we do not stress these results.

In none of the estimated equations is there evidence of first-order autocorrelation or non-normally distributed residuals. Models using *QXb* were also estimated, which yielded very similar results. Hence they are not reported here.

Conclusions and Qualifications

Export demand is significantly negatively related to the relative price of Indian and competitor-country exports. The price elasticity of demand for exports is about 1.1 in the short run and 3.0 in the long run, with 80 percent of the long-run effect coming through within two years after the current year. Exports also depend positively on change in world income but this effect is not quite significant statistically.

Export supply is significantly positively related to the domestic relative price of exports and other goods. The price elasticity of supply of exports is about 0.7 in the short run and 1.1 in the long run, with over 80 percent of the effect coming through within one year after the current year. Export supply is also significantly negatively related to the pressure of aggregate demand on the home market.

Finally, we note several reasons for thinking that the above estimate of price elasticity of export demand is on the low side.

- The use of "unit value" as a proxy for export price introduces a downward bias into the demand elasticity of exports. This is because the unit value index does not have fixed weights. For example, a price increase for an individual export commodity, which results in a decline in exports, will reduce the weight of the commodity in the index, biasing the coefficient on the export price toward zero.
- Our estimate of demand elasticity is for nonoil exports as a whole and includes many primary commodities. Demand elasticities for manufactured

goods can be expected to be considerably higher than the overall elasticity. Over time, the composition of India's exports has shifted toward manufactured goods. Hence, the measured elasticity is likely to be an underestimate of the true elasticity at present.

- There are not enough degrees of freedom in annual data to allow satisfactorily for the long lags in the effects of exchange rate changes due to the difficulty of breaking into export markets and the lags in export-oriented investment.
- Price elasticities are reduced below their unrestricted levels in a quantity-controlled regime.

Data Sources for Export Equations

1. *Export volume. QXc* from table 11.3, *QXa* and *QXb* from Government of India, DGCIS; and Government of India, Ministry of Finance (various years), *Economic Survey.*
2. *Export unit values for India.* Government of India, DGCIS; and Government of India, Ministry of Finance (various years), *Economic Survey.*
3. *Export unit values for industrial countries and nonoil developing countries.* IMF (1988).
4. *Industrial-country GDP.* IMF, *International Financial Statistics Yearbook* (various years).
5. *World GDP (net of the former Soviet Union and Eastern Europe).* IMF, *International Financial Statistics Yearbook* (various years).
6. *Export volume of nonoil developing countries.* IMF, *International Financial Statistics Yearbook* (various years).
7. *Indian wholesale prices.* Government of India, Ministry of Finance (various years), *Economic Survey.*
8. *Indian money supply.* Table 10.1.
9. *Indian GDP and total final expenditure.* Government of India, CSO (various years), *National Accounts Statistics.*
10. *India's real effective exchange rate.* Table 11.3.
11. *Indian export subsidies and incentives.* Table 11.3.
12. *India's consolidated fiscal deficit.* Government of India, Ministry of Finance (various years), *Indian Economic Statistics: Public Finance.*

Chapter Twelve

The Deficits and Surpluses of the Public and Private Sectors

In chapter 9 on fiscal policy we discussed the deficits of the consolidated government and the economy as a whole. The sustainability of these deficits was analyzed. In this chapter we consider separately the balance of savings and investment of the public, corporate, and household sectors, concentrating on savings and their determination. In chapter 13 we concentrate on public and private investment, and on its efficiency and contribution to growth.

It is beyond the scope of this book to attempt a complete explanation of the determinants of savings. We concentrate on suggesting ways in which macroeconomic policy may have been influential. Table 12.1 shows savings and investment for the three sectors, as well as for India as a whole. It also shows implicitly how total investment is financed by the savings of the three sectors and by foreign savings. We first consider household savings.

Household Saving

Household saving accounts for 60 to 80 percent of domestic saving. Households by the national accounts definition include unincorporated enterprises. The national accounts divide household savings into their physical and financial components. Household physical saving is defined as identically equal to household investment; its estimation is very unreliable. (For a description of the methodology, see appendix A on the quality of statistics.[1]) The national accounts do not distinguish between domestic and national saving; current transfers from Indian emigrants and net factor incomes from abroad are recorded as part of domestic saving. The household saving rate increased from around 8 percent of GDP in the early 1960s to over 15 percent in the late 1970s. It then dipped to around 13 to 14

Table 12.1 Public, Corporate, and Household Savings and Investment, 1960/61 to 1989/90
(current prices, percentage of GDP)

Year	Public			Corporate			Household			Total		
	Invest-ment	Savings	Deficit	Invest-ment	Savings	Deficit	Invest-ment	Savings	Surplus	Invest-ment	Savings	Deficit
1960/61	7.1	2.6	4.4	3.3	1.7	1.6	5.4	8.4	3.0	15.7	12.7	3.0
1961/62	6.7	2.9	3.8	4.3	1.8	2.5	3.2	7.5	4.3	14.2	12.2	2.0
1962/63	7.8	3.1	4.8	2.9	1.8	1.1	5.1	8.5	3.4	15.8	13.4	2.4
1963/64	7.9	3.3	4.6	4.1	1.8	2.3	3.4	8.2	4.8	15.4	13.3	2.1
1964/65	7.9	3.3	4.6	3.6	1.5	2.1	3.6	7.8	4.2	15.1	12.7	2.4
1965/66	8.5	3.1	5.4	2.7	1.5	1.2	5.7	9.9	4.2	16.8	14.5	2.3
1966/67	7.2	2.3	5.0	2.1	1.4	0.7	9.1	11.6	2.5	18.4	15.3	3.1
1967/68	6.7	1.9	4.8	2.3	1.2	1.1	6.3	9.9	3.6	15.4	13.0	2.4
1968/69	5.9	2.3	3.6	2.1	1.2	0.9	6.0	9.3	3.3	13.9	12.8	1.1
1969/70	5.6	2.6	3.0	1.6	1.3	0.3	8.3	11.1	2.8	15.6	15.0	0.6
1970/71	6.5	2.9	3.6	2.4	1.5	0.9	7.8	11.3	3.5	16.6	15.7	0.9
1971/72	7.1	2.8	4.3	2.8	1.6	1.2	7.6	11.8	4.2	17.3	16.2	1.0
1972/73	7.3	2.6	4.7	2.6	1.5	1.1	6.3	11.2	4.9	15.9	15.4	0.6
1973/74	7.7	2.9	4.8	2.6	1.7	0.9	8.7	13.8	5.1	19.1	18.4	0.6
1974/75	7.6	3.7	3.9	3.7	2.0	1.7	6.8	11.8	5.0	18.3	17.4	0.9
1975/76	9.6	4.2	5.4	2.7	1.3	1.4	6.4	13.4	7.0	18.8	19.0	-0.2
1976/77	10.1	4.9	5.2	1.5	1.4	0.1	8.1	15.0	6.9	19.7	21.2	-1.5
1977/78	8.2	4.3	3.9	2.4	1.4	1.0	8.9	15.3	6.4	19.5	21.1	-1.5
1978/79	9.5	4.6	4.9	2.2	1.6	0.6	11.9	17.0	5.1	23.3	23.2	0.1

(table continues on next page)

Table 12.1 (continued)

Year	Public Invest-ment	Public Savings	Public Deficit	Corporate Invest-ment	Corporate Savings	Corporate Deficit	Household Invest-ment	Household Savings	Household Surplus	Total Invest-ment	Total Savings	Total Deficit
1979/80	10.3	4.3	6.0	2.7	2.1	0.6	9.2	15.2	6.0	22.1	21.6	0.5
1980/81	8.7	3.4	5.3	2.5	1.7	0.8	11.5	16.1	4.6	22.7	21.2	1.5
1981/82	10.5	4.5	6.0	5.7	1.6	4.1	6.4	14.9	8.5	22.6	21.0	1.6
1982/83	11.3	4.4	6.9	5.7	1.6	4.1	3.6	13.1	9.5	20.6	19.1	1.4
1983/84	9.8	3.3	6.5	3.4	1.5	1.9	6.8	14.0	7.2	20.0	18.8	1.2
1984/85	10.8	2.8	8.0	4.4	1.7	2.7	4.5	13.7	9.2	19.6	18.2	1.4
1985/86	11.1	3.2	7.9	5.5	2.0	3.5	5.5	14.5	9.0	22.1	19.7	2.4
1986/87	11.7	2.7	9.0	5.3	1.7	3.6	3.6	13.9	10.3	20.6	18.4	2.2
1987/88	10.4	2.2	8.2	3.6	1.7	1.9	8.3	16.5	8.2	22.4	20.3	2.1
1988/89	9.9	2.0	7.9	4.2	2.1	2.1	9.8	17.1	7.3	23.9	21.1	2.8
1989/90	10.7	1.7	9.0	3.9	2.1	1.8	9.4	17.8	8.4	24.1	21.7	2.4

Note: Errors and omissions in total investment are attributed entirely to household investment.

Source: Government of India, CSO (1989a); Government of India, CSO (1991), National Accounts Statistics; and Government of India, CSO (1991), Quick Estimates of National Income 1989/90.

percent from 1982/83 to 1986/87; the rising trend seemed to have reached a plateau.[2] However, there was a further rise to over 17 percent in the closing years of the decade. Within the total, financial savings and private physical savings (investment) moved somewhat differently.

Household Financial Saving

Table 12.2 gives the breakdown of household saving into its components. Household financial savings as a proportion of GDP show a tendency to stagnate or fall during or immediately following episodes of high inflation/recession when real interest rates turn sharply negative, for example 1966/67 to 1968/69, 1974/75, and 1979/80 to 1981/82.[3] (For real interest rates see table 12.6 at the end of the chapter). Looking at changes over longer periods, the notable feature is the rapid growth of financial savings in the 1970s, particularly in the latter half of the decade. The following factors may be advanced to explain this phenomenon.

- The decade of the 1970s closely followed bank nationalization in 1969. The policy of spreading bank branches throughout the country had been initiated a few years before nationalization but was most vigorously pursued during this period. (Note the fall in population per bank branch in table 12.6). It seems that the new opportunities to hold bank deposits increased savings (particularly rural savings) as well as their financial component.[4]
- The second half of the 1970s was the first five-year period since 1960/61 when real bank deposit rates were positive. (See table 12.6.)
- Another feature of importance in the 1970s was the rapid rise in remittances from Indian workers who emigrated to the Gulf countries in response to the oil boom. Foreign remittances rose from 0.2 percent of GDP to 1.5 percent of GDP during the course of the decade.
- Another explanation (though more speculative) of the rise in the saving rate in the second half of the 1970s is that agriculture's terms of trade against industry worsened quite sharply in this period, causing a shift in income distribution away from agriculture. There is some evidence that the marginal propensity to save is lower in rural areas than it is in urban areas.
- Household financial savings as a proportion of GDP continued to rise, albeit more slowly, in the 1980s. The spread of banking has slowed down considerably and so has the increase in remittances from the Middle East. Real deposit rates averaged a small negative figure between 1980/81 and 1984/85 and a small positive figure since.

Table 12.2 Components of Household Savings, 1960/61 to 1989/90
(percentage of GDP at market prices, unless otherwise indicated)

Year	Total	Period average	Financial	Period average	Physical	Period average	Percent financial[a]	Period average
1960/61	8.4		2.8		5.6		33.3	
1961/62	7.5		2.9		4.6		38.7	
1962/63	8.5		2.7		5.8		31.8	
1963/64	8.2		3.5		4.6		42.7	
1964/65	7.8	8.1	2.9	3.0	4.9	5.1	37.2	37.0
1965/66	9.9		4.1		5.8		41.4	
1966/67	11.6		2.9		8.7		25.0	
1967/68	9.9		2.5		7.4		25.3	
1968/69	9.3		2.2		7.1		23.7	
1969/70	11.1	10.4	2.3	2.8	8.8	7.6	20.7	26.9
1970/71	11.3		3.2		8.1		28.3	
1971/72	11.8		3.4		8.5		28.8	
1972/73	11.2		4.2		7.0		37.5	
1973/74	13.8		5.8		8.0		42.0	
1974/75	11.8	12.0	3.2	4.0	8.5	8.0	27.1	33.3

1975/76	13.4		5.0		8.4		37.3
1976/77	15.0		5.7		9.2		38.0
1977/78	15.3		6.1		9.2		39.9
1978/79	17.0		6.4		10.6		37.6
1979/80	15.2	15.2	5.3	5.7	9.9	9.5	34.9	37.5
1980/81	16.1		6.3		9.7		39.1
1981/82	14.9		6.0		8.8		40.3
1982/83	13.1		7.2		6.0		55.0
1983/84	14.0		6.4		7.6		45.7
1984/85	13.7	14.3	7.7	6.7	6.0	7.6	56.2	46.9
1985/86	14.5		7.1		7.4		49.0
1986/87	13.9		7.9		6.1		56.8
1987/88	16.5		7.8		8.6		47.3
1988/89	17.1		7.3		9.8		42.7
1989/90	17.8	16.0	8.9	7.8	8.9	8.2	50.0	48.8

a. Share of financial in total household saving.

Note: Household physical savings is identical to household investment (unadjusted).

Source: Government of India, CSO (1989a); Government of India, CSO (1991), *National Accounts Statistics*; and Government of India, CSO (1991), *Quick Estimates of National Income 1989/90.*

Household Physical Saving

Household physical saving has also increased substantially over the period. Unlike financial saving, it has shown no tendency to stagnate during periods of high inflation. This may be because of the tendency to substitute real assets for financial assets at such times. Even so, the large jump during the inflation of the mid-1960s is hard to explain. It continued on a slowly rising trend until the end of the 1970s. Since then this trend has reversed itself, falling from about 10 percent of GDP to about 8 percent. The reasons for this are conjectural. It has been suggested that the slowing down of the green revolution has reduced the profitability of private investment in agriculture. Another possibility is that the rise in public borrowing (see below) has crowded out investment in the small-scale industrial sector, which is included under "households."

Macroeconomic Policy and Household Savings

To what extent can long-term movements in household saving be attributed to macroeconomic policy? The answer depends on how macroeconomic policy is defined. If it is taken to mean short-term crisis management, it is difficult to see any direct influence except perhaps through the generally anti-inflationary use of monetary and fiscal policy (see chapters 9 and 10). In contrast, we believe that the general style of macroeconomic policy was influential. An important determinant of the rate of saving appears to have been the spread of banking. This was deliberate policy aimed at promoting monetization of the economy and increasing financial saving. These aims were achieved. Moreover, total household saving increased; that is, financial saving did not merely substitute for physical saving.

The other important influence on saving has been through the real interest (deposit) rate. The general style of policy was to rely on controls, including financial controls. So the nominal interest rate was an administered price, changed at infrequent intervals, and the real interest rate moved with the rate of inflation. In general, over five-year periods real deposit rates were slightly negative or slightly positive; there was no attempt to promote or allow high rates. Evidently whatever discouragement this might have given to the growth of saving was outweighed by the positive effect of the spread of banking. A tendency for high inflation (and concomitant sharply negative real deposit rates) to discourage financial saving *can* be discerned in the data. It is of some importance, therefore, that macroeconomic policy had an anti-inflationary stance and that high inflation and sharply negative real deposit rates were not allowed to persist for long. In the last thirty years, *ex post* real deposit rates were less than –5 percent in only 5 years, and less than –15 percent in only 1 year. The generally stable financial climate also probably helped the growth of foreign remittances in the second half of the 1970s, although of course they also had exogenous causes.

Corporate Saving

We have not researched the determinants of corporate savings, and therefore have little to say about this sector, which in any case accounts for only around 10 percent of total savings in recent years. The sector is always in deficit, its own savings financing about 40 percent of investment in the 1980s and rather more in earlier years. Savings have very gradually risen as a percentage of GDP, but investment has risen a little more. Investments fluctuate much more from year to year than savings, so that the deficit has effectively varied from almost nothing to about 4 percent of GDP. However, we are doubtful about the validity of the annual fluctuations in investment (see chapter 13).

Public Saving

Indian plans have strongly emphasized the role of public savings as a support for public investment. In practice, public saving as a proportion of GDP has stagnated, except for an upturn in the second half of the 1970s. After 1981/82 there was a pronounced fall, which contributed to rising public deficits. In the three years 1987/88 to 1989/90 public saving averaged only 2 percent of GDP, which is lower than in any earlier three-year period.

It is instructive to break down public saving into saving by different components of the public sector. Table 12.3 gives separate estimates for government administration and public enterprises. The latter are further subdivided into financial and nonfinancial enterprises.

Government

From 1960/61 to 1964/65 government saving rose above the levels attained in earlier periods, primarily due to increased tax effort. But in the second half of the decade, government saving fell. This reflected the fall in tax revenue during a period of recession combined with the fact that expenditure cuts were directed at investment, not current expenditure.

In the 1970s government savings rose. This happened even during the crisis years of 1973/74 and 1974/75 because in these years (unlike the crisis years in the 1960s) there were drastic cuts in current expenditure. In the second half of the decade there were sizable increases in government expenditure, a trend which was to persist, and even accelerate later. But government revenue also rose strongly, partly because of the economic recovery during this period; consequently there was little change in government saving.

In the 1980s there was a sharp deterioration in government saving, which became increasingly negative after 1984/85 and has helped to contribute to a danger-

Table 12.3 Components of Gross Public Saving, 1960/61 to 1989/90
(percentage of GDP at market prices)

Year	Total public	Period average	Government administration	Period average	Public enterprises Total	Period average	Financial	Period average	Non-financial	Period average
1960/61	2.6		1.3		1.4		0.1		1.3	
1961/62	2.9		1.4		1.5		0.1		1.4	
1962/63	3.1		1.5		1.6		0.2		1.4	
1963/64	3.3		1.5		1.9		0.2		1.7	
1964/65	3.3	3.0	1.9	1.5	1.4	1.6	0.2	0.2	1.2	1.4
1965/66	3.1		1.5		1.6		0.3		1.3	
1966/67	2.3		0.9		1.3		0.1		1.2	
1967/68	1.9		0.8		1.2		0.2		1.0	
1968/69	2.3		1.1		1.3		0.1		1.2	
1969/70	2.6	2.4	1.1	1.1	1.4	1.4	0.2	0.2	1.2	1.2
1970/71	2.9		1.3		1.6		0.2		1.4	
1971/72	2.8		1.2		1.6		0.2		1.4	
1972/73	2.6		1.0		1.6		0.3		1.3	
1973/74	2.9		1.5		1.4		0.4		1.0	
1974/75	3.7	3.0	2.0	1.4	1.6	1.6	0.5	0.3	1.1	1.2

Year									
1975/76	4.2		2.7		1.6		0.5		1.1
1976/77	4.9		2.5		2.4		0.7		1.7
1977/78	4.3		2.2		2.2		0.6		1.6
1978/79	4.6		2.4		2.2		0.7		1.5
1979/80	4.3	4.5	2.3	2.4	2.1	2.1	0.7	0.6	1.4	1.5
1980/81	3.4		1.9		1.5		0.6		0.9
1981/82	4.5		2.4		2.2		0.8		1.4
1982/83	4.4		1.6		2.8		0.9		1.9
1983/84	3.3		0.6		2.7		1.0		1.7
1984/85	2.8	3.7	-0.1	1.3	3.0	2.4	0.9	0.9	2.1	1.6
1985/86	3.2		-0.2		3.4		1.1		2.3
1986/87	2.7		-0.8		3.6		1.1		2.5
1987/88	2.2		-1.6		3.8		1.0		2.8
1988/89	2.0		-2.1		4.1		1.1	1.1	3.0	2.7
1989/90	1.7	2.4	-2.6	-1.5	4.2	3.8	—		—

Source: Government of India, CSO (1989a); Government of India, CSO (1991), *National Accounts Statistics*; and Government of India, CSO (1991), *Quick Estimates of National Income 1989/90*.

303

ous fiscal crisis. This arose from changes in political economy, which had been occurring in creeping fashion for a long time. But they first clearly surfaced in the 1970s and intensified in the 1980s. These changes consisted of a move toward a more populist style of government at both the center and in the states, the growth of various powerful interest groups including public sector trade unions, the assertion of states' rights, and the growth of the black economy—all factors making for looser fiscal control (see chapters 3 and 9).

These tendencies manifested themselves in various ways, some of which are apparent in the data on government revenue and expenditure already given in table 9.1. Subsidies as a proportion of GDP have been on a rising trend over the whole period since 1960/61. There was a sharp rise in the second half of the 1970s, with a short lived plateau during the IMF program at the beginning of the 1980s. Since 1982/83 there has been another sharp rise to over 3.5 percent of GDP. Interest payments have also risen rapidly from about 1 percent at the end of the 1970s to about 3 percent in 1987/88 and 1988/89, due mainly to a rise in the debt. Other features that have probably contributed to the rise of expenditure are the growth in corruption and the sharp increases in central transfers to the states after the award of the Seventh Finance Commission in 1978.

Public Enterprises

Public enterprise investment has grown significantly as a proportion of GDP.[5] But the saving performance of public enterprises has been inadequate, with the implication that the public sector is relying to a growing extent on capturing private savings for its own use (see table 12.3). From 1960/61 to 1974/75 there was virtually no change in public enterprise savings, which hovered around 1.6 percent of GDP, apart from a dip below that level for a few years after the crisis of 1966. There was a slight increase to around 2.2 percent of GDP during the second half of the 1970s, partly resulting from bank nationalization and consequently higher recorded savings in financial enterprises. Savings of nonfinancial enterprises showed no growth trend as a proportion of GDP until the 1980s. The savings of these enterprises doubled from around 1.5 percent of GDP in the late 1970s to 3 percent in 1988/89. But this change is almost entirely on account of the highly profitable oil sector and masks the low or negative profitability of a large proportion of other public enterprises (see chapter 13).

The causes of low public enterprise profitability are manifold—multiplicity of objectives, lack of adequate project selection procedures, inappropriate pricing, lack of penalties for inefficiency in an economy in which the public sector is substantially insulated from international and domestic competition, and political interference with management (see chapters 1 and 9 for further discussion). The only factor in this list with an obvious macroeconomic connection is pricing—there is a tendency to hold down administered prices of key goods to avoid cost-push pressures. Most of the other factors mentioned derive from the general style and philosophy of economic policymaking.

Macroeconomic Policy and Public Savings

Our brief survey of the behavior of public savings does not indicate any obvious relationships with short-term macroeconomic policy except perhaps in two respects. There appears to be some tendency for subsidies to move to permanently higher levels after they are increased during macroeconomic crises (for example, after 1966/67 and 1974/75); and the attitude toward price controls may have contributed to keeping down public enterprise profits.

But these are asides to the main story. The causes of low public enterprise savings lie principally in the style and philosophy of economic policy. The belief in "planning without prices" reduces efficiency in public enterprises and keeps their savings low. This mattered less while a certain austerity prevailed in government administration, and while government savings were positive. But in recent years this austerity has been eroded and the government is dissaving. Consequently, overall public savings have fallen sharply.

Though the inadequacy of public sector savings does not have obvious macroeconomic causes, it undoubtedly has potentially adverse macroeconomic effects. Why India has so far escaped these and whether it can continue to do so is discussed below and in chapter 9.

The Financing of Public Investment

Table 12.4 presents information on the financing of public investment by public saving, public domestic borrowing, and public foreign borrowing. There was no growth trend in public sector borrowing from 1960/61 to 1974/75, during which period it averaged about 4.4 percent of GDP. However, borrowing was temporarily reduced during the 1966/67 and 1974/75 crises. This contrasts with the 1980/81 crisis, during which borrowing rose to 6 percent and has continued to rise to 9 percent in 1989/90. The rise seems to have begun after 1974/75 with a dip only in 1977/78. The reasons for the rise differed as between the second half of the 1970s and the 1980s. In the first period public deficits rose, despite some rise in public savings, because public investment was growing strongly. In the second period the growth of public investment slowed but public deficits increased because public savings fell. The rising public sector deficits have principally been covered by domestic borrowing, although in the 1980s foreign borrowing also rose as a proportion of GDP (see also chapter 9).

Table 12.5 divides domestic borrowing between the Reserve Bank, the commercial banks, and the nonbank public. All categories have shown substantial increases. Since 1984/85 borrowing from the commercial banks and the nonbank public (through small savings schemes, for example) has continued apace. The rise in borrowing from the commercial banks has been achieved by increases in the statutory liquidity ratio. Direct borrowing from the public has in recent years

Table 12.4 Financing of Public Investment, 1960/61 to 1989/90

(percentage of GDP at market prices)

Year	Public GDCF	Period average	Gross public saving	Period average	Total	Period average	Public sector borrowing			
							Foreign	Period average	Domestic	Period average
1960/61	7.1		2.6		4.5		1.9		2.6	
1961/62	6.9		2.9		4.0		1.7		2.3	
1962/63	7.8		3.1		4.7		2.0		2.7	
1963/64	7.9		3.3		4.6		2.2		2.4	
1964/65	7.9	7.5	3.3	3.0	4.6	4.5	3.1	2.2	1.5	2.3
1965/66	8.5		3.1		5.4		2.3		3.1	
1966/67	7.2		2.3		4.9		2.9		2.0	
1967/68	6.7		1.9		4.8		1.8		3.0	
1968/69	5.9		2.3		3.6		1.6		2.0	
1969/70	5.6	6.8	2.6	2.4	3.0	4.3	1.2	2.0	1.8	2.3
1970/71	6.5		2.9		3.6		1.0		2.6	
1971/72	7.1		2.8		4.3		1.2		3.1	
1972/73	7.3		2.6		4.7		0.8		3.9	
1973/74	7.7		2.9		4.8		0.8		4.0	
1974/75	7.6	7.2	3.7	3.0	3.9	4.3	1.1	1.0	2.8	3.3

1975/76	9.6		4.2		5.4		1.8		3.6	
1976/77	10.1		4.9		5.2		1.5		2.7	
1977/78	8.2		4.3		3.9		1.2		2.7	
1978/79	9.5		4.6		4.9		0.8		4.1	
1979/80	10.3 9.6		4.3 4.5		6.0 5.1		0.8 1.2		5.2 3.9	
1980/81	8.7		3.4		5.3		1.2		4.1	
1981/82	10.5		4.5		6.0		0.7		5.3	
1982/83	11.3		4.4		6.9		1.0		5.9	
1983/84	9.8		3.3		6.5		0.9		5.6	
1984/85	10.8 1C.2		2.8 3.7		8.0 6.5		1.4 1.0		6.6 5.5	
1985/86	11.1		3.2		7.9		1.1		6.8	
1986/87	11.7		2.7		9.0		1.6		7.4	
1987/88	10.4		2.2		8.2		1.3		6.9	
1988/89	9.9		2.0		7.9		1.3		6.6	
1989/90	10.7 10.8		1.7 2.4		9.0 8.4		1.1 1.3		7.9 7.1	

Source: Last two columns from World Bank (various years), "India: Country Economic Memorandum"; other columns as for table 12.1.

307

Table 12.5 Sources of Public Domestic Borrowing, 1960/61 to 1989/90
(percentage of GDP at market prices)

Year	Total	Period average	Reserve bank	Period average	Commercial banks	Period average	Banking system	Period average	Nonbank public	Period average
1960/61	2.6		—		—		—		—	
1961/62	2.3		0.9		0.3		1.2		1.1	
1962/63	2.7		1.2		0.0		1.1		1.6	
1963/64	2.4		0.9		0.2		1.1		1.3	
1964/65	1.5	2.3	0.5	0.9	0.3	0.2	0.8	1.1	0.7	1.2
1965/66	3.1		1.4		0.4		1.8		1.3	
1966/67	2.0		0.4		0.3		0.7		1.3	
1967/68	3.0		0.5		0.3		0.8		2.2	
1968/69	2.0		0.9		0.3		1.2		0.8	
1969/70	1.8	2.3	-0.2	0.5	0.3	0.3	0.1	0.9	1.7	1.4
1970/71	2.6		0.7		0.5		1.2		1.4	
1971/72	3.1		1.9		0.7		2.6		0.5	
1972/73	3.9		1.6		1.1		2.7		1.2	
1973/74	4.0		1.2		0.3		1.5		2.5	
1974/75	2.8	3.3	0.5	1.2	0.6	0.6	1.1	1.8	1.7	1.5

Year										
1975/76	3.6		0.2		0.5		0.7		2.9	
1976/77	2.7		0.3		0.8		1.1		1.6	
1977/78	2.7		0.6		2.3		2.9		-0.2	
1978/79	4.1		1.2		0.8		2.0		2.1	
1979/80	5.2	3.9	2.6	1.0	0.8	1.0	3.4	2.0	1.8	1.9
1980/81	4.1		2.6		1.2		3.8		0.3	
1981/82	5.3		2.5		0.6		3.1		2.2	
1982/83	5.9		1.3		1.3		2.6		3.3	
1983/84	5.6		1.9		0.7		2.6		3.0	
1984/85	6.6	5.5	2.6	2.2	0.9	0.9	3.5	3.1	3.1	2.4
1985/86	6.8		2.4		1.4		2.8		3.0	
1986/87	7.4		2.6		2.1		4.7		2.7	
1987/88	6.9		1.9		1.8		3.7		3.2	
1988/89	6.6		1.6		1.3					
1989/90	7.9	7.1	3.1	2.3	1.5	1.6				

Note: The second, third, and fourth columns refer to government borrowing only. The last column includes nongovernment public borrowing from the commercial banks.

Source: First column, table 12.4; second, third, and fourth columns, RBI (various years), *Report on Currency and Finance*. Fifth column, residual.

been carried out at sharply rising effective interest rates (particularly given the very substantial tax breaks).

A standard hypothesis is that high public sector borrowing will tend to crowd out private investment. We see no evidence of this except in the period 1982/83 to 1986/87 when there was a clear dip in household physical savings; that is, investment (see table 12.2). As we shall see in chapter 13 (table 13.1), total *fixed* private investment was also relatively low in this period, but this was more than entirely due to the household sector, as corporate investment was relatively high. This was also a period of high public sector borrowing from the commercial banks and the public (see table 12.5). In this connection it must be remembered that household investment includes that of unincorporated enterprises. It is thus possible that some investment in this sector was crowded out. That the rising public deficit did not crowd out private investment to a greater extent was because it was increasingly financed by a deterioration in the current amount of the balance of payments, shown in the last column of table 12.1.

The Sustainability of Public Deficits

The general conditions governing the size of long-run sustainable public sector deficits were derived in chapter 9. It was shown that India's public sector and current account deficits, and associated increases in domestic and foreign debt, have reached levels (relative to GDP and exports) far higher than could be sustained for long. It was in fact the level of foreign debt, together with the current account deficit, that caused the crisis of 1990/91.

On the domestic front, the rising public deficits have not thus far produced any dramatic adverse effects with respect to the crowding out of private investment or inflation. This is mainly to be attributed to the continued growth in household savings and in the demand of households for real financial assets. In addition, banks were forced to channel a greater proportion of the credit counterpart of deposit creation to financing public sector deficits. New public instruments have also been introduced with very attractive post-tax rates of return to attract household savings.

However, the relative ease of the domestic situation was, of course, partly due to the increase in foreign borrowing, which was far from benign. The urgency of reducing the public deficit is also underlined by the fact that the authorities cannot rely on household savings rates rising yet further. Many of the factors favorable to household savings (for example, the spread of banking and foreign remittances) have lost their impetus. In the absence of continued strong growth of household savings, rising real interest rates would be required to induce household lending to the government, which would create crowding out problems and further worsen public deficits. The technique of capturing household savings by forcing banks to lend to the government at below-market interest rates is also reaching its limits.

Summary

Households including unincorporated enterprises account for nearly 80 percent of total savings in recent years—some 16 percent of GDP. They seem now to be on a plateau, having experienced a notable rise earlier, especially in the 1970s. The rise was largely the result of the rapid spread of banking, though remittances from workers overseas also played a part. Private corporate saving accounts for only about 10 percent of total saving, and shows no clear trend. Public savings have been disappointing. They grew to a peak of nearly 5 percent of GDP in the mid-1970s, and then fell away to about 2 percent, much the same as private corporate investment. In the early days of Indian planning, it was expected that public savings would provide much of the finance for public investment. In fact, the public deficit has grown, especially in the 1980s, to 8 to 9 percent of GDP. This has been mainly because of the rapid growth of current government expenditure, especially subsidies and interest, so that government administration (apart from public enterprises) is dissaving to the extent of over 2.5 percent of GDP. There is an urgent need to reduce the public sector deficit.

Table 12.6   Spread of Banking and Interest Rate Indicators, 1960/61 to 1989/90

Year	Population per bank branch/1,000	Period average	Deposit rate[a]	Inflation[a] (WPI)	Real deposit rate (ex post)[a]	Period average
1960/61	88		3.3			
1961/62	89		4.0	0.2	3.8	
1962/63	88		4.0	3.8	0.2	
1963/64	85		4.0	6.3	−2.3	
1964/65	81	86	4.8	10.8	−6.1	−1.1
1965/66	79		5.5	7.7	−2.2	
1966/67	75		6.0	13.9	−7.9	
1967/68	73		6.0	11.6	−5.6	
1968/69	68		5.5	−1.2	6.7	
1969/70	59	71	5.5	3.8	1.7	−1.5
1970/71	48		6.0	5.5	0.5	
1971/72	43		6.0	5.6	0.4	
1972/73	39		6.0	10.0	−4.0	
1973/74	35		6.0	20.2	−14.2	
1974/75	33	40	8.0	25.2	−17.2	−6.9
1975/76	30		8.0	−1.1	9.1	
1976/77	26		8.0	2.1	5.9	
1977/78	23		6.0	5.2	0.8	
1978/79	21		6.0	0.0	6.0	
1979/80	20	24	7.0	17.1	−10.1	2.3
1980/81	18		7.5	18.2	−10.7	
1981/82	16		8.0	9.3	−1.3	
1982/83	16		9.0	2.6	6.4	
1983/84	15		8.0	9.5	−1.5	
1984/85	13	16	8.0	7.1	0.9	−0.7
1985/86	13		8.5	5.7	2.8	
1986/87	13		8.5	5.3	3.2	
1987/88	13		9.0	7.6	1.4	
1988/89	12		9.0	7.4	1.6	
1989/90	12	13	9.0	7.4	1.6	2.1

a. Percentage per year.

Source: First column, Reserve Bank of India (various years), *Report on Trends and Progress of Banking in India*; second column, Reserve Bank of India (various years), *Report on Currency and Finance*; third column, Government of India, Ministry of Finance (various years), *Economic Survey* for WPI.

Chapter Thirteen

Investment and Growth

Macroeconomic policy is undoubtedly a major determinant of the real growth of an economy. In the short to medium run it causes changes in the intensity of use of resources, and the efficiency with which they are used. It also influences the level of both material investment and investment in people, these being the main determinants of long-run growth in income per head.[1]

Fiscal, monetary, and trade and exchange rate policies have been independently discussed and assessed in chapters 9, 10, and 11. These policies were judged by the short- to medium-run success with which they were used to maintain internal and external balance, while keeping changes in the price level within tolerable bounds. But we also tried to indicate their probable longer run effects on efficiency and on investment. These indications will be brought together in our concluding chapter 14.

In this chapter we concentrate directly on public and private investment as normally defined in the national accounts, paying particular attention to its apparent efficiency. We ignore investment in human beings only because we have done no work on that subject. Consideration of the effects of macroeconomic policy are limited to the changes in public investment that were part of that policy. The macroeconomic crises and the political changes that account for the erratic path of public sector investment—erratic at least until about 1976/77—have been described in chapters 4 to 8. In this chapter we try to make a more synoptic and long-term assessment, and also bring private investment more into the picture.

Figure 13.1 portrays the growth of public and private investment. More detail of investment and its fluctuations is given in tables 13.6 through 13.8. Where possible, the story is told in terms of gross fixed investment, partly because we believe that figures for investment in inventories are even less reliable than those for fixed investment, but also because fixed investment is probably more controllable and hence relatable to stabilization measures. We use gross investment because there are theoretical grounds for believing that it is more relevant for growth than net investment, as normally estimated.[2]

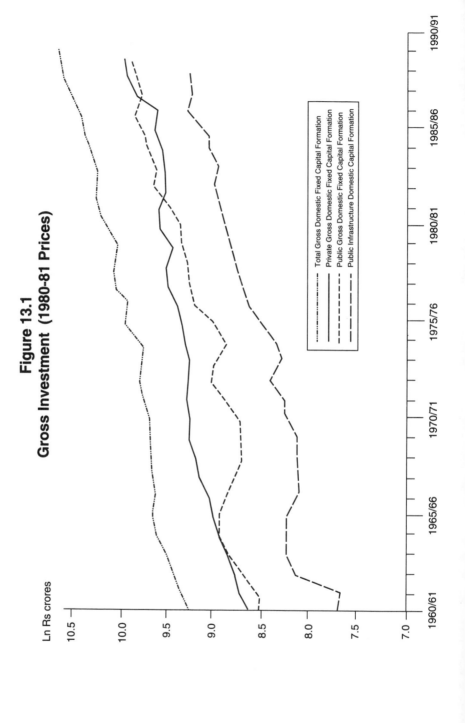

Figure 13.1
Gross Investment (1980-81 Prices)

Ln Rs crores

Total Gross Domestic Fixed Capital Formation
Private Gross Domestic Fixed Capital Formation
Public Gross Domestic Fixed Capital Formation
Public Infrastructure Domestic Capital Formation

The Relationship between Public and Private Investment

The relationship between public and private investment can be very complex. It is widely believed by Indian economists that the two are complementary. On the demand side, if there is some slack one would expect a change in public investment to push private investment in the same direction. But if there is no slack, then by one means or another some private investment will probably have to be "crowded out." However, these are not strictly relationships between public and private investment, but rather between the whole fiscal stance of the public sector, and investment in the private sector. We have already briefly discussed the hypothesis of crowding out in chapter 12.

There are also potential supply side relations. The private sector relies on public investment in most of the infrastructure, because this is either a natural or a legal public monopoly. Therefore public infrastructure and private investment should be complementary, in that infrastructure deficiencies will hold back both private production and private investment. Infrastructure investment is separated out for this reason, and also because it has been argued that infrastructure investment should be sheltered when public investment is cut for stabilization reasons.[3] It has been argued in India that the failure to shelter infrastructure investment had adverse long-run consequences.

In India the boundaries of the infrastructure are less clear than in many economies. This is because the Industrial Policy Resolutions reserve production of many widely used intermediate and capital good items for the public sector, and at the same time import controls may make foreign procurement difficult or impossible. There is therefore a case for including some parts of the manufacturing sector as infrastructure.[4] Nevertheless the line for public infrastructure investment in figure 13.1 excludes manufacturing. It includes agriculture, construction, electricity and gas, communications, railways and other transport, and other services.[5] Gross investment (including stocks) for these sectors is given in table 13.7. Power and the railways account for about half the total in recent years (and more in earlier years).

Private fixed investment is separated into corporate and household in table 13.6 (there was no room to include them separately in figure 13.1). It is notable that private corporate investment is extremely unstable with a standard deviation of the growth rate of about 26 percent in the period up to 1975/76, and 32 percent in the subsequent period up to 1989/90. Private household investment growth, which includes the investment of unincorporated enterprises, is also unstable with standard deviations of about 12 and 24 percent in the two periods. But the two taken together have much lower standard deviations of 5 and 9 percent. Thus these two components of private investment offset each other to a large extent—indeed in all but eight of the twenty-nine years they move in opposite directions. This strongly suggests that there are major year-to-year errors in corporate investment offset by errors in household investments, the latter being a residual. It is certainly hard to imagine sound economic reasons why the two components should usually vary inversely.

Gross fixed capital formation (GFCF) has grown at 4.9 percent a year over the whole period, the public and private sectors contributing about equally.[6] The period opened with a five-year investment boom at the unsustainable rate of over 8.5 percent a year. There was then a setback in 1966/67, followed by seven years of slow growth until 1973/74 (2.9 percent a year). In 1973/74 and 1974/75 there was a second setback, followed by a four-year boom until 1978/79, which brought GFCF as a percentage of GDP back to the levels of the late 1960s. This was followed by another relatively minor fall in 1979/80 and recovery in 1980/81. From 1980/81 to 1989/90 the growth has been reasonably stable at 5.4 percent a year, a little above the long-run trend.

The fact that two of the setbacks followed unsustainable high rates of growth of investment might suggest that the investment boom resulted in overheating of the economy, which in turn necessitated some deflationary measures. This, however, does not seem to have been the case. The investment boom of the first half of the 1960s could not continue for ever—the deficits and borrowing were too high to be sustainable. But a soft landing (on the ceiling) was prevented, not by any general overheating or balance of payments crisis induced by excess demand, but by the two disastrous droughts of 1965/66 and 1966/67. The setback in 1974/75 followed a period of slow total investment growth. That of 1979/80 admittedly followed another investment boom that had, however, already flattened out. But a soft landing was again prevented by the very bad harvest of 1979/80.

The relative movements of public and private investment are of considerable interest. While public investment slumped sharply in 1966/67 and 1967/68 and did not begin to recover until 1970/71, private investment continued to boom until 1969/70, thus stabilizing the total. It is remarkable that total investment never fell below its trend in this period. From 1969/70 to 1972/73 public investment recovered to its long-term trend level. During this period, private investment stagnated, thus again stabilizing total investment. In 1974/75, when public investment again slumped, private investment began to recover.

After 1974/75 the story becomes more incoherent, though it remains true that high growth in one sector is more often than not associated with low growth or decline in the other. Private investment did not offset the recovery in public investment from 1974/75 to 1977/78. After that public investment became sluggish for three years before building up to a new boom in 1982/83. In this period private investment was very erratic, with sharp setbacks in 1979/80 (when total GFCF also fell) and 1982/83. But in five of the seven years after 1982/83, when public investment growth is above trend, private investment in growth is below trend, or vice versa. The year 1987/88 is especially remarkable with a fall in public investment accompanied by a 25 percent rise in private investment.

From table 13.6 it can be seen that in the first period (up to 1975/76) private investment is far more stable than public investment. After 1976/77 public investment becomes more stable, although there are booms in 1981/82, 1982/83, and 1986/87, followed by slow growth or decline. In contrast, private investment became much less stable, indeed less stable than public investment. The reason for the increased stability of public investment is clear—in the first period public investment was severely cut on two occasions, primarily in order to combat inflation, and this did not happen in the second period. The reasons for the increased instability of private investment in the second period are unclear, and further research is needed to throw light on this.

In both periods total investment is more stable than either public or private investment taken separately; this is especially true of the second period when the standard deviation of the annual changes in total investment was 4.3 percent, against 7 percent for the public sector and 9.1 percent for the private sector. Thus, over the whole period, but especially in the second half, changes in public and private investment offset each other. But we have found little evidence of any reliable mechanism that brings this result about. As we saw in chapter 12 there may have been some crowding out of private household investment from 1982/83 to 1986/87, when public sector investment was on a high plateau averaging nearly 10 percent of GDP, this being also associated with high public borrowing from the public and commercial banks. But this, even if true, does not adequately explain the persistent tendency for high *annual* increases in public investment to be offset by low or negative increases in private investment, and vice versa. A theoretical possibility is that changes in public investment were deliberately planned to smooth total investment in the face of unstable private investment. This possibility can easily be dismissed. Only in the earlier period were there planned cuts in public investment, and these were made primarily in response to inflation that was only very remotely connected, if at all, with private investment. In the 1980s the boom in public investment in 1981/82 and 1982/83 came just after a strong recovery in private investment in 1980/81. In any case the public authorities cannot be aware of movements in private investment, especially household investment, until long after the event.

Although we have no satisfactory explanation of the offsetting changes in public and private investment, it is clear that they lend no support to the idea that public and private investment are complementary. However, Bardhan (1984) has claimed to establish a positive relationship between private corporate investment and public investment, lagged by one year.[7] Working with the new national income figures over a longer period we find a negligible *negative* simple correlation between these two variables. In any case, we have already cast strong doubt on the measure of private corporate investment.

However, as we have seen, it is likely that the extraordinary short-term swings in private corporate investment are the result of the methods of estimation. Therefore longer run averaging might show some relationship with public investment. Expressed as a percentage of GDP, private corporate investment was continuously below average for the whole period from 1965/66 to 1979/80 (and in no other year). Public investment was below average from 1967/68 to 1975/76 (as well as in a few other years). We doubt if this can be counted as evidence of any relationship. It should also be noted that private household investment was above average for the whole of the period during which private corporate investment was below average; and that much of private household investment—that of unincorporated enterprises—should be as much subject to any influences of complementarity as private corporate investment (though small enterprises are more likely to be crowded out than corporations).

Finally it has been suggested above that private investment, whether corporate or total, might be related to public infrastructure investment for supply side reasons. Figure 13.1 shows that public infrastructure investment growth follows a very similar path to that of total public investment. Substituting the former for the latter makes no significant difference to the story told above.

The Distribution and Instability of Public Sector Investment

Table 13.8 shows public sector investment disaggregated into seven sectors. The line for infrastructure investment in figure 13.1 is also relevant.

It has been argued by several Indian authors that public sector, especially infrastructure, investment cutbacks in the 1960s and 1970s seriously damaged the long-run performance of the economy. We have already remarked that infrastructure investment shows much the same pattern as total investment. However, it was somewhat protected, as the lower line of figure 13.1 shows. After the cuts in 1966/67 and 1967/68, infrastructure investment recovered more quickly than total investment, and in 1974/75 the infrastructure also suffered less. In the second half of the 1960s the largest cuts were suffered by the railways, by manufacturing, and by administration and defense. In chapter 4 it was pointed out that the fall in railway investment followed large increases in the early 1960s, and that the railway authorities were not apparently forced to cut below what they believed was required. It should also be noted that railway investment has never recovered to the levels of the mid-1960s. This would seem to imply that serious underinvestment in the railways, if that can be substantiated, has been chronic and has little to do with the investment cuts made in periods of crises.[8]

In the case of electricity the evidence of chronic excess demand is compelling. There can be little doubt that both overall production and investment have suffered as a result. But it could be argued that it would have been bad policy to provide for more investment when the load factor was so poor (and was caused by gross supply inefficiencies rather than any exceptional demand variability). Furthermore, electricity for many purposes is sold far below marginal cost, and highly power-intensive industries are promoted. Be that as it may, it should also be noted that, although investment was cut significantly in 1966/67 and again in 1973/74, it recovered rapidly. So, as in the case of the railways, shortages must be regarded as chronic and not in large measure due to the cutbacks of 1966/67 and 1973/74.

Manufacturing, some parts of which may be regarded as infrastructure given India's import control system and emphasis on self-reliance, suffered very heavily from 1966/67 to 1970/71. But large parts of public sector manufacturing were suffering from low capacity utilization. This was sometimes because of technological failures, or bad management and bad labor relations. But it was also because domestic demand for plant and equipment was less than had been planned for, and very probably less than would have been forthcoming even if total investment had never fallen below its long-run viable growth path.

Some other features of public investment that emerge from table 13.8 deserve mention. There was surprisingly no rise in agricultural investment at the time of the green revolution in the second half of the 1960s. But during the 1970s it rose by about 50 percent, only to fall back in recent years to the lowest recorded proportion of GDP. There has been a very large rise in mining and quarrying as a result of oil exploration and discovery prompted by the 1973/74 oil price rise.

Finally the table discloses an extraordinary instability of investment. We have already discussed the instability of total public fixed investment. Table 13.8 shows that this applies equally to particular sectors. We also saw above that total public investment, especially infrastructural investment, became notably less unstable in the second half of the period. The main reason for this, as we have already stated, is that after 1975/76 there were no major cuts in public investment as a response to inflation or balance of payments problems—India borrowed abroad instead. This greater stability applies also to some, but not to all, sectors. Investment in electricity, and in administration and defense, became much more stable, but investment in manufacturing and "other" sectors became less stable.

Although we have argued that the public investment cuts of 1966–68 and 1974/75 had no serious long-run influence as a result of causing infrastructural deficiency, nevertheless it remains true that the stop and go course of investment in most sectors must surely have reduced the efficiency of investment. We thus surmise that the greater stability of public investment may be one of the reasons for the higher growth rate after 1975.

The Efficiency of Investment

In the past decade there has been much concern among Indian economists and journalists about the apparent inefficiency of the Indian economy. Apart from an almost unlimited number of anecdotes, the main evidence lies with its slow growth combined with a rather high level of investment for such a poor country. Also investment has grown faster than output. Over the period 1960/61 to 1989/90 it grew at a compound rate of 4.8 percent a year against 4.2 percent for GDP.

There has been a good deal of work in India on capital output ratios,[9] and on total factor productivity.[10] There is no doubt that capital to output ratios have risen, and continue to rise, both for the economy as a whole and for manufacturing. For the whole economy this may have been due more to broad intersectoral shifts than to intrasectoral rises (see Panchmukhi 1986); but for manufacturing it was due much more to intrasectoral rises, where all manufacturing groups experienced rises in the period 1959/60 to 1979/80 as shown by Ahluwalia (1985) and confirmed by Dholakia (1983). The rises were large. For the whole economy Chitale (1986) shows a clearly rising trend in capital output ratios (1951/52 to 1982/83) from about 2.5 to 4.5.

Incremental capital output ratios are highly erratic and it is more difficult to produce unquestionable figures.[11] Chitale (1986) suggests some rise between the 1960s and 1970s, when an average figure of 6.0 may not be far wrong. Other works cited tend on the whole to confirm some upward trend at least until 1980.

The work on total factor productivity (TFP) also yields a clear message. Ahluwalia (1985) found zero or negative growth in total factor productivity in manufacturing from 1959/60 to 1979/80. Goldar (1986), making different assumptions, leading to a slower estimated growth of the capital stock, found a positive growth in TFP of 1.3 percent a year for the same period, but pointed out that this still accounted only for about one-sixth of the growth of manufacturing output, both figures being very much lower than are found in most other economies, whether developing or industrial (usually TFP accounts for half or more of increases in GDP).

All this suggests that the efficiency of production and investment in India has been low. This is confirmed for the public sector by evidence produced by the recently created Ministry of Program Implementation, by many reports of the Planning Commission and other committees on management failure in various parts of the public sector, by the Centre for Monitoring the Indian Economy,[12] and by other authors.[13]

The 1987/88 report of the Ministry of Program Implementation is certainly disturbing. Delays are described as endemic, and average cost overruns for major projects completed in 1986/87 in the coal, power, railways, and manufacturing sectors exceeded 100 percent. It describes the cost of delay as "truly enormous," and remarks that this "would seriously vitiate the initial appraisal of a project with regard to its financial viability." To this may be added the widespread undercapacity working after completion. The causes of delay are manifold, but the most pervasive may be starting too many projects in the face of limited planning, infrastructure, and financial resources.

On paper the procedures for appraising and selecting public sector projects, at least for those over Rs 20 crores,[14] (approximately $150 million) seem to be good.[15] These larger projects require the recommendation of the Public Investment Board (PIB), and must be approved by the cabinet. But some sectors—the railways, defense, atomic energy, space and electronics—do not have to jump the PIB hurdle. The PIB consists of secretaries of the main economic ministries, and is chaired by the expenditure secretary of the Finance Ministry.

Projects go through two stages, first a feasibility report in which costs and benefits are orders of magnitude based largely on past projects. If the feasibility report is favorably regarded (by a committee of the PIB), the expenditure required for a full technical and economic report is approved. If this in turn is approved by the PIB it goes to the cabinet.

The PIB receives reports from the Project Appraisal Division (PAD) of the Planning Commission, which became operative in 1972, and from various other bodies.[16] The PAD is supposed to check the responsible ministry's estimates, and then calculate economic rates of return or present values based on shadow pricing. An extensive set of shadow prices was calculated in 1974 by a consultant, Deepak Lal (see Lal 1980). PAD receives about 250 feasibility reports a year. Those not dropped after preliminary discussions with the ministry concerned constitute less than one-third of public investment, because of the exclusion from the PIB's demesne of certain important sectors (see above), and because of the large number of projects of less than Rs 20 crores. At the time of our visit in 1989 its professional staff numbered only thirteen, though the number of posts had recently been raised to twenty-three. It was claimed that its preliminary appraisals resulted in some 30 percent of projects being dropped, modified, or deferred by the ministry. PIB nearly always agreed with its views. A few large projects had finally been rejected as a result.

We interviewed a good many serving and retired civil servants about the effectiveness of the project planning procedures. Their opinions ranged all the way from almost unqualified denunciation (how can a set of senior civil servants open to all kinds of pressures make good economic decisions?) to almost equally unqualified approval (of course, there had been certain weaknesses but these were being dealt with—a typical civil servant's response). But there was a consensus that PAD did some good. It should not be judged only by the few bad projects it caused to be rejected. It also had an educative function in the ministries, and many of the wilder schemes that might have been put forward in the past would no longer get a hearing. A common criticism was that it had previously reported only at the feasibility stage, and the final proposal could look very different; but it was emphasized that this had been changed with the introduction (in March 1985) of the two-tier procedure described above (but as yet no project had run the gauntlet).

Our own impressions follow. First, the PAD is inadequately staffed, both as to numbers and expertise.[17] We very much doubt whether it can, as presently constituted, be an effective watchdog so far as most ministry proposals are concerned, either on technical matters including alternative technologies, or on matters of supply, timing, or market demand. Second, their calculations of economic rates of return (as opposed to financial) are based on a rudimentary methodology. Only one shadow price is used. Foreign exchange is given a premium of 25 percent, which does not vary with changes in the real exchange rate and has remained unchanged for a decade or more. No calculation appears to be made of the marginal foreign exchange cost of anything procured in India. This results in a bias in favor of any project that produces import substitutes which are counted as saving foreign exchange, that is, most manufacturing projects or exports. Labor is not shadow priced. However PAD's defense of this omission is not altogether unreasonable. They are asked only to evaluate capital-intensive projects.[18] In the above respects, it is clear that PAD has regressed in the past decade. We do not think that PAD offers an effective counter to the chronic Indian preference for self-reliance over comparative advantage. India still invests heavily in sectors where it is difficult to believe that she has any comparative advantage—for example, highly capital- and energy-intensive industries such as nonferrous metals.

We also believe that the whole procedure is far from immune from political influence.[19] We were told that internal political or external diplomatic reasons played a part in the choice of some of the projects that seemed to us doubtful on economic grounds. But perhaps it is too much to expect that this should not be the case.

Finally it is not altogether irrelevant that a great many public sector enterprises make losses. Indeed, apart from the oil and natural gas industry, and financial enterprises, losses outweighed profits in 1984/85.[20] While much of the loss is incurred by state enterprises in electricity, irrigation, and public transport (see chapter 1), central enterprises do not perform very well either. Of 196 central, nondepartmental, industrial enterprises outside the profitable petroleum sector, reported on by the Public Enterprise Board in 1984/85, 104 made profits and 91 losses. The pretax profits only exceeded the losses by a narrow margin. There was some improvement later. In 1989/90 about three-quarters of central industrial public enterprise profits of Rs 3,782 crores came from a handful of oil and natural gas companies. Of about 220 nonoil companies, 98 made losses. However, total nonoil profits were positive at Rs 882 crores.[21]

Unfortunately such figures do not throw a very clear light on the efficiency of investment, since much of the loss can be attributed to price and other controls. While this makes the monitoring of investment very difficult, it is unfortunately true that it also makes the economic and social appraisal of new investments very difficult.

There is very much less to go on for any account of the efficiency of private investment. All one can really say is that there is a good deal of government control that may well reduce the profitability of private investment without any gain to society.[22] Thus private investment is often subject to delay, and the choice of technology from private foreign sources is restricted. Import controls encourage excessive stock holding. Controls over the expansion of large private firms under the Monopoly and Restrictive Trade Practices (MRTP) and Foreign Exchange Regulation Act (FERA) regulations have probably reduced the efficiency of economic development in some industries.[23] The strong bias of the price mechanism in favor of production for the domestic market compared with exports clearly reduces both private and social profitability below its potential. These and other influences are briefly reviewed, with references, in Ahluwalia (1985).

Some observers, notably the World Bank[24] and at least one of our most well-informed interviewees, believe that there has been an improvement in the quality of both public and private investment since the early 1970s, when the procedures described above were instituted.

For the above reason, but also for its intrinsic interest, we have estimated real returns to investment in the public sector[25] and in organized manufacturing (public and private separately) for the two periods 1960/61 to 1975/76 and 1976/77 to 1986/87.[26] The essentials of the method are due to Scott (1989).[27] The figures on which the calculations are based are given in tables 13.9, 13.10, and 13.11. It is important to note that the method attributes all growth either to gross investment or to changes in the size and quality of the labor force. The rate of return for a given period is estimated as

$$r_1 = \frac{G_Y - (G_L \times WL/Y)}{I/Y}$$

or as

$$r_2 = \frac{G_Y - (G_{LA} \times WL/Y)}{I/Y}$$

where Y is gross value added at current prices; G_Y is the exponential trend growth rate of Y at 1980/81 prices; G_L is the exponential trend growth rate of labor input; WL is employees' compensation at current prices; I is gross investment at current prices (including stocks); G_{LA} is the growth rate of labor input adjusted for quality, estimated as the growth rate of nominal earnings divided by an appropriate cost of living index. This assumes no change in the real price of labor.

The required figures and estimates of r_1 and r_2 for the public sector are calculated from table 13.9, and are given in table 13.1. It is to be noted that G_L is certainly an underestimate of the true labor input, since there must have been some improvement in the quality of labor. G_{LA} would be a good estimate of the true growth rate of labor input if wage rates rose in the same proportion as the quality of labor, that is if the real price of labor was unchanged. We would expect that in fact the real price of labor has risen. This implies that r_1 is a high estimate and r_2 is a low estimate.

Table 13.1   Calculations of Rates of Return in the Public Sector[a]

(percentages and percentages per year)

	1960/61 to 1975/76	*1976/77 to 1986/87*
G_Y	7.8	6.5
I/Y	103.0	83.0
WL/Y	54.0	51.0
G_L	4.1	2.7
G_{LA}	6.8	7.4
r_1	5.4	6.2
r_2	4.0	3.3

a. Excluding banking, administration and defense, and other services. The meaning of the symbols is explained in the text.

Source: Calculated from data in table 13.9.

Table 13.2   Calculations of Rates of Return in Public Sector Manufacturing
(percentages and percentages per year)

	1960/61 to 1975/76	*1976/77 to 1986/87*
G_Y	7.0	6.8
I/Y	190.0	96.0
WL/Y	52.0	51.0
G_L	5.8	3.7
G_{LA}	13.1	7.5
r_1	2.1	5.2
r_2	0.1	3.1

Note: The meaning of the symbols is explained in the text.
Source: Calculated from data in table 13.10.

Comparing the two periods, we note that the return to investment has risen from about 5 to 6 percent if no allowance is made for a rise in the quality of labor; and with probably excessive allowance for this rise in quality it has fallen from about 4 to about 3.5 percent. This is clearly compatible with no change. Either way, in both periods the returns are extremely low (of which more below).[28]

It might be thought that such low returns result from the inclusion of infrastructure investment where low returns may result from price controls. It is however possible to calculate returns on public manufacturing. These are given in table 13.2. The calculations are based on table 13.10.

In both periods the returns are lower than in the public sector as a whole. In the first period the returns are close to zero. There is a considerable improvement after 1975/76, but the returns remain very low, probably less than the real rate of interest. The improvement comes because while the growth of output is scarcely changed, investment input as a proportion of output is halved, and the growth of the labor force as well as the growth of the real wage bill is reduced by about a third.

Calculations for private sector manufacturing, based on table 13.11, are given in table 13.3. Its record is much less dismal than that of the public sector. The great improvement comes because a rise in the growth rate of output of about 75 percent has been achieved with an actual reduction in the ratio of investment to output. The growth rate of labor productivity has also risen despite the lower investment ratio. The improvement in efficiency is impressive, and probably brings returns in this sector in line with those that have been achieved in industrial countries.[29] Unfortunately the social rate of return on private sector manufacturing is almost certainly lower than the private rate of return, as argued in the following paragraph.

Our various estimates of real rates of return to investment are summarized in table 13.4. The calculations have been based on market prices, not on social or accounting prices. Unfortunately it was beyond our resources to attempt estimates

Table 13.3   Calculations of Rates of Return in Private Sector Organized Manufacturing
(percentages and percentages per year)

	1960/61 to 1975/76	*1976/77 to 1986/87*
G_Y	3.9	6.8
I/Y	30.0	26.0
WL/Y	51.0	49.0
G_L	1.1	1.9
G_{LA}	3.1	5.0
r_1	11.1	22.6
r_2	7.7	16.7

Note: The meaning of the symbols is explained in the text.
Source: Calculated from data in table 13.11.

of social returns, but we can offer a few observations concerning the differences that the use of social prices might make. Probably over half of the public sector investment in the sectors that we have included is in nontradable commodities. Here shadow pricing would raise the rate of return. Shadow wages would be less than actual wages—if, for instance, the shadow wage were two-thirds the actual wage this would raise the rates of return by roughly 1 percent. Public sector outputs in much of the important nontraded sectors (electricity, transport, and communications) are probably underpriced, and thus would also raise the rate of return, by how much we cannot say. However, in public sector manufacturing shadow pricing would reduce the rate of return. Here outputs are protected, while a shadow wage rate would make a negligible difference in this capital-intensive area. Moreover, manufacturing may have the benefit of underpriced nontraded inputs. It is thus probable that public sector manufacturing made a negative contribution to GDP in the earlier period, and this could even be true of the later period also. Private sector manufacturing, which accounts for most of India's exports, is almost certainly less protected than public sector manufacturing; nevertheless, the respectable private returns of about 20 percent in the second period probably overstate the social returns.

Table 13.4   Real Rates of Return to Investment

Period	Whole public sector[a]	Public sector manufacturing	Private sector manufacturing
1960/61 to 1975/76	4.0–5.4	0.1–2.1	7.7–11.1
1976/77 to 1986/87	3.3–6.2	3.1–5.2	16.7–22.6

a. Excluding banking, administration and defense, and other services.
Source: Tables 13.1, 13.2, and 13.3.

Table 13.5   Investment and Savings as Percentages of GDP

	1960/61	1965/66	1970/71	1975/76	1980/81	1985/86	1989/90
Investment at current prices	13.7	16.8	16.6	18.8	22.7	22.1	24.1
Investment at 1980/81 prices	18.1	20.8	18.7	18.9	22.7	20.6	21.8
Domestic savings	12.7	14.5	15.7	19.0	21.2	19.7	21.7

Note: In this table the investment figures used are those that are adjusted to equal the estimates of domestic plus foreign savings in the national accounts.

Source: Government of India, CSO (1989a); and Government of India, CSO (1991), *National Accounts Statistics.*

Table 13.5 shows that the investment ratio at current prices has risen more than the investment ratio at 1980/81 prices. This implies that the prices of investment goods have risen more than the GDP deflator. In other words, saving buys less investment.

The relative rise in the price of investment goods occurred mainly in two periods, from 1973/74 to 1975/76 and again from 1980/81 to 1986/87. One possible explanation might be import substitution in machinery and equipment, which might have raised their domestic prices relative to the GDP deflator. However, the price rises of investment occurred mainly in the price of construction rather than machinery and equipment. One reason may have been the decontrol of the prices of steel and cement, another possible reason could be a rise in the wages of construction workers as a result of the demand for their services in the Middle East. This hypothesis is supported by the fact that the price rises occurred in periods subsequent to the oil price shocks. Even so, this is little more than speculation (see also chapter 6).

In our calculations of the returns to investment we have used the mean of the ratios of I/Y at *current* prices. Since this ratio has been rising faster than I/Y at 1980/81 prices, the means are a little higher than if the latter ratio had been used, and consequently the estimates of the returns to investment a little lower. Our figures are properly described as estimates of the returns to savings devoted to the sector in question. This indeed is what should be estimated, for it is the return to consumption sacrificed, or to foreign savings used, that matters. It is also worth noting that until 1976/77 domestic savings had to substitute for a reduction in foreign aid as well as buy more expensive investment goods. In the decade 1965/66 to 1975/76, as a proportion of GDP, domestic savings rose 31 percent, investment at current prices rose 12 percent, and investment at 1980/81 prices *fell* by 9 percent. From 1975/76 to 1989/90 domestic savings rose 15 percent, investment at current prices rose 27 percent (there was recourse to foreign borrowing), and investment at 1980/81 prices rose 15 percent.

Explaining a Rise in the Growth Rate of GDP

There has been a considerable rise in the trend rate of growth of real GDP since the mid-1970s. From 1960/61 to 1975/76 it was 3.4 percent a year, and from 1976/77 to 1989/90 it was 4.7 percent a year. If we dated the change from 1980/81 the difference would be still greater.

The question arises as to whether there is anything to explain. Could the change in the trend be simply due to chance? The standard statistical test (the Chow test of parameter constancy) yields the result that one can reject the hypothesis that there was no significant change in the trend with 95 percent confidence.[30] Thus there is something to explain. The main sectors with large rises in the rate of growth have been manufacturing and mining. But many other sectors show some rise, the main exceptions being agriculture, electricity, construction, railways, and public administration and defense.[31]

We consider five explanations of faster growth that would seem to exhaust the possibilities: greater pressure of demand; more efficient use of existing resources; higher investment; higher rate of growth of the quality of the labor force; and more efficient investment.

- *Greater pressure of demand.* Very strong demand will surely induce some extra output from an economy. But this 'bonus' may be unsustainable, either because it also results in an unacceptable inflation (or an inflation which so reduces efficiency that the bonus disappears), or an unsustainable level of foreign borrowing. Some part of the higher growth in India in the 1980s is due to this "Keynesian" effect. We have argued in chapter 9 that it is unsustainable.
- *More efficient use of existing resources.* There has been some liberalization of industrial, trade, financial, and tax policies, starting in the late 1970s. Economic theory (and common sense!) suggests that this will have led to some increase in efficiency, but there is no way of either proving or quantifying this.
- *Higher investment.* Real investment (at 1980/81 prices, adjusted for errors and omissions) averaged 18.9 percent of GDP in the first period and 20.7 percent in the second period. This may have contributed, but the rise is too small to be an important element in the achievement of higher growth. Unadjusted investment can be broken down into public and private. Public real investment averaged 7.7 percent of GDP in the first period and 9.9 percent in the second period. Private real investment averaged 12.0 percent of GDP in the first period and 11.7 percent in the second period. Thus the whole of the rise in the investment level took place in the public sector (ignoring errors and omissions). However, the rate of growth of public sector GDP declined (from 7.8 to 7.2 percent a year), while that of the private sector rose (from 2.6 to 3.7 percent a year).[32] Evidently the latter figure was not due to a rise in the level of investment.

- *Higher rate of growth of the quality of the labor force.* Such little evidence as can be presented derives from the above section on efficiency of investment. A comparison of the rates of growth of the labor force (G_L) and the real wage bill (G_{LA}) shows that real earnings per worker in public manufacturing rose considerably less fast in the second period as compared with the first—in private manufacturing real earnings per workers rose rather faster in the second period. For manufacturing as a whole, there can have been little change. Insofar as the growth of real earnings per worker is a good indicator, it thus seems that the quality of the labor force grew no faster in the second period than in the first. But for the public sector as a whole the growth in real earnings per worker was somewhat higher in the second period; this however, can form no part of any explanation of the higher growth rate of GDP in the second period, since the growth rate of public sector GDP was actually lower.

- *More efficient investment.* In the section on efficiency of investment we found that there was an increase in the productivity of investment, most especially in private manufacturing. In the section dealing with the distribution and instability of public sector investment we found that there had been a large reduction in the instability of public investment, especially public infrastructure investment. This may have contributed to the rather minor rise in the productivity of public investment. Although there was no rise in the public sector GDP growth rate, a rise in the productivity of public investment implies that growth was achieved with less call on investment resources, which would help growth elsewhere in the economy. It is also possible that this reduction in instability would make some contribution to the productivity of private investment as well as to the efficiency of the use of existing resources by reducing the problem of bottlenecks in the supply of power, transport, and communications.

It may seem that the most important causal element that we have been able to isolate was the rise in the real yield of private investment in manufacturing. Any such conclusion must however be qualified. Any increase in the rate of growth of output due to other causes, especially those discussed under the first two points above, feeds into our measure of the yield of investment (public or private). In other words the increase in the returns to investment may be due to the strong demand of the 1980s, and to a general improvement in the efficient use of existing resources, rather than to any improvement in the selection and implementation of investment projects.

Deeper research into the causes of the improvement in the growth of GDP than we have been able to do would be possible. Our conclusions can be only tentative. On the negative side, neither a rise in investment, nor an acceleration in the improvement in the quality of the labor force, seems to have been significant. We think there has been some improvement in the general efficiency of the use of resources, and an improvement in the quality of investment. We fear, however, that an important part of the explanation may be the high level of demand in the 1980s. As we have argued in chapter 9, this cannot be sustained.

Summary

Over the whole period, fixed capital formation has grown at nearly 5 percent a year, about equally in the public and private sectors. Until the 1980s private investment was more stable than public investment. This was because changes in public investment were made with the intention of controlling inflation and stabilizing the economy. In particular there was a trough in public investment from 1965/66 to 1975/76, but this was offset by a continued boom in private investment. While the instability of public investment probably reduced the rate of growth of the economy, we do not think that chronic infrastructure shortages, especially of power, can be explained by the public investment cuts made in response to the crises of 1965/66 and 1973/74.

Investment in India is high for a very poor country. In current prices it has risen from about 17 percent in 1965/66 to about 24 percent of GDP in 1989/90. In constant prices the rise has been quite small (the relative price of investment goods has risen sharply) but the ratio has been quite high throughout, between 18 and 22 percent of GDP. However, the growth rate of GDP has been modest, just over 4 percent a year, which, along with other research, suggests that the efficiency of investment, especially public investment, has been low. We estimated real rates of return to investment, using a method developed by Scott (1989), as given in table 13.4.

The reader should consult the previous section for certain reservations. We do not believe that they upset the conclusion that public sector investment is extraordinarily inefficient, especially in manufacturing. We think that choice procedures for public investment are partly to blame. In the later period, private sector manufacturing has achieved returns comparable to those found in industrial countries.

Finally, we sought to explain an acceleration of growth of GDP from 3.4 percent a year from 1960/61 to 1975/76, to 4.7 percent a year from 1976/77 to 1989/90. This does not seem to have been due either to a rise in the ratio of investment to GDP or to an acceleration of the growth of the quality of the labor force. There may have been some increase in the efficiency of the use of existing resources, due to liberalization, though this cannot be proven. An increase in the efficiency of private manufacturing investment is apparent, and a reduction in the instability of public investment may have helped. But we fear that much was due to a rise in the pressure of demand that cannot be sustained.

Appendix

Appendix tables 13.6 to 13.11 follow.

Table 13.6 Unadjusted Gross Fixed Capital Formation, 1960/61 to 1989/90
(1980/81 prices, percentage of GDP)

Year	Total		Total public		Public infrastructure		Total private		Private corporate		Private household	
	Percent GDP	Annual growth (percent)	Percent GDP	Annual growth (percent)	Percent GDP	Annual growth (percent)	Percent GDP	Annual growth (percent)	Percent GDP	Annual growth (percent)	Percent GDP	Annual growth (percent)
1960/61	15.5	—	7.6	—	3.2	—	7.9	—	2.4	—	5.5	—
1961/62	15.9	6.2	7.2	-1.0	3.1	-1.8	8.6	13.0	3.5	48.9	5.1	-2.9
1962/63	16.7	8.3	8.1	15.1	4.6	55.9	8.6	2.7	2.6	-22.2	6.0	19.6
1963/64	17.3	10.5	8.5	12.6	5.0	13.6	8.8	8.6	3.6	45.6	5.2	-7.7
1964/65	18.0	11.6	8.9	12.1	4.6	0.9	9.1	11.2	3.0	-12.3	6.1	27.6
1965/66	19.5	6.0	9.6	5.2	4.7	-0.4	10.0	6.8	1.9	-36.2	8.0	27.5
1966/67	18.7	-4.7	8.4	-13.1	4.2	-11.8	10.3	3.4	1.8	-8.0	8.5	6.1
1967/68	18.0	4.0	7.2	-8.0	3.7	-6.2	10.9	13.7	1.8	9.2	9.1	14.6
1968/69	17.8	2.2	7.0	1.2	3.6	1.1	10.8	2.8	1.7	-3.6	9.1	4.1
1969/70	17.2	3.2	6.4	-2.1	3.5	3.3	10.8	6.6	1.3	-16.9	9.5	10.9
1970/71	16.5	0.5	6.3	2.5	3.7	13.3	10.2	-0.7	1.6	27.8	8.6	-4.6
1971/72	17.2	6.2	6.8	10.6	3.8	2.5	10.4	3.5	1.9	21.2	8.5	0.2
1972/73	18.2	5.2	8.1	18.7	4.4	16.4	10.1	-3.7	1.8	-4.9	8.2	-3.4
1973/74	17.5	-1.0	7.7	-2.2	3.9	-9.4	9.8	-0.1	2.1	17.0	7.7	-3.8
1974/75	16.7	-3.1	6.5	-14.5	4.0	4.1	10.2	6.0	1.7	-15.3	8.5	11.6
1975/76	16.8	9.7	7.0	17.9	4.3	18.9	9.8	4.4	2.1	34.9	7.6	-1.8
Mean	17.3		7.6		4.0		9.8		2.2		7.6	
Standard deviation		4.9		10.7		16.3		5.0		25.8		11.7

1976/77	18.6	12.6	8.5	23.7	4.7	11.6	10.0	4.6	1.3	-36.9	8.7	16.2
1977/78	19.0	9.6	8.5	6.5	4.7	5.3	10.5	12.2	1.7	35.6	8.8	8.7
1978/79	18.1	0.9	8.1	-0.3	4.8	9.0	10.1	1.4	1.1	-31.3	9.0	7.6
1979/80	18.6	-2.9	8.7	2.8	5.2	2.6	9.8	-7.4	1.6	38.9	8.3	-13.0
1980/81	19.3	10.9	8.6	4.9	5.3	8.0	10.7	16.2	2.6	74.6	8.1	4.9
1981/82	19.4	6.9	9.1	12.5	5.2	6.1	10.3	2.4	3.7	51.6	6.6	-13.4
1982/83	19.5	4.3	10.1	15.9	5.3	5.0	9.3	-5.9	4.4	22.3	5.0	-21.7
1983/84	18.3	1.2	9.6	2.0	4.7	-4.0	8.7	0.2	3.3	-18.4	5.4	16.5
1984/85	18.4	3.9	9.8	5.7	5.0	8.6	8.6	1.9	3.7	15.4	4.9	-6.4
1985/86	18.7	7.1	9.7	3.9	4.9	1.3	9.0	10.8	3.9	10.5	5.1	10.9
1986/87	18.6	3.9	10.4	12.6	5.6	22.0	8.1	-5.5	4.2	14.4	3.9	-20.5
1987/88	19.4	9.5	9.6	-3.0	5.2	-1.7	9.7	25.4	3.2	-20.2	6.5	74.9
1988/89	19.0	7.8	9.1	3.8	4.8	0.6	9.9	11.8	3.2	7.9	6.7	13.7
1989/90	18.9	4.6	9.1	4.5	4.7	4.1	9.9	4.7	3.1	3.4	6.8	5.3
Mean	18.8	4.3	9.2	7.0	5.0	6.4	9.6	9.1	2.9	31.9	6.7	23.9
Standard deviation												

Source: Tables 4.14, 5.16, 6.15, and 7.9, except for public infrastructure, which is taken from table 13.7. Public infrastructure includes stocks.

331

Table 13.7 Public Gross Infrastructural Investment, Including Stocks, 1960/61 to 1989/90

(1980/81 prices, Rs crores)

Year	Agriculture	Construction	Electricity and water	Railways	Communication	Other transport	Other services	Total	Percentage of GDP	Annual percentage growth
1960/61	589	25	496	779	74	146	96	2,205	3.2	—
1961/62	600	30	821	960	72	218	64	2,165	3.1	-1.8
1962/63	694	35	1,010	1,292	115	160	70	3,376	4.6	55.9
1963/64	725	37	1,198	1,451	170	173	80	3,834	5.0	13.6
1964/65	765	45	1,175	1,434	181	171	96	3,867	4.6	0.9
1965/66	798	50	1,349	1,256	126	230	44	3,853	4.7	-0.4
1966/67	696	47	1,210	901	165	319	61	3,399	4.2	-11.8
1967/68	688	43	1,263	774	154	171	96	3,189	3.7	-6.2
1968/69	775	29	1,198	656	151	324	91	3,224	3.6	-2.9
1969/70	775	41	1,375	568	162	282	127	3,330	3.5	3.3
1970/71	789	50	1,529	669	137	492	106	3,772	3.7	13.3
1971/72	851	46	1,475	716	192	455	131	3,866	3.8	2.5
1972/73	1,049	55	1,441	745	277	678	255	4,500	4.4	16.4
1973/74	993	92	1,321	624	216	558	271	4,075	3.9	-9.4
1974/75	919	149	1,454	580	235	680	226	4,243	4.0	4.1
1975/76	1,041	100	2,039	598	276	818	171	5,043	4.3	18.9
1976/77	1,378	117	2,158	734	323	705	214	5,629	4.7	11.6
1977/78	1,534	215	2,465	526	326	635	228	5,929	4.7	5.3
1978/79	1,697	237	2,606	572	353	711	288	6,464	4.8	9.0
1979/80	1,772	141	2,775	686	327	632	297	6,630	5.2	2.6

1980/81	1,796	292	2,951	814	321	667	317	7,158	5.3	8.0
1981/82	1,779	253	3,399	829	467	517	354	7,598	5.2	6.1
1982/83	1,725	117	3,712	798	477	765	385	7,979	5.3	5.0
1983/84	1,707	11	3,705	830	519	542	344	7,658	4.7	-4.0
1984/85	1,673	170	3,797	882	596	828	370	8,316	5.0	8.6
1985/86	1,516	138	4,315	914	565	518	460	8,426	4.8	1.3
1986/87	1,428	34	5,367	1,241	610	1100	500	10,280	5.6	22.0
1987/88	1,456	127	5,618	1,005	790	624	485	10,105	5.2	-1.7
1988/89	1,346	99	5,330	1,111	1,048	713	522	10,169	4.8	0.6
1989/90	1,169	52	5,621	983	1,206	1,017	541	10,589	4.7	4.1

Source: Government of India, CSO (1989a); Government of India, CSO (1991), *National Accounts Statistics*; and Government of India, CSO (1991), *Quick Estimates of National Income 1989/90*.

Table 13.8 Public Gross Capital Formation, 1960/61 to 1988/89

(1980/81 prices)

Year	Agriculture and fisheries Percent GDP	Annual growth (percent)	Mining and quarrying Percent GDP	Annual growth (percent)	Manufacturing Percent GDP	Annual growth (percent)	Electricity Percent GDP	Annual growth (percent)	Railways Percent GDP	Annual growth (percent)	Administration and defense Percent GDP	Annual growth (percent)	Other Percent GDP	Annual growth (percent)
1960/61	0.9	—	0.2	—	1.6	—	0.7	—	1.1	—	1.8	—	0.7	—
1961/62	0.9	1.6	0.2	-7.7	1.2	-24.4	1.2	65.5	1.4	23.2	1.3	-22.2	0.7	7.2
1962/63	1.0	16.1	0.3	50.0	1.1	-1.5	1.4	23.0	1.8	24.6	1.6	25.0	0.7	1.0
1963/64	1.0	4.0	0.4	36.9	1.4	31.2	1.6	18.6	1.9	12.3	1.5	-3.7	0.8	16.4
1964/65	1.0	5.9	0.3	4.4	1.3	5.9	1.4	-1.9	1.7	-1.2	1.6	19.7	0.8	7.9
1965/66	1.0	5.1	0.2	-37.1	2.0	43.0	1.7	14.8	1.5	-12.4	1.7	0.0	1.0	27.2
1966/67	0.9	-12.8	0.4	62.9	2.1	5.3	1.5	-10.3	1.1	-28.3	1.1	-33.1	1.0	1.3
1967/68	0.9	-0.3	0.3	-21.4	1.6	-16.3	1.5	4.4	0.9	-14.1	1.5	40.0	1.1	17.7
1968/69	0.9	11.0	0.2	-27.2	1.4	-7.8	1.3	-5.2	0.7	-15.3	0.8	-44.7	0.9	-16.8
1969/70	0.9	-0.1	0.2	28.3	1.2	-11.1	1.4	14.8	0.6	-13.4	1.1	50.4	0.9	-0.5
1970/71	0.8	1.8	0.2	-4.2	1.1	-7.1	1.5	11.2	0.7	17.8	1.2	18.7	1.4	74.5
1971/72	0.9	8.2	0.2	12.3	1.3	21.7	1.4	-3.5	0.7	7.0	1.6	33.2	1.3	-4.8
1972/73	1.1	21.2	0.3	45.4	1.4	13.2	1.4	-2.3	0.7	4.0	2.0	20.2	1.9	44.4
1973/74	1.0	-5.4	0.4	28.5	1.8	30.8	1.3	-8.3	0.6	-16.2	1.8	-5.6	1.6	-11.2
1974/75	0.9	-7.4	0.4	8.2	2.1	16.2	1.4	10.1	0.5	-7.1	1.1	-38.9	1.8	9.2
1975/76	0.9	13.4	0.7	67.0	1.8	-8.9	1.8	40.2	0.5	3.1	1.0	3.1	2.8	72.9
Standard deviation		9.0		32.5		19.6		20.2		17.2		29.2		27.7
Mean	0.9		0.3		1.5		1.4		1.0		1.4		1.2	

1976/77	1.2	33.0	0.8	20.6	2.0	18.6	1.8	5.8	0.6	232.7	1.1	12.4	2.8	-0.1
1977/78	1.3	11.2	0.7	-9.6	1.7	-9.8	1.9	14.2	0.4	-28.3	1.1	8.6	1.1	-58.3
1978/79	1.3	10.6	0.6	-6.4	1.8	12.7	1.9	5.7	0.4	8.8	1.4	26.2	1.9	80.9
1979/80	1.5	4.3	0.7	12.4	2.4	22.8	2.2	6.5	0.5	19.9	1.5	5.9	1.5	-24.7
1980/81	1.4	2.3	0.7	3.0	0.9	-61.3	2.2	6.3	0.6	18.7	1.6	11.7	1.4	-0.6
1981/82	1.3	-0.7	0.9	49.7	2.1	162.0	2.4	15.2	0.6	1.8	1.6	7.5	1.6	24.2
1982/83	1.2	-1.1	1.5	66.5	2.2	7.9	2.5	9.2	0.5	-3.7	1.7	6.6	1.5	-4.8
1983/84	1.1	-0.8	1.4	-2.0	1.5	-27.8	2.3	-0.2	0.5	4.0	1.5	-4.7	1.3	-2.8
1984/85	1.1	-1.1	1.3	-4.9	1.9	33.0	2.3	2.5	0.5	6.3	1.6	11.4	1.9	47.4
1985/86	0.9	-10.5	1.5	20.8	2.2	20.1	2.4	13.6	0.5	3.6	1.6	7.1	1.2	-31.5
1986/87	0.8	-5.0	1.4	2.1	1.8	-12.5	2.9	24.4	0.7	35.8	1.6	6.1	1.5	26.3
1987/88	0.8	1.4	1.3	-5.4	2.0	18.6	2.9	4.7	0.5	-19.0	1.4	-8.0	0.8	-46.3
1988/89	0.7	-6.7	1.2	-1.0	1.4	-27.2	2.5	-5.1	0.5	10.6	1.3	1.3	1.5	114.6
Standard deviation		10.9		23.2		52.3		7.6		17.0		8.4		49.3
Mean	1.1		1.1		2.1		2.3		0.5		1.5		1.5	

Source: Government of India, CSO (1989a); Government of India, CSO (1991), *National Accounts Statistics*; and Government of India, CSO (1991), *Quick Estimates of National Income 1989/90.*

Table 13.9 Public Sector, Excluding Banking, Administration, Defense, and Other Services: Various Indicators

Year	GDP (current prices)	GDP (1980/81 prices)	GDCF (current prices)	GDCF/GDP (current prices)	Labor input (L)	Wage bill (WL)	Real wage bill (WL/CPI)	WL/GDP (current prices)
1960/61	711	2,589	811	1.14	32.49	384	376	0.54
1961/62	801	3,004	906	1.13	34.39	417	401	0.52
1962/63	936	3,588	1,128	1.21	36.72	477	442	0.51
1963/64	1,091	3,959	1,339	1.23	38.88	535	473	0.49
1964/65	1,209	4,234	1,489	1.23	41.13	629	487	0.52
1965/66	1,391	4,712	1,752	1.26	42.55	737	530	0.53
1966/67	1,584	5,000	1,786	1.13	43.55	840	535	0.53
1967/68	1,767	5,284	1,793	1.01	44.28	954	545	0.54
1968/69	2,063	5,847	1,838	0.89	45.51	1,073	617	0.52
1969/70	2,340	6,066	1,762	0.75	46.53	1,217	687	0.52
1970/71	2,620	6,395	2,234	0.85	48.41	1,362	732	0.52
1971/72	2871	6,663	2,468	0.86	51.16	1,493	778	0.52
1972/73	3,191	7,171	2,671	0.84	55.61	1,723	832	0.54
1973/74	3,823	8,180	3,542	0.93	58.56	2,217	887	0.58
1974/75	5,035	8,596	4,944	0.98	59.32	3,021	953	0.60
1975/76	6,025	9,384	6,538	1.09	61.93	3,555	1,136	0.59
Exponential trend[a]		7.76			4.05		6.82	
Mean				1.03				0.54

Year							
1976/77	7,413	10,332	7,308	0.99	64.63	3,929	1,305	0.53
1977/78	8,166	10,702	6,404	0.78	67.02	4,410	1,361	0.54
1978/79	9,114	11,215	7,974	0.87	69.58	4,922	1,487	0.54
1979/80	10,721	11,775	9,526	0.89	71.63	5,682	1,578	0.53
1980/81	12,694	12,694	11,150	0.88	73.81	7,109	1,773	0.56
1981/82	16,173	13,200	14,408	0.89	75.84	8,248	1,829	0.51
1982/83	20,143	14,533	16,487	0.82	77.78	9,467	1,948	0.47
1983/84	23,451	15,544	17,690	0.75	79.74	11,256	2,058	0.48
1984/85	27,240	16,433	21,253	0.78	81.63	13,075	2,247	0.48
1985/86	32,842	17,974	24,247	0.74	83.32	15,764	2,543	0.48
1986/87	39,250	19,895	27,643	0.70	84.41	18,840	2,795	0.48
Exponential trend[a]	6.53				2.68		7.43	
Mean				0.83				0.51

a. Percent per year.
Source: Columns 1 to 4, Government of India, CSO (1989a); Government of India, CSO (1989), *National Accounts Statistics*. Column 5, Government of India, Ministry of Finance (various years), *Economic Survey* (data adjusted to allow for nationalization of banks and post-1975 change in industrial classification). Column 6, from columns 1 and 8. Column 7, wage bill (column 6) deflated by consumer price index for industrial workers. Column 8, Government of India, CSO (1989), *National Accounts Statistics* through 1984/85, then assumed constant.

Table 13.10 Public Sector Manufacturing: Various Indicators

Year	GDP (current prices)	GDP (1980/81 prices)	GDCF (current prices)	GDCF/GDP (current prices)	Labor input (L)	Wage bill (WL)	Real wage bill (WL/CPI)	WL/GDP (current prices)
1960/61	57	475	280	4.91	540	28	28	0.49
1961/62	75	718	212	2.83	584	36	35	0.48
1962/63	105	984	253	2.41	640	51	47	0.48
1963/64	153	1,111	291	1.90	724	73	65	0.48
1964/65	199	1,213	367	1.84	783	96	74	0.49
1965/66	221	1,307	503	2.28	847	113	81	0.50
1966/67	251	1,298	575	2.29	899	128	82	0.51
1967/68	303	1,340	533	1.76	915	164	94	0.54
1968/69	360	1,456	469	1.30	939	198	114	0.55
1969/70	463	1,496	439	0.95	967	232	131	0.50
1970/71	541	1,530	436	0.81	1,017	287	154	0.53
1971/72	535	1,449	559	1.04	1,022	284	148	0.53
1972/73	630	1,600	678	1.08	1,165	340	164	0.54
1973/74	841	1,776	1,021	1.21	1,227	446	178	0.53
1974/75	1,274	2,074	1,496	1.17	1,318	713	225	0.56
1975/76	1,310	1,969	1,445	1.10	1,396	746	238	0.57
Exponential trend[a]		6.98			5.78		13.1	
Mean				1.90				0.52

1976/77	1,564	2,251	1,737	1.11	1,498	845	281	0.54
1977/78	1,742	2,474	1,607	0.92	1,583	993	306	0.57
1978/79	1,978	2,541	1,870	0.95	1,636	1,088	329	0.55
1979/80	2,325	2,581	2,657	1.14	1,678	1,232	342	0.53
1980/81	2,823	2,823	3,136	1.11	1,738	1,412	352	0.50
1981/82	3,357	2,767	3,623	1.08	1,844	1,578	350	0.47
1982/83	4,023	3,095	3,894	0.97	1,893	1,931	397	0.48
1983/84	4,886	3,411	4,139	0.85	1,989	2,394	438	0.49
1984/85	5,764	3,592	5,277	0.92	2,040	2,767	475	0.48
1985/86	7,267	4,046	6,455	0.89	2,103	3,488	563	0.48
1986/87	8,920	4,870	6,083	0.68	2,157	4,282	635	0.48
Exponential trend[a]	6.83			3.68		7.50		
Mean				0.96				0.51

a. Percent per year.

Source: Columns 1 to 7, as in table 13.9. Column 8, independent estimates for 1970/71 to 1979/80 from Government of India, CSO (1983), *Transactions of the Public Sector*. For other years we have assumed that the figure was the same as for organized manufacturing as a whole, as taken from Government of India, CSO (1989), *National Accounts Statistics*.

Table 13.11 Private Organized Manufacturing: Various Indicators

Year	GDP (current prices)	GDP (1980/81 prices)	GDCF (current prices)	GDCF/GDP (current prices)	Labor input (L)	Wage bill (WL)	Real wage bill (WL/CPI)	WL/GDP (current prices)
1960/61	1,132	4,125	370	0.33	3,166	556	545	0.49
1961/62	1,231	4,302	372	0.30	3,272	589	566	0.48
1962/63	1,389	4,525	385	0.28	3,407	672	622	0.48
1963/64	1,591	5,021	377	0.24	3,575	759	672	0.48
1964/65	1,745	5,425	502	0.29	3,764	857	664	0.49
1965/66	1,894	5,549	586	0.31	3,812	955	687	0.50
1966/67	2,072	5,564	885	0.43	3,728	1,056	673	0.51
1967/68	2,115	5,298	602	0.28	3,766	1,141	652	0.54
1968/69	2,255	5,631	384	0.17	3,738	1,232	708	0.55
1969/70	2,709	6,822	851	0.31	3,752	1,341	758	0.50
1970/71	2,865	6,986	984	0.34	3,890	1,495	804	0.52
1971/72	3,169	7,221	942	0.30	3,681	1,705	888	0.54
1972/73	3,470	7,346	496	0.14	3,785	1,860	899	0.54
1973/74	4,061	7,611	1,135	0.28	3,862	2,156	962	0.53
1974/75	5,086	7,407	2,235	0.44	3,937	2,479	782	0.49
1975/76	5,337	7,608	2,025	0.38	3,938	2,842	908	0.53
Exponential trend[a]		3.9			1.1		3.1	
Mean				0.30				0.51

1976/77	6,000	8,522	680	0.11	4,174	2,885	958	0.48
1977/78	6,589	9,022	1,324	0.20	4,262	3,361	1,037	0.51
1978/79	7,647	10,209	3,024	0.40	4,434	3,703	1,119	0.48
1979/80	8,722	9,901	2,557	0.29	4,644	4,277	1,188	0.49
1980/81	9,458	9,458	2,789	0.29	4,774	4,729	1,179	0.50
1981/82	11,061	10,461	3,920	0.35	4,872	5,199	1,153	0.47
1982/83	12,535	11,406	3,617	0.29	4,945	6,017	1,238	0.48
1983/84	15,422	13,218	4,420	0.29	4,913	7,557	1,382	0.49
1984/85	17,609	14,455	3,544	0.20	4,974	8,452	1,452	0.48
1985/86	20,509	15,837	3,984	0.19	5,017	9,844	1,588	0.48
1986/87	22,566	16,889	5,770	0.26	5,039	10,832	1,607	0.48
Exponential trend[a]	6.8			1.9		5.0		
Mean				0.26				0.49

a. Percent per year.

Source: Columns 1 to 7 as in table 13.9, Column 8, except for the years 1970/71 to 1979/80, the figure is assumed to be the same as for organized manufacturing as a whole, as taken from Government of India, CSO (1989), National Accounts Statistics. For 1970/71 to 1979/80, the independent estimate for public sector manufacturing given in table 13.10 implies that private sector figures are a residual.

Chapter Fourteen

Concluding Remarks

The Dichotomy of Macroeconomics and Microeconomics

India is widely thought of as a country with good macroeconomic management at least until the early 1980s, but with pervasive controls over economic activities, which mostly serve no social purpose but which undermine the efficiency of the economic system and are thus a prime cause of India's rather slow growth of income per head.

Unlike many such caricatures, this one is in our opinion essentially just. Macroeconomic management was good in the simple sense that in the face of considerable adverse exogenous shocks, primarily caused by droughts and secondarily by oil-price rises, both high inflation and any very serious industrial recessions were avoided without an excessive build up of debt (until the 1980s). We are not saying that it was perfect; greater stability with less loss of productive investment and output could have been achieved. We also think that the rate of inflation influenced policy to a rather greater extent than it should have. Not only was there a tendency to overreact to price rises caused by drought, but also, when inflation was low, it tended to be wrongly assumed that everything in the garden was lovely, and so the build-up of debt was ignored. We have made significant criticisms along these lines especially in chapters 8 to 13. But compared with many other developing countries, reasonably stable progress was sustained until the breakdown of fiscal discipline in the 1980s.

However, the simple dichotomy between macroeconomic and microeconomic management cannot be maintained. India's macroeconomic management has involved controls. If controls are bad for efficiency and growth, then India's macroeconomic management was bad for growth, even if reasonably good for stability. Were the controls really needed for macroeconomic management? Perhaps they were not only not needed, but were actually counterproductive.

Rather than again summarizing our views on stabilization, the analysis of which has been the core of this book, we therefore now turn to the macroeconomic consequences of India's control regime, a subject which has been only incidentally treated in earlier chapters. In the next section we give further consideration to India's crucial fiscal problem, and deal more fully with its long-run aspects than was done in chapter 9. We conclude with a summary of our relevant economic beliefs.

Macroeconomic Consequences of the Control Regime

Controls of all kinds tend to create parallel or black markets and this diversion of economic activity undermines tax morality and reduces government revenue. Discretionary controls also create opportunities for corruption, and the resulting payments or kickbacks raise the cost of both public and private economic activities, especially investment; they also undermine commercial and civil service morality. We turn to a more detailed discussion of the various controls that purport to have some macroeconomic function. Of these, import controls are the most important.

Import Controls

The need for import controls, and the possibility of doing without, depends crucially on other macroeconomic policies. An unsustainable demand for imports may arise from a general excess demand for goods. It should be a major function of fiscal and monetary policy to avoid such excess demand. If instead import controls were used to frustrate the demand for imports, then the general excess demand would translate into excess demand for domestic output. This would result in inflation, or in extensive price controls and hence quantitative allocation and rationing of goods in general. Surely no more need be said.

Alternatively an unsustainable demand for imports may arise without such general excess demand, in which case there is a deficiency of demand for domestic goods. This is the case of an overvalued exchange rate. A real devaluation, making imports more expensive and exports more profitable, can always cure this situation. The elasticities of supply and demand for exports are, as we have shown, clearly such that the result will be a much greater value and volume of imports than if import controls are used. There is not the slightest doubt that the efficiency of use of India's resources, both capital and labor, would have been greater if India had traded more. India missed out on the great boom of the late 1960s and 1970s in exports of clothing and light engineering goods from developing countries. This was a direct result of her trade and industrial policies.

It may be argued that import controls are needed to affect not the total value of imports, but their composition. Some have in mind mainly imports of luxury consumer goods, but distributional concerns of this kind can surely be met by high taxation (of both imports and indigenous production). Others believe that some industries need to be promoted by the total protection given by rigid quotas on all competitive imports. In contrast, we believe that such total protection has been a major contribution to the admitted inefficiency of Indian manufacturing.

It is arguable that the ability to limit imports in a crisis, either by quota or by advance deposits, should be retained. Although such crises should be avoidable by sound macroeconomic policies, including the maintenance of reserves and credit-worthiness, we would not oppose this. But such emergency trade intervention is a very different matter from the permanent use of controls, and the accompanying ov ervaluation of the currency, which has so reduced imports that any further reduction in an emergency necessarily impinges on current production and capital investment.

Other Quantitative Controls

Capital movements have been strictly controlled throughout the period. Their efficacy is questionable—they have not prevented the buildup of large illegal holdings of foreign assets, but they may serve to reduce rapid destabilizing movements of "hot" money. Given sound macroeconomic policies, they can probably be abandoned. But this is not a high priority in the drive for reform.

India's other main quantitative controls are those over industrial investment and production. These are described in chapter 2, where we indicate that such controls are deleterious from a macroeconomic point of view because they reduce the flexibility of response of the economy to shifts in the levers of macroeconomic policy. The same is true of much labor market legislation, especially the restrictions on making workers redundant. Policymakers appear to be extraordinarily short-sighted in failing to see that employment in industry is reduced by making it difficult to sack workers. There is little doubt that labor market legislation is partly responsible for the slow growth of industrial employment in India.

Price Controls

Apart from interest rates, which we deal with in the next section, the most important price control is that of foreign exchange. Except in the rare case of "clean floating," meaning that the monetary authorities refuse to buy or sell foreign exchange, the exchange rate is always administered. In discussing import controls we have already implied that the exchange rate should be managed in conjunction with fiscal and monetary policy so as to permit a wide-ranging freedom to import and export.

Prominent among the reasons why India and many other countries were reluctant to devalue (until after 1983) was the fear that devaluation would be inflationary, and that the real effects would be quickly wiped out. We have seen that this fear was unfounded in India's case and that devaluation had very positive effects on the balance of trade and payments (see chapter 11). Furthermore, a fixed rate has been seen by some as an anti-inflationary "anchor" that restrains governments from pursuing the loose fiscal and monetary policies which lead to inflation and unsustainable current account deficits. The cogency and force of these arguments in the case of India and seventeen other developing countries over the past twenty-five years have been closely examined in chapter 8 of Little and others (1993). Many countries ran into severe inflationary problems while maintaining a fixed rate. Tightened import controls followed, but sooner or later "import starvation" and severe price distortions forced a major devaluation. In other countries with a strong commitment to price stability, a bout of inflation arising from supply-side forces (as in the case of Indian droughts) was followed by a devaluation, or the adoption of a variable peg (or managed float), after which low inflation was again achieved. A traditional historical commitment to low inflation, together with the avoidance of wage indexation, was more important than any nominal anchor. In every case, including India, a nominal depreciation of the currency resulted in a real depreciation that lasted for a considerable time, and exports rose.[1]

We can deal more briefly with other controlled prices (for an account of their prevalence and supposed objectives see chapter 2). One of their purposes has been to suppress inflation. Shortages and arbitrary inefficient allocation follow, while reduced profits or losses result in inadequate investment and high-cost production later. The fiscal problem that lies at the heart of inflation is exacerbated. But it should be noted here that we do not include under price controls the government's influencing of prices by buying (without compulsion) or selling in the market. The primary examples of this are buying and selling foreign exchange when the exchange rate is flexible ("dirty" floating) and buying and selling cereals (buffer stock operations). If successful in achieving their objectives, these activities will produce a profit—except when the government deliberately subsidizes the sale of food.

The Effect of Controls on Government Revenue and Expenditure

For a long time the balance of payments was considered the key problem faced by developing countries, including India, in their drive for development. We believe, on the contrary, that the fiscal problem is central, and that this is particularly true of India and other countries that see a very large and necessary role for the public sector in promoting development while at the same time suffering from a narrow revenue base. If the public finances are in good shape, and the exchange rate is flexible, the balance of payments and inflation will rarely be a major problem.[2]

It is therefore important to note that trying to manage the balance of payments and inflation by controls invariably exacerbates the fiscal problem. Until at least recently quotas were the effective limitation on most imports; this implies that there was excess demand at the landed (cum tariff) price, and that the government could have earned more revenue if tariffs had been relied on to limit imports. Only in the 1980s have tariffs been so greatly increased that in some cases there is no excess demand (when quotas become redundant). At least as important is the fact that import controls permit the rupee value of foreign exchange to be lower than otherwise, and so reduce the profitability of exporting (but high tariffs have much the same effect). Exports, and consequently imports, become so restricted that the government finds it essential to institute export subsidies.

The manner in which India has managed the balance of payments is only one example, albeit an important one, of the way in which India's use of price and quantity controls creates fiscal problems. Other controls with macroeconomic objectives, such as the suppression of inflation, also increase government expenditure or reduce revenue. To that extent, India's style of managing the economy creates its own problems. We elaborate on this theme next.

The Fiscal Problem

The fiscal problem has often changed the course of history. In modern times it has been argued that it is more of a problem for democracies than for autocracies. This disputable argument is discussed below. However, it is surely more of a problem for developing countries than for the industrial countries for two reasons. First, in nearly all developing countries a development role is assigned to government implying high expenditures relative to GNP. Second, the revenue base is more restricted in a poor country, with the exception of a few countries where production of a particular commodity is a large part of GNP. The problem has been exacerbated in many developing countries by the growth of inefficient parastatal industrial enterprises, which the central government has found difficulty in controlling. This has been the main reason for recent massive privatization measures, for example, in Mexico and Argentina.

India is a prime example. An exceptional development role was assigned to government. In particular, her industrial policies led to the creation of a large public manufacturing sector, which is very high cost both because of the usual inherent tendencies of public sector monopolized industries, and because industries were promoted without regard to comparative advantage, consequently needing high even total protection. The need for tax revenue was thus magnified by high public investment that was inadequately supported by public sector profits (see chapters 1, 9, 12, and 13). At the same time the tax base is exceptionally restricted by the center-state relations, which give insufficient incentive to the states to raise revenue and avoid subsidies, and by the constitutional fact that the center cannot tax agricultural incomes (or the land). These limitations have long been recognized and indeed emphasized, but nothing has been done.

Despite the above difficulties, Indian government and public sector deficits were for a long time kept at levels that could be financed without either excessive inflation or any excessive creation of debt. This was partly because of concessional foreign finance, and partly because the government paid very low rates of interest on domestic (nonmonetized) borrowing. However, the latter was achieved in ways that had costs as well as benefits, and which led eventually to serious weakness of the banking system—see below. The fiscal problem thus did not become overt until the mid 1980s, and it became serious mainly because of a rapid growth of hidden and explicit subsidies. Part of the reason for this rapid growth of subsidies can be traced back to the general style of India's macroeconomic management, and to its development philosophy or ideology.

The Style of Economic Management and the Fiscal Problem

We have already shown how managing the balance of payments by controls led to expenditure on export subsidies, and to loss of revenue from tariffs. We now give further examples of how controls have exacerbated the fiscal problem. Much the largest explicit subsidy is that for fertilizers; it accounted in 1989/90 for almost half the total of explicit central budget subsidization, and was about 1 percent of GDP.

The fertilizer subsidy is partly a subsidy to farmers (bringing the administered price of fertilizers below the imported cost) and partly a subsidy to the fertilizer industry (bringing the price paid to the industry above the imported price). The relative magnitude of these parts varies with the import price; in 1989/90 they were roughly equal. Insofar as the subsidy is a production subsidy, it arises from the supposed need to keep high-cost fertilizer plants in operation, and, at one further remove, from India's project selection procedures and neglect of comparative advantage. From the agricultural point of view, the fertilizer subsidy is only one of several subsidies on agricultural inputs. Irrigation and electricity are also heavily subsidized. Although these subsidies do not appear directly in the budgetary accounts, they reduce profits or give rise to losses in state enterprises, thus contributing to the overall deficit of the public sector. In all, these input subsidies amounted to about 2.5 percent of GDP in 1989/90, or about 32 percent of the public sector deficit.[3] Finally agricultural credit is subsidized, as described in the next section.

For what economic reason are these large subsidies paid? They do not result in positive effective protection of agriculture.[4] In the aggregate, agriculture has been disprotected, especially in the case of the major food grain crops and cotton (oilseeds and sugar have heavy effective protection). Thus the subsidies are a partial offset to the relatively high input prices and low output prices for agriculture (compared with world prices) that are largely a consequence of India's controlled trade.[5] This is an example of the way in which the fiscal problem is related to the management of foreign trade.

The Fiscal Problem and the Banking System

Until the 1980s the Indian (consolidated) government was able to run substantial fiscal deficits averaging somewhat over 5 percent of GDP without incurring any dangerous rise in the level of debt relative to GDP. This success was for two main reasons. First, there was substantial external borrowing (averaging 1.3 percent of GDP), around 85 percent of which was on highly concessionary terms, so that although the ratio of foreign debt to exports was high, the total debt service was very low (see tables 9.1 and 9.2).

The second reason is the one that concerns us here. The government also managed to borrow domestically at very low (real) interest rates. As we saw in chapter 2, the organized or formal domestic financial system has been under almost total control, virtually every interest rate being administered. The commercial banks and other financial institutions—most importantly life insurance and pension funds—have been forced to lend to the government at negative real interest rates. The benefit of this for the government is obvious. The counterparts of this benefit are low deposit rates for savers, and high lending rates for nonpriority sectors (mainly organized industry, services, and trade); and an erosion of the profits of financial institutions. Since these institutions are predominantly in the public sector, the benefits of cheap public borrowing are to some extent illusory. The government borrows cheaply, but it has to borrow more as these institutions generate less public savings.

Apart from compulsory lending to the government, the commercial banks are now required to direct 40 percent of bank credit to priority sectors, including agriculture (16 percent) at subsidized (sometimes negative) real rates of interest. In addition to low interest rates, nearly half of all agricultural loans are in default. The credit subsidy to farmers in a typical year is of the same order of magnitude as each of the other major subsidies—fertilizers, irrigation, and electricity.

It is difficult to sum up the macroeconomic effects of India's system of controlling interest rates and directing credit. Prima facie it helped the government to sustain for some twenty years, from 1960/61 to 1979/80, a fairly high public sector domestic borrowing requirement of about 3.5 percent of GDP (inclusive of borrowing from the RBI) without running into the 'debt trap' or unacceptable inflation. We have not found any clear evidence of offsetting costs in the form of discouraging private investment in the organized sector, or discouraging household savings (the spread of branch banking, itself part of the system, probably overcompensated for the possible effects of low deposit rates). However, the apparent ease with which deficits could be financed encouraged the current spending spree of the government in the 1980s when interest rates rose and deficits reached levels that could no longer be financed without excessive increases in debt. Furthermore, the system encouraged the payment of credit subsidies, the growth of irresponsible lending, and the condonation of default (a large loan write-off scheme for agriculture was initiated in 1990). It is not only the profitability, the portfolio quality, and the capital of the banking system that have been seriously eroded, but also probably its prudence and probity. The government squeezed the financial sector too hard and for too long. Recent committee enquiries show serious concern.[6] The extensive structural liberalization of the economy that is in progress requires the support of a strong financial system.

Political Economy and the Fiscal Problem

We have traced India's recent macroeconomic problems to the proliferation of controls and the breakdown of fiscal discipline. Thus, reform requires the breakdown of controls and the restoration of fiscal discipline.

The ideology of Indian development emphasized state ownership and controls. The collapse of this ideology in the world at large has already had some influence on Indian thinking, and this influence will surely increase. But controls are hard to get rid of, since both controllers and some of the best organized and influential sections of the controlled economy benefit. However, the quite dramatic reforms of 1991/92 give ground for hope that the process can continue though a larger and more effective constituency for reform needs to be created.

Greater reliance on the price mechanism will help the fiscal problem. But far more than that is needed. Fiscal laxity is a danger whatever the system of regulation. Indeed, it is a danger whatever the political system. It is often supposed that the pressures that may lead to fiscal laxity are more keenly felt in a democracy. As against this, elections have to be won and inflation is unpopular. Autocratic governments may be more insulated from pressure groups, but this has not stopped some charismatic autocratic rulers from initiating wild bursts of public expenditure.

Until the early 1970s India may have had the best of both worlds. It was effectively a genuine one-party democracy. The Congress party could mediate conflicting claims through its own internal democracy. Although it had little fear of losing elections, the civil service and the austerity and high-mindedness of the first generation of postindependence politicians were effective restraints on inflationary finance.

We have described in chapter 3 how this system was weakened, indeed destroyed, in the 1970s. Mrs. Gandhi's style of government, including the emergency, was a major cause, although some dissolution of such a convenient kind of democracy was inevitable, and perhaps desirable. Now the mediating role of the Congress party has been lost. Furthermore the restraining role of the civil service has been weakened. This can be seen in its compliance with the fiscal laxity of the 1980s. It seems that civil servants could no longer stand up to their political masters after the Emergency. In short, the officials of even the Finance Ministry and the Reserve Bank became subject to political pressures.

Economic stability in a democracy would seem to require a stable center insulated from excessive demands. This may be provided by the bureaucracy, especially of course the Finance Ministry. But some political analysts, fearing that politicians cannot be restrained by their civil servants, advocate independence of the central bank. Clearly a lot depends on the history and traditions of the country in question. India must somehow rediscover her earlier prudence.

A Summary of What We Believe

We agree with those who believe that controls have been a major cause of the inefficiency of use and the maldistribution of resources that have characterized the Indian economy since independence. We have also shown that these controls are, with very few exceptions, unnecessary for achieving macroeconomic stability. Mainstream methods, as briefly described below, of securing internal and external balances of supply and demand, are fully applicable to India, and can and should operate within a framework of very extensive reliance on the price mechanism. We believe that such methods are more conducive to long-run growth and equity than the highly interventionist style of economic management that has prevailed in India for forty years. But we do not agree with the so-called 'new classical' macroeconomists that all systematic government intervention is necessarily futile. In particular, we advocate some government action to influence aggregate demand as well as the supply of a few major commodities.

Long-run fiscal policy should limit public sector deficits to amounts that can be financed without an inflationary growth of the money supply, or imprudent increase in the domestic or the external debt. In the short run larger or smaller deficits (or surpluses) may be used to restrict or stimulate demand, if a private imbalance of investment and savings results in excessive or deficient demand: but it has to be recognized that timely and successful use of fiscal policy in this manner is difficult, and that any such attempt to stimulate demand has to be avoided for the present, given existing levels of the public deficit and the debt. In the past fiscal policy has been used to counter inflation arising from drought; but inflation arising from the supply side is better met by the use of reserves, of either foreign exchange or commodities (especially food), or both.

In the long run money supply should match the growth in the demand for money, and this limits the desirable size of the public sector deficits, given the limitations on sources of borrowing other than the RBI. But in the short run monetary policy is partly independent of fiscal policy. The government can vary its borrowing from non-RBI sources—furthermore, the economy is not so open financially that the money supply is endogenous for this reason. Thus, in the short run the authorities can expand or contract the growth of the base money supply, and also by varying reserve requirements restrict or expand the extension of credit by the banking system. While in the long run real interest rates are determined by savings and investment, the monetary authorities can also use the discount rate to influence demand in the short run. These methods, as well as fiscal policy, can be used to counter any excess or deficiency of demand that may be generated in the private sector.

Turning to the balance of external payments, we have made it clear that trade controls (or even variations in trade taxes) should not be used to maintain a viable balance of payments on current account. There is no doubt that imports and exports are sufficiently responsive to variations in the exchange rate for it to be an effective instrument for this purpose, provided that fiscal and monetary policy are used to maintain an overall balance of supply and demand. Of course, the trade balance takes some time to respond. The maintenance of adequate reserves and borrowing capacity is therefore important. Only in the event of mismanagement, or a very large exogenous shock, need resort to control be contemplated.

The above is no more than a condensed account of an orthodoxy to which the industrial countries subscribe in principle, although there have been some serious deviations in practice. It will be objected to by some who believe that the extreme poverty of a high proportion of the Indian population requires unorthodox solutions. The poverty problem is not one that has been examined in this book, but we should here emphasize that we believe, with many other economists, that the promotion of labor-demanding growth is the most effective means open to government of reducing poverty. The unorthodox elements in Indian economic policy have all served to restrain demand for labor. Trade policies have produced a bias against exports and agriculture, both of which are relatively labor-intensive. The government has directly created capital-intensive import-substituting industries in the public sector, most of which are highly protected and often otherwise subsidized. Credit at low interest rates to favored sectors also encourages capital-intensity. Finally, protective labor legislation and high wages in the public sector have further discouraged the use of labor-intensive methods. Attempts to offset some of this bias, for instance by the reservation of products for small-scale industry, have been of very doubtful value.[7]

We have no doubt that greater reliance on the price mechanism would result in a more labor-demanding development, and in a reduction in poverty. This is not to say that further measures are not required. Well-targeted schemes for public employment and other forms of poverty relief are both desirable and in no way incompatible with the much more open economy and the greatly increased reliance on the price mechanism that we advocate.

Appendix A

The Quality of Economic Statistics

Indian economic statistics are among the best in the developing world.[1] A great deal of detail—especially of public transactions—is provided. However, the basis for the estimates made is often very shaky. Conscious of the futility and even deception involved in interpreting the effects of economic policies on the basis of false reflections of reality, the authors have studied the quality of the statistical information used. Fortunately, absolute magnitudes and even proportions of GDP are not usually very important either for research or for macroeconomic policy itself. It is periodic changes that matter. Bearing this in mind the authors hope that they have not often been guilty of reading too much into the data, although this may occasionally have happened.

There is far more information available for research after the event, with a lag of sometimes several years, than for the timely operation of the instruments of economic policy. Researchers are in danger of assuming that policymakers were better informed than was the case. We therefore start with a very brief survey of the information on the basis of which economic decisions have been made. This describes the situation in the early 1980s. Since then there have been some improvements in the speed with which statistics become available.

Statistics Available for Macroeconomic Management

Many indicators of aggregate supply and demand that are available to decision-makers in most industrial countries are lacking in India. Only limited production data are available, for example the unreliable index of industrial production. No expenditure or demand data are available. Employment figures refer only to the public sector and the "organized" private sector, which probably account for about 7 percent of total employment; and there is a lag of about a year in their availability. There are few meaningful unemployment figures. Capacity-use figures refer only to large-scale industry, suffer from conceptual confusion, and are anyway highly unreliable. There are no regular surveys of expenditure plans by business or households.

Statistics that are available (but of little use because of lags, unreliability, or minor relevance) include all the GDP estimates, and its components. The Index of Industrial Production with recently revised base is available monthly with a three- to four-month lag. Rail transport figures (lag of two to three months) and electricity production (lag of six months) are available. These are sometimes used in other countries as indicators of industrial activity, but they are unreliable for this purpose in India because of supply problems.

Agricultural production is rather special. Estimates for the principal crops are made throughout the growing and harvesting period, based on area under the crops, rainfall, and the crop conditions, but are not very reliable. They are anxiously watched. However, it may well be that they are dominated by food prices as far as policy changes are concerned. The statistics most likely to influence policy are those for foreign trade, the balance of payments, banking, money and public finance, and prices. We consider these below. Among them foreign trade is probably of least importance, and prices of most importance.

Foreign Trade

Statistics on merchandise trade are compiled by the Directorate of Commercial Intelligence and Statistics (DGCIS) and by the Reserve Bank of India (RBI), the former from returns filed by customs offices all over the country, the latter from returns filed by "authorized dealers" in foreign exchange (principally commercial banks) as part of the mechanism of exchange control. The two sources do not match and there are substantial discrepancies.

Total values of merchandise exports and imports are available to the government with a two-month lag, and the same totals with broad commodity classifications (nearer one digit than two digits) with a four-month lag, subject to revisions of course. Detailed external trade statistics with commodity and country classification take about three years to appear. DGCIS also has the responsibility for calculating unit value and volume indices. These are available with a three-year lag, and there are considerable doubts about their reliability.

Balance of Payments

Complete balance of payments data take at least two years to prepare. "Quick" estimates of merchandise trade based on authorized dealers' returns to the RBI's exchange control department are available to the government with a two-month lag. But, as seen above, these do not match the DGCIS estimates. The RBI is the only source of information on invisibles, and here the delays are shocking. A well-organized sample survey system to estimate remittances and earnings from travel, for example, does not exist. As a result, for short-term policy formulation, the government's information regarding invisibles is little better than wild guesswork. On capital flows, the Finance Ministry monitors aid, external borrowing, and debt service closely; and the RBI has current information on certain categories of capital inflows, for example deposits made by nonresidents as part of special schemes to attract such inflows. But that still leaves a large part of the capital account in a state of mystery. Even when it finally appears, there is very little detail in the capital account, and errors and omissions can be large. There is, however, one item in the balance of payments that is known on an up-to-the-minute basis—this is the foreign exchange reserves, and they are consequently a focus of much official attention.

Money, Banking, and Finance

Aggregate money and banking data are based on weekly (unfortunately recently changed to fortnightly) returns by commercial banks to the RBI. These are collated quickly, so that provisional data are available with a lag of only two weeks and partially revised data with a lag of six weeks. Continuous monitoring of both the money supply and reserve money is therefore possible. Central government revenues and expenditures are also known with a short time lag (about two months). Finances of the state governments present more of a problem but not an acute one.

Prices

The movement of prices is probably more influential than anything else, except foreign exchange reserves. Consumer price index numbers are compiled monthly for industrial workers, nonmanual workers, and agricultural laborers. Wholesale price indices are compiled weekly. The consumer price indices that are mostly used in the text are widely based, but the expenditure weights are very outdated, being based on 1958/59 surveys. For this reason they may give somewhat distorted indications. New indices are available for 1983/84 and later, based on 1980/81 surveys. The WPI is based on a large number of commodities, the weights being the value of total supplies in 1970. It is available with a time lag of only two to three weeks, and is the inflation indicator that is most commonly referred to. A new index is now available based on 1981/82. Finally, changes in interest rates (except in the informal sector) are quickly known, but convey little information since they are controlled.

It is evident from the above that short-term macroeconomic management cannot but be essentially monetary. Very little is reliably known about aggregate supply until too late. There are no useful employment figures. Excess supply or demand has to be judged on the basis of price movements, with some rather remote help from money supply and credit figures, and movements in the reserves. We are in a land where Keynes's *Treatise on Money* may be more easily applied than *The General Theory*.

National Income Statistics

Though these are too delayed to be of any use for short- and even medium-term economic policy formulation, they are essential for judging the real effects of policies and are therefore a core input for our book. They are also of course essential for measuring longer-run growth, and the contribution of savings and investment to such growth. We therefore give a highly compressed account of how the estimates are made, and a summary of our views concerning their reliability.

Gross Domestic Product

AGRICULTURE (35 PERCENT OF GDP).[2] The quantity of agricultural output for the major crops is assessed from estimates of the area sown, and yields derived from crop-cutting surveys. The first estimates can be quite influential but are not very reliable. The value of output is derived using wholesale prices prevailing in primary markets during peak marketing periods. Value added uses estimates of inputs derived from a wide variety of sources. Frequent revisions are made, and fully revised estimates for gross value added are available only after about three years. Estimates for many minor crops and livestock have little validity. Our general assessment is that the trend of the main physical outputs and gross output values, and year-to-year movements in the same, are fairly reliable. Slightly less faith attaches to changes in gross value added in agriculture as a whole.

MANUFACTURING (18 PERCENT OF GDP).[3] Roughly two-thirds of the value added in manufacturing is believed to come from the registered sector, which supposedly consists of all units employing ten persons or more if using power, or twenty persons or more if not using power (but probably many fail to register). Estimates for the registered sector are based on the Annual Survey of Industries, which can be considered to be fairly reliable, albeit with a lag of three years. Preliminary estimates are extrapolated using the less reliable Index of Industrial Production and the WPI.

Estimates for unregistered manufacturing are highly unsatisfactory, being based on out-of-date and incomplete surveys and on unreliable indicators of quantity changes. It is possible that both the trend and annual changes are significantly misstated.

OTHER SECTORS (47 PERCENT OF GDP).[4] In a good many sectors, recourse is had to out-of-date surveys to determine value added per worker. The decennial population censuses are then used to produce estimates for benchmark years. Intermediate years are estimated using a variety of indicators of the volume of activity in the particular sector. In other cases more reliable estimates can be made using the account of public sector and private corporate enterprises. The sectors for which the estimates are relatively reliable include the railways; mining; electricity, gas, and water; communications; and banking and public administration—totalling about 12 percent of GDP. Overall, the percentage of estimates based on direct current data, which may therefore be deemed to be relatively reliable, was about 64 percent in 1980/81 (see Government of India, CSO (1989b) table 1.1). For the rest one has to hope that there are no very significant cumulative errors.

Investment and Savings

First, total gross fixed capital formation is estimated by the commodity flow approach. We believe that very considerable errors may result both for the total of construction, and of plant and machinery. Second, partly independent estimates of fixed capital formation are made for sixteen sectors using the expenditure approach. These estimates would seem to be reasonably reliable only for the organized sectors, or the organized parts of other sectors. The sectoral total diverges from the total arrived at by the commodity flow approach. Changes in stock are then estimated for each sector, and the total is added to the sectoral fixed capital formation estimates (arrived at by the expenditure method) to give total domestic capital formation unadjusted—see below. The sector-by-sector breakdown of stock changes is not given in the national accounts. For some sectors the methods used seem very untrustworthy, but one hopes that errors cancel out in arriving at the total. From 1975/76 to 1981/82 the addition to stocks varied between 7.6 and 20.3 percent of total gross capital formation, but in most years it was close to 20 percent.

Savings estimates are prepared for the public, private corporate, and household sectors. The public estimates may be considered as reasonably reliable. Private corporate savings estimates are, like the investment estimates, derived mainly from RBI samples of company accounts. These estimates should be relatively reliable, though in chapter 13 we doubted the validity of the extraordinary annual variations in corporate investment that have mostly been offset by variations in household investment.

The household sector is a residual including everything that is neither government nor a corporation. Its saving is divided into physical and financial additions to assets. The physical is a residual derived by subtracting government and corporate investments from total investment, as arrived at by the commodity flow method (so physical savings and investment are identical). The household sector's financial savings is also largely a residual, arrived at by deducting the government and corporate sector's holding of financial assets (such as currency, bank deposits, and shares and debentures) from the total of such assets in the economy, while also deducting its liabilities to the other sectors. For insurance and provident funds, however, the estimates are prepared directly. Considerable errors may arise, the information being often that of sample studies or periodic surveys. Foreign savings, estimated from the balance of payments accounts, is added to give an estimate of total gross savings, which should equal gross investment. However there is a gap, so that the savings and investment estimates need to be reconciled.

The CSO treats the savings estimates as the more reliable. It therefore adjusts the total investment estimate arrived at by the commodity flow method. Errors and omissions are thus ascribed to investment. This new adjusted total is then used to adjust the estimates for the industrial sectors, arrived at by the expenditure method. The organized sectors (or parts thereof) for which direct data are available are not adjusted, while the others are adjusted pro rata. Published data do not reveal the extent of the sectoral adjustments, but it seems probable that agriculture, forestry and logging, fishing, unregistered manufacturing, construction, transport other than railways, trade (including hotels and restaurants), real estate and business services, and other services, suffer the bulk of adjustment. These together comprise a little over half of total gross investment. The size of the adjustment as a percentage of the final figure for total gross investment ranged from –10.3 to –0.2 percent in the period 1975/76 to 1981/82. The Raj committee has given the adjustment figures back to 1950/51. They are usually negative and it should be noted that the figure of –10.3 percent for 1975/76 was exceptionally high.

The Raj committee questioned the presumption of the superiority of the savings estimates. But we are not convinced by their arguments, and accept the adjusted investment estimates as the best that could be made, despite our considerable doubts about their reliability. Household physical savings and investment is a large residual (ranging from about 35 to about 48 percent in the period 1970/71 to 1981/82), which could easily accommodate quite large errors in the total. The reliability of sectoral savings and investment estimates for the private sector is still more questionable.

Appendix B

Structuralist Macroeconomics and the Indian Economy

Structuralist thinking has been, and still is, influential in India. The first and most important structuralist theory was that growth may be limited by the availability of foreign exchange rather than savings. This was prevalent in India in the 1950s. In Little (1960) it was stated that "A large element of foreign aid is, for a decade at least, indispensable. This is not so much because it is impossible to increase savings in India, but because savings cannot be transformed into the kind of capital development which will later permit India to grow without continued reliance on foreign aid." In other words, savings could not be transformed into foreign exchange. In more up-to-date language, India was operating under a trade constraint (or foreign exchange constraint), not a savings constraint. Little later renounced this idea. For an early forceful critique see Joshi (1970).

All forms of structuralism involve the assumption of rigidities. The foreign exchange constraint implies that reduced domestic consumption cannot be made to result quickly in reduced imports or increased exports. It is by now rather widely accepted that this particular assumed rigidity was greatly exaggerated (export pessimism), the effect of which was to reduce growth by over-emphasis on import substitution. The effective constraint on Indian growth was doctrinal rigidity, not any real rigidity.

The language of "constraints" is the linguistic and mathematical counterpart of the assumed rigidities. Models of the economy are built with fixed exogenous coefficients reflecting absolute constraints. Output or growth in such a model is maximized when one of the independent variables reaches a supply limit, since there is no substitution. Output or growth is then "constrained" by that variable, for instance in the example given, by foreign exchange. Other variables are "slack," that is, in economic terms they are not scarce; their shadow price is zero. Structuralists, discounting the possibilities of substitution, typically ignore (relative) prices.

Supposed constraints have since been multiplied in India. It is now held that foreign exchange was only sometimes the constraint; at other times it was the output of food. Ignoring population growth, if the amount of food demanded is rigidly related to the total output (and hence income) of the economy, and if that demand cannot be denied, and if food cannot be made available through foreign trade, then the output of food determines total output. And therefore the limit to the rate of growth of income and output is the rate of growth of food output divided by the exogenously given income elasticity of demand for food. The proviso "if food cannot be made available through foreign trade" makes it clear that there cannot be a food constraint independently of a foreign exchange constraint; unless another rigidity is introduced to the effect that food cannot be imported even though foreign exchange is available.

It is held by some commentators—not only structuralists—that in the second half of the 1970s there were no supply-side constraints. Food and foreign exchange stocks were being built up, so there were no constraints there. It was also held that the more traditional savings constraint was slack. This is just another way of asserting that there was slack in the economy; that is, output and investment, and therefore growth, could have been higher. Structuralists express this by saying that output (and growth) were demand-constrained, and imply that the government should have increased demand. We agree that in principle demand can be deficient, and that it may be right for a government to try to increase demand. One does not have to be a structuralist to believe that! But our own views concerning this period take other considerations and difficulties into account, and are therefore more qualified.

Yet another constraint has been recently introduced—a fiscal constraint on output and growth. The idea is that the infrastructure (whether physical or human) can be built up only by the public sector. And infrastructure limits total output so that public investment may constrain output and growth. Public investment is not limited by a shortage of total domestic or national savings, for belief in the independent validity of a fiscal constraint implies a denial of a savings constraint. In effect it is suggested that the economy would grow faster, without any rise in the propensity to save, if there were more public savings. Several further rigidities are implicit in this argument. More private savings cannot be borrowed by the public sector. The public sector cannot substitute infrastructural for other investments that the private sector could make. The private sector itself cannot supply any of the infrastructure whose deficiency is held to be restraining output or growth.

Structuralists take a nonmonetarist view of inflation. Demand and supply are not fundamental. More traditionally, until the last fifteen to twenty years, inflation would have been regarded as a symptom of a generalized supply constraint. However, recently the phenomenon of "stagflation" has been diagnosed, implying that inflation may occur with generalized slack in the economy. This results from malfunctioning of the labor market, usually with some element of "inertial" inflation by which past price rises influence present wage rises and hence future price rises. These conditions are considered to be quite prevalent in many industrial countries, and also in the chronic inflationary countries of Latin America. However, unlike some structuralists, we believe that in a country like India any persistent tendency to inflation is a symptom of general excess demand. This is not of course to deny that supply failure—caused by drought in particular—may almost inevitably give rise to a temporary inflation accompanied by some industrial slack, and several such episodes are analyzed in the main body of this book.

Since we believe that great harm was done by structuralist emphasizing of a single constraint (apart from savings), we should perhaps welcome the multiplication of constraints that we have just described. At least attention is drawn to a variety of possible problems. However, we have not found recent structuralist accounts of India's economic history and current situation enlightening.[1] The economy jumps from one constraint to another in a manner and with timing that is not transparent. The assumed coefficients and relationships are not based on firm evidence or research, and the particular constraint that is deduced may be very sensitive to the choice of a coefficient.

More fundamentally we find the essential feature of structuralism—rigidities, and their model counterparts of fixed coefficients—to be unacceptable. Of course, everything is rigid if no time is allowed to elapse. It is the function of reserves to tide over the lag before substitution becomes significant. Where firm medium- or long-run rigidities exist they are almost always created by controls. In other cases substitution is possible, and prices become important. In reality, almost everything has a price—in contrast to a constrained economy where only one thing is scarce. Of course, we recognize that these prices do not always properly reflect scarcities; that is, economic quantities may have shadow prices that differ from actual prices. We may want to assert that a crucial problem facing the Indian authorities is, say, the fiscal deficit. In formal language this can be translated as "public income has a shadow price greater than unity." It does not say that nothing else is scarce. In most economies almost everything is a constraint—more or less.

Structuralist thinking was most prominent in the 1950s and 1960s. One only had to have a feel for a few key "orders of magnitude" and their relationships, and one could tell what was wrong with an economy, and deduce the most desirable thrusts of economic policy—the development strategy. Oxford used to be the home of lost causes. They have moved to India.

Notes

Chapter 1. Recent History and a Profile of the Economy

1. For an account of the antecedents of planning in India see Hanson (1966), chapter 2.
2. Until the Janata party was stitched together in 1977, the Communist party of India, formed in the 1920s, was the only other all-India party of any consequence, although it never had much influence at the national level.
3. "... the Congress inherited an administrative structure, which it had to use for a new purpose. Its ideas became, not to disrupt the status quo, but to build up its "socialistic pattern" of economy on the foundation of the existing order without any violent disturbance. In the prosaic task of reformation, the Congress Party, in the opinion of its critics, has tried to convert every problem of rational reconstruction into an administrative problem ... There is an effort to continually add to new responsibilities, instead of a desire to stimulate the growth of non-official endeavors to any appreciable extent." N. K. Bose, "Social and Cultural Life of Calcutta," *Geographical Review of India*, December 1958, pp. 27–8, quoted by Rosen (1966:71).
4. An exception to this has been the supposedly temporary overdraft facilities accorded by the Reserve Bank of India, which in some years (usually preceding an election, or when there was a drought) reached amounts equal to about half of the central government's deficit. This loophole is reported to have been closed in 1986.
5. The states themselves have no constitutional say in the creation of states, which is done by simple majority in the Lok Sabha.
6. There are now twenty-five states. In 1966 the Punjab was split into Hindi-speaking Haryana and Punjabi-speaking Punjab. Sikkim has been turned from a protectorate into a state, and three more mini-states have been created in response to ethnic demands. These demands are still continuing. Himachal Pradesh was also split off from the Punjab, and became a state in 1971.
7. But since the late 1960s the public sector has entered the consumer good field to a significant extent by nationalizing "sick" units. In India, exit from an industry is even more difficult than entry.
8. For a more extended discussion of the political economy of Indian inflation, see Joshi and Little (1987).
9. Except when otherwise stated figures come from the World Bank's *World Development Report* (various years), and from *World Debt Tables* (1991–92), or from tables in later chapters where original sources are given.
10. In terms more familiar to some, this is 1.14 acres per person.
11. The "organized" sector consists of government and public enterprises, and all private enterprises employing ten persons or more (or twenty or more if not using power). All such private enterprises are supposed to register and so be counted—but many do not. The vast proportion of agricultural labor is, of course, in the unorganized sector.
12. Some defense expenditure is classified as capital. Total defense expenditure in 1989–90 officially amounted to 3.25 percent of GDP.

Chapter 2.   The Structure and Working of Markets

1. In the long run the structure of land ownership and the market for land have important implications, especially for agricultural output. But land, in the medium-run context of macroeconomic policy and behavior, which is the focus of this work, is much less important than labor and capital, and is not considered in this chapter.
2. Estimates of total employment in manufacturing range from 25 to 35 million (see Fallon 1986:3).
3. Madhya Pradesh, Manipur, Orissa, and Rajasthan.
4. See Fallon (1986:9). In earlier years, minimum wages were revised only at fairly long intervals, thus often lagging behind the going wage in small enterprises, which is believed to be the standard commonly used by wage boards.
5. See Little, Mazumdar, and Page (1987), chapter 14.
6. It can, however, also be argued that the existence of indexation may help to reduce the level of nominal wages demanded at any point in time when some positive but unknown rate of inflation is expected.
7. Fallon and Lucas (1991) found conclusive evidence that job security legislation reduced employment, but not the flexibility of employment in response to changing market conditions. The latter non-result may have been due to the fact that only annual figures were available.
8. The only continuous time series of agricultural wages comes from Government of India, Ministry of Agriculture, *Agriculture Wages in India*, various years. These figures are collected in a very unscientific manner (see V. M. Rao 1972). But they are probably good enough to substantiate the statement that agricultural wages have grown far less than wages in organized industry.
9. These figures are unreliable. See previous note.
10. A good recent survey is Drèze and Mukherjee (1987). A much more extensive but now somewhat dated survey is Bardhan (1977).
11. See Acharya and Madhur (1983).
12. For useful surveys see Chakravarty Committee (Reserve Bank of India 1985), Morris (1985), and Narasimhan Committee (Government of India 1991).
13. On May 14, 1991, an incremental CRR of 10 percent was introduced, making the upper limit 16.5 percent.
14. Current figures of the CRR and SLR are taken from the Narasimhan Committee (Government of India 1991).
15. Narasimhan Committee (Government of India 1991).
16. Narasimhan Committee (Government of India 1991).
17. See Little, Mazumdar, and Page (1987) for an extensive discussion of India's promotional policies toward small manufacturing enterprises, and of the grounds for such policies, and their effects.
18. World Bank (1987) "India: Country Economic Memorandum," chapter 4, section D.
19. World Bank (1987) "India: Country Economic Memorandum," chapter 4, section D.
20. The role of temporary price and wage control in breaking inflationary expectations when trying to reduce high and persistent levels of inflation is much debated. But there is probably a consensus that they may be a necessary component of a stabilization package, depending on the particular conditions of wage and price formation in the country in question. However, this debate is of little or no relevance in the Indian context. India is a low-inflation country where expectations of persistent unrelenting inflation are not endemic. Furthermore, wage indexation is still very limited, and finally India's price controls are not temporary.
21. See Madhur and Roy (1986).

Chapter 3.   A Sketch of Political and Macroeconomic Developments from 1964 to 1991

1.   See Government of India, Ministry of Finance (1985a).
2.   The terms "political awakening" and "political decay" come from Manor (1983), but similar accounts can be found in Kohli (1990) and Rudolph and Rudolph (1987). The brilliant analysis of India's political economy by Bardhan (1984) is also relevant. For a critique of Bardhan, see Dhar (1987) and Joshi and Khilnani (1991).
3.   See the evidence on the occupational background of members of central and state legislatures given by Panandikar and Sud (1983).

Chapter 4.   The Crisis of 1965–67: Antecedents and Consequences

1.   In a subcontinental country, aggregate figures conceal wide variations. A famine occurred in Bihar where foodgrain production fell by 40 percent in 1966–67. Prices of cereals in Bihar were four times prices in Haryana.
2.   The term "quiet crisis" comes from the title of a well-known book by Lewis (1962). Some aspects of the crisis of 1965–67 are carefully analyzed by Bhagwati and Srinivasan (1975), Frankel (1978), and Toye (1981).
3.   Our account may not be altogether correct. It is reconstructed from interviews and without access to key documents. But we believe it is substantially correct.
4.   The actual size of the devaluation was negotiated only with the IMF.
5.   The *Economic Survey* for 1967/68 states that the consortium agreed a "target" of $950 million of nonproject aid in April 1967 but could not translate it into firm authorizations because of difficulties with International Development Association (IDA) replenishment and the cut in U.S. aid appropriations.
6.   One possible explanation of events is that the donors promised $900 million a year of nonproject aid inclusive of PL 480. But this cannot be correct as India was already receiving non-project aid inclusive of PL 480 of more than $900 million in 1965–66 and the devaluation package was clearly negotiated on the understanding of an increase in nonproject aid. J. P. Lewis (1970) states clearly "Back in 1966, the Consortium ... rallied in support of India's import liberalization with a solid (roughly 50 percent) increase in nonproject assistance to $900 million. But the assumption was it was to be sustained for several years. In fact, it was sustained only one year ...." A more likely explanation of the events is that $900 million of nonproject aid was "promised" but the United States could not deliver its share because of opposition in congress.
7.   For an excellent analysis of famine management in Bihar see Drèze (1990). Drèze claims that famine was "declared" late in Bihar for political reasons, namely the impending general election of February 1967. (The "declaration" of famine is an essential first step in setting in motion the provisions of famine codes concerning relief works.) Drèze (1990) and Drèze and Sen (1990) point out the superiority in many contexts of cash-for-work programs over free-feeding programs. But their argument partly depends on free movement of food, which did not exist in India.
8.   Of course, the fiscal deficit as a proportion of GDP could be expected to rise endogenously with the downturn in GDP. Note, however, that the calculation of a cyclically adjusted deficit yields a small negative "fiscal impulse" (see chapter 9).
9.   The peculiar nature of a "balanced" budget, which takes credit for long-term borrowing from the RBI, must be remembered.
10.   This, of course, was the result of devaluation—in dollar terms net foreign "borrowing" (almost entirely aid) was slightly lower than in 1965–66.

11. The shift of attention and resources to agriculture, although begun earlier, may also be considered to be partly a crisis measure. But beyond saying that it was not reversed, as was the more open trade regime that devaluation was supposed to bring about, it does not require further attention from a macroeconomic viewpoint.

12. Bhagwati and Srinivasan (1975). This work exhaustively analyzes in an illuminating manner all aspects of the devaluation and its consequences. For this reason our own account can be limited to emphasizing the essentials.

13. The rationalization and liberalization of trade policy accompanying the devaluation was reversed in the following sequence: export subsidies were reduced and controls on "competitive" imports were tightened in the second half of 1966–67 under pressure from interest groups; "noncompetitive" imports were tightened from 1968–69 onward. By 1970–71 the control-subsidy system had returned to its erstwhile complexity.

14. Bhagwati and Srinivasan (1975) present econometric evidence that exports of engineering goods and of iron and steel responded favorably to the devaluation.

15. A detailed account of this opposition is given by Bhagwati, Srinivasan, and Sunderam (1972).

16. Moreover, Bhagwati and Srinivasan (1975) are surely correct when they argue that foreign pressure, far from strengthening the hand of those who favored the right policies compromised their political credibility.

17. Our account of the politics of devaluation owes much to Bhagwati and Srinivasan (1975), chapters 10 and 11, who deal with the matter in much greater detail.

18. We believe that Mrs. Gandhi was open to argument concerning the costs and benefits of any economic measure. Her opposition was not dogmatic, but rather that of an intensely political person.

19. See chapter 9.

20. Unfortunately, we do not have monthly data based on the wholesale price index with 1970–71 as the base. Our remarks are based on the 1952–53 index (which has a somewhat different coverage) as reported in the *Economic Survey* 1968–69.

21. The industrial breakdown of public gross fixed capital formation is not available at 1980–81 prices.

22. This statement in the *Economic Survey* is barely consistent with and certainly has a different flavor from the account, based on a private communication from L. K. Jha given by Toye (1981:136). To quote, "In 1967, L. K. Jha, then head of the Prime Minister's Secretariat, succeeded in persuading both the Prime Minister and the Finance Minister that it was desirable that the Railways Board should place additional orders for capital equipment. But the Government's suggestion to this end was successfully resisted by the Railways Board."

23. The buoyancy of private investment is to be attributed to the household component. Corporate investment fell sharply. One possible explanation is that corporate investment is complementary to public investment, but we do not find firm evidence to support this (see chapter 13). Other reasons have been suggested. Immediately after the devaluation, adding to capacity in order to secure import licenses became less important in view of liberalization. At the end of the decade there were restrictions on investment by MRTP firms. Probably the most important reason is the uncertain economic climate. The strength of household investment is hard to understand, but see the remarks in chapter 13 on the unreliability of investment statistics.

24. Ahluwalia (1985) warns us of the shortcomings of the index of industrial production. The National Accounts Statistics (NAS) does not give output figures for capital goods as a whole. NAS March 1975 does, however, confirm the sharp fall in the output of transport equipment in the second half of the 1960s.

25. One might think that demand must eventually catch up. But by that time the theoretical capacity would no longer be economically useful—for reasons of lack of maintenance, inappropriate product potential, and obsolete technology.

26. This "missing inflation" can be explained in roughly the same way as the more dramatic "missing inflation" episode in the second half of the 1970s—see chapter 5.

27. Other sources give slightly different accounts. Rudolph and Rudolph (1987) say on the basis of the *Pocket Book of Labor Statistics* (1983) that there was a 6 percent drop in real wages from 1965 to 1967.
28. This is consistent with a fall in the share of profits during these years, recorded in the national accounts (old series). But the magnitude of the recorded fall is hard to believe.
29. Madhur and Roy (1986).
30. But the reliability of the agricultural wage figures is open to question.
31. However, it should not be ruled out that the policies might have been less effectively and stringently implemented if Morarji Desai had not been minister of finance.
32. Our own judgment is more complex. See the extended discussion in chapter 8.

Chapter 5.   The Crisis of 1973–75: Causes and Resolution

1. A good analysis of some aspects of the crisis of 1973–75 can be found in Ahluwalia (1986).
2. Arguably, these figures understate the increase in the current account deficit. See note 7 below.
3. In fact, it is unlikely that the entire increase in import costs could have been passed on. So 16 percent is the upper limit of the rise in WPI attributable to world prices.
4. Some of the monetary expansion in the early 1970s can also be attributed to an increase in the money multiplier. Not only was there a secular decline in the currency-to-deposit ratio, but the Reserve Bank was lax about enforcing the cash reserve ratio.
5. In this connection, see the appendix to chapter 10.
6. Monetary control proved to be difficult because banks began with large excess holdings of government securities which they could liquidate; if the banks were pressing against cash limits, they could seek accommodation from the Reserve Bank. The Reserve Bank's lending rate was increased by 1 percent in 1973–74 but was ineffective since industrial demand for credit was buoyant and banks could increase their lending rates. The Reserve Bank was also fighting itself, in the sense that it was not tough enough about enforcing the required cash and liquidity ratios. The Reserve Bank did not at that stage entirely believe in the connection between reserve money and total money. See Singh, Shetty, and Venkatachalam (1982).
7. This statement is based on balance of payments data that are constructed by the Reserve Bank. An estimate of the current account using DGCIS data for exports and imports shows a small surplus in 1972–73 and a deficit of $1,200 in 1974–75 (25 percent of exports and 1.4 percent of GDP).
8. See table 5.3.
9. The formula used for the terms of trade effect (TOTEFF) in year t is

$$TOTEFF_t = EXP_t \; \frac{PM_{t-1}}{PM_t} \div \frac{PX_{t-1}}{PX_t}$$

where EXP is the dollar value of exports, and PM and PX are unit value indices for imports and exports respectively. $TOTEFF_t$ is expressed in the table as a percentage of EXP_{t-1} and GDP_{t-1}. This formula is conventional and widely accepted by national income statisticians. For a critical discussion of this and other formulas, see Scott (1979).
10. Net imports of food were negative in 1972 but they went up to 3.6, 5.2, and 7.5 tonnes in the following three years. See table 5.1.
11. Some cushioning of the real consumption levels of the poor was achieved through (a) the sale of subsidized food through government shops in urban areas, and (b) cash-for-work programs for the rural poor in some states, particularly in Maharashtra. For a detailed and illuminating account of the latter see Drèze (1990) and Drèze and Sen (1990).

12. The political situation, which is critical to an understanding of the sequence of events, has already been described in chapter 3.

13. The cash reserve ratio (which had been reduced from 7 to 5 percent at the end of June 1974) was left untouched.

14. For a definition of the concept of "fiscal impulse," see chapter 9.

15. We do not believe that this effect is usefully summed up by calculating an inflation-adjusted (or "operational") fiscal deficit. See chapter 9.

16. Though the fiscal deficit increased as a proportion of GDP, M1 growth fell because the growth of government borrowing from the Reserve Bank continued to fall sharply. The fiscal deficit was covered to a greater extent by external assistance, which rose during this year in response to the oil crisis.

17. There was a large reduction in central government grants and loans to the states as a proportion of GDP. We speculate that the difference relative to the first crisis arises from the different political power balance between the central government and the states.

18. See table 5.12.

19. See chapter 13 for some qualifications.

20. Domestic prices of petroleum products were considerably above cost, insurance, and freight (cif) prices even before the oil crisis. After the oil crisis, domestic prices were increased sharply but the ratio of domestic-to-cif prices fell.

21. The improvement in the trend of India's growth rate can be dated from 1975–76. See chapter 13 for a discussion of the causes.

22. The behavior of savings and investment and their public and private components is discussed in chapters 12 and 13.

23. See chapter 12.

24. See Reserve Bank of India (1983a).

25. See Singh, Shetty, and Venkatachalam (1982).

26. See table 5.19.

27. More accurately, exports grew fast in 1976–77 and in 1978–79. There was a drop in export volume in 1977–78, a year in which the growth of world trade declined and the real exchange depreciation was arrested.

28. The width of the band was increased in January 1979 from ±2.25 percent to ±5 percent to accommodate this change.

29. See table 11.3.

30. This view is also taken by Sen (1987).

31. See tables 5.14, 5.15, and 5.16.

32. The increase was not consistent, however. An increase to 5.4 percent in 1976–77 was followed by a decline to 4.9 percent in 1977–78, mainly as a result of a cautious central government budget.

33. Remarkably, in this period the growth of foreign assets was a more important source of increase in reserve money than fiscal deficits. See chapter 10. The Reserve Bank was worried about the pace of money supply growth and took various measures to restrain it (for example, increases in cash and statutory liquidity ratios). But banks managed to get round these by defaulting on reserve requirements and raising cash from unrestricted nonbank institutions. See Singh, Shetty, and Venkatachalam (1982).

34. Policy was important, however, in that the authorities did not fight the real depreciation by upvaluing the nominal exchange rate.

Chapter 6.   The Crisis of 1979–81 and Its Aftermath

1. The "fiscal impulse" was strongly positive in 1975–76 (1.4 percent) but this was after three consecutive years of negative impulse. In 1976–77 and 1977–78 the fiscal impulse was close to zero. See chapter 9.

2. But the "fiscal impulse" was negative in 1979/80.
3. We do not wish to imply that populism began with the Janata government (see chapter 3).
4. See Singh, Shetty, and Venkatachalam (1982).
5. Note, however, that bank loan rates were lowered in 1977 in response to fears of an industrial recession.
6. The banks increased loans on the basis of borrowing in the form of "participation certificates" from nonbanks. Such borrowing was not included in the definition of bank liabilities that were subject to a cash reserve ratio, and credit extended against such borrowing was not subject to credit ceilings.
7. Monthly price data can be found in Government of India, Ministry of Finance, *Economic Surveys*.
8. Net bank credit and domestic credit had been growing at average annual rates of 26 and 22 percent respectively in the previous two years. However, monetary tightening from July 1981—perhaps in anticipation of the IMF program—had reduced credit growth, so by November 1981 the ceilings did not look particularly tough.
9. The government also instituted a "no-questions-asked" bearer bond scheme to mop up unaccounted money. The consequent reduction in the public's currency holdings also reduced reserve money.
10. There is a noticeable divergence between actual inflation in 1983–84 and the fitted value for that year in our inflation model estimated in the appendix to chapter 10. This arises mainly because our model is based on annual data that show money growth slowing in 1982–83; in fact money growth accelerated substantially from the second quarter of 1982–83 to the second quarter of 1983–84. (See table 6.12.)
11. Data for real public fixed investment by industry are not available after 1980–81. The above statements are supported by data on real public investment inclusive of stocks. See chapter 13.
12. The rising price of construction is reflected in the pronounced difference between the current price and constant price ratio of fixed capital formation to GDP (see table 6.15), particularly in the household sector. For further discussion, see chapter 13.
13. One of our interviewees observed that it was just as well that the Bombay High Field was outside territorial waters and hence outside the jurisdiction of Customs.
14. This story has focused on the evolution of the current account deficit. We could instead focus on the resource deficit. This would require Indian savings figures to be doctored to fall in line with conventional concepts of domestic saving. We have done so and find that the basic outline of the story is unaltered. The resource deficit fell by about 0.6 percent of GDP though the (redefined) public gap increased by about 1 percent of GDP. This was because of the (largely fortuitous) squeeze in household investment. But the resource deficit needed to fall a lot more to make a dent in the current account deficit. Since private financial savings grew rapidly and could not reasonably have grown faster, a fall in the public deficit (through higher public savings) was required.
15. It should be kept in mind that the budgetary classification of expenditures between "current" and "capital" is not coterminous with the distinction between consumption and investment. An economic classification is available only for the central government. That shows central government support for capital formation to be increasing from 1978–79 onward as a proportion of GDP, which is consistent with national accounts data on public capital formation.
16. de Janvry and Subbarao (1986) show that in recent years procurement prices for wheat and rice have risen faster than the cost of production.
17. Note that the center's revenue position actually worsened while that of the states improved. But this change resulted from the changes in center-state fiscal transfers. Note also that some of the revenue-raising measures undertaken in 1981–82 were increases in administered prices that would show up in improvements in the finances of public enterprises, not directly in the budget.
18. Budget data, however, show government savings becoming negative earlier (in 1982–83). On this basis, government savings changed from 1.3 percent of GDP in 1978–79 to –1.9 percent in 1984–85.
19. The oil sector was more efficient than most public sector enterprises but it was also favored with high product prices.
20. See Narasimham (1988) and Aghevli, Kim, and Neiss (1987).

Chapter 7. The Road to Crisis, 1985/86 to 1990/91

1. The cutoff of foreign loans was not an exogenous shock but an endogenous reaction to the unsound macroeconomic position. It must be admitted, however, that political instability and the absence of a government with a secure parliamentary majority also played some part in the sudden collapse of confidence on the part of foreign creditors.
2. It appears that low inflation and constant money supply growth were mistakenly regarded as indicating the sustainability of fiscal expansion. (See chapter 9).
3. The shift from IDA to IBRD in multilateral lending to India followed upon India's designation as a "blend" country. Note that nonresident deposits were an expensive form of borrowing—the interest rates paid were well above world rates.
4. See also the discussion of saving-investment balances in chapters 6 and 8.
5. On this matter, we disagree with the thrust of the argument in Rakshit (1991).
6. Foodgrain prices, more narrowly defined, rose 8.5 percent on an average-of-weeks basis, but more than 20 percent on a year-end to year-end basis.

Chapter 8. Crisis and Short-Term Macroeconomic Policy: An Appraisal

1. This judgment is somewhat open to question as regards the first crisis. Exogenous shocks (two successive droughts) were obviously important in causing the crisis, but past macroeconomic policies were equally important in creating the fragile initial condition of the economy.
2. In the third crisis this change was from a very small deficit. In the second crisis the apparent deterioration in the current deficit was quite small but that is only because current account adjustment began almost immediately (see chapter 5). A better measure of the external impact is the terms of trade shock, which in both crises was substantial (see chapters 5 and 6).
3. This assumes that the optimum degree of stabilization will not be provided by rational, far-sighted private stock-holding and by speculative activity. But there are many reasons why such an outcome may not occur, including diseconomies of scale in individual action, lack of well-functioning credit markets, and the possibility under certain circumstances of rational but destabilizing speculation.
4. In principle, stabilization of food prices could also be achieved by reducing fluctuations in food production (for example by increased irrigation), but that is clearly only a long-term measure.
5. Some studies (for example World Bank 1986) have concluded that an optimal stabilization scheme should rely mainly on international trade. One of the main supporting arguments is that the cost of running a buffer stock rises sharply as the size of the stock increases.
6. Even if trade is cheaper than buffer stocks, stabilization through buffer stocks may be better than no stabilization at all. In India, which for much of the period was ideologically anti-trade, a domestic buffer stock was politically a far easier option than reliance on trade. However, the position has changed over time. Given reasonably efficient management, it is doubtful whether maintaining foodgrain stocks in excess of 20 million tonnes, as in some recent years, is a sensible policy.
7. However, in the case of raw materials private traders may stabilize as well as the government if permitted to do so, that is if they are free to import and hold stocks. The Indian government has conducted some buffer stock operations in industrial raw materials but of a very limited nature. Private trade has been heavily controlled, so price fluctuations in raw materials have been avoidably large.
8. For an illuminating analysis of India's income-support policies during famines see Drèze (1990) and Drèze and Sen (1990).
9. See Bhattacharya, Coondoo, Maiti, and Mukherjee (1985).
10. This applies particularly to fiscal restriction through higher income taxes, compulsory deposit schemes, and higher indirect taxes on non-necessities (these do not enter the CPI and hence do not

qualify for indexation). Expenditure reduction does not have large effects on unskilled labor incomes in the organized sector because of indexation and employment protection. (During the first two crises there was some fall in private organized employment. In no crisis did total organized employment fall. This can be checked from employment data given in the annual *Economic Surveys*.) But it should be noted that (a) the growth of employment and hence growth of labor incomes is reduced and (b) firms in trouble may postpone wage payments even if they do not sack workers. Nonwage incomes in the organized sector are of course affected by fiscal expenditure reduction. Incomes in the urban unorganized sector are insulated from direct tax measures but they would be affected through the production chain by the multiplier effect of expenditure policies. Standards of living in this sector are cushioned to some extent by the public distribution system that covers urban areas quite well. The rural poor are insulated from the effects of fiscal retrenchment (and incidentally of exchange rate depreciation as well). Their standards of living decline because of the droughts themselves, which reduce income and employment and increase food prices (agricultural laborers are net buyers of food). Thus, from the viewpoint of the poor, fiscal retrenchment, which reduces food demand of the relatively well-off, combined with subsidized public distribution of food and income-support policies may well be the optimal policy.

11. See chapters 4 and 5. Note that industrial raw materials also fell in price in early 1967 in spite of the droughts of 1965–66 and 1966–67. This phenomenon was not observed in the third crisis but that is understandable as the deflationary policies were extremely mild.

12. See Madhur and Roy (1986).

13. It should be noted that our econometric work shows very clearly the importance of monetary and fiscal factors in explaining inflation. See the appendix to chapter 10.

14. The "fiscal impulse" calculations referred to in this chapter are based on the discussion in chapter 9.

15. Budgetary figures of government capital expenditure for 1966–67 do not show a slowdown but it is evident in the conceptually more accurate economic and functional classification of central government expenditure. Both sources show a further slowdown in the next three years. See also the figures for real public investment in table 8.1 and chapter 13.

16. Note that the measured fiscal deficit fell in 1973–74 and 1974–75 but the "fiscal impulse" was negative not only in these two years but in 1972–73 as well.

17. See, for example, P. Sen (1987 and 1991).

18. The role of import controls as a macroeconomic policy device is further considered in chapter 11.

19. Of course, the drought of 1966 could not have been forecast but it would have been wise to wait until the end of the rainy season before deciding whether or not to implement such a package.

20. Given the attitude of the donors, the Indian government had little leeway on the timing and magnitude of the devaluation-liberalization package. Even so, the government can be criticized in two respects. Public investment cuts from 1967–68 were overdone. Aid utilization did not have to fall so sharply, even though aid authorizations did. More fundamentally, it would have been wise to carry on with the liberalization program even though donor support was inadequate. But this was not politically feasible.

21. We argue in chapter 7 that the alternative view that the persistence of the current account deficit was principally due to import liberalization is untenable.

22. A large increase in the private sector surplus would have been impractical or unwise. For details, see chapter 7.

23. Our views on this matter do not accord with those of Rakshit (1991).

Chapter 9.   Fiscal Policy

1. The explicit subsidies shown in table 9.1 may be dwarfed by further subsidies that do not appear as such in the government's budget accounts. See Mundle and Rao (1991).

2. The identification of the current balance with savings and of the deficit with the fiscal deficit, both assume that revenue and expenditure exclude the sale or purchase of assets to or from the private sector. In the case of India such transactions have been negligible.

3. See for example Heller, Haas, and Mansur (1986).

4. Output may be below trend because of a drought. A positive fiscal impulse can do nothing about that, but it can alleviate the induced fall in industrial output. It can also help to stabilize consumption, but this is possible only if the reserves position is comfortable.

5. The government acquires command over real resources by creating money and spending it. When this gives rise to inflation because the public does not willingly hold the extra money without a rise in prices, then the real value of the money that the public already holds is reduced. Therefore this form of acquisition of resources by the government may be described as a tax. In the words of Keynes, "what is raised by printing notes is just as much taken from the public as a beer duty or an income tax" (Keynes 1923:37).

6. The algebra of this and the following arguments is presented in the appendix to this chapter.

7. It could be argued that logically it should be the debt-to-tradable output ratio. But this would be hard to estimate, and more importantly creditors look to the debt-to-exports ratio, or the debt service ratio. For our rough purposes the debt-to-exports ratio can be used.

8. The doubt about the sustainability of 5.3 percent depends partly on the conclusions as to the sustainability of the levels of borrowing of the 1980s. Note that 4.5 percent is roughly the growth trend from 1975–76 to 1989–90.

9. The gross deficit of the nonfinancial public sector in 1989–90 was 10.1 percent according to the national accounts. Net interest payments of the consolidated government sector were 2.1 percent, and would be somewhat higher for the whole nonfinancial public sector—say 3.4 percent. Subtracting this from the gross deficit leaves a primary deficit of 6.7 percent.

10. In the nineteenth century the world rate of interest on safe bonds was about 3 percent. But the world rate of growth has risen, which would tend to raise the rate, perhaps to 4 percent. On top of this, with India's level of indebtedness, a risk premium has to be allowed.

11. The unsustainability of the growth of the debt—and how to deal with the problem—is carefully considered in Chelliah (1992). The problem of the subsidies is further considered in chapter 14, while a much more detailed account of both explicit and implicit subsidies is given in Mundle and Rao (1991).

12. The manner in which the system of controls has generated corruption and tax evasion is well described in Acharya and associates (1985). See also Acharya (1988).

Chapter 10.   Monetary Policy

1. In principle, an independent central bank could also place limits on its lending to the government. In India, this is not possible.

2. See Gupta (1979).

3. That money supply growth responds to food prices with a lag is borne out by our econometric model of inflation (see the appendix to this chapter.). Of course some increase in growth of money supply is quite rational in a good agricultural year, since the demand for money would rise due to higher real income and lower expected inflation. Problems arise from (a) the lagged response of money supply growth so that monetary expansion may coincide with a poor harvest, and (b) an "excessive" increase in money growth—more than can be justified by the fall in velocity. Note that velocity may fall abnormally for short periods only to rise with a vengeance later.

4. Evidence for the above points is given in previous chapters and in the excellent review of monetary policy by Singh, Shetty, and Venkatachalam (1982).

5. Note that higher expected inflation brings about a portfolio shift toward food stocks in the private sector, thereby exacerbating inflation.

6. If we consider the course of the velocity of M1 and the velocity of M3 over the whole period 1960–61 to 1989–90, there were deviations greater than ±5 percent in relation to trend in thirteen and seventeen out of thirty years respectively. This is, however, reduced to six and seven cases if trends are estimated separately for the periods 1960–61 to 1970–71 and 1971–72 to 1989–90. Velocity data are given in table 10.1.

7. See for example, Singh, Shetty, and Venkatachalam (1982) and the studies reported in the Chakravarty Committee Report (Reserve Bank of India 1985).

8. The income-elasticity of demand for money shifted upward after 1970–71. The demand for money equations satisfy the standard statistical tests over the period as a whole but the fit is much better if the subperiods are separately considered.

9. See Hendry (1985).

10. Note that the model in the appendix to this chapter includes an estimated policy reaction function. It suggests that policymakers react to faster inflation by reducing monetary expansion. But the reaction is sequential not simultaneous. Reverse causality does not appear to be a problem in the relationship between money, production, and prices.

11. See the Chakravarty Committee Report (Reserve Bank of India 1985). It is notable, however, that the committee gives no guidance as to how the target should be adjusted in response to shocks. We have discussed this issue in the previous section.

12. See Rangarajan and Singh (1984). Note also that in the period 1973–74 to 1986–87 the maximum annual deviation from trend was 1.2 percent for the adjusted multiplier for M1, and 1.5 percent for the adjusted multiplier for M3. For figures on money multipliers see table 10.1.

13. See Chakravarty Committee Report (Reserve Bank of India 1985). This view has also been strongly supported by the recent Narasimham Committee (Government of India 1991).

14. The extra interest cost would apply only to new government borrowing since coupon payments on the outstanding stock of government bonds will not change. But commercial banks will suffer a write-down in the value of their holding of government debt, a problem that would have to be solved by creative accounting.

15. Note also that financial liberalization may transitionally make monetary control more difficult by making velocities and money multipliers less stable.

16. This is important as open-market operations are a more sensitive instrument than the cash-reserve ratio. Nevertheless, the cash ratio should be retained as it is a more reliable instrument than open-market operations.

17. Econometric evidence for this proposition is given in the section on reaction functions in the appendix to this chapter. See in particular table 10.5.

Chapter 11.   Trade and Payments Policy

1. Studies by Bhagwati and Desai (1970) and by Bhagwati and Srinivasan (1975) are recognized as landmarks in the analysis of the efficiency effects of Indian trade policies. See also Srinivasan (1992).

2. For terminology, concepts, and analysis of exchange rate policy see Williamson (1981 and 1982), Joshi (1984 and 1990), Collier and Joshi (1989), Edwards (1989), Corden (1990), and Little and others (1993).

3. Our measure of export incentives includes premia on import replenishment licenses for exporters. But we cannot allow for variations in anti-export bias arising from the tightness of the import control regime generally since this is impossible to measure accurately.

4. The above estimates do not make an allowance for capital flight through underinvoicing of exports and overinvoicing of imports. Surprisingly, estimates of this phenomenon for India show it

not to be a problem. It appears that underinvoicing of imports is an important feature in India (presumably to escape high tariffs) and exceeds underinvoicing of exports. See Rishi and Boyce (1990). But our conclusions concerning the magnitude of capital flight are different from those of Rishi and Boyce, who do not allow for exchange rate valuation effects.

5. Note, however, that only a part (and probably a small part) of the demand for black foreign exchange was for capital flight. Most of the demand was for imports of smuggled gold.

6. See Haque and Montiel (1990).

7. Bhagwati and Srinivasan (1975) have analyzed the effects of import restrictions in India in considerable detail. Economic theory further suggests that if there are distortions in the working of domestic markets they should be corrected by domestic taxes and subsidies, not by trade intervention.

8. Sometimes the government can bind itself within a crawling peg, for example a rule that it would keep the real exchange rate constant—a "rule-based crawling peg."

9. Another channel through which nominal exchange rate changes affect the current account is variations in real money balances and the consequent changes in spending. We ignore these effects, which in any case are unlikely to be sizable in India given the small size of the traded sector in relation to GDP.

10. Nonfulfillment of the Marshall-Lerner condition does not, however, prove the case for trade intervention to improve the current account; it suggests that appreciation of the exchange rate is the answer. In theory, there is no long-run case for trade intervention other than on terms of trade grounds. We saw above that trade intervention also has severe limitations as a macroeconomic device as borne out by Indian experience.

11. See Joshi (1984) and Gupta and Srinivasan (1984).

12. Ghosh (1990) plots the NER and the RER over time, and concludes that nominal depreciation does not stick in real terms. The above discussion indicates why this is a misleading procedure.

13. If inflation in foreign countries is low, the price level in a country hit by a negative real shock may have to fall in absolute terms to secure the appropriate real exchange rate. This is a tall order in a country in which inflation is determined by political acceptability.

14. All this is clear enough in the case of a permanent negative real shock such as an oil price increase. What about temporary real shocks such as a drought? A depreciation is not called for since no permanent increase in competitiveness is required; deficits should be financed using reserves. But the following qualification is worth making. A drought may leave the price level permanently higher than other countries (since prices are not as flexible downward as they are upward); in that case maintenance of a constant RER would require a nominal depreciation.

15. This position is supported by Faini and de Melo (1990).

16. In fact, the concealed depreciation had begun in 1972 but at least the government did not fight it. It maintained the sterling peg, which provided the cover for the depreciation.

17. Most econometric work on India's exports has been confined to estimating single-equation models that mix up demand and supply factors, a highly dubious procedure. Notable exceptions to this general tendency are Das-Gupta (1990) and Virmani (1991).

Chapter 12.   The Deficits and Surpluses of the Public and Private Sectors

1. See also Krishnaswamy, Krishnamurti, and Sharma (1987).

2. See Virmani (1988).

3. Several studies of Indian savings find a significant positive correlation between real interest rates and household savings, for example Krishnaswamy, Krishnamurti, and Sharma (1987).

4. See Krishnaswamy, Krishnamurti, and Sharma (1987).

5. The old national accounts statistics give figures of 5.4, 8.5, and 9.7 percent for 1970–71, 1980–81, and 1984–85. The new statistics give 6.4, 8.9, and 7.8 percent respectively for 1980–81, 1984–85, and 1988–89.

Chapter 13. Investment and Growth

1. We do not accept the so-called neoclassical growth model that makes the long-run rate of growth independent of the ratio of investment to GNP. The model requires that technical progress is exogenous. If investment causes technical progress, one is free to believe that a higher investment ratio will result in a higher rate of growth for ever.
2. See especially Scott (1989), chapter 1.
3. See Blejer and Khan (1984).
4. There are also manufacturing sectors where both public and private investment are permitted. Here the two are much more likely to be competitive than complementary.
5. It is believed that almost all public agricultural investment is of the infrastructural type, for example irrigation, training, and research. Banking and insurance is excluded, mainly because the bank nationalization of 1969 would somewhat distort the figures. But banking is included in total public investment where its relatively small size makes an insignificant difference.
6. These are compound growth rates and differ from the mean annual growth rates given in table 13.6.
7. See Bardhan (1984), chapter 4.
8. Ahluwalia (1985: 91–95) argues strongly that there has been insufficient investment, and that railway transport has been a major bottleneck. Although the arguments there presented—principally, that the railways move a decreasing proportion of the total supply of a number of bulk commodities—are not totally compelling, we have no reason to believe that she is wrong.
9. See Dholakia (1983), Panchmukhi (1986), and Chitale (1986).
10. See Ahluwalia (1985) and Goldar (1986).
11. The figures vary considerably with the concept chosen (net or gross), whether current or constant prices are used, whether or not lags are introduced, and over what period averages are taken.
12. See Centre for Monitoring the Indian Economy (1986), especially chapter 14.
13. See, for example, Ahluwalia (1985), chapters 5 and 8.
14. Under Rs 20 crores the responsible ministries do their own appraisal. Approval is given by the Expenditure Finance Committee, chaired by the Finance Ministry.
15. The following account of project appraisal and selection procedures is based on interviews conducted in 1989. There may have been changes since then.
16. In 1970 one of the present authors persuaded Pitamber Pant, a member of the Planning Commission, of the need for PAD. He in turn convinced the Planning Commission, and steps were taken to institute it, but there was some delay in getting final approval.
17. The Sengupta Committee (December 1984) recommended some increase in the functions of the PAD, and recommended that it should be strengthened (p 4.11).
18. The counterattack is of course that they might be offered more labor-intensive projects, or technologies, if it were known that labor was shadow-priced.
19. See also Centre for Monitoring the Indian Economy (1986).
20. Centre for Monitoring the Indian Economy (1986).
21. See Government of India, Department of Public Enterprises (1991).
22. These controls have since been greatly reduced, especially in 1991.
23. See the discussion in Little, Mazumdar, and Page (1987), chapter 4.
24. See World Bank, "India: Country Economic Memorandum" (1988), pp. 4–6.

25. Parts of the public sector were excluded—defense and administration—because measurable returns are not to be expected; and banking—because the nationalization in 1969 would tend to falsify any comparison of the two periods.

26. For most other sectors, and the whole economy, there are no figures for labor input or labor earnings. Mixed incomes dominate the compensation of employees. Investment and value added figures are also less reliable. We have therefore confined our estimates to the sectors mentioned.

27. Scott (1989) rejects the production function approach, which requires estimates of the stock of capital. Such estimates are economically arbitrary and conceptually unsound. Only changes in output can be explained. They result wholly from investment (which is widely defined as the cost of changing economic arrangements) and changes in the quantity and quality of labor. The concept of exogenous technical progress is rejected. It is impossible to convey in a brief paragraph the full force of Scott's critique of conventional growth accounting, and to justify his own methods. It may be noted that the so-called New Growth Theory, of which the seminal article is Romer (1986), shares with Scott the important feature of endogenizing technical change. We have used Scott's theory because it can be empirically tested and applied, whereas it is not apparent how this could be done for those of Romer or Lucas (1988). Moreover, Scott's methods were available to use before the New Growth Theory got going.

28. Also, of course, the implicit incremental capital output ratios (ICORs) are extremely high, about thirteen, with only a slight fall in the second period.

29. The following returns to gross investment, excluding housing and public investment in education, health, and general services, and after allowing for improvements in the quality of the labor force (that is, r_2) can be calculated from table 7.1 in Scott (1989).

Japan	1961–73	23.6 percent
United Kingdom	1964–73	20.4 percent
United States	1948–73	16.9 percent

30. This also applies if the period is broken at 1980–81. See also Bhargava and Joshi (1990).

31. Some writers have voiced concern that faster growth in India is largely to be attributed to public administration and defense. This concern seems misplaced. If the period is broken at 1975–76 there was no increase in the growth rate of public administration and defense. If the period is broken at 1980–81 the growth rate rose by 1.7 percent, but this is statistically insignificant.

32. Nationalization in the 1960s and 1970s affects these comparisons, but it is probably safe to say that there was no rise in the growth rate of the public sector adjusted for such changes in coverage. Note that public sector manufacturing does show a sizable (but statistically insignificant) rise in the growth rate after 1980–81.

Chapter 14.   Concluding Remarks

1. By 1990 all eighteen countries, except for Mexico and those in the franc zone, had adopted some form of managed floating exchange rate regime. We need not examine the policy of temporarily fixing the exchange rate, and using other price and wage controls in very high-inflation countries, to break inflationary expectations. This has been done with varied success in Argentina, Israel, and Mexico. But India is not a case in point.

2. Among the eighteen countries examined by Little and others (1993), Chile is the only case where private sector excesses led to crisis and chaos.

3. The input subsidies are from World Bank, "India: Country Economic Memorandum" (1991), volume II, table 2.1.

4. See World Bank "India: Country Economic Memorandum" (1991), volume II, table 2.10.

5. We are not here concerned with the social or distributional effects of these input subsidies, but there seems to be wide agreement that the benefits go mostly to large farmers. It must also be recognized that freeing agricultural trade would result in a rise in cereal prices, and hence a rise

in the issue prices of the public distribution service (PDS) unless food subsidies were increased. While this would certainly present a problem, it is to be noted that subsidized food supplies from the PDS have been criticized as a costly and ineffective method of poverty relief. The poor are not well targeted, first because a high proportion of PDS supplies go to urban areas while most poor people are in rural areas; and second because a high proportion of the urban supplies go to middle-class consumers.

6. Government of India (1991), *Report of the Committee on the Financial System.*
7. Little, Mazumdar, and Page (1987).

Appendix A. The Quality of Economic Statistics

1. The main sources are Government of India, CSO (1980 and 1989b); and Reserve Bank of India (1982).
2. Approximate percentages for 1980/81.
3. Approximate percentages for 1980/81.
4. Approximate percentages for 1980/81.

Appendix B. Structuralist Macroeconomics and the Indian Economy

1. Some recent examples are P. Sen (1987 and 1991) and Taylor (1988b). But strands of structuralist thinking are to be found in much Indian economic writing.

Bibliography

In addition to the works referred to in the text, this bibliography incorporates others that the authors have found informative, stimulating, or useful in understanding India's political economy and macroeconomics, whether or not they agree with them.

Acharya, Shankar. 1988. "India's Fiscal Policy." In R. Lucas and G. Papanek, eds., *The Indian Economy: Recent Developments and Future Prospects.* Boulder, Colo.: Westview Press.

Acharya, Shankar, and associates. 1985. *Aspects of the Black Economy in India.* New Delhi: National Institute of Public Finance.

Acharya, Shankar, and Srinivasa Madhur. 1983. "Informal Credit Markets and Black Money: Do They Frustrate Monetary Policy?" *Economic and Political Weekly* 18(41): 1751–56.

Aghevli, Bijan, In-Su Kim, and Hubert Neiss. 1987. "Growth and Adjustment in South Asia." *Finance and Development* 24(3): 12–16.

Ahluwalia, Isher J. 1985. *Industrial Growth in India.* New Delhi: Oxford University Press.

———. 1991. *Productivity Growth in Indian Manufacturing.* New Delhi: Oxford University Press.

Ahluwalia, Montek S. 1986. "Balance of Payments Adjustment in India, 1970/71–1983/84." *World Development* 14(8): 937–62.

Alagh, Yoginder K. 1986. *Some Aspects of Planning Policies in India.* Allahabad: Vohra Publishers.

Asia Society. Various years. *India Briefing.* Boulder, Colo.: Westview Press.

Bagchi, Amaresh. 1992. "Fiscal Finances and Money Supply." In Subroto Roy and William James, eds., *Foundations of India's Political Economy: Towards an Agenda for the Nineties.* London: Sage Publications.

Balakrishnan, Pulapre. 1991a. "Current Deficit and its Malcontents." *Economic and Political Weekly* 26(7): 353–54.

———. 1991b. *Pricing and Inflation in India.* New Delhi: Oxford University Press.

Balasubramanyam, V. N. 1984. *The Economy of India.* London: Nicholson and Weidenfeld.

Bardhan, Kalpana. 1977. "Rural Employment, Wages and Labour Markets in India: A Survey of Research." Sections I, II, and III. *Economic and Political Weekly* 12(26): A34–54, 12(27): 1062–74, 12(28): 1101–18.

Bardhan, Pranab. 1984. *The Political Economy of Development in India.* Oxford: Basil Blackwell.

Bhagwati, Jagdish. 1993. *India in Transition.* Oxford: Clarendon Press.

Bhagwati, Jagdish, and Padma Desai. 1970. *India: Planning for Industrialization.* Oxford: Oxford University Press.

Bhagwati, Jagdish, and T. N. Srinivasan. 1975. *Foreign Trade Regimes and Economic Development—India.* New York: National Bureau of Economic Research.

Bhagwati, Jagdish, T. N. Srinivasan, and K. Sundaram. 1972. "Political Response to the 1966 Devaluation." *Economic and Political Weekly* 7(36): 1835–36.

Bhalla, Surjit. 1981. "India's Closed Economy and World Inflation." In R. C. Williams and others, eds., *World Inflation and Developing Countries.* Washington, D.C.: Brookings Institute.

———. 1989. "Droughts and Economic Growth: Myth and Reality." *The Economic Times*, February 21.

Bhargava, Sandeep, and Vijay Joshi. 1990. "Faster Growth in India: Facts and a Tentative Explanation." *Economic and Political Weekly* 25(48–9): 2657–62.

Bhattacharya, B. B. 1984. *Public Expenditure, Inflation and Growth.* New Delhi: Oxford University Press.

Bhattacharya, Nikhilesh, D. Coondoo, P. Maiti, and R. Mukherjee. 1985. *Relative Price of Food and the Rural Poor: The Case of India.* Calcutta: Indian Statistical Institute.

Bhole, L. M. 1987. "Definition, Measurement and Determination of Money Supply." *Economic and Political Weekly* 22(24): 945–50.

Blejer, Mario I., and Mohsin S. Khan. 1984. "Government Policy and Private Investment in Developing Countries." *IMF Staff Papers* (31)2: 379–403.

Brahmananda, P. R. 1982. *Productivity in the Indian Economy: Rising Inputs for Falling Outputs.* Bombay: Himalaya Publishing House.

Brass, Paul. 1990. *The Politics of India Since Independence.* Cambridge: Cambridge University Press.

Cassen, Robert H. 1978. *India: Population, Economy, Society.* London: Macmillan.

Centre for Monitoring the Indian Economy (CMIE). 1984. *Basic Statistics Relating to the Indian Economy.* Bombay.

———. 1986. *Public Sector in the Indian Economy.* Bombay.

Chakravarty, Sukhamoy. 1974. "Reflections on the Growth Process in the Indian Economy." Reprinted in Charan Wadhwa, ed., *Some Problems of India's Economic Policy.* New Delhi: Tata McGraw Hill.

———. 1979. "On the Question of Home Market and the Prospects for Indian Growth." *Economic and Political Weekly* 14(30–2): 1229–42.

———. 1986. "Report of the Committee to Review the Working of the Monetary System: A Re-examination." Sir Purushotandas Thakurdas Memorial Lecture, Indian Institute of Bankers, Bombay, December 29.

——. 1987. *Development Planning: The Indian Experience*. Oxford: Clarendon Press.

Chandok, H. L. 1978. *Wholesale Price Statistics: India 1947–1978*. New Delhi: Economic and Scientific Research Foundation.

Chaudhuri, Pramit. 1974. *The Indian Economy*. London: Crosby, Lockwood and Staples.

Chelliah, R. J. 1992. "Growth of Indian Public Debt." In Bimal Jalan, ed., *The Indian Economy*. New Delhi: Viking-Penguin Books.

——. 1983. "The Economic and Equity Aspects of the Distribution of Financial Resources between the Centre and the State in India." In *Seminar on Centre-State Relations: Papers, Group Reports, and Conclusions*. Bangalore: Government of Karnataka.

Chitale, V. P. 1986. *Capital Output Ratio in the Indian Economy*. New Delhi: Radiant Publishers.

Chitre, Vikas S., and Rohini Paranjape. 1987. "Keynesian, Monetarist and New Classical Economics and Short-Run Dynamics of Output and Inflation in India." *Prajnan* (16)4: 431–43.

Coats, Warren L. Jr., and Khatkhate, Deena R. 1980. "Money and Monetary Policy in Less Developed Countries." In Warren L. Coats, Jr. and Deena R. Khatkhate, eds., *Money and Monetary Policy in Less Developed Countries*. Oxford: Pergamon Press.

Collier, Paul, and Vijay Joshi. 1989. "Exchange Rate Policy in Developing Countries." *Oxford Review of Economic Policy* (5)3: 94–113.

Corden, W. Max. 1990. "Macroeconomic Adjustment in Developing Countries." In Maurice Scott and Deepak Lal, eds., *Public Policy and Economic Development*. Oxford: Clarendon Press.

Dandekar, V. M. 1986. "Monetary Policy for Independent Monetary Authority." *Economic and Political Weekly* 21(4): 169–74.

——. 1992. "Forty Years after Independence." In Bimal Jalan, ed., *The Indian Economy*. New Delhi: Viking-Penguin Books.

Das-Gupta, Bejoy. 1990. "Exports and Exchange Rate Policy: The Case of India." D. Phil. diss., Oxford University.

Datta-Chaudhuri, Mrinal. 1990. "Market Failure and Government Failure." *Journal of Economic Perspectives* 4(3): 25–40.

Desai, Ashok V. 1988. "Technology Acquisition and Application: Interpretations of the Indian Experience." In R. E. B. Lucas and G. F. Papanek, eds., *The Indian Economy: Recent Developments and Future Prospects*. Boulder, Colo.: Westview Press.

de Janvry, Alain, and Kalanidhi Subbarao. 1986. *Agricultural Price Policy and Income Distribution in India*. New Delhi: Oxford University Press.

Dhar, P. N. 1987. "The Political Economy of Development in India." *Indian Economic Review* 22(1): 1–118.

——. 1990. *Constraints on Growth: Reflections on the Indian Experience*. New Delhi: Oxford University Press.

Dholakia, Bakul H. 1983. *Behaviour of Capital Output Ratios in the Indian Economy*. Ahmedabad: Indian Institute of Management.

Drèze, Jean. 1990. "Famine Prevention in India." In Jean Drèze and Amartya Sen, eds., *The Political Economy of Hunger*. Vol. 2. Oxford: Clarendon Press.

Drèze, Jean, and Anindita Mukherjee. 1987. "Labour Contracts in Rural India: Theories and Evidence." Discussion Paper 7. London School of Economics, Development Economics Research Programme, London.

Drèze, Jean, and Amartya Sen. 1990. *Hunger and Public Action*. Oxford: Clarendon Press.

Edwards, Sebastian. 1989. *Real Exchange Rates, Devaluation and Adjustment: Exchange Rate Policy in Developing Countries*. Cambridge, Mass.: MIT Press.

Faini, Riccardo, and Jaime de Melo. 1990. "Adjustment, Investment and the Real Exchange Rate in Developing Countries." *Economic Policy* 5(2): 491–519.

Fallon, P. R. 1986. "The Effects of Labour Regulation upon Industrial Employment and Output in India." DRD Discussion Paper 296. World Bank, Washington, D.C.

Fallon, P. R., and R. E. B. Lucas. 1991. "The Impact of Changes in Job Security Regulations in India and Zimbabwe." *The World Bank Economic Review* 5(3): 395–413.

Frankel, Francine R. 1978. *India's Political Economy 1947–1977*. Princeton: Princeton University Press.

Frankel, Francine R., and M. S. A. Rao. 1989. *Dominance and State Power in Modern India*. Volumes I and II. Oxford: Oxford University Press.

Ghani, Ejaz. 1987. "Money and the Real Economy: A Study of India 1960–1984." D. Phil. diss., Oxford University.

———. 1991. "Rational Expectations and Price Behaviour: A Study of India." *Journal of Development Economics* 36(2): 295–311.

Ghosh, Jayati. 1990. "Exchange Rates and the Trade Balance: Some Aspects of Indian Experience." *Economic and Political Weekly* 25(9): 441–45.

Goldar, B. N. 1986. *Productivity Growth in Indian Industry*. New Delhi: Allied Publishers.

Goldsmith, Raymond W. 1983. *The Financial Development of India 1860–1977*. New Haven: Yale University Press.

Goldstein, Morris, and Mohsin S. Khan. 1977. "The Supply and Demand for Exports: A Simultaneous Approach." *Review of Economics and Statistics* 60(2): 275–86.

Government of India. 1984. *Report of the Committee on Trade Policies* (Abid Hussain, Chairman). New Delhi.

Government of India, Central Statistical Organization (CSO). Various years. *National Accounts Statistics*. New Delhi.

———. 1980. *National Accounts Statistics: Sources and Methods*. New Delhi.

———. 1983. *Transactions of the Public Sector 1960–61 to 1979–80*. New Delhi.

———. 1989a. *National Accounts Statistics (new series) 1950–51 to 1979–80*. New Delhi.

——. 1989b. *National Accounts Statistics: Sources and Methods*. New Delhi.

——. 1991. *Quick Estimates of National Income 1989/90*. New Delhi.

Government of India, Department of Public Enterprises. 1991. *Monograph on the Performance Status of Central Public Enterprises*. New Delhi.

Government of India, Directorate General of Commercial Intelligence and Statistics (DGCIS). Various years. *Monthly Statistics of the Foreign Trade of India*. Calcutta.

Government of India, Ministry of Agriculture. Various years. *Agricultural Wages in India*. New Delhi.

Government of India, Ministry of Commerce. 1978. *Report of the Committee on Import-Export Policies and Procedures* (P. C. Alexander, Chairman). New Delhi.

Government of India, Ministry of Finance. Various years. *Economic Survey*. New Delhi.

——. Various years. *Indian Economic Statistics: Public Finance*. New Delhi.

——. 1985a. *Long-Term Fiscal Policy*. New Delhi.

——. 1985b. *Report of the Committee to Examine Principles of a Possible Shift from Physical to Financial Controls* (M. Narasimham, Chairman). New Delhi.

——. 1986. *Administered Price Policy: A Discussion Paper*. New Delhi.

Government of India, 1991. *Report of the Committee on the Financial System* (M. Narasimham, Chairman.) New Delhi.

Government of West Bengal. 1981. *The IMF Loan: Facts and Issues*. Calcutta.

Guha, Ashok. ed., 1990. *Economic Liberalization, Industrial Structure and Growth in India*. New Delhi: Oxford University Press.

Guhan, S. 1986. "Fiscal Policy, Projections and Performance." *Economic and Political Weekly* 21(15): 631–38.

Gulati, Ashok, and G. D. Kaira. 1992. "Fertiliser Subsidy: Issues related to Equity and Efficiency." *Economic and Political Weekly* 27(13): A43–48.

Gulati, Iqbal S. ed., 1987. *Centre-State Budgetary Transfers*. Bombay: Oxford University Press.

Gupta, Anand. 1988. "Financing Public Enterprise Investments." *Economic and Political Weekly* 23(51): 2687–702.

Gupta, Suraj B. 1979. *Monetary Planning for India*. New Delhi: Oxford University Press.

Gupta, S. P., and T. N. Srinivasan. 1984. "Inflation and the Role of Administered Prices." *Economic and Political Weekly* 19(36): 1579–82.

Gwin, Catherine. 1983. "Financing India's Structural Adjustment." In J. Williamson, ed., *IMF Conditionality*. Washington, D.C.: Institute for International Economics.

Hanson, A. H. 1966. *The Process of Planning*. Oxford: Oxford University Press.

Haque, Nadeem, and Peter Montiel. 1990. *Capital Mobility in Developing Countries: Some Empirical Tests*. IMF Working Paper WP/90/117. Washington, D.C.

Hardgrave, R. L., and S. A. Kochanek. 1986. *India: Government and Politics in a Developing Nation*, fourth edition. New York: Harcourt, Brace Jovanovitch.

Harriss, John. 1987. "The State in Retreat? Why has India Experienced Such Half-hearted Liberalisation in the 1980s?" *Institute of Development Studies Bulletin* 18(4): 31–8. Brighton: University of Sussex.

Heller, P. S., R. D. Haas, and A. S. Mansur. 1986. *A Review of the Fiscal Impulse Measure.* IMF Occasional Paper 44. Washington, D.C.

Hendry, David. 1985. "Monetary Economic Myth and Econometric Reality." *Oxford Review of Economic Policy* 1(1): 72–84.

———. 1986. "Empirical Modelling in Dynamic Econometrics." Applied Economics Discussion Paper 1. Oxford University.

International Monetary Fund (IMF). Various years. *International Financial Statistics Yearbook.* Washington D.C.

———. Various years. *World Economic Outlook.* Washington D.C.

———. 1988. "International Financial Statistics: Supplement on Trade Statistics." Supplement Series 15. Washington D.C.

Jalan, Bimal. 1991. *India's Economic Crisis.* New Delhi: Oxford University Press.

Jalan, Bimal, ed., 1992. *The Indian Economy.* New Delhi: Viking-Penguin Books.

Jha, Prem Shankar. 1980. *India: A Political Economy of Stagnation.* Bombay: Oxford University Press.

Jose, A. V. 1988. "Agricultural Wages in India." *Economic and Political Weekly* 23(26): A46-58.

Joshi, Vijay. 1970. "Saving and Foreign Exchange Constraints." In P. P. Streeten, ed., *Unfashionable Economics.* London: Weidenfeld and Nicholson.

———. 1984. "The Nominal and Real Effective Exchange Rate of the Indian Rupee 1971–1983." *Reserve Bank of India Occasional Papers* 5(1): 27-87.

———. 1990. "Exchange Rate Regimes in Developing Countries." In Maurice Scott and Deepak Lal, eds., *Public Policy and Economic Development.* Oxford: Clarendon Press.

Joshi, Vijay, and I. M. D. Little. 1987. "Indian Macroeconomic Policies." *Economic and Political Weekly* 22(9): 371–78.

———. 1989a. "Indian Macroeconomic Policies." In G. Calvo, R. Findlay, P. Kouri, and J. B. de Macedo, eds., *Debt, Stabilization and Development.* Oxford: Basil Blackwell.

———. 1989b. "Les Politiques Macroéconomiques Indiennes." *Revue Tiers Monde* 30(120): 796–821.

Joshi, Vijay, and Sunil Khilnani. 1991. "The Erosion of India's Stability." *Times Literary Supplement*, June 14.

Kaldor, Nicholas. 1984. "An Exchange Rate Policy for India." *Economic and Political Weekly* 19(28): 1093–95.

Kaviraj, Sudipta. 1986. "Indira Gandhi and Indian Politics." *Economic and Political Weekly* 21(38–9): 1697–708.

Kelkar, Vijay, and Rajiv Kumar. 1990. "Industrial Growth in the Eighties: Emerging Policy Issues." *Economic and Political Weekly* 25(4): 209–22.

Kelkar, Vijay, Rajiv Kumar, and Rita Nangia. 1990. *India's Industrial Economy: Policies, Performance and Reforms*. Manila: Asian Development Bank.

Keynes, J. M. 1923. *A Tract on Monetary Reform*. London: Macmillan.

Khatkhate, Deena R. 1992. "Running with the Hare and Hunting with the Hounds." *Economic and Political Weekly* 27(1): 21–23.

Khilnani, Sunil. 1992. "India's Democratic Career." In John Dunn. ed., *Democracy: The Unfinished Journey 508 B.C.–1993 A.D.* Oxford: Oxford University Press.

Khusro, A. M. 1988. "Management of the Indian Economy: Macroeconomic and Sectoral Policies." Sir Purushottamdas Memorial Lecture, Indian Institute of Bankers, Bombay.

Kohli, Atul, ed., 1988. *India's Democracy*. Princeton: Princeton University Press.

——. 1989. "Politics of Economic Liberalization in India." *World Development* 17(3): 305–28.

——. 1990. *Democracy and Discontent*. Cambridge: Cambridge University Press.

Kothari, Rajni. 1970. *Politics in India*. New Delhi: Orient Longmans.

Krishnamurti, K., and Vishwanath Pandit. 1985. *Macroeconometric Modelling of the Indian Economy*. New Delhi: Hindustan Publishing Corporation.

Krishnaswamy, K. S. 1985. "The Reserve Bank and Government: A Broad-Brush Picture." *Commerce*, September 7.

——. 1991. "On Liberalisation and Related Matters." *Economic and Political Weekly* 26(42): 2415–22.

Krishnaswamy, K. S., K. Krishnamurti, and P. D. Sharma. 1987. *Improving Domestic Resource Mobilization through Financial Development: India*. Manila: Asian Development Bank.

Lal, Deepak. 1980. *Prices for Planning*. London: Heinemann.

——. 1988. *The Hindu Equilibrium*. Oxford: Clarendon Press.

Lewis, J. P. 1962. *Quiet Crisis in India*. Washington, D.C.: The Brookings Institution.

——. 1970. "Wanted in India: A Relevant Radicalism." *Economic and Political Weekly* 5(29–31): 1202–10.

Lipton, Michael, and John Toye. 1990. *Does Aid Work in India?* London: Routledge.

Little, I. M. D. 1960. "The Strategy of Indian Development." *National Institute Economic Review* 9: 20–24.

Little, I. M. D., Richard N. Cooper, W. Max Corden, and Sarath Rajapatirana. 1993. *Boom, Crisis, and Adjustment: The Macroeconomic Experience of Developing Countries*. New York: Oxford University Press.

Little, I. M. D., Dipak Mazumdar, and John Page. 1987. *Small Manufacturing Enterprises: A Comparative Study of India and Other Economies*. New York: Oxford University Press.

Lucas, R. E. 1988. "On the Mechanics of Economic Development." *Journal of Monetary Economics* 22(1): 3–42.

Lucas, R. E. B. 1986a. "An Overview of the Labour Market in India." DRD Discussion Paper 153. World Bank, Washington D.C.

———. 1986b. "Demand for India's Manufactured Exports." *Journal of Development Economics* 20.

Lucas, R. E. B., and G. F. Papanek. 1988. *The Indian Economy: Recent Developments and Future Prospects.* Boulder, Colo.: Westview Press.

Madhur, Srinivasa, and Pronnoy Roy. 1986. "Price Setting in Indian Industry." *Journal of Development Economics* 20(2): 205–24.

Majumdar, N. A. 1989. "Monetary Targeting: Objectives and Appropriate Indicators." *Economic and Political Weekly* 24(34): 1959–62.

Malhotra, R. N. 1989. *Growth and Current Fiscal Challenges.* L. K. Jha Memorial Lecture, Fiscal Research Foundation, New Delhi.

Manor, James. 1983. "The Electoral Process amid Awakening and Decay." In Peter Lyon and James Manor, eds., *Transfer and Transformation: Political Institutions in the New Commonwealth.* Leicester: University of Leicester Press.

———. 1987. "Tried, Then Abandoned: Economic Liberalisation in India." *Institute of Development Studies Bulletin* 18(4): 39–44. Brighton: University of Sussex.

———. 1992. "The State of Governance." In Subroto Roy and William James, eds., *Foundations of India's Political Economy: Towards an Agenda for the Nineties.* London: Sage Publications.

Marathe, Sharad S. 1989. *Regulation and Development: India's Policy Experience of Controls over Industry.* New Delhi: Sage Publications.

Mason, Edward S., and Robert E. Asher. 1973. *The World Bank Since Bretton Woods.* Washington D.C.: The Brookings Institution.

Menon, K.A. 1988. "Reserve Money, Money Stock and the Money Multiplier." *Economic and Political Weekly* 23(41): 2121–25.

Minhas, Bagicha S. 1987. "The Planning Process and the Annual Budgets: Some Reflections on Recent Indian Experience." *Indian Economic Review* 22(2): 115–49.

Mitra, Pradeep K., and Suresh D. Tendulkar. 1986. "Coping with Internal and External Shocks: India 1973–74 to 1983–84." CPD Discussion Paper 1986–21. World Bank, Country Economics Department, Washington, D.C.

Mohan, Rakesh. 1992. "Industrial Policy and Controls." In Bimal Jalan, ed., *The Indian Economy: Problems and Prospects.* New Delhi: Viking Press.

Morris, Felipe. 1985. *India's Financial System: An Overview of Its Principal Structural Features.* World Bank Staff Working Paper 739. Washington, D.C.

Mozoomdar, Ajit. 1989. "The Rise and Decline of Planning in India." Paper presented to conference on the State and Development Planning in India. School of Oriental and African Studies, London, April 21.

Mulji, Sudhir. 1990. "Vision and Reality of Public Sector Management: The Indian Experience." In Maurice Scott and Deepak Lal, eds., *Public Policy and Economic Development.* Oxford: Clarendon Press.

Mundle, Sudipto, and M. Govinda Rao. 1991. "The Volume and Composition of Government Subsidies in India 1987–88." *Economic and Political Weekly* 26(18): 1157–72.

Nagaraj, R. 1990. "Growth Rate of India's GDP 1950/51 to 1987/88: Examination of Alternative Hypotheses." *Economic and Political Weekly* 25(26): 1396–403.

Nandy, Ashish. 1984. *The Intimate Enemy*. New Delhi: Oxford University Press.

Narasimham, M. 1988. "Adjustment with Growth: The Indian Experience with IMF Loans." In M. Narasimham, *World Economic Environment and Prospects for India*. New Delhi: Sterling Publishers.

Nayar, Baldev Raj. 1992. "The Politics of Economic Restructuring in India." *Journal of Commonwealth and Comparative Politics* 30(2): 145–71.

Nayyar, Deepak. 1976. *India's Exports and Export Policies in the 1960s*. Cambridge: Cambridge University Press.

———. 1987. "India's Export Performance, 1970–85: Underlying Factors and Constraints." *Economic and Political Weekly* 22(19): 73–90.

Pai Panandikar, V. A., and Arun Sud. 1983. *Changing Political Representation in India*. New Delhi: Centre for Policy Research.

Panchmukhi, V. R. 1986. *Capital Formation and Output in the Third World*. New Delhi: Radiant Publishers.

Pandit, Vishwanath. 1978. "An Analysis of Inflation in India." *Indian Economic Review* 13(2): 89–115.

Patel, I. G. 1987. "On Taking India into the Twenty-First Century." *Modern Asian Studies* 21(2): 209–31.

Patnaik, Prabhat. 1986. "Public Debt as a Mode of Financing Public Expenditure: Some Comments." *Economic and Political Weekly* 21(35): 1545–52.

Raj, K. N. 1984. "Economic Growth in India 1952/3–1982/3." *Economic and Political Weekly* 19(41): 1801–04.

Rajaraman, Indira. 1991. "Impact of Real Exchange Rate Movements on Selected Indian Industrial Exports." *Economic and Political Weekly* 26(11-12): 669–78.

———. 1992. "Trade-Relevant External Value of the Rupee: 1974–1989." *Journal of Foreign Exchange and International Finance* 5(4): 284–89.

Rakshit, Mihir. 1987. "On the Inflationary Impact of the Budget Deficit." *Economic and Political Weekly* 22(19): 35–42.

———. 1991. "The Macroeconomic Adjustment Programme: A Critique." *Economic and Political Weekly* 26(34): 1977–88.

Rangarajan, C. 1982. "Process of Policy Formulation in Central Banks." *Reserve Bank of India Bulletin* 36: 523–27.

———. 1988. "Issues in Monetary Management." Presidential Address at the 71st Annual Conference of the Indian Economic Association, Calcutta, 29 December.

———. 1990. "Industrial Growth in the Eighties—Facts and Some Issues." Convocation Address, Indian Institute of Management, Lucknow, 6 April.

Rangarajan, C., and Anoop Singh. 1984. "Reserve Money: Concepts and Policy Implications for India." *Reserve Bank of India Occasional Papers* 5(1): 1–26.

Rangarajan, C., Anupam Basu, and Narendra Jadhav. 1989. "Dynamics of Interaction between Government Deficit and Domestic Debt in India." *Reserve Bank of India Occasional Papers* 10(3): 163–220.

Rao, C. H. H., S. K. Ray, and Kalanidhi Subbarow. 1988. *Unstable Agriculture and Droughts*. New Delhi: Vikas Publishing House.

Rao, J. C. 1983. "Money and Prices: An Empirical Study of the Indian Experience 1970–1982." *Reserve Bank of India Occasional Papers* 4(1): 1–38.

Rao, Narhari. 1985. "Exchange Rate and Commercial Policy in a Controlled Trade Regime: A Case Study of India." D. Phil. diss., Oxford University.

Rao, V. M. 1972. "Agricultural Wages in India: A Reliability Analysis." *Indian Journal of Agricultural Economics* 27(3): 38–62.

Reserve Bank of India. Various years. *Reserve Bank of India Bulletin*. Bombay.

——. Various years. *Report on Currency and Finance*. Bombay.

——. Various years. *Report on Trend and Progress of Banking*. Bombay.

——. Various years. *Annual Report*. Bombay.

——. 1982. *Capital Formation and Saving in India 1950/51 to 1979/80*. Report of the Working Group Appointed by the Ministry of Planning, Government of India (K. N. Raj, Chairman). Bombay.

——. 1983a. *Report of the Working Group on Bank Deposits*. Bombay.

——. 1983b. *Reserve Bank of India: Functions and Working*. Bombay.

——. 1985. *Report of the Committee to Review the Working of the Monetary System* (S. Chakravarty, Chairman). Bombay.

Riedel, James, Chris Hall, and Roger Grawe. 1984. "Determinants of Indian Export Performance in the 1970s." *Weltwirtschaftliches Archiv* 120(1): 40–63.

Rishi, Meenakshi, and James Boyce. 1990. "The Hidden Balance of Payments: Capital Flight and Trade Misinvoicing in India 1971–1986." *Economic and Political Weekly* 25(50): 1645–48.

Romer, Paul. 1986. "Increasing Returns and Long-Run Economic Growth." *Journal of Political Economy* 94(5): 1002–37.

Rosen, George. 1966. *Democracy and Economic Change in India*. Berkeley: University of California Press.

——. 1992. *Contrasting Styles of Industrial Reform: China and India in the 1980s*. Chicago: University of Chicago Press.

Roy, Subroto, and William E. James. 1992. *Foundations of India's Political Economy*. London: Sage Publications.

Rubin, Barnett R. 1982. *Private Power and Public Investment in India*. Ph.D. diss., Department of Economics, University of Chicago.

——. 1985. "Economic Liberalisation and the Indian State." *Third World Quarterly* 7(4): 942–57.

——. 1986. "Financing Gross Capital Formation in the Indian Public Sector." *Economic and Political Weekly* 21(44–5): 1943–50.

Rudolph, Lloyd, and Suzanne Rudolph. 1987. *In Pursuit of Laxmi*. Chicago: University of Chicago Press.

Scott, Maurice F. G. 1979. "What Price the National Income." In Michael J. Boskin, ed., *Economics and Human Welfare, Essays in Honor of Tibor Scitovsky*. New York: Academic Press.

———. 1989. *A New View of Economic Growth*. Oxford: Oxford University Press.

Sen, Abhijit. 1987. "A Note on Employment and Living Standards in the Unorganized Sector." New Delhi: Jawaharlal Nehru University.

Sen, Pronab. 1986. "The 1966 Devaluation in India: A Reappraisal." *Economic and Political Weekly* 21(30): 1322–28.

———. 1987. *India: Stabilization and Adjustment Policies and Programmes*. Helsinki: World Institute for Development Economics Research.

———. 1991. "Growth Theories and Development Strategies: Lessons from Indian Experience." *Economic and Political Weekly* 26(30): PE62–72.

Seshan, A. 1987. "The Burden of Domestic Debt in India." *Reserve Bank of India Occasional Papers* 8(1): 45–78.

Shetty, S. L. 1990. "Saving Behaviour in India in the 1980s." *Economic and Political Weekly* 25(11): 555–60.

Shroff, Manu R. 1984. *Public Enterprise Banks and Financial Institutions in India*. Ahmedabad: Indian Institute of Management.

Singh, Ajit, and Jayati Ghosh. 1988. "Import Liberalisation and the New Industrial Strategy." *Economic and Political Weekly* 23(45–7): 2331–42.

Singh, Anoop, S. L Shetty, and T. R. Venkatachalam. 1982. "Monetary Policy in India: Issues and Evidence." *Reserve Bank of India Occasional Papers* 3(1) Supplement: 1–33.

Singh, Manmohan. 1964. *India's Export Trends and Prospects for Self-Contained Growth*. Oxford: Clarendon Press.

Srinivasan, T. N. 1992. "Planning and Foreign Trade Reconsidered." In Subroto Roy and William E. James, *Foundations of India's Political Economy*. London: Sage Publications

Srinivasan, T. N., and N. S. Satyanarayana. 1977. "Economic Performance Since the Third Plan and Its Implications for Policy." *Economic and Political Weekly* 12(6): 225–40.

Subbarow, Kalandhi. 1992. "The Economics of Food and Agriculture." In Subroto Roy and William E. James, *Foundations of India's Political Economy*. London: Sage Publications.

Subramanian, K. N. 1977. *Wages in India*. New Delhi: Tata McGraw Hill Publishing Company.

Sunderam, K., and Suresh Tendulkar. 1987. "Administered Prices and Inflation." *Economic and Political Weekly* 22(22): 853–57.

———. 1986. "Financing the Step-up in Plan Investment: Administered Prices or Increased Deficit Financing." *Economic and Political Weekly* 21(25–26): 1109–13.

Sunderarajan, V. 1986. "Exchange Rate Versus Credit Policy: Analysis with a Monetary Model of Trade and Inflation in India." *Journal of Development Economics* 20: 75–105.

Taylor, Lance. 1983. *Structuralist Macroeconomics*. New York: Basic Books.

———. 1988a. *Varieties of Stabilization Experience*. Oxford: Oxford University Press.

———. 1988b. "Macro Constraints on India's Economic Growth." *Indian Economic Review* 23(2): 145–65.

Thimmaih, G. 1985. *Burning Issues in Centre-State Financial Relations.* Bombay: Ashish Publishing House.

Toye, John. 1981. *Public Expenditure and Indian Development Policy, 1960–1970.* Cambridge: Cambridge University Press.

———. 1988. "Political Economy and the Analysis of Indian Development." *Modern Asian Studies* 22(1): 97–122.

Tully, Mark, and Zareer Masani. 1988. *From Raj to Rajiv.* London: BBC Books.

Tulpule, Bagaram, and R. C. Datta. 1988. "Real Wages in Indian Industry." *Economic and Political Weekly* 23(44): 2275–79.

Varshney, Ashutosh. 1984. "Political Economy of Slow Industrial Growth." *Economic and Political Weekly* 29(35): 1511–17.

Veit, Lawrence A. 1976. *India's Second Revolution.* New York: McGraw Hill.

Verghese, S. K. 1984. "Management of Exchange Rate since its Basket Link." *Economic and Political Weekly* 19(28): 1096–105.

Virmani, Arvind. 1988. *Saving Performance and Prospects: A Historical Perspective.* Economic Research Paper 2. Planning Commission, Government of India, New Delhi.

———. 1989. *Trends in the Current Account and the Balance of Trade: Separating Facts from Prejudices.* Economic Research Paper 6. Planning Commission, Government of India, New Delhi.

———. 1991. "Demand and Supply Factors in India's Trade." *Economic and Political Weekly* 26(6): 311–13.

Wadhwa, Charan D. 1988. "Import and Export Policy 1988–1991." *Economic and Political Weekly* 23(26): 1331–37.

Wadhwa, Charan D. ed., 1977. *Some Problems of India's Economic Policy.* New Delhi: Tata McGraw Hill.

Wall, John. 1979. "Foodgrain Management: Pricing, Procurement, Distribution, Import and Storage Policy." In World Bank, *India: Occasional Papers.* World Bank Staff Working Paper 279. Washington, D.C.

Weiner, Myron. 1989. *The Indian Paradox.* New Delhi: Sage Publications.

Williamson, John, ed., 1981. *Exchange Rate Rules.* London: Macmillan.

———. 1982. "A Survey of the Literature on the Optimal Peg." *Journal of Development Economics* 43(1): 56–60.

———. 1989. "Comment on Joshi and Little." In G. Calvo, R. Findlay, P. Kouri, and J. de Macedo, eds., *Debt, Stabilization and Development.* London: Basil Blackwell.

Wolf, Martin. 1982. *India's Exports.* Oxford: Oxford University Press.

World Bank. Various years. "India: Country Economic Memorandum." World Bank, South Asia Country Department 2, Washington D.C.

———. Various years. *World Debt Tables.* Washington D.C.

———. Various years. *World Development Report.* New York: Oxford University Press.

———. 1986. *Poverty and Hunger: Options for Food Security in Developing Countries.* Washington D.C.

Index